MW00511164

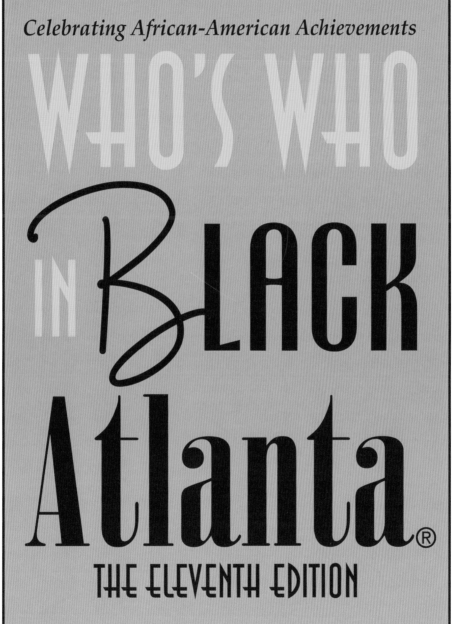

Celebrating African-American Achievements

WHO'S WHO
in BLACK
Atlanta®
THE ELEVENTH EDITION

Scenes from the 2007 Atlanta Unveiling Reception

Celebrating African-American Achievements

WHO'S WHO
IN BLACK
Atlanta®
THE ELEVENTH EDITION

Who's Who In Black Atlanta®
is a registered trademark of
Real Times Media

Purchase additional copies online @
www.whoswhopublishing.com

Corporate Headquarters
Who's Who Publishing Co., LLC
1801 Watermark Drive, Suite 250
Columbus, Ohio 43215

All Credit Cards Accepted
*Inquiries for bulk purchases for youth
groups, schools, churches, civic or
professional organizations, please call
our office for volume discounts.*

Corporate Headquarters
(614) 481-7300

Photo Credits
C. Sunny Martin
Denise Gray

Cover Design by: Kimberly Byers

ISBN # 1-933879-75-0 Hardback
$50.00 each-U.S. Hardback
Commemorative Edition

ISBN # 1-933879-74-2 Paperback
$34.95 each-U.S. Paperback

Diversity + Inclusion = Success

Comcast is a proud supporter of Who's Who in Black Atlanta whose mission is to ensure that our industry reflects our amazingly diverse world.

We honor this year's extraordinary employees spotlighted in this 2009 edition:

Michael Hewitt	Steve Gillenwater
Angela Gray	Tina Capers-Hall
Stacy Cole	Robert Harris
Shauna Gordon	Jason Biske
Herb Linsey	Bridgett Shields-Wilson
	Veree Freeman

Table of CONTENTS

MEET THE TEAM

WHO'S *Who*
PUBLISHING CO., LLC

C. Sunny Martin
Founder & CEO

Yolanda Reynolds
Atlanta Associate Publisher

Monica Cabbler
Sr. Account Executive

Ernie Sullivan
Senior Partner

Paula Gray
V.P. Customer Care

Melanie Diggs
Executive Editor

Carter Womack
Regional VP

Tamara Allen
Production Manager

Reghan Jones
Business Manager

Carlton Butler
Distribution Manager

Nathan Wylder
Senior Editor

Sarah Kalb
Webmaster

Alicia Dunlap
Production Assistant

Corey E. Favor
Sr. Graphic Designer

Monica Sherchan
Graphic Designer

Kimberly Byers
Graphic Designer

Earron West
Graphic Designer

Lori Haramia
Graphic Designer

Rachel Bobak
Copy Editor

Danielle Solomon
Copy Editor

Keenan Sourelis
Copy Editor

Jackie Nash
Copy Editor

Amanda Forbes
Copy Editor

Steve Clark
Sales Representative

Meagan Culley
Customer Service Rep.

Sarah Longacre
Executive Assistant

Tracy Trammell
Administrative Assistant

Stephanie Longacre
Administrative Assistant

CORPORATE OFFICE
1801 Watermark Drive, Suite 250 • Columbus, Ohio 43215 • (614) 481-7300
Visit Our Web Site - www.whoswhopublishing.com

THIS BOOK WAS MADE POSSIBLE BY THE GENEROUS SUPPORT OF OUR

SPONSORS

PLATINUM SPONSOR

WHO'S who OFFICIAL AIRLINE

DIAMOND SPONSORS

EMERALD SPONSOR

UNVEILING RECEPTION SPONSORS

EDUCATION SPONSORS

MEDIA SPONSORS

IT'S TIME
TO LEAD BY EXAMPLE

Brian Cohen
VP NJ Metro Region

Marvin Ellison
EVP U.S. Stores

Anne Marie Campbell
VP In-Store Service

Jocelyn Hunter
**VP & Assoc. General
Counsel-Legal**

Arlette Decuir Guthrie
VP Talent Management

Gloria Johnson-Goins
Chief Diversity Officer

The Home Depot's commitment to diversity begins at the top.
We believe that our work environment, where all associates are valued
and supported to do their best, helps us grow competitively and keeps
us connected to today's consumer in the global marketplace.

You can do it. We can help.®

Foreword

by The Honorable William "Bill" Edwards

"As we face the unpredictable future, we do so in the faith that our objectives are sound, that our means of achieving them are practicable, and that man and God will assist us all the way."
- Benjamin E. Mays

When I first arrived in Atlanta in 1968 to attend Morehouse College, I was filled with an incredible excitement to live in a city and a county that was quickly becoming known as a place of opportunity for African Americans. Thanks to the efforts of remarkable leaders such as Dr. Martin Luther King Jr., the Honorable Maynard H. Jackson, Dr. Benjamin Elijah Mays, Rev. Andrew Young and numerous other outstanding leaders, African Americans have achieved unparalleled success in our community and throughout this country and abroad.

It is an honor to be selected to write the foreword for this edition of **Who's Who In Black Atlanta**®, which honors outstanding African Americans who have excelled in business, government, education, clergy, public service, nonprofit, sports, entertainment and philanthropic arenas. In particular, Fulton County Government, the City of Atlanta and the metropolitan area have a strong tradition of ensuring opportunities for African Americans and other minorities.

In my own experience as a businessman and an elected official for Fulton County Government, I've learned the importance of continuing the commitment of maintaining a level playing field through our Minority and Female Business Enterprise programs. These programs have helped make Fulton County, the city of Atlanta and the metropolitan area an outstanding place of opportunities for minorities for decades to come.

Looking through the pages of this publication, several of our local leaders will tell their stories – many against incredible odds of efforts and struggles to bring change to our community. As we applaud their success, let us also remember those who are no longer with us, but whose efforts have also led us to the incredible achievements and accomplishments that we are enjoying today.

As you read their stories, please recall their journeys as well as the journey that we have all traveled, and be sure to reflect on how far we have come, particularly at this magnificent moment in history. The people profiled in this publication have set the standard for our future generations. We have so much to be proud of, and I applaud each of you for your outstanding accomplishments.

Sincerely,

William "Bill" Edwards

William "Bill" Edwards
Vice Chairman
Fulton County Board of Commissioners
District 7

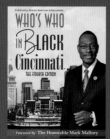

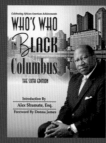

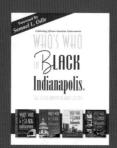

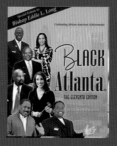
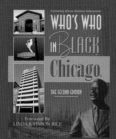

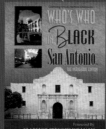

Nine different people. Nine paths to success. One company that thrives on diversity.

WHAT CAN BROWN DO FOR YOU?®

UPS Salutes Who's Who In Black Atlanta.

1st row: James Mallard, *VP Procurement Services*; Jim Winestock, *SVP U.S. Operations*; Lisa Hamilton, President, *The UPS Foundation*; Gerard Gibbons, VP Sales Strategy Worldwide Services; Teri McClure, *SVP Legal and Compliance, General Counsel and Corporate Secretary*

2nd row: George Brooks, *VP Operations, Southeast Region*; Bill Gummer, *VP Corporate Transportation*

3rd row: Mike Johnson, *VP Human Resources*; Michael Turner, *VP Strategic Account Sales*

"It took us longer to play the course
than it did to get to Bermuda."

Eight world-class golf courses. Over 70 fantastic tennis courts. And dozens of delightful spas. There's no place like Bermuda when it comes to indulging all your passions. And at just under two hours from the East Coast, there's no island paradise that's easier to reach. So come relax, hit the ball, and feel the love in Bermuda.

For full details, and to book tickets and reservations, call **1-800-BERMUDA**, or visit **www.bermudatourism.com**

BERMUDA
feel the love.

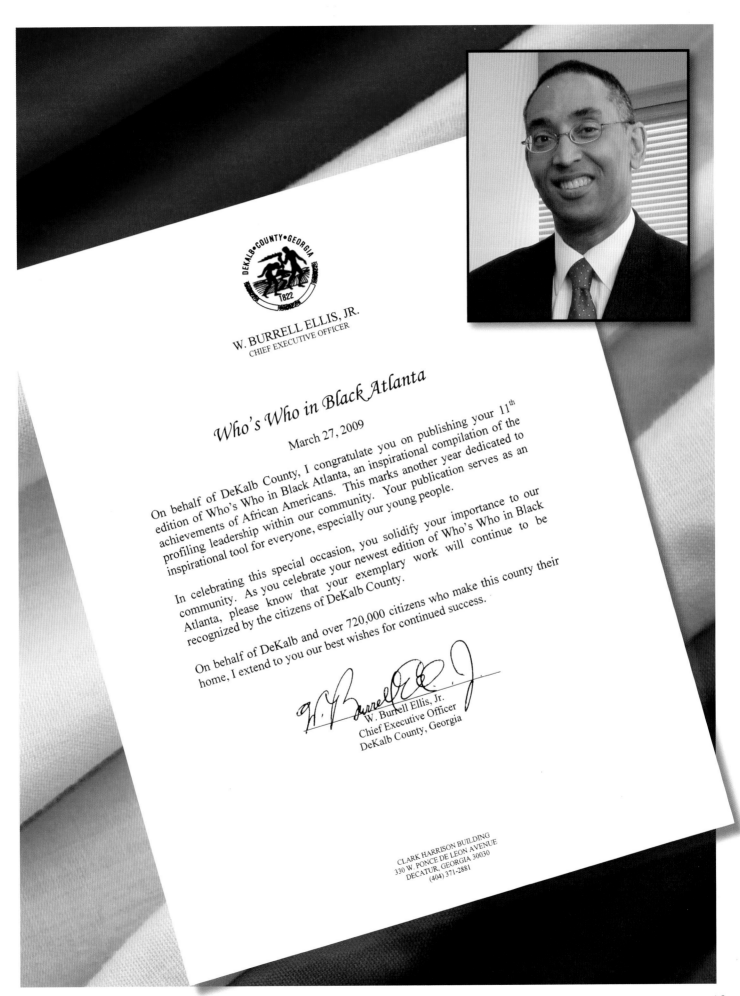

W. BURRELL ELLIS, JR.
CHIEF EXECUTIVE OFFICER

Who's Who in Black Atlanta

March 27, 2009

On behalf of DeKalb County, I congratulate you on publishing your 11th edition of Who's Who in Black Atlanta, an inspirational compilation of the achievements of African Americans. This marks another year dedicated to profiling leadership within our community. Your publication serves as an inspirational tool for everyone, especially our young people.

In celebrating this special occasion, you solidify your importance to our community. As you celebrate your newest edition of Who's Who in Black Atlanta, please know that your exemplary work will continue to be recognized by the citizens of DeKalb County.

On behalf of DeKalb and over 720,000 citizens who make this county their home, I extend to you our best wishes for continued success.

W. Burrell Ellis, Jr.
Chief Executive Officer
DeKalb County, Georgia

CLARK HARRISON BUILDING
330 W. PONCE DE LEON AVENUE
DECATUR, GEORGIA 30030
(404) 371-2881

V-103
The People's Station

Frank & Wanda in the Morning
6am-10am   with Miss Sophia

Elle Duncan
10am-2pm

Ryan Cameron
2pm-6pm

Greg Street
6pm-10pm

Joyce Littel
10pm-2am

SALUTES WHO'S WHO
IN BLACK ATLANTA

A MESSAGE FROM THE
Founder & CEO
C. SUNNY MARTIN

Greetings Atlanta!

It's good to journey back where my Who's Who Publishing endeavors first began. Now in our eleventh edition, I can see the growth that has taken place in Atlanta – economically, politically, educationally and culturally. It makes me wonder what so many of our most beloved leaders, such as Dr. Martin Luther and Coretta Scott King, Hosea Williams and Maynard Jackson, might say. With the election of Barack Obama as president of the United States, the last few decades have seen a tremendous amount of change.

Would they be compelled to tell us that now the real work begins in our cities – to ensure that the increasing numbers of homeless families are sheltered and fed; to not get comfortable with past economic prosperity and open the doors of our companies a little wider to mentor the next generation of titans; to find creative solutions to educate the masses of young people who need to find their place in our global marketplace; and to march longer and cry louder when civil injustice takes place in our courts and on our streets? While I think they would be proud, I also surmise they would roll up their sleeves a little higher to ensure our gains do not ultimately result in loss, greed or complacency.

So, as I write I am inspired to continue to make a difference by persisting in my mission to uplift and highlight the achievements of African Americans. Without the support of our local and national advertisers and sponsors, our efforts would flounder. Therefore, I give my utmost gratitude for your ongoing support. I also thank you, our loyal readers who also continue to support our products and events. Our progress should not be a secret, so please make sure you share copies with schools and youth organizations in your area through our 1,000 Books for a 1,000 Kids initiative.

I also thank Yolanda Reynolds for another year of leadership in the Metro Atlanta market. Each year, she finds creative ways to showcase the finest of Atlanta. To that end, we are proud to pay special tribute to Bishop Eddie Long and the ministry of New Birth Missionary Baptist Church, an example of how the spiritual and secular communities make a difference by rolling up their sleeves and working together.

Live life to the fullest,

C. Sunny Martin

Criteria for Inclusion

Who's Who In Black Atlanta is an opportunity for us to afford a measure of recognition to the men and women who have made their mark in their specific occupations, professions, or in service to others in the Atlanta community.

A sincere effort was made to include those whose positions or accomplishments in their chosen fields are significant and whose contributions to community affairs, whether citywide or on the neighborhood level, have improved the quality of life for all of us.

The names of those brief biographies included in this edition were compiled from customary sources of information. Lists of a wide variety were consulted and every effort was made to reach all whose stature or civic activities merited their inclusion.

In today's mobile society, no such publication could ever claim to be complete; some who should be included could not be reached or chose not to respond, and for that we offer our apologies. Constraints of time, space and awareness are thus responsible for other omissions, and not a lack of good intentions on the part of the publisher. Our goal was to document the accomplishments of many people from various occupational disciplines.

An invitation to participate in the publication was extended at the discretion of the publisher. Biographies were invited to contribute personal and professional data, with only the information freely submitted to be included. The editors have made a sincere effort to present an accurate distillation of the data, and to catch errors whenever possible. However, the publisher cannot assume any responsibility for the accuracy of the information submitted.

There was no charge for inclusion in this publication and inclusion was not guaranteed; an annual update is planned. Comments and other concerns should be addressed to:

C. Sunny Martin, CEO
Who's Who Publishing Co., LLC
1801 Watermark Drive, Suite 250
Columbus, Ohio 43215
Phone: (614) 481-7300

E-mail: sunny@whoswhopublishing.com
www.whoswhopublishing.com

Atlanta

ASSOCIATE PUBLISHER

Yolanda Reynolds

Whatever you do, work at it with all your heart, as working for the Lord, not for men, since you know that you will receive an inheritance from the Lord as a reward. It is the Lord Christ you are serving. Colossians 3:23, 24 NIV

The words that were so eloquently spoken by Apostle Paul mirror my heart's sentiments as I go about my daily occupation. A paraphrase of the scripture would put it this way, "Whatever you do, do it well." With this in mind, I am sincerely delighted to present to you another edition of **Who's Who In Black Atlanta**®. As we chronicle the achievements of African-Americans, I know you will easily identify with others who are also committed to doing their best. They have done such an exemplary job that it has caught our attention.

I would like to thank our founder and CEO, Sunny Martin, for the awesome leadership role that he played in helping to make this book a success. I also commend the team at our headquarters, as well as our local team members. All of you have done an excellent job of pulling together to make it happen.

This year's edition focuses on one of the business community's most vital issues, diversity. In today's harsh economic climate, it is essential that every individual do all they can to remain competitive, adding value to their organizations and ultimately their communities. It is times like these that have made it clear that attaining additional education and skills is no longer an option, but a necessity. This edition takes a look at the value of diversity and the role it plays in Atlanta's business sector.

The realities of the economy also made it obvious that the decision of advertising is one that needs to be

more carefully made than in previous years. As such, I applaud each of our sponsors and advertisers for the sacrifices that were made. I truly appreciate your support.

To Bishop Eddie L. Long and Commissioner Bill Edwards, I salute you for the leadership roles you have exemplified in your respective areas. We count it an honor to share examples of the invaluable contributions that you have made.

And, to two of the most wonderful sons that a mother could ever hope for, Ashton and Wildon, I want to say, thank you for being who you are. I appreciate you for always understanding the many sacrifices I make as I prepare to make your futures brighter. You are such good sons, and I thank God for you every day. My prayer is that the work I am doing and the seeds I plant in your life will yield fruit that will last a lifetime and set a lasting foundation for you to build upon. I love you!

Enjoy the book.

Sincerely,

Y Reynolds

Yolanda R. Reynolds

**Many diverse minds. One dedicated vision.
Making a difference in Atlanta and northwest Georgia.**

The difference is Kennesaw State.

Back row (left to right): *Adrian L. Epps, Associate Dean, College of Science and Mathematics; Jennifer Wade-Berg, Chief Diversity Officer; Arlethia Perry-Johnson, Special Assistant to the President for External Affairs; Daniel S. Papp, President; Flora B. Devine, University Attorney and Special Assistant to the President for Legal Affairs; Barry J. Morris, Director of Cabinet Strategic Projects*

Front Row (left to right): *Jerome Ratchford, Interim Vice President of Student Success and Enrollment Services; Linda M. Lyons, KSU's Customer Service Champion; Akanmu Adebayo, Executive Director, Institute for Global Initiatives; Valerie Whittlesey, Assistant Vice President for Academic Affairs; Michael S. Heard, Associate Dean, University College*

www.kennesaw.edu

BE HEARD
your world, your voice, our work

INTEGRATED MARKETING   MULTI-MEDIA   EXTENDED NETWORK

Let Real Times Media create unique and innovative marketing experiences for your brand.

REAL TIMES MEDIA

Real Times Media 535 Griswold, Suite 1300, Detroit, MI 48226 ■ 313-963-8100

Atlanta's
CORPORATESPOTLIGHT

INTEREST

LIMELIGHT

ATTENTION

comcast.

PROMINENCE

HIGHLIGHT

CELEBRATE

HEADLINE

FOCUS

RECOGNITION

Jason Biske

Regional Director, Sales & Retention
Comcast Cable Communications, Inc.

Tina A. Capers-Hall

Director, Human Resources
Comcast Cable Communications, Inc.

Jason Biske is regional director of sales and retention for Comcast Atlanta. In this position, he is responsible for strategy formation and implementation for all inbound sales and retention activities. Since taking over inbound sales responsibilities in 2003, Jason has been instrumental in growing Comcast Atlanta's subscriber base from 250,000 to more than 800,000, and his sales staff has grown from 50 to more than 240.

Jason received a Master of Science degree in management from Georgia Tech in 1995. He completed undergraduate work at Tulane University and received a Bachelor of Arts degree in economics.

Originally hailing from St. Thomas in the U.S. Virgin Islands, Jason is married to Sheraunda Biske and is the proud father of his two sons and best friends, Michael and David.

Tina Capers-Hall is human resources director for the Atlanta Metro System of Comcast Cable Communications. In this role, she manages a wide array of human resources functions, including recruitment, employee relations, compliance, compensation and benefits, and employee and organizational development.

Prior to joining the cable industry, Tina's career has spanned the pharmaceutical, electronics and defense, financial services, and food and beverage industries in various leadership roles. She has also served as an adjunct professor in the academic arena, and is a former assistant-to-the-editor of the *Journal of Black Psychology*.

A Georgia 100 alumna, Tina is a member of the Cable Television Human Resources Association and the Cornell University Black Alumni Association. She also serves on the advisory board of Jazz 91.9 WCLK and attends Cascade United Methodist Church.

Tina holds a Bachelor of Science degree from Cornell University and a Master of Business Administration degree from Clark Atlanta University. She and her spouse of 23 years, John Hall, proprietor of Hall's of Fine Wines, have two children, Ian (Hampton University) and Gabrielle (Woodward Academy).

Stacy Cole

Director, Government Affairs
Comcast Cable Communications, Inc.

Veree Freeman Jr.

Senior Technical Operations Manager
Comcast Cable Communications, Inc.

Stacy Cole is director of government affairs for the Atlanta region of Comcast Cable Communications, Inc., the largest provider of cable television and broadband services in the country. In her role, she is responsible for maintaining relationships with elected officials and ensuring compliance of the cable franchise agreements in the Atlanta region.

Prior to joining Comcast, Cole served as director of government relations with Charter Communications. Additionally, she served as a law clerk for the honorable Vernon R. Pearson, former chief justice of the Washington State Supreme Court, and was a senior assistant city attorney with the City of Atlanta Law Department representing the Mayor's Office of Communications on cable and telecommunication matters.

Active in many professional and community organizations, Cole is a member of GABWA and NAMIC. She also serves on the boards of directors for Cool Girls, Inc., Literacy Action, Inc. and the Dogwood City Chapter of The Links, Inc.

Cole received a Bachelor of Arts degree from Washington State University and a juris doctorate degree from the Gonzaga University School of Law.

Veree Freeman Jr. is senior technical operations manager for Comcast Cable in the Atlanta region. In this position, he is responsible for 205 employees who maintain services, installation and manage the distribution plant for 206,000 subscribers that reside within DeKalb and Gwinnett counties.

Veree has been in the telecommunication industry for 16 years. He moved to Atlanta in 1995 from Paterson, New Jersey. He swiftly moved through the technical ranks, accepting a role in management as a supervisor in 2000, and was promoted to senior technical manager in 2002.

Veree is a member of the National Association for Multi-Ethnicity in Communications and the Society of Cable Telecommunication Engineers (SCTE). He is also on the board of directors for the Chattahoochee Chapter of the SCTE. He studied communications at Southern Connecticut State University and electrical engineering at DeVry University.

A native of Paterson, New Jersey, Veree is the husband of Genevia Freeman and the proud father of three daughters, Sakeema, Maya and Kianna.

Steve Gillenwater

Vice President, Human Resources, Field
Operations & Labor/Employee Relations
Comcast Cable Communications, Inc.

Shauna M. Gordon

Director, Dispatch
Comcast Cable Communications, Inc.

Steve Gillenwater has been a human resources (HR) professional for more than 18 years. Prior to joining Comcast in 2000, Steve was director of HR for Wesley Industries, Inc., a tier-one automotive supplier in Bloomfield Hills, Michigan. He also worked for the Warren/Conner Development Coalition in Detroit, Michigan, where he led the HR and administration functions for a large community-based nonprofit located in a former enterprise zone.

Steve has held several senior leadership positions in three different divisions of Comcast. In his current role as vice president of HR, field operations and labor/employee relations with the Southern Division of Comcast, he is responsible for employee relations and labor relations, including negotiating collective bargaining agreements. He has held similar positions in the former Midwest and Atlantic divisions of Comcast as well as regional HR lead positions.

Steve holds a master's degree in organizational management from the University of Phoenix in Southfield, Michigan, and a Bachelor of Science degree in communications from Western Michigan University in Kalamazoo, Michigan, where he was a scholarship athlete. He is a certified senior professional in human resources.

Shauna M. Gordon is director of dispatch for Comcast's Atlanta Metro System, where she oversees the Dispatch Department, supporting installation, service and outage restoration for customers in the city of Atlanta, as well as South Fulton, DeKalb, Fayetteville, Clayton, Rockdale and Walton counties.

Gordon has been a part of several successful product launches in Atlanta, including Comcast Digital Voice and High-Definition Television. Additionally, she has taken a leadership role in launching new applications that help manage technicians' productivity in the field, resulting in the reduction of missed customer appointments and increased customer satisfaction.

A member of Women in Cable Telecommunications, Gordon earned an associate degree in paralegal studies from Phillips Junior College in Carson, California. She is currently attending Jones International University where she is working on a Bachelor of Business Administration degree in communications. A native of Los Angeles, California, she is a proud parent of two children, Jessika and Anthony.

Angela Gray

Vice President, Human Resources
Comcast Cable Communications, Inc.

Robert Harris

Director, Technical Operations
Comcast Cable Communications, Inc.

Angela Gray is vice president of human resources for Comcast's Atlanta region, where she provides strategic direction for all aspects of human resources. Previously, she served as director of learning and development for Comcast's Southern Division and held leadership roles at Sprint, Circuit City and Carmax.

Gray holds a Bachelor of Science degree in education from Southern University and A&M College in Baton Rouge, and is currently enrolled at the University of Central Michigan, where she is pursuing a master's degree in administration. She earned a senior professional human resources certification from the Society for Human Resource Management, and holds certifications from the Institute for Applied Management and Law, the DOL and the EEOC.

A graduate of Comcast's Executive Leadership Forum, Gray is a fellow of the Betsy Magness Leadership program. She is a member of Women in Cable Telecommunications and was awarded the 2006 Red Letter Award for corporate mentoring. She is also a member of the Society for Human Resource Management, the National Association for Multi-Ethnicity in Communications and the National Association for Female Executives.

Robert Harris is director of technical operations for the Atlanta Metro System for Comcast. He oversees all technical operations, including construction, maintenance, fiber optics, installation and service for more than 444,000 subscribers in the city of Atlanta, as well as South Fulton, DeKalb, Fayetteville, Clayton, Rockdale and Walton counties.

Robert has been instrumental in launching new products, such as High-Definition Television, On Demand and Comcast Digital Voice in Atlanta, Georgia, and Baltimore, Maryland. He has been recognized by *Communications Technology* magazine as an outstanding manager and leader within the cable television industry. He is also an active member of the Society of Cable Television Engineers.

A native of Baltimore, Robert received a Bachelor of Science degree in electronics engineering technology from the DeVry Institute of Technology in Columbus, Ohio. He and his wife, Debra, are the proud parents of four children, Javonna, Christopher, Shannon and Janel.

Michael Hewitt

Regional Vice President, Operations
Comcast Cable Communications, Inc.

Herbert Linsey Jr.

Senior Construction Manager
Comcast Cable Communications, Inc.

Michael Hewitt, regional vice president of operations for Comcast's Atlanta region, focuses on strengthening the region's field operations. He works directly with the leadership of Atlanta's two systems and the call centers to align processes thus ensuring customer satisfaction throughout the service process. Throughout his career, he has been credited for consistently delivering results that demonstrate growth in Comcast's video and high-speed Internet business, and was instrumental in launching new products such as High-Definition Television, On Demand and Comcast Digital Voice.

Hewitt started his career in the cable industry in 1995 as area director for TCI's Baltimore/Washington, D.C. market. In 1999 he joined AT&T Broadband as the director of technical operations for the West Technical Center in Atlanta. Following the acquisition by Comcast, he was named vice president and general manager, overseeing operations in the city of Atlanta and South Fulton, Gwinnett and DeKalb counties. He was promoted to his current position in May of 2006.

Hewitt holds an undergraduate degree in mechanical engineering from Stony Brook University and a Master of Business Administration degree from Hofstra University.

Herbert Linsey Jr. is senior construction manager for Comcast Cable in Metro Atlanta. In his position, he manages the designing, engineering and building of cable plants for homes, apartments and businesses in the Atlanta area. Herbert began in the cable industry in 1980, starting as an installer and being promoted to service technician, maintenance technician and technical supervisor. He became one of the first black construction managers for Comcast in Atlanta. He was a 2004 nominee for the Circle of Success Team Award. In 2008 Herbert was promoted to senior construction manager.

A native of Atlanta, Herbert attended Morris Brown College, majoring in music education. In 1978 he gave his life to Christ, dedicating his musical talent to the Lord. He and his wife have conducted marriage seminars and several pre-marital counseling sessions. He gives God praise, glory and honor for his work in ministry and in the cable industry.

Herbert has been married to his high school sweetheart, Goddess Linsey, for 26 years. They are the parents of four sons, Joshua, Daniel, Caleb and Isaiah, and one daughter, Faith.

Since joining Comcast in 1999, Bridgett Shields-Wilson has held numerous positions. In her new role as senior manager for service center operations, she will lead all 17 Comcast service center locations in the Atlanta region, representing the largest group of service centers in Comcast's Southern Division and servicing more than 285,000 customers.

A native of Atlanta, Bridgett graduated from Southwest Atlanta High School in 1981 and received a Bachelor of Science degree from the DeVry Institute of Technology in 1994. She is also active in her community, working with organizations such as Cool Girls, Inc. and Unlock the Waiting Lists. Additionally, she leads the Comcast Cares Day effort for Clifton Elementary School in DeKalb County, Georgia. Bridgett is on the board of directors for The Smart Place Adult and Children Services, Inc., an organization dedicated to providing services to the mentally impaired. She is also a member of Alpha Kappa Alpha Sorority, Inc.

An excellent cook, Bridgett is known for her sweet potato pies and her love of gardening. She and her husband, Kevin, reside in Rex, Georgia.

Bridgett Shields-Wilson

Manager, Service Centers
Comcast Cable Communications, Inc.

Hello, Georgia.

We're American Family Insurance. Although we may be new to you, for more than 80 years we've been protecting millions of customers across the country. From our first policy (written for a Wisconsin farmer) to your policy, our protection is backed by our people—experienced agents who make it easy to get all the coverage you need at a competitive price. Call 1-800-MYAMFAM (1-800-692-6326) or visit **amfam.com** to find an agent near you.

Auto. Home. Life. Business. And more.

Michael Riggs,
here for you in Atlanta

AMERICAN FAMILY
INSURANCE ®

All your protection under one roof ®

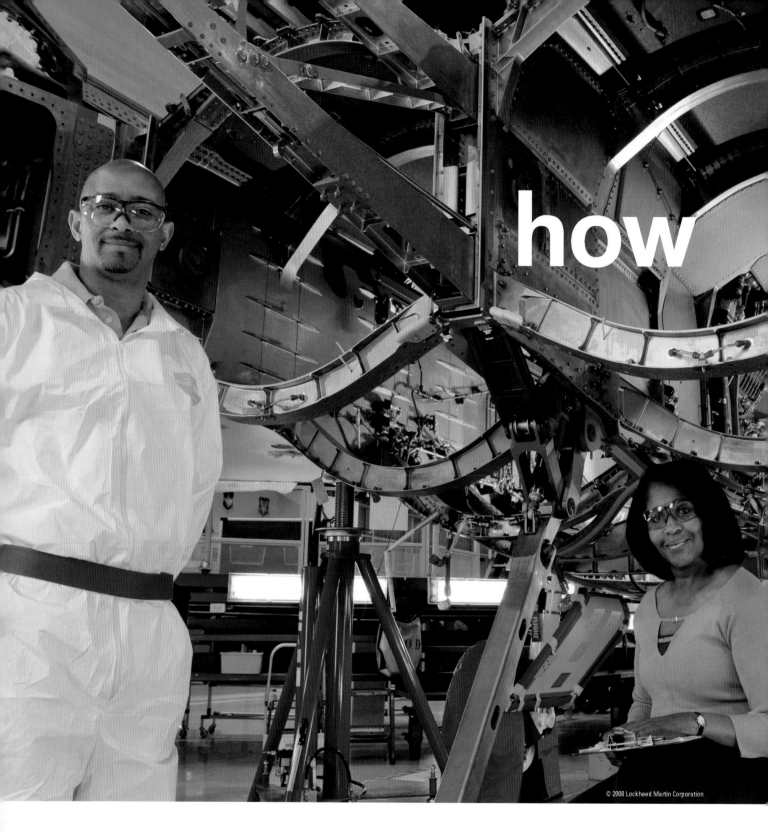

© 2008 Lockheed Martin Corporation

BETWEEN THE CHALLENGE AND THE SOLUTION, THERE IS ONE IMPORTANT WORD: HOW.

Diversity. It's not a goal. It's a necessity. When facing down the most important projects in the world, you need fresh ideas. And unique perspectives. Delivering the most complete answers to solve complex problems is all a question of how. And it is the how that makes all the difference.

lockheedmartin.com/how

LOCKHEED MARTIN
We never forget who we're working for®

BISHOP EDDIE L. LONG

BRIDGING THE GAP BETWEEN THE CHURCH AND THE COMMUNITY

BY ALONIA JERNIGAN

It has been commonly stated that the church cannot live apart from the community. In essence, the church/community relationship is one that can reflect that truth is spoken, grace is given without exception, lives are changed, people are empowered, and finally, but more importantly, God's love is revealed.

For anyone who has witnessed the ministry of Bishop Eddie L. Long, senior pastor of Lithonia's New Birth Missionary Baptist Church, there is a strong assurance that his leadership embodies these attributes. It is these attributes that underscore the fact that the church needs the community and the community needs the church.

While Long has gained a profound reputation as the leader of a congregation that exceeds 25,000 members, what few seem to grasp is that his focus has not been on numerical growth as much as it has been on nurturing people to the point where they experience life-changing, positive advancements. Consequently, the New Birth ministry is making an impact. After all, the church is the oldest formal institution known to mankind. The programs and outreach efforts of New Birth are quite meritorious, to say the least. In fact, they are an asset to the community.

Understanding the vital connection between the church and the community, Long imparts the importance of understanding that living a victorious life is not a bad thing. "All people, especially those who are in the body of Christ,

should understand that spiritual information without application leads to spiritual constipation," he shares. In other words, when one is taught principles of wholesome and successful living, the next task is to believe that the end result is actually within reach. Then, they must apply those principles to their daily lives.

Long adds, "Megachurches come under great criticism, yet have the power to confront power and make opportunities as far as health care, education, feeding the hungry and entrepreneur training. All of these additional arms that the church can give further empowers people to walk the life that Christ has ordained. It's relevant to the time, and the church must communicate, educate and empower."

The news of Long and the church's involvement has almost remained a well-kept secret – at least until now. Their relationships with many community organizations and community-related initiatives are paramount. For example, New Birth has continually played an active role in American Red Cross blood drives, simultaneously educating its members on the importance of giving blood, while also encouraging them to take an active stand in making donations.

Moreover, the church has been a major and consistent supporter of Hosea Feed the Hungry and Homeless, donating thousands of dollars and tons of food. Long has also been a strong voice for the need to support the organization. For 13 years, New Birth has made its way to the Georgia Dome for Easter services, while at the same

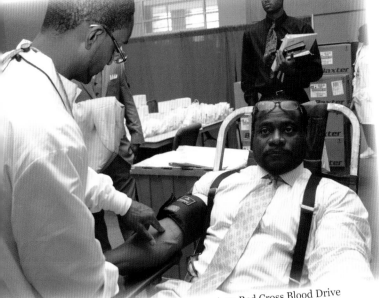

Bishop Long gives blood at the American Red Cross Blood Drive held at New Birth, December, 2008

Bishop Long fellowships during the church's Annual Outreach Project in 2007

time offering haircuts, clothing, meals and other services to members of the Atlanta community who may be in need.

Health and wellness are a major concern of Long's, which is evident in the church's involvement in activities that are related to such. He says, "Good health is a part of spiritual wholeness." In addition to being the centerpiece of the church's worship site, the sprawling 250-acre campus is also home to a state-of-the art wellness center. Additionally, New Birth plays a major role in its annual 5k walk, which raises awareness of and generates financial support for cancer patients and their families. Spearheaded by New Birth's first lady, Elder Vanessa Long, this effort shows the church's sincere concern for all people.

Long is a well-known proponent for excellence in education, and a testament to this fact is evidenced through the New Birth Christian Academy, a fully functioning, onsite school of excellence that he founded. His heart for the children was felt when asked what makes him cry. His response was, "When I see little kids stand up before large crowds and express themselves through their speeches. There's something about watching them. It invokes an awesome feeling that lets me know that our future is in great hands."

What's more, in 2004 Long established a mentorship program called the Longfellows Summer Academy to assist in the mental,

physical and spiritual development of young men between the ages of 13 and 16. What began as an eight-week program quickly developed into a year-round character development program that has graduated more than 200 young men since its inception.

Prior to becoming a pastor, Long had a successful career in corporate America. He thoroughly understands the tenets of business and applies them to his leadership at the church. It is no surprise, then, that he would envision the Embassy International Chamber of Commerce (EICC). Launched in 2008, EICC's vision is to build an international network of businesses that will help facilitate the transfer and release of billions of dollars and resources into the Kingdom of God. As such, the organization's membership is comprised of faith-based business owners who are committed to practicing biblical business principles and teachings. Cognizant that there are many outstanding

Bishop Long poses for a quick shot at the New Birth Annual 5K Run/Walk for Cancer sponsored by the Heart to Heart Ministry

"GOOD HEALTH IS A PART OF SPIRITUAL WHOLENESS."

entrepreneurs outside of New Birth, EICC's membership is not exclusive to the church.

As if these involvements and achievements are not enough, the impact of New Birth and Long is also felt across the globe. He has gained a special affinity for the African nation of Kenya and has planted many seeds there. Among them is the Bishop Eddie Long Bondeni Women and Children's Hospital. This health clinic that was started in the 1940s was upgraded to include a maternity ward and a children's hospital in 1999 with support from Long. The hospital is located in Nakuru, Kenya, and provides care to more than 200,000 low-income people. Since 1999, Long has donated $250,000 in equipment and funds to the project.

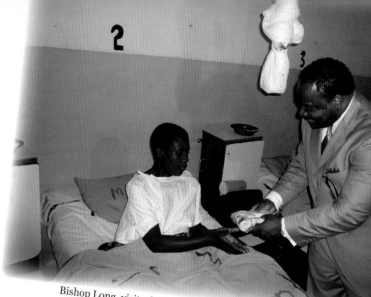

Bishop Long visits the Eddie L. Long Bodeni Hospital Kenya

"ALL PEOPLE, ESPECIALLY THOSE WHO ARE IN THE BODY OF CHRIST, SHOULD UNDERSTAND THAT SPIRITUAL INFORMATION WITHOUT APPLICATION LEADS TO SPIRITUAL CONSTIPATION."

Additionally, the Center of Hope was established in 2001 for the purpose of helping the disadvantaged community of Nakuru, Kenya. Young men and women attend the center to study technical skills, with an average of 230 people enrolled at one time. Long provides financial support for this initiative and has an onsite representative. Another initiative is the King's Orphanage. Located in

Nakuru since 2003, the orphanage provides housing for 300 street children. Similar to the Center of Hope, Long provides financial support for the center and an onsite representative.

Since 2005, the Moi Africa Foundation Institute, located in Nairobi, Kenya, is responsible for negotiating peace in troubled regions such as Somalia, Sudan and Liberia. Long is a board member of the foundation and has donated $70,000 to the group since its inception. Continuing his commitment to education, Long has awarded $38,000 annually in scholarships to young Kenyan leaders since 2003. His goodwill has allowed the beneficiaries to attend college in the United States. Two students graduated in 2008 and returned to Kenya to minister and establish churches.

This is an incredible list of accomplishments for a young man who shared a bed with his brother until he was in the 10th grade. "I had three brothers and we all slept in one bedroom," says Long. He goes on to chuckle and say, "I was so glad when my two older brothers got old enough to go to college." Long was the third of four sons born into his family, but he insists, "I acted like the baby, though."

After witnessing his father serve many years as a Baptist pastor, it was no surprise that the young Long found himself mimicking his father every chance he got. "I played church all the time," he says. But many people do not realize that with the task of pastoring also comes a lot of pain in addition to a world of responsibilities. "As I grew older, being a leader in the church became the furthest thing from my mind. I diverted my attention. I was determined to be a businessman," he shares.

Groundbreaking ceremony in Eldoret, Kenya, for the television/radio station, 2006

Upon completing high school, he left home to pursue a college education. Successful in this endeavor, he earned an undergraduate degree in business administration from North Carolina Central University. Still not totally rid of the undeniable fire of the gospel that continued to burn inside his bones, Long journeyed to Atlanta to enter seminary at the Interdenominational Theological Center (ITC), where he later earned a master's degree in divinity. He further earned a doctorate degree in pastoral ministry from the International College of Excellence, an affiliate of Life Christian University in Tampa, Florida.

By 1997, Long found himself serving as pastor of a 300-member congregation. The members were dedicated and he was committed to preaching the unadulterated gospel of Jesus Christ. Perhaps the church's explosive growth could be attributed to the manner in which Long presented the gospel, or one may surmise that the principles he learned in business proved to be the foundation that would later allow him to successfully grow a ministry.

What, then, is success in Long's eyes? "Success is being able to discern God's call on your life. It is when you know for what purpose you were born and you have a peace in knowing that," he says.

Naturally, the demands of being a pastor of Long's magnitude is no simple task, but he is truly grateful for a loving and supportive wife and children. He recalls his most touching moment in ministry when he read the tribute that his children gave him during his 20th pastoral anniversary. Of this moment he says, "I wept. My kids described me as being very special to them and they talked about how they appreciated me making them feel important. This only goes to show that you can win the world, but if you lose your family you have nothing." He adds that his family adds balance to his life. "I keep a very busy calendar, but it's very important

that I sacrifice and make special time for my family. Vanessa does a wonderful job in making sure things stay right on the home front, and I can't begin to tell her how much I value that."

From a pastoral perspective, his assistant, Elder April McLaughlin says, "I don't think he sees the flowers he's grown. Sometimes I look around and see the lives he's transformed. Whether through the Internet, our broadcasts, his international involvement or so many other endeavors; he's made a tremendous impact that can never be measured. People have killed some strongholds that he spoke to. He'll never know the people he's touched. It actually has a trickle-down effect because if he touched me, I've touched someone else in return, etc. That's a huge accomplishment."

Nonetheless, when it's all said and done, everything Bishop Eddie L. Long has done is to the glory of God. He says, "I'm not afraid of trying and failing. I am, however, afraid of succeeding at the wrong thing."

"I KEEP A VERY BUSY CALENDAR, BUT IT'S VERY IMPORTANT THAT I SACRIFICE AND MAKE SPECIAL TIME FOR MY FAMILY."

Long Family Photo, 2007

Operating as a true warrior who is described as visionary, giving, energetic, compassionate and loyal, his life is a testament to the fact the world is a much better place simply because he wasn't afraid to try to make a difference.

Photo Credit:

"I'M NOT AFRAID OF TRYING AND FAILING. I AM, HOWEVER, AFRAID OF SUCCEEDING AT THE WRONG THING."

Together we care.

LexisNexis is a leading provider of technology, information and analytic solutions to professionals across a variety of industries.

It is our belief that a corporation must be a positive force in society. We harness our unique capabilities through volunteerism, technology donations and strategic nonprofit partnerships to positively impact the communities.

We are a proud sponsor of **Who's Who in Black Atlanta** and congratulate those being honored this year.

Celebrating

diversity

in our **workplace**.

And yours.

Creating a diverse workplace isn't just **"the right thing to do,"** it's a business advantage. The byproduct of Humana's commitment to diversity is increased creativity. Every associate's contribution counts, and our differences produce superior business results. To learn more about Humana's commitment to diversity, visit **Humana.com/diversity**.

HUMANA®
Guidance when you need it most

Join us in saluting Atlanta's diverse workplace

Group health   Medicare   Individual health   Dental, Life, Vision

Champions OF
Diversity

HOT 107.9

MAJIC 107.5 97.5
-ATLANTA'S BEST MIX OF R&B-

Praise 102.5
Atlanta's Inspiration Station

RADIO ONE
THE URBAN MEDIA SPECIALIST

www.HOT1079ATL.com • www.MAJICATL.com • www.PRAISE1025.com
RADIO ONE ATLANTA | 101 Marietta Street 12th Floor Atlanta, Ga 30303 | (404) 765-9750

Atlanta's
CORPORATE SPOTLIGHT

INTEREST

LIMELIGHT

ATTENTION

PROMINENCE

DELTA

HIGHLIGHT

CELEBRATE

HEADLINE

FOCUS

RECOGNITION

Lisa Abraham-Brown

Director, Human Resources
Delta Air Lines, Inc.

Sandy Palmer Gordon

Managing Director, Flight Attendants
Delta Air Lines, Inc.

Lisa Abraham-Brown is director of human resources at Delta Air Lines. She leads the global human resource strategy for Delta's largest division, Airport Customer Service, which includes more than 15,000 employees worldwide. In her role, she is responsible for leading the people strategy surrounding Delta's cultural transformation.

An experienced and proven human resources professional, Lisa joined Delta Technology in 1999 as a human resource consultant. In 2003 she became a human resource manager in in-flight service. Lisa was promoted to general manager of human resources in reservation sales and customer care in 2004, and to her current position in 2006. With each position, her scope of responsibility has increased. Lisa has demonstrated an impressive depth of business knowledge, a strong drive for results and effective relationship-building skills with her clients, team and constituents.

Prior to Delta, Lisa held various human resource and leadership positions at Prudential, Bank of Atlanta, Concessions International and Florist Transworld Delivery.

Lisa holds a bachelor's degree in human resources from Michigan State University, and a Master of Business Administration degree from Kennesaw State University.

Sandy Palmer Gordon is managing director of flight attendants for Delta Air Lines, the fastest-growing international airline. In this position, she is responsible for managing the daily customer service performance of the Delta flight attendants.

A 19-year Delta veteran, Sandy began her career as a flight attendant. She has held numerous leadership positions, specifically within the In-Flight Services Department. Prior to her current position, Sandy served as director of customer service of Song and played a key role during its startup, which led the way for many of Delta's new innovative customer products.

Previously, Sandy served as general manager of in-flight scheduling, where she was responsible for managing the daily scheduling logistics of more than 18,000 flight attendants. In this role, she was the recipient of the REACH Award, recognizing her decisive and effective leadership during the 9/11 tragedy.

A native of Atlanta, Sandy received a Bachelor of Science degree in finance from Hampton University in 1990. Today she resides in Fairburn, Georgia, with her husband and their two children.

Esther L. Hammond

Director
Equal Opportunity & Compliance
Delta Air Lines, Inc.

Melanee Haywood

Vice President, Engineering &
Common Services
Delta Technology, LLC

Esther L. Hammond is director of equal opportunity and compliance at Delta Air Lines. She spent the first 17 years of her career with Delta in Chicago, Illinois, relocating to Atlanta in 1995. In her current role, Esther is responsible for Delta's affirmative action plans, OFCCP audits, substance testing programs, criminal history record checks and employee networking groups.

Esther sits on the boards of directors for the Delta Community Credit Union and the Jesse Draper Boys & Girls Club.

Esther holds a Bachelor of Science degree. She also received a Master of Science degree in organization/management, with a concentration in human resources, from Capella University. She has maintained the designation of certified professional in human resources for more than nine years.

Melanee Haywood is vice president of engineering and common services at Delta Technology, LLC, a wholly owned subsidiary of Delta Air Lines. Her responsibilities include providing leadership and strategic direction for 200 architects, engineers and developers who design technology solutions for Delta Air Lines.

Melanee began her career with Delta Air Lines in 1980, and has held various positions of increased responsibility within Delta and its information technology subsidiaries. As an experienced leader, Melanee consistently seeks to influence direction throughout the company. One of her primary objectives is to build strong leadership competencies at all levels of the organization. She is committed to leadership development through formal mentoring to facilitate positive individual career growth.

Melanee received a Bachelor of Arts degree in psychology from Spelman College in Atlanta, Georgia. She is a member of the Infrastructure Executive Council of the Corporate Executive Board, the Information Technology Senior Management Forum, the Delta Air Lines Women's Employee Network, and serves as executive sponsor of Delta Technology's Medallion Toastmasters Chapter.

She resides in Smyrna, Georgia, and is a member of Cascade United Methodist Church.

Keyra Lynn Johnson

Director, Internal Communications
Delta Air Lines, Inc.

Thonnia Lee

Senior Manager & Editor
Corporate Communications
Delta Air Lines, Inc.

Keyra Lynn Johnson is director of internal communications for Delta Air Lines. She sets the course for the company's employee communications strategies, and oversees Delta's internal news vehicles, leadership communications and the corporate intranet. She is an advocate for Delta's goal of direct, honest, collaborative communications with its more than 45,000 employees worldwide.

Keyra began her career with Delta in 1994 as a customer service agent. In 2000 she joined Delta's corporate communications team as manager of strategic communications. She served as general manager and program director of internal communications before being promoted to her current position in 2005.

Prior to joining Delta, Keyra was a consultant for the Parents Resource Institute for Drug Education (PRIDE), representing the organization in 17 states, Canada and Japan. She also co-authored a grant to establish and manage PRIDE youth teams throughout the Atlanta Public Schools.

Keyra graduated from Georgia State University with a Bachelor of Arts degree in speech communication. A believer in giving back to the community, she is the co-founder of Girls In Transition, a youth mentoring program.

Thonnia Lee is senior manager and editor in corporate communications at Delta Air Lines. She is responsible for the monthly employee magazine, *NewsDigest*, as well as the editorial direction, look and feel for company news on the intranet. Her team provides employee news in real time on a site that is updated with breaking news several times a day.

Prior to joining Delta, Lee was editor of the Morehouse College alumnus magazine and acted as lead on the media team as interim director of public relations. An award-winning journalist, she has written for *Atlanta*, *Essence*, *Black Enterprise* and a number of other local and regional magazines. She spent six years with *The Atlanta Journal-Constitution*.

A graduate of Hampton University, Lee has served as an adjunct professor of journalism at Clark Atlanta University, and taught magazine freelance writing at the Callanwolde Fine Arts Center. Under her leadership, Delta's *NewsDigest* has received several awards from the International Association of Business Communicators, and is acknowledged by communications professionals as an industry leader in internal communications.

Valerie S. Nesbitt

General Manager, Supplier Diversity
Delta Air Lines, Inc.

Scarlet Pressley-Brown

Director, External Affairs
Delta Air Lines, Inc.

Valerie S. Nesbitt is general manager of supplier diversity for Delta Air Lines. She is responsible for developing and implementing the corporation's strategy for building and maintaining partnerships with small, minority- and women-owned businesses. Prior to joining Delta, she held the position of purchasing manager at Scientific-Atlanta, Inc., where she was responsible for the purchase of general office and computer supplies, and capital equipment.

Earlier in her career, Valerie spent 12 years with Martin Marietta Specialty Components Inc. (formerly General Electric), where she gained an extensive background in supply chain management through a variety of assignments.

A native of Aiken, South Carolina, Valerie is a certified purchasing manager. She earned a Bachelor of Arts degree in psychology from the University of South Carolina, and a master's degree in public administration from Golden Gate University.

Valerie and her husband, Donas, reside in Smyrna, Georgia.

Scarlet Pressley-Brown is director of external affairs and community relations for Delta Air Lines, Inc. and vice president of the Delta Air Lines Foundation.

Recognized by the Atlanta Business League among Atlanta's Top Black Women of Influence, Scarlet has received the Trumpet Awards Foundation High Heels in High Places Award, among others. In addition, *Atlanta Tribune: The Magazine* featured her and her husband, Wendell, as one of Atlanta's Power Couples in 2006.

Scarlet serves on the boards of the Atlanta Business League, the Juvenile Diabetes Research Foundation, the Atlanta Medical Association and Ron Clark Academy. She is a member of various organizations, including the National Black MBA Association and the National Coalition of 100 Black Women, Inc. In addition, Scarlet is a proud graduate of the Leadership Atlanta Class of 2008.

She received a bachelor's degree in communication from Oglethorpe University and a Master of Business Administration degree from the University of Phoenix.

Scarlet and Wendell are the proud parents of Wendell Jr., April Partridge (Kenya), Amber French (Jason), Kiesha and Dexter, and the proud grandparents of Ryan Michelle French.

William E. Settle

Program Manager, Global Diversity
Talent Acquisition & Retention
Delta Air Lines, Inc.

William E. Settle is program manager for global diversity, talent acquisition and retention for Delta Air Lines at the world headquarters in Atlanta, Georgia. Settle is responsible for the management of Delta's global diversity community outreach initiatives. For 12 years, he served as dean of students and vice president for student affairs at Morris Brown College in Atlanta. He entered the corporate world with Delta Air Lines on June 1, 1998.

A native of Charleston, South Carolina, Settle received a bachelor's degree from Fisk University in Nashville, Tennessee, and a master's degree in education from Western Carolina University in Cullowhee, North Carolina.

Settle serves on the minority advisory council of the Metropolitan Atlanta Chapter of the American Red Cross. He is a board member of the Salley Foundation and a vice chair of the Southern Region of the General Alumni Association of Fisk University.

He and his wife, Michelle, have two sons, Matthew and Christopher. They currently reside in Fayetteville, Georgia.

Atlanta's
CORPORATE SPOTLIGHT

INTEREST

LIMELIGHT

ATTENTION

PROMINENCE

HIGHLIGHT

CELEBRATE

HEADLINE

FOCUS

RECOGNITION

At The Home Depot, we believe we are at our best when we bring all of our diverse talents to bear on creating a great customer and associate experience. As a global retailer, our company's success is directly tied to how well we reflect the markets we serve, including the $20 billion African-American home improvement market.

Celebrating diversity and practicing inclusion are not only the right things to do – these goals are necessary to stay competitive. Along with having the best products and services, we aim to hire the best: associates who feel respected, who can relate to our customers' diverse needs and who can speak our customers' language. When we create a diverse and inclusive working and shopping environment, a ripple effect of positive action follows: a highly engaged workforce thrives; customer service improves; and customer satisfaction increases.

The Home Depot was founded with an entrepreneurial spirit, and we know that instilling diversity in our core business approach is the catalyst for continued innovative thinking and the new ways of building our markets and communities.

We are committed to remaining the retailer, employer, neighbor and investment of choice. We realize that our competitive advantage lies in our ability to effectively nurture the future generations of The Home Depot customers and associates by enriching and celebrating the diversity that exists within the communities in which we do business. To deliver on this commitment, it is critical that we continue to focus our attention on the changing demographics of the communities that have embraced The Home Depot for almost 30 years.

Tonnice Charles

Director of
Global Supplier Performance
The Home Depot

Marvin R. Ellison

Executive Vice President of U.S. Stores
The Home Depot

Tonnice Charles is the director of global supplier performance for The Home Depot. She joined the company in 2002 and is currently responsible for supplier scorecard, supplier compliance, supplier social and environmental responsibility, supplier communications and electronic exchange enablement for The Home Depot enterprise.

Tonnice began her career as a product engineer and marketing manager with Intel in Phoenix, Arizona, and Portland, Oregon. Prior to joining The Home Depot, she was a consultant with Cap Gemini Ernst & Young.

A native of New Orleans, Louisiana, Tonnice holds a Bachelor of Science degree in electrical engineering from Southern University and A&M College, and a Master of Business Administration degree from The University of North Carolina Kenan-Flagler Business School.

Tonnice currently serves as treasurer and recording secretary of the Velvet Hammers, an organization of executive women within The Home Depot whose mission is to promote professional and personal development, and involvement inside and outside the company.

Marvin Ellison is executive vice president of U.S. stores for The Home Depot. He is responsible for driving sales and execution across the company's retail divisions and overseeing operations of more than 1,950 stores and more than 240,000 employees in the United States, Guam, Puerto Rico and the U.S. Virgin Islands.

Marvin has more than 25 years of retail experience, and has served in a variety of operational roles at The Home Depot since joining the company in 2002, including president of the Northern Division, senior vice president of global logistics, and vice president of loss prevention. Prior to joining The Home Depot, he spent 15 years with Target Stores in a variety of operational roles, including corporate and store assets protection.

Marvin is actively involved in philanthropic efforts, including inner-city school renovations as well as mentoring programs aimed at developing inner-city youth. He earned a business administration degree in marketing from The University of Memphis, and a Master of Business Administration degree from Emory University.

Marvin and his wife, Sharyn, reside in Marietta, Georgia, with their two children, Donavan and Gabrielle.

Gloria Johnson Goins

Chief Diversity Officer
The Home Depot

Sabrina M. Green

Director of Talent Management &
Organizational Effectiveness
Northern Division
The Home Depot

Gloria Johnson Goins is chief diversity officer for The Home Depot, responsible for creating and implementing companywide diversity and inclusion initiatives for the world's second-largest retailer. In this role, she is charged with leveraging diversity and inclusion to enable The Home Depot to become the company of choice.

She is active in numerous professional and civic organizations, including the United Way of America, the NAACP and Leadership Atlanta. Additionally, she is a member of the Florida and Georgia bar associations. An honors graduate of Stanford University, Goins also received a law degree from the University of Pennsylvania, and a Master of Business Administration degree from Mercer University.

In 1992 Goins joined the BellSouth Telecommunications Legal Department, where she handled employment/labor law, general litigation, and state/federal regulatory matters. From 1997 to 2000, she was a general attorney with BellSouth Cellular Corporation, and had responsibility for general and employment litigation. From 2000 to 2002, she served as vice president of diversity for Cingular Wireless, the nation's largest wireless communications company.

Goins is married to Prince Leon Goins, and they have one daughter, Grace Princess.

Sabrina Green is a human resources professional who has worked in the human resources field for 27 years. Her professional experience includes developing human capital strategies and processes to support the organization's strategic objectives. More specifically, Sabrina provides counsel to executives regarding the total human resources function, including talent management, organizational effectiveness, staffing and employment practices.

Sabrina works closely with all levels of management in advising and making recommendations that significantly impact operations. Her mantra is delivering quality results, setting strategic priorities, influencing and collaborating at all levels.

Sabrina attended the University of Phoenix and the University of Michigan Business School's Human Resources Executive Program. She is a certified senior professional in human resources.

Sabrina has served in many organizations which provide support to women and children, including the Atlanta Girls Foundation (role model); the Northwest Georgia Girl Scout Council (former board member); Quality Care for Children (board member) and the Atlanta Women's Foundation Destiny Fund. Additionally, she was appointed by Governor Barnes in 2002 to serve on the Commission for Service and Volunteerism.

Arlette Decuir Guthrie, Ph.D.

Vice President, Talent Management
The Home Depot

Jocelyn J. Hunter

Vice President of Legal for
Employment & Labor Law
The Home Depot

Dr. Arlette Decuir Guthrie serves as the vice president of talent management for The Home Depot enterprise, leading the organizational effectiveness, executive staffing and talent management teams. In this capacity, she oversees succession planning and human resource review, executive staffing, and pipeline leadership development programs. Arlette joined The Home Depot in 1999, and with increasing levels of responsibility, she has continued to make contributions focused on building and retaining a high-performing, diverse workforce.

Prior to joining The Home Depot, Arlette served as the research leader for an international workplace research consortium and an assessment center consultant through the department of psychology at Texas A&M University in College Station, Texas. She holds a bachelor's degree from Dillard University in New Orleans, Louisiana, and Master of Science and Doctor of Philosophy degrees in industrial-organizational psychology from Texas A&M.

A native of Louisiana, Arlette relocated to Houston, Texas, during early childhood, and she still considers that her home. She currently resides in Atlanta with her husband, Oral, and son, Jonathan.

Jocelyn Hunter is the vice president of legal for employment and labor law at The Home Depot. She has been a member of The Home Depot Legal Department since 1997. Prior to her appointment to vice president, she has served in the roles of corporate counsel and senior corporate counsel at the company.

In her current role, Hunter has responsibility for the worldwide labor and employment matters for The Home Depot and its subsidiaries. The Home Depot has 355,000 associates and more than 2,104 locations enterprisewide.

Hunter began her career in a small labor and employment firm in Atlanta in 1987. In 1989 she became an associate at the law firm of Paul Hastings Janofsky & Walker LLP. There, Hunter served in an advisory role to employers, and litigated individual and class action employment matters. In 1993 she left Paul Hastings and joined Dun and Bradstreet Software Services, Inc., where she was assistant general counsel responsible for employment law, commercial litigation and contracts.

CORPORATE SPOTLIGHT

K. Michelle Sourie Johnson

Director of Supplier Diversity
The Home Depot

Troy Saunders

Senior Director
Corporate Services &
Facilities Management
The Home Depot

K. Michelle Sourie Johnson is director of supplier diversity for The Home Depot. In her nearly ten-year tenure with the company, she has led several areas of the organization through successful growth and change processes.

In 2003 Michelle assumed the role as director of supplier diversity and designed the company's first formalized supplier diversity strategy and supporting processes. The team's efforts gained industry recognition. Notably, Michelle was also selected as Advocate of the Year for the Georgia Minority Supplier Development Council in 2007 and 2008.

An Oklahoma native, she earned a Bachelor of Science degree in organizational administration from Oklahoma State University and a juris doctorate degree from The University of Kansas. Michelle serves on several boards, including the Georgia Minority Supplier Development Council, the Women's Business Enterprise National Council, the Diversity Information Resources and The National Center for American Indian Enterprise Development. An active member of Leadership Atlanta, she is also active within her church and community where she serves on the Howard University School of Communications board of visitors and the SafeHouse board of directors.

Troy Saunders is responsible for The Home Depot's non-product real estate, property management, food service, branded merchandise, and corporate office services enterprisewide.

His responsibilities include a portfolio of corporate, regional and district offices, and call and training centers. He is also responsible for real estate planning, project management, portfolio analysis, strategic space planning, office services, development of food service strategies, construction management, and branded merchandise management programs. Troy serves as a key contributor of real estate, property management, and corporate services expertise on strategic initiatives that continue to help drive key priorities and improve execution across 2,200 stores in the United States, Canada, Mexico and China.

He previously served as senior director of corporate asset management at Black Entertainment Television Inc., headquartered in Washington, D.C. He was responsible for real estate, supply chain management, strategic sourcing, property management, construction management, travel programs, and security for all offices and broadcast facilities.

Troy served as an officer in the Navy after graduating from the U.S. Naval Academy, where he earned a Bachelor of Science degree in engineering.

Anika Clement Wharton is the merchant of pipe for all U.S. stores for The Home Depot. She has P&L responsibility for more than $500 million in sales, and is responsible for establishing product retails, product innovation, product assortment.

Anika has been with The Home Depot for seven years, and has served in a variety of roles at The Home Depot since joining the company in 2002, including director of merchandise planning, project manager of capital resets, and manager of strategic financial analysis. Prior to joining The Home Depot, she worked with Accenture's Strategy Consulting Group and with Arthur Andersen.

An active mentor, Anika has volunteered with the Dance Theatre of Harlem's youth program and Junior Achievement.

She earned aBachelor of Arts degree in Economics from Spelman College, and a Master of Business Administration degree from The Wharton Business School. Additionally, she is a Certified Public Accountant.

Anika and her husband, Steve, reside in Atlanta, Georgia, with their two children, Patricia and Alexander.

Anika Clement Wharton

Merchant
The Home Depot

CELEBRATE 35 YEARS

1974 - 2009

radio

broadcasting

excellence

On April 10, 1974, Jazz 91.9 FM WCLK aired its very first jazz selection, "Maiden Voyage," by Herbie Hancock. Under the direction of former Clark College President Vivian Henderson, and former Director of Mass Communications Charles Hobson, WCLK became the first black federally licensed educational FM station in Georgia. Transmitting from Clark College's McPheeters-Dennis Hall at a mere 54 watts from noon - midnight. WCLK marked the beginning of an exciting journey to cultivate an Atlanta public radio entity that would educate, inform and entertain listeners.

BE A PART OF THE CELEBRATION!

VISIT WWW.WCLK.COM

Celebrating 35 Years of Radio Broadcasting Excellence

Atlanta's
GOVERNMENT SPOTLIGHT

INTEREST

LIMELIGHT

ATTENTION

PROMINENCE

HIGHLIGHT

CELEBRATE

HEADLINE

FOCUS

RECOGNITION

FULTON COUNTY

FULTON COUNTY

Fulton County's MFBE Program Opens Doors to Vendor Opportunities

Getting a foot in the door of any sales client can be difficult, but the Fulton County Minority/Female Business Enterprise (MFBE) program – a vendor initiative that monitors and ensures opportunities for minority and female business enterprises – helps that door open wider.

For the past three years (2005-2008), the County has awarded minority and female firms more than 35 percent of all contracts for goods and services.

That improvement – not a goal, quota or set-aside – is the result of a comprehensive program of vendor awareness, inclusion and program monitoring.

"Our progress over the years has been slow, steady and an uphill climb, but we're making inroads towards ensuring opportunities for participation for all who want to do business with us," says Fulton County Manager Zachary Williams.

The Department of Purchasing and Contract Compliance employs an aggressive, multi-pronged outreach effort to solicit and encourage MFBEs to bid on County contracts:

Targeted Notification of Bids – Advertisements and notifications of all County contracts are placed in minority newspapers and trade publications, posted on the Georgia Procurement Registry and the Fulton County Web site (www.fultoncountyga.gov) and aired on Fulton's television station, FGTV, Channels 21 or 23.

MFBE Online Application – A new online process allows vendors to submit certification and recertification applications by logging on to the Web site www.occfultoncountyga.com. After the application is submitted, vendors can track the status of their application, verify their certification expiration date, verify payments and modify their profile information at any time.

MFBE Certification – This designation ensures businesses are what they claim to be. In order to qualify as an MFBE, a business entity has to be at least 51 percent owned and controlled by one or more minorities or females.

MFBE Directory – This valuable online resource lists approximately 580 active certified minority and female entrepreneurs available to do business with the County's 36 departments, as well as with prime contractors.

Vendor Self-Service System – All vendors use this online tool to register their businesses with Fulton County so they can receive bid notifications in their specialty areas, track their quotes and receive award notifications.

Vendor Education – Free hands-on vendor training workshops are held throughout the year on subjects such as how to become a registered vendor and how to submit and track bids, as well as how to become certified as a Minority/Female Business Enterprise.

Vendor Networking – Fulton staffers partner with professional and trade organizations, attend area vendor fairs and establish liaisons with local, small minority and women business groups to explain the MFBE program and upcoming bids.

Insurance and Bonding – A redeveloped and redefined Surety Assistance Insurance and Bonding Program offers access to advice on various aspects of surety bonding, such as an insurance and surety bonding overview, obtaining a first bond or increasing present capacity, project management techniques, and legal issues of surety bonding.

For more information, call 404-612-6300.

FULTON COUNTY

Larry Few
Fire Chief
Fulton County Fire Department

Cassandra A. Jones
Chief of Police
Fulton County Police Departmen

Larry Few is fire chief of the Fulton County Fire Department. He directs and manages all fire fighting, fire prevention and fire service activities, and develops recommendations for the protection of life and property in Fulton County. Appointed by the county manager on August 8, 2006, he manages a $33 million budget and 398 employees.

Few previously served in many divisions of the Fulton County Fire Department. He has held chief officer positions in Fire and Emergency Medical Services, Operations, Fire Administration, Support Services and Community Risk Reduction.

Few earned a bachelor's degree in business management from Shorter College in Rome, Georgia.

Cassandra A. Jones is chief of police for Fulton County. She was sworn in as interim chief of police on July 13, 2007, and was appointed chief on October 9, 2007.

Jones achieved many firsts in her career since joining the department in 1979. She became the first female sergeant in 1982, and later became the first female promoted to lieutenant, captain and major. Jones is also the first and only female to hold the rank of deputy chief in the department. That promotion made her the commander over the Uniform Division in the North and South Precinct Patrol Division and Special Services Division North and South.

Jones has also been a patrol officer, patrol sergeant and captain of the Special Services Division in charge of the Traffic Unit, Crime Prevention Units and Juvenile Detectives. As commander of the Major Case Division, she oversaw the SWAT Team, Narcotics and K9 units.

A Military Police School honor graduate, Jones is trained as a military intelligence officer. She holds a degree in criminal justice from Georgia State University.

GOVERNMENT SPOTLIGHT

GOVERNMENT SPOTLIGHT

FULTON COUNTY

Dr. Barbara Lattimore

Behavioral Health

Veronica Williams Njoku

Director, Fulton County Arts Council
Fulton County

Dr. Barbara Lattimore is director of the Fulton County Department of Mental Health, Developmental Disabilities and Addictive Diseases, a position she has held since 2003. The department is the largest public behavioral health organization in the southeast U.S., serving approximately 6,000 consumers annually and representing more than 75,000 contacts.

Lattimore has implemented an innovative system-of-care program involving many public care agencies, including schools, physical health, human and social services, and others. She played a lead role in developing Fulton County's first mental health treatment jail diversion program.

Lattimore has more than 25 years of experience in behavioral health treatment, advocacy and administration. Previously, she managed an outpatient substance abuse and mental health program for more than 6,000 military and civilian families. She also worked with the American Red Cross in Mannheim, Germany, approving emergency funds and providing trauma and grief counseling for soldiers and families.

An adjunct faculty member at Argosy University, Lattimore holds a Doctor of Philosophy degree in community health, master's degrees in health services administration and counseling, and a Bachelor of Science degree in psychology.

Veronica Williams Njoku is director of the Fulton County Arts Council (FCAC), which is responsible for the development and implementation of Fulton County Arts initiatives. Additionally, she oversees the management of four county-owned neighborhood arts centers and a fifth facility operated through a public/private partnership.

Njoku is also responsible for establishing prototypes for policies and procedures in the governmental granting process. Appointed by the county manager on July 10, 2000, she manages a $5.7 million budget and 25 employees. She was previously the FCAC deputy director and the director of community relations for the Alliance Theatre.

Currently, Njoku serves on the boards of the National Guild of Community Schools of the Arts, Americans for the Arts, Arts Supporting Agencies Partnership, the Metropolitan Atlanta Arts Fund and the Atlanta Convention & Visitors Bureau Cultural Tourism. She is also the Fulton County liaison to the board of the National Black Arts Festival.

Njoku earned a bachelor's degree from Georgia State University and holds a diploma from the University of Paris in Paris, France.

FULTON COUNTY

R. David Ware

County Attorney
Fulton County

Zachary Williams

County Manager
Fulton County

R. David Ware is the county attorney for Fulton County. Appointed November 19, 2008, he is responsible for a team of attorneys and staff who counsel the Board of Commissioners, county manager and county staff on legal matters related to policy and services.

Ware joined the County Attorney's Office in September of 2004. Previously, he was the senior attorney in charge of the Employment/Personnel Division. Prior to that, he was senior attorney in charge of risk management and a staff attorney in the Public Safety Division.

Before joining Fulton County, Ware practiced privately, specializing in litigation and was a well-known sports attorney. A past president of the Gate City Bar Association, he has served as a magistrate judge in state and superior courts.

Ware earned a bachelor's degree in English from West Georgia College and received a juris doctorate degree from The University of Georgia School of Law. A member of the State Bar of Georgia, he is admitted to practice in all federal and state trial and appellate courts. He is also executive pastor at Light of the World Christian Ministries.

Zachary Williams was selected by the Fulton County Board of Commissioners to serve as county manager after a national search. He was sworn into office on January 2, 2008, bringing nearly 20 years' experience in local government, with emphasis on efficiency, innovation, customer service and communications. He supervises 40 departments serving more than 960,000 residents, with 6,000 employees and a budget of nearly $1 billion. Williams has sought ways to maintain services during a time of reduced revenue due to municipalization and the housing crisis, and was able to propose a balanced budget for 2009.

Williams previously served as assistant county administrator for Broward County, Florida, since 2004. He led more than 80 departments, divisions and agencies, and helped develop an outcome-based process that reduced the county's budget by more than $90 million. He was also assistant city manager for Coral Gables, Florida, and worked in the City Manager's Office in Santa Fe Springs, California.

Williams holds a Master of Public Administration degree and a Bachelor of Science degree in criminal justice, both from California State University, Long Beach.

A COMMITMENT
To Excellence
since **1990**

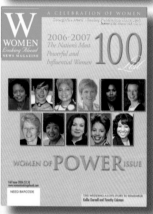

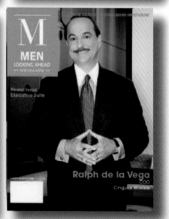

Women Looking Ahead was the first company (1990) and publication (1993) that caters exclusively to the wants, needs and lifestyles of today's business woman. These women range from your average college student to the retired woman.

Men Looking Ahead has an allure that appeals to men readers of all backgrounds, ethnic groups, races and diversities. It is a celebration of the printed word designed to highlight the accomplishments of men, provide viable information and serve as an echoing voice for every man of the 21st century.

Rebecca Franklin is the spirit behind Women Looking Ahead, Inc. Women Looking Ahead, Inc. is a company that recognizes the progress and achievements of people across the globe and works endlessly to further the prosperity and growth of all individuals

WOMEN WORKS PUBLISHING, INC.

Mailing Address: P.O. Box 767277
Roswell, Georgia 30076
Phone: 770.993.1173
Fax: 770.993.1179
Email: wlanews@bellsouth.net
Website: www.womenlookingahead.com

Atlanta's
CORPORATE SPOTLIGHT

INTEREST

LIMELIGHT

ATTENTION

PROMINENCE

HIGHLIGHT

CELEBRATE

HEADLINE

FOCUS

RECOGNITION

The heart of UPS

It's not often you meet someone who flies jumbo jets and devotes virtually every moment of free time in service to others. From coaching and mentoring kids to assisting with the March of Dimes, Habitat for Humanity, aviation camps and his church ministries, UPS Captain Norman Seawright, Jr., is out there making a difference. What's more, he sings a breathtaking baritone for the sheer enjoyment of others.

Indeed, Captain Seawright flies high and sings out loud in all his actions. And, he is a fine example of UPS's talented and diverse workforce. UPS, in fact, thrives on its diversity and supports minority-focused organizations that promote the cultures, ideas and well being of those they represent.

It's the right thing to do, and it's a commitment that's as much a part of UPS as our brown trucks.

Diversity: at the heart of UPS.

community.ups.com

UPS is proud to support Who's Who in Black Atlanta.

WHAT CAN BROWN DO FOR YOU?

Gerard Gibbons

Vice President
Sales Strategy Worldwide Services
UPS

A s vice president for corporate sales strategy at UPS, Gerard Gibbons is responsible for creating sales strategies on a global scale.

Gibbons joined UPS in 1989, starting as a driver in Los Angeles. In 1992 he was promoted to management and became a manager supporting consignee sales initiatives, working from the company's corporate headquarters in Atlanta. Gibbons headed west to Phoenix, Arizona, in 1995 when he was promoted to director of sales. In 2001 he moved to Dallas after being named business development manager for UPS' Southwest Region. He stayed there until being promoted to his current position in Atlanta in October of 2005.

Gibbons holds a bachelor's degree in marketing from Howard University in Washington, D.C., and a Master of Business Administration degree from Arizona State University.

Lisa M. Hamilton

Vice President
Public Relations
UPS

A s vice president of public relations for UPS, Lisa Hamilton directs all media relations, reputation management, executive communications, financial communications and marketing public relations activities for the company worldwide.

A native of Atlanta, Georgia, she holds a Bachelor of Science degree in commerce from the University of Virginia and a juris doctorate degree from the University of Michigan. Hamilton began her career as a tax attorney in private practice with the Atlanta law firm of Chamberlain, Hrdlicka, White, Williams & Martin.

Hamilton joined UPS in 1996 in the Tax Department as tax research and planning manager. She later served as program director of The UPS Foundation and subsequently a public affairs manager in Washington, D.C., focusing on tax, health care, financial services and legal reform issues. Prior to her current position, Hamilton served as president of The UPS Foundation and was responsible for The UPS Foundation's global philanthropic initiatives.

In addition to her corporate responsibilities, Hamilton serves on the board of the Annie E. Casey Foundation, the U.S. Chamber of Commerce Business Civic Leadership Center and the Atlanta Education Fund.

Michael G. Johnson

Vice President of Human Resources
U.S. Operations
UPS

James E. Mallard

Vice President
Global Procurement Services
UPS

Mike Johnson is vice president of human resources for the domestic operation of UPS, and has global health and safety operations reporting to him. A key member of the Senior Leadership Team for U.S. operations, he is responsible for aligning human resource strategy with business goals for the $30 billion domestic small package unit to sustain the company's high performance, people-oriented culture. He manages all aspects of UPS health and safety processes and strategies for its 420,000 employees worldwide.

Mike holds a Bachelor of Arts degree in human resource management and organizational development from DePaul University. He completed Executive Human Resources programs at the University of Michigan and Emory University.

Mike is national board chair of the National Black Child Development Institute, a board trustee of the National Merit Scholarship Corporation and an advisory board member of the Executive Leadership Council Institute for Leadership Development. A member of the Executive Leadership Council, 100 Black Men of Atlanta, Inc., the Society for Human Resource Management and the Employment Management Association, he is on the executive advisory board for the National Association of African Americans.

James E. Mallard is vice president of global procurement services for UPS. He is responsible for managing the company's annual global spend of approximately $20 billion. He is also responsible for the company's Supplier Diversity Program.

A native of Mississippi, Mallard earned a Bachelor of Science degree in accounting from Jackson State University in Jackson, Mississippi, with continuing education at Nova Southeastern University in Miami, Florida. A UPS employee for 30 years, he has vast experience in the company's international and domestic operations. He even drove the truck as a UPS driver.

In keeping with UPS' long-standing commitment to diversity and the community, Mallard serves on the board of directors and executive committee for the National Minority Supplier Development Council, where he chairs the Field Services Committee. He was named Executive of the Year by the Georgia Minority Supplier Development Council. Under his leadership, UPS was named Corporation of the Year by the National Minority Supplier Development Council as well as the Women's Business Enterprise National Council.

Teri Plummer McClure

Senior Vice President
Legal & Compliance,
General Counsel
UPS

Michael K. Turner

Vice President
Strategic Account Sales
Worldwide Services
UPS

As senior vice president of legal for UPS, Teri McClure oversees the company's compliance and public affairs activities worldwide. She received a bachelor's degree in marketing and economics from Washington University in St. Louis and a law degree from the Emory University School of Law in Atlanta.

Teri began her legal career in 1985, practicing labor and employment law in Atlanta, and representing employers in all aspects of state and federal civil litigation matters. She joined UPS in 1995 as employment counsel for the Corporate Legal Department. She is now responsible for managing the relationships between the company and its Core Counsel Network, a group of law firms that represent UPS around the world.

A member of various bar associations, Teri serves on the boards of The Annie E. Casey Foundation, Junior Achievement of Georgia, Children's Healthcare of Atlanta, the Atlanta Legal Aid Society, Equal Justice Works and the Lawyers' Committee for Civil Rights Under Law. She also serves as co-chair of the Equal Justice Commission Committee on Civil Justice, and is active with many other civic and professional organizations.

Mike Turner began his career with UPS in 1983 as a part-time unloader in the northwest Ohio district. He later became a part of the sales organization as an account executive in 1990. Mike has held various positions in sales, including account executive, sales manager and national account manager. In 1998 he became director of sales in the South Carolina district, and after two years, he moved to the Bay Area as director of sales in Northern California.

In 2004 Mike relocated to the corporate office in Atlanta as a vice president of strategic accounts. He has managed the Northeast and East Central regions of the United States, and is now aligned with the Southeast and Southwest regions. He manages a team of 65 managers and directors, with more than $2 billion in sales revenues annually originating from more than 300 strategic clients.

Mike holds a bachelor's degree in marketing from The University of Toledo. He lives in Alpharetta with his wife and two sons. He enjoys reading, exercising and knowledge acquisition, and is a member of Stonecreek Church in Alpharetta.

There's something important we'd like you to know about Publix: showing our appreciation to our customers is the cornerstone of our culture. It's not just something we do when we think about it. It's who we are. We want you to always feel good about shopping at Publix, and that everything you buy will meet your expectations. In fact, we feel so strongly about it that we've put it in writing. Come by and let us prove it. Publix Super Markets. Where shopping is a pleasure.

www.publix.com

Madam President.

Today, anything is possible and by the time this little girl grows up, she could be President.

Creating the leaders of tomorrow, starts with meeting the needs of children today. It takes basic ingredients to give a child the ability to succeed: the opportunity to live in a healthy community and to get a great education. Cast your vote for tomorrow's leaders by supporting plans to give families a choice about where to live. Your support today will help end concentrated poverty in Atlanta once and for all.

In Atlanta, public and private partners are working together to transform distressed neighborhoods into healthy, mixed-income communities with high performing schools.

www.atlantahousing.org

ATLANTA'S
INTERESTING PERSONALITIES

PROFOUND

CAPTIVATING

DISTINCT

IMPASSIONED

ORIGINAL

INSPIRING

REMARKABLE

INDIVIDUAL

PRODIGIOUS

EMPOWERING OTHERS: NOTHING ELSE MATTERS

BARNEY SIMMS

Senior Vice President/Chief External Affairs Officer
Atlanta Housing Authority

By Alonia Jernigan

Barney Simms hasn't simply dreamed the impossible dream; he has opened his eyes and lived it, too. The leadership roles in which he has been entrusted puts thousands of lives in his hands, but springing from humble beginnings in the segregated South, just a few miles outside of Orlando, Florida, helping others seemed the least he could do.

Simms remembers, "I came up at a time when you had to be a credit to your race, not just your family." With this principle in mind, he set out on a quest for success that has allowed him to make his race and family proud. He has spent more than 30 years of his life empowering others, and as far as Simms is concerned, nothing else matters.

Self-described as a caring and sensitive person, Simms says, "I'm genuinely concerned about the welfare of people, especially people who have not had advantage and opportunity as a birthright." His concern is made evident through the many organizations with which he has shared his time, talents and treasures. Outside of his executive responsibilities with the Atlanta Housing Authority, Simms is also board chairman for the Fulton County Division of Family and Children Services. Additionally, he holds board membership and other leadership roles with numerous organizations that support children, families and neighborhoods.

With Atlanta being often referred to as a melting pot for economic development, Simms is a key player in this ever-evolving perspective, particularly as it relates to the BeltLine project. He is credited as being co-chair of the Mayor's BeltLine Tax Allocation District Feasibility Study Steering Committee, a task he shared with Georgia State University's president, Dr. Carl Patton.

He is also vice chairman of the Atlanta Development Authority, wherein he will help provide oversight for the BeltLine's success.

The second of three boys raised by a single mom, Simms shares, "It was nothing for my mother to make us sit down and study. She also instilled within us the values of respect for authority, discipline and integrity." Holding fast to his mother's insistence on education, he received a bachelor's degree in English from Knoxville College, becoming the first in his family to earn a college degree. Intrigued by the excitement and attention Maynard Jackson created for the city, Simms pressed his way to Atlanta, furthered his education and earned a Master of Library Science degree from Clark Atlanta University.

Simms is a proud member of Antioch Baptist Church North, faithfully serving as a part of the Trustee Ministry under the leadership of Rev. Cameron Alexander. Of the preacher who would subsequently become his mentor, he says, "He certainly taught me patience, the art of persuasion and how to negotiate for the betterment of the community."

While it is widely known that Simms spends a lot of time attending to the needs of others, what may be a surprise is the fact that he is a connoisseur of camellias. "My garden has been featured in several publications. It has even taken two days to film a 30-minute segment for the garden channel," he says.

But beautiful camellias aren't the only things Simms has raised. "I raised my two adult children, Natalie and Justin, as a single parent," he states. This proud papa is an even prouder grandfather to 5-year-old Jeremiah.

Photo by: DENISE GRAY

PRETTY AND POISED, POLISHED AND POWERFUL

THE HONORABLE PENNY BROWN REYNOLDS

Presiding Judge & Owner
Family Court with Judge Penny

By Alonia Jernigan

"God will call into existence those things that do not exist if you only believe," is the daily affirmation that gives Judge Penny Brown Reynolds the motivation to make every day a great day. She also lives by the scripture found in Jeremiah 29:11, which essentially reminds her that God has good plans for her life. "I live by that. I believe that there is a master plan," she says.

It is apparent that God's master plan for the good judge was to use her as an inspiration to millions. Her life is a living testimony that, with God, all things are possible. As a wife, mother, grandmother, minister, judge and entrepreneur, her many accomplishments are admirable, to say the least. Executing each responsibility with a combination of beauty and grace, she has emerged from life's fiery furnace as pure gold. In a few words, Penny is pretty and poised, yet polished and powerful.

Every individual has a story. Oftentimes, people of prominence are overshadowed by their public presentation. Generally, people don't know the trials and tribulations that were endured to reach their place of prestige. Penny is no exception. Her humble beginnings identified her as the oldest of four daughters born to a single mother. She never knew her father, and she was raised by her grandparents in what she would later realize was extreme poverty. An angelic visitation at the age of 12 informed her that she would one day grow up to impact millions. "I'll never forget that experience," she recalls. "My grandmother and I were hanging clothes in the backyard on her clothesline. I really didn't know how that could be, but I always kept it in my heart and mind."

By the time Penny was a young adult, she had packed her bags, left New Orleans and headed for Atlanta in search of a better life. Living in her car, she and her young son endured a life of homelessness. Yet, she held fast to the wisdom of her grandparents, which taught her that education was the only escape from poverty. Initially landing three jobs, she began her college career, ultimately earning not one, but three degrees. She earned an undergraduate degree, cum laude, from Georgia State University after only three years of study, as well as a juris doctorate degree from the same institution. She most recently completed studies at the Interdenominational Theological Center, majoring in theology and graduating with a 4.0 grade point average.

Penny makes an indelible mark wherever her feet tread. She has served as Georgia's assistant attorney general and presided over trial court cases. She made history as the first African American in Georgia's history to become executive counsel to the governor (Roy Barnes). What's more, she served as the first African-American chief of staff and executive counsel to Georgia's Lieutenant Governor Pierre Howard. She impressively serves as host and owner of *Family Court with Judge Penny*, wherein she helps families work through difficult situations from a legal perspective.

Penny enjoys spending time with her husband and best friend, Rev. Edward Reynolds, senior pastor of Midway Missionary Baptist Church, where she serves as an associate minister. She is also proud of her two sons, granddaughter and daughter-in-law.

FROM REBOUND TO REBIRTH

MICHAEL "WOODY" WOODSON
Head Coach
Atlanta Hawks

By Alonia Jernigan

Standing tall at a solid 6 feet 5 inches, the future for a young Mike "Woody" Woodson looked bright and clear. Excelling as a student-athlete at Indiana University (IU) and majoring in physical education, it seemed the best was yet to come. But an unexpected injury during his senior year sent him to surgery and caused many to pronounce his future doomed. Over. Done. "Everybody wrote me off and said I'd never play again," he recalls.

Such was not the case, according to the divine will of God. Woodson was able to amazingly bounce back after only eight weeks. The rest, as is popularly said, is history. Today, his record boasts of more than two decades in the NBA as both player and coach. Woodson didn't let his injury stop him. Instead, it has proven to be fuel that blazed the path to make him the incredible sports professional he is today.

Growing up the 11th of 12 children in his family, Woodson always wanted to succeed in life. His parents instilled within him the principles of hard work and humility. After the death of his father when Woodson was a mere 12 years old, he says, "My main aspiration became to help take care of my mom."

Accordingly, he developed an interest in basketball and began playing in the 8th grade with the hope of someday making it to the NBA. In the meantime, he figured he could help his mom with the bills by working during high school. He did so by taking jobs such as a janitor at an elementary school and a housing project complex, and as a worker in a book factory. By the time he reached his junior year, he had earned a basketball scholarship to IU. His experience at IU engraved him in the school's history as the fifth leading scorer with 2,061 points. He averaged 19.8 points and 5.6 rebounds in 104 games. Woody's acumen on the court caught the eye of the New York Knicks, who selected him in the first round of the 1980 draft as the 12th overall pick. He was able to retire from the game in 1991 after having played for the Kansas City and Sacramento Kings, as well as teams in New Jersey, Los Angeles, Houston and Cleveland. Woodson became the Hawks' head coach after having served as assistant coach for the Detroit Pistons. He was an assistant under his mentor, Larry Brown, in Philadelphia and Detroit, and he served in the same capacity with the Cleveland Cavaliers and the Milwaukee Bucks.

On and off the court, Woodson is committed to putting his best foot forward, and he encourages his players to do the same. He lives by the mantra, "When a job has once begun, never leave it until it's done. If the task is great or small, do it well or not at all."

Woodson would like to believe that he has done just that, both personally and professionally. He has been married to his high school and college sweetheart, Terri, for 28 years this year. They are the proud parents of two beautiful and athletically inclined volleyball players, Alexis and Mariah.

Photo by: DENISE GRAY

QUEEN OF HEARTS

JOVITA MOORE
News Anchor & Reporter
WSB-TV, Channel 2 Action News

By Alonia Jernigan

The adage, "You see the glory, but you don't know the story," could easily summarize the life of one who has captured the hearts of millions to whom she breaks the evening news. Behind the glitz and glamour that comes with the territory of being a television news anchor and reporter lies an ordinary girl of humble beginnings who sprang from New York's Bronx/Queens community.

In the broadcasting industry since 1990, the award-winning media professional is full of grace and humility. She is one who does not take her success for granted. "I realize that I could have easily been one who never emerged from my humble beginnings," states the daughter of a single black mother and white father, "but here I am today." Loved by many, it can easily be said that Jovita Moore is truly a queen of hearts.

Beautiful on the inside as she is on the outside, there is a particular aura that surrounds Moore that makes one feel a sisterly connection. Colleague and mentor Monica Pearson describes her as one who is genuinely very caring and empathetic. She states, "There is a sensitivity about Jovita that's quite admirable. I remember when the station announced her as my successor, she cried. That's a realness that you just don't see every day."

Today, Moore can attribute who she is to the careful upbringing she received from her mother. "My mom was very loving and nurturing, yet very stern. Her protectiveness definitely kept me on the straight and narrow," she recalls.

Through her mother's insistence that she study and make good grades, Moore was able to successfully matriculate through high school and make it to college. While attending Vermont's Bennington College, where she earned an undergraduate degree in literature, a professor took notice of her writing abilities and encouraged her to consider a career as a journalist.

A later life experience connected her with a founding member of the New York Association of Black Journalists. This mentor further encouraged her to consider internships. "That was such valuable information because I learned that internships, mentors and networking are so important in this business. Mentors can help you navigate, and it's important to understand that you have to know more than just the people you see in your everyday surroundings," she says.

Perhaps this is one of the wisdom nuggets that can be attributed to Moore's sensitivity to others. "I really believe in the scripture that says, 'To whom much is given, much is required.' It's important for me to remember that there were those who took the time to pour into me. Acknowledging such makes it easier for me to take a little time to help someone else."

Moore subsequently furthered her education and earned a master's degree in journalism from Columbia University Graduate School of Journalism. Prior to joining WSB-TV Channel 2, she was a weekend anchor/reporter in Memphis. Early on, she launched her career as a reporter in Fayetteville, Arkansas.

Happily married, Moore and her husband are the parents of three children. In her spare time, the new vegetarian enjoys reading fiction and biographies. She also loves outdoor walking and bicycling.

INTERESTING PERSONALITIES

Bank of America Plaza

GIVING BACK, SHAPING THE WORLD

MILTON H. JONES JR.
President, Georgia
Bank of America

By Alonia Jernigan

A familiar quote from Mahatma Gandhi says, "The best way to find yourself is to lose yourself in the service of others." Milton H. Jones Jr. embraces Gandhi's words so well that they are clearly woven into the fabric of his essence. For some, it would seem their life's plateau is to serve as the highest-ranking African-American executive for one of the nation's largest retail banks. While Jones doesn't take this feat for granted, he still believes a key to his success comes from serving others.

His combination of career excellence and community involvement easily makes him a model for the epitome of corporate excellence. As he humbly puts it, "I'm a caring person who really gives all he has to make the world a better place, one person at a time."

Jones, a native Atlantan, fondly recalls the caring way in which his parents and the community at-large affected him. He says, "I've benefited from very loving parents and other adults that cared not just about their own children. The whole village helped raise us, and it was very important for us as kids to learn from any adult we ran into. I try to be involved with organizations that help do that."

From all indications, Jones is doing just that. In addition to serving as Bank of America's president for the state of Georgia, which includes more than 8,000 employees, he has also been, since 1993, a member of the 100 Black Men of Atlanta, Inc., becoming chairman and president of the board of directors in November of 2008. Likewise, he is chairman for the Bank of America Atlanta Football Classic, a signature event of the

organization for life advancement. Jones serves on the executive committee of the Metro Atlanta Chamber of Commerce and the boards of the Metro Atlanta YMCA, Woodruff Arts Center and the Commerce Club, among others. He is also chairman of Meharry Medical College's board of trustees and Audit Committee chair for the United Negro College Fund.

Jones' impact is felt not only within the organizations he serves, but his employees view him as a strong leader who is extremely insightful and passionate. Regarding this, Jones modestly adds, "I'm told that I'm a very good coach and that people who work for me tend to perform quite well. That's the key. You succeed or fail based on the strength of the people you manage. You have to give them feedback and help them grow."

Just as he has helped countless others grow, so has he helped Bank of America grow. He is the recipient of the company's Crystal Grenade, an award bestowed for strong performance and service.

Jones is also pleased to note that he played an instrumental role as president of the MidSouth region (Georgia and Tennessee) in 2000, advancing his team to second in the country, rebounding after having been in sixth place out of seven regions only the previous year.

Sharing the joys of Jones' life is his wife of 34 years, Shelia, the one who has impacted him in the most significant way. He is also the proud father of two adult children, Milton Clarence and Tiffany M. Harris, and grandfather of the most recent addition, Peyton Grace Harris.

INTERESTING PERSONALITIES

DISCOURAGED BUT NOT DEFEATED

RODNEY G. MOORE
President, National Bar Association
Partner, Adorno & Yoss, LLP

By Alonia Jernigan

If Rodney Moore had listened to an undergraduate professor, he never would have pursued his dream of becoming an attorney. A trip back in time reminds Moore of how the professor shook his head when he asked for a reference letter to accompany his law school application. "He said I'd never make it," Moore recalls. "That was quite stunning, but it reminded me that you cannot allow another person's perception of you to dictate your destiny. Their words or actions may be discouraging, but you don't have to accept it as defeat."

Thus, Moore was determined. With early aspirations of becoming a professional football player, the harsh reality of segregation quickly gave him a change of heart. The evils of segregation sparked a desire for him to right the world's wrongs. In essence, he believed the best way for him to make a difference was to pursue a career in law. Moore earned a bachelor's degree in political science from the University of Washington and a Doctor of Jurisprudence degree from Santa Clara University School of Law in California. His education served as the foundation for him to build a highly regarded reputation as one of the best in the business. A partner at Adorno & Yoss, LLP, he has been lauded with such distinctions as Lawyer of the Year, one of 50 Most Influential Minority Lawyers in America and listed as one of the Best Lawyers in America.

But the pinnacle of it all came in August of 2007 when he became president-elect of the National Bar Association (NBA). One year later, he became the first Georgia lawyer to serve as NBA president in the 82-year history of the association. He has been a member of the organization that represents a network of 44,000-plus lawyers, judges and law professionals for more than 20 years. During this time, he served as general counsel from 1997 to 1999 and vice president from 2002 to 2004.

As the son of a military officer, the Birmingham, Alabama, native traveled quite a bit during his childhood. When his father retired in California, the door was open for him to choose California as the place for him to grow where he was planted. After completing law school, Moore ran his own law firm. He was also very active with the Santa Clara business sector, serving as general counsel for their black chamber of commerce. An avid supporter of education, Moore spent three years as general counsel of the East Side Union High School District, in San Jose, California.

In 2000 Moore accepted the position as general counsel and chief legal officer of the Atlanta Public Schools (APS), fulfilling a nationwide search and making him the first African-American general counsel. "I would have to say that helping reform APS into the system it is today, one that is well-respected around the country, is my greatest professional success story," he says.

Personally, he is proud to have raised three healthy children, along with his wife, Yaslyn. His oldest, Nyosha, is a graduate of Bennett College. He is also proud of his two youngest, Rodney and Imari. When not busy working, Moore simply enjoys spending time with family and attending sporting events.

INTERESTING PERSONALITIES

COMPUCREDIT

Photo by: DENISE GRAY

A HEART OF GOLD AT THE TOP

DENISE HALES HARROD
Vice President, Corporate Affairs
CompuCredit Corporation

By Alonia Jernigan

It didn't take a long time for a young Denise Hales Harrod to realize she wanted to spend a lifetime helping people. In fact, it was her early aspiration to become a math teacher. Her pursuit of destiny led her from Vandergrift, Pennsylvania, to Pennsylvania State University. Refocusing her love for mathematics, she earned an undergraduate degree in accounting and successfully climbed the corporate ladder to her current position.

As the vice president of corporate affairs for CompuCredit Corporation, she is enabled to fulfill her commitment to increasing minority professional participation in the financial services industry. Specifically, she is charged with promoting CompuCredit's business model, which is designed to help empower consumers who are financially underserved by traditional financial institutions. Appointed to this position in 2005, Harrod reports directly to CEO and Chairman David G. Hanna on matters related to government and regulatory affairs, minority joint ventures, public relations and community affairs.

A retrospective look at Harrod's career path illustrates that she has tread an admirable path. Besides her work in financial services, she has held executive management positions in the telecommunications and utility industries. Rightfully so, her leadership has yielded a significant measure of commendation. The Trumpet Awards Foundation presented her with its 2007 High Heels in High Places Award, wherein she was recognized for her success in breaking the glass ceiling. The National Organization of Black Elected Legislative Women presented her with its Shining Star Award for outstanding achievement and leadership in public policy. And, most recently, the Southern Christian Leadership Conference presented her with its Reverend Dr. Martin Luther King, Jr. Presidential Award in 2008. Yet, the corporate executive maintains a spirit of humility. She has a sense of connectivity that reassures those whom she serves that there is someone out there who truly cares and understands. "The challenge we face in shaping national economic policy is to ensure that the true voice of Americans who are financially underserved is heard in Washington and throughout our country. Everyone deserves the opportunity to be a part of our nation's financial mainstream," states Harrod, whose company has implemented policies in the financial services industry that provide consumers on Main Street with the opportunity to join the economic mainstream.

Although such sentiments are reflective of her company's philosophy, they are also a mirror image of her own way of thinking. With a heart of gold, she never hesitates to do what she can to make a difference, whether in a corporate setting or not. For example, during a celebration of her daughter Devyn's birthday, the mother-daughter team donated the gifts that were given to an Atlanta women's shelter. She reflects, "After the party, we took all the gifts to the shelter, visited with the kids there and gave the gifts to them. It was like a midsummer Christmas. It's the simple things in life that help make a difference."

When she saw a family member in need recently, she took the proper steps to reach out to him and send him to college. She says, "God fulfills needs every day. I just think that's what He wants us to do in return."

When she is not busy traveling, Harrod simply enjoys spending time with her 12-year-old daughter and cooking family meals.

Photo by: DENISE GRAY

A NOBLE CALLING

W. BURRELL ELLIS JR.
Chief Executive Officer
DeKalb County

By Alonia Jernigan

A fundamental fact of life states that every person is born for a purpose. When these purposes are identified, they are often labeled as one's calling. Though diverse in nature, the value of purpose can never be denied. Why? Because one's individual purpose is a visible and relevant part of their very being. This principal is written all over their faces, it is shown in their footprints in the sand, following them wherever they go. An evaluation of the life of W. Burrell Ellis Jr. makes it clear that he was called to lead. He was called to serve. Such is a noble calling for a noble man.

Born in Washington, D.C., and raised at the height of the civil rights movement, (through the early influences of the day, coupled by parents who worked in government), Ellis obtained a firsthand glimpse of two of life's most vital realities: the injustices of the world and the need for public service. "It seems that much of the civil rights movement unfolded right in front of me," states Ellis. "I remember the whole Watergate era and when Nixon resigned. I remember John Kennedy as president; he was assassinated on my birthday. I learned of the assassination of Dr. King while watching television. I'll never forget the look on my parents' faces when I ran and told them."

These activities, along with the work that he saw his parents lay their hands to, instilled within a young Ellis his heart's desire to make a difference. By the time he was in 6th grade, his quest had begun. He ran for class president. He didn't stop there, though. Ellis progressed to earn an undergraduate degree from the Ivy League's Wharton School of the University of Pennsylvania. He was later elected student body president at The University of Texas School of Law, one of the nation's largest and most prestigious law schools. The transition from a boy to a man was further enhanced by the major influence Ellis' father had on him. "He taught us, my brother, sister and me, character and responsibility," says Ellis. "I remember being in college and running up a phone bill. My parents loaned me the money to pay that bill. My mother was compassionate because she knew that as a student I didn't have much money. My dad, on the other hand, made sure I paid it back. Later, after he passed away, we found all these checks that I'd written for the loan that had never been cashed. My father didn't really care about the money, but he was teaching me about responsibility. It was that kind of lesson that helped shape my character."

It is the same character that made Ellis stand out in a crowd among DeKalb County voters. In a field of five, he almost obtained his current position without a runoff. "It's an honor to serve," he says. Described by colleagues as a focused man of honor and integrity, he is committed to assuring excellent leadership that addresses the needs of all people.

Ellis and his wife, Philippa, enjoy spending quality time with their children, Victoria and Burrell III. Very health-conscious, the vegetarian is physically fit and gets a real kick out of collecting soapbox derby memorabilia.

JOURNEY TO EXCELLENCE

RONALD E. FRIESON

Senior Vice President, External Affairs
Children's Healthcare of Atlanta

By Alonia Jernigan

Just a simple glance at his title is an instant indication of a solid track record of admirable leadership. He has spent the last 25-plus years traveling the highways of the corporate community, and recently, the nonprofit sector, ultimately rising to another level of prominence. Ronald E. Frieson is senior vice president of external affairs for Children's Healthcare of Atlanta, where his journey has allowed him to make a name for himself that could be an equivalent to excellence.

Yet, the leading role doesn't necessarily have to be the given persona in order for this remarkable leader to get the job done. "I don't mind going above and beyond the call of duty to do that which I have been commissioned to do. That's the least I can do," says Frieson. "But I am also of the firm conviction that there's no limit to the good one can do if they don't care who gets the credit. This thought process keeps me focused on the end result. Too many people worry strategically, 'How do I position things so that people will know the role I played in making it happen?' However, if people know you and your work ethic, they will clearly see your handwriting all over it."

Considering this notion, Frieson's handwriting has left many calligraphic markings that are individually stamped "winner," "consensus maker," "bridge builder" and "high achiever."

Born in Memphis, Tennessee, Frieson sprang from modest beginnings under the loving guidance of parents who believed in hard work and the value of a good education. His mother was an educator while his father was as a postal worker. The fruit of their labor is three accomplished children.

Frieson's identical twin brother, Donald, is a senior vice president of a major national retail chain, and his sister is a principal in the Memphis City Schools system. While attending high school, Frieson was athletically inclined, excelling in track and basketball. Still, he insists his participation in sports was contingent upon high academic performance. Upon high school graduation, he furthered his education and earned a bachelor's degree in finance from The University of Tennessee and an MBA in information systems from Georgia State University.

He credits his grandfather, Charlie Lemons, with being his greatest role model. As an ex-sharecropper who later worked from machines that picked cotton, he was by far one of the smartest men Frieson ever knew. "He was a natural leader in anything he would have chosen to become a leader in," he states. He had such an impact on his life that Frieson and his wife, Belinda Stubblefield, created the Charlie Lemons Endowment, which supports the black cultural center at The University of Tennessee at Knoxville.

A down-to-earth guy, Frieson loves life and is living it like it's golden. He thoroughly enjoys traveling and cites Italy as one of his favorites. He also has an appreciation for good food. Perhaps the combination of Italy's influence and high-quality cuisine was the inspiration for him and his wife to explore their chosen business ventures. Married for six years, they are owners of WineStyles Cascade, a wine retail and gift store, and co-owners of Landon's Restaurant, an upscale casual dining establishment. Frieson is also the father of adult twins.

Photo by: DENISE GRAY

AN ATTITUDE OF GRATITUDE

SHERYL RILEY GRIPPER
Vice President, Community Relations
WXIA-TV/11Alive

By Alonia Jernigan

"Every man and woman is born into the world to do something unique and something distinctive..." Dr. Benjamin E. Mays

Dr. Mays was absolutely right. For Sheryl Riley Gripper, that "something unique, something distinctive" is simply to make a difference. She has, indeed, made an indelible mark on the Metro Atlanta community at-large, using her gift of communication on the platforms of newspaper, television and radio for the past 25 years. Though the path she has trod has taken her on a detour from her original destination, she still made it through the doorway called success. Most importantly, she maintained an attitude of gratitude along the way.

A talented writer, young Sheryl had early aspirations as a student at Spelman College to become a newspaper reporter. She won the coveted Princeton Newspaper Fund scholarship and interned at the now-defunct *Houston Post Newspaper*. Preparing for a future beyond Spelman's gates in her chosen career path, she later voluntarily wrote articles for a local newspaper. When the sought-after newspaper job took a while to manifest, Sheryl was not discouraged. Instead, she signed up with the Black Women Employment Program, headed at that time by former Secretary of Labor Alexis Herman. The organization helped her launch a career in the media as a promotions manager in public radio and television.

She remembers, "I created a children's character, Captain 30, and wrote a jingle for him. I was also the voice of Cee Metric in a series the public stations produced. I also spent time as a volunteer for the United Negro College Fund." That experience gave her the opportunity to meet the executives of 11Alive. "When they had a position open, they called me to interview for it," she explains.

Today, she is entrusted with managing public service events and cause-related marketing campaigns for the station. Most notably, she serves as executive producer of the *11Alive Community Service Awards*, a program that annually honors outstanding volunteers, and the 11Alive Holiday Can-a-Thon, Georgia's largest televised food-raising event. In 2008 alone, the event generated almost 300,000 pounds of food.

In addition to her work at 11Alive, the Waco, Texas, native is also founder of the Black Women Film Preservation Project, an organization that celebrates the history of women in film. Now in its 12th year, the organization has earned a solid reputation as a trailblazer, opening doors for many women who are interested in film and broadcast. A multi-Emmy Award winner, the documentary Sheryl produced on the children of Dr. Martin Luther and Coretta Scott King merited a CEBA Award for Excellence in recognition of Achievement to Black Audiences. Another documentary she made, *I Didn't Make Him, God Did*, explores the impact of tragic murders on families, and explores the 2006 unsolved murder of her own son, as well as those of media colleagues who have endured similar tragedies.

Sheryl's quiet and humble spirit should not be discounted. Underneath it all is a woman of strength, power and faith. She has faced tragedy yet emerged with peace and fortitude. She is thankful for a loving and supporting husband, Jeff, along with her surviving sons, Edward and Ellis. She says, "No matter what happens, God is good."

Photo by: DENISE GRAY

MAN WITH THE HORN

MELVIN M. MILLER
Musician Extraordinaire

By Alonia Jernigan

Musical mastermind, magnificent maestro and mystically mellow all accurately describe one of the music world's most amazing phenomena. His name is Melvin M. Miller, and from the time he was a kid growing up in Chicago, it was evident that jazz would be a major component of his life. Today, Miller has emerged as a world-renowned composer, educator, musician, conductor and performing artist. But after all the accolades, after the final curtains are drawn and when the music stops, Miller's bottom line is that music must remain an essential part of our children's educational journey. "There's no doubt that our children need to be adequately prepared to meet and surpass the requirements of standardized testing," says the music educator. "Still, it is equally important that the commitment to the arts remains intact. I am an artist at heart, and I teach from an artistic perspective."

So, when the opportunities come for Miller to present his artistic abilities, he seizes every moment by putting his best foot forward, and the records show that he is a real crowd pleaser. Having shared the stage with a list of superstars that would leave even the most critical spectator breathless, Miller is a force to be reckoned with. His credits range from the African American Philharmonic Orchestra to the UniverSoul Circus to *Madea's Family Reunion*. From the time he blew his trumpet at the very first Trumpet Awards, he has remained the instrumental voice of the annual event, later serving as musical director for the event. Superstars like the original Dream Girl Jennifer Holliday and disco queen Gloria Gaynor have also relied on him to serve as their musical director. Additionally, he is a former member of Five Men on a Stool. Humble for all that he has been able to accomplish, Miller can still remember the days when he wasn't so fearless. "My first encore performance was when I was in elementary school. I was performing George Benson's 'Masquerade,' but I didn't do so well. But my mom came to me and encouraged me to get back out there and do it again. I'm so glad she did. She's the one who gave me the nickname 'Young Man with a Horn.'"

Miller also recollects his father encouraging him to nurture his love for music. "I initially started out playing the trombone, but my dad encouraged me to play the trumpet, too. He was actually my first trumpet teacher," he shares. Trained to perform, produce and present everything from classical to pop to jazz, the Tennessee State University alumnus remembers his early days of participating with every band the school had: marching, concert and jazz.

Miller also acknowledges the influences of Miles Davis, Freddie Hubbard, Clifford Brown, Lee Morgan, Maynard Ferguson and Doc Severinsen, to name a few. "I'd listen to their records and learn all I could from their distinctive styles," he says.

Miller is pleased to have released his third recording, *In the Moment*, in 2009. When not blowing his horn, the internationally acclaimed Miller enjoys tinkering with his computer, playing pool and spending time with his family. He is a member of Alpha Phi Alpha Fraternity, Inc. and Phi Mu Alpha Sinfonia Fraternity, Inc., a professional music fraternity.

INTERESTING PERSONALITIES

LIFTING AS SHE CLIMBS

OLIVIA C. BROWN, CPA
Hotel Manager
The Ritz-Carlton, Buckhead

By Alonia Jernigan

"Excellence is never an accident; it is the result of skillful execution," is the mantra that inspires Olivia C. Brown to be the shining star she is today. With many years under her belt as a successful accountant, she had a task of tactfully proving herself to be an ideal candidate for the InterContinental Hotel's strenuous two-year general manager training program when she decided to make a career change. She made this choice before joining The Ritz-Carlton team. "The stigma was there. 'She's an accountant. How could she possibly make a smooth transition into operations,' was the thought I knew inhabited the minds of my superiors. But I was up for the challenge. I had to make my ability to excel in this industry a known fact," Brown says.

Brown effectively conveyed her message, and her ability to achieve this feat made her the 2007 Road Less Traveled Award recipient from the National Association of Black Accountants. The award is presented to one who has utilized accounting education and training as a springboard into a unique position, or to one who provides a unique service that is nontraditional of an accountant or certified public accountant (CPA).

But perhaps one of the most notable and admirable aspects of her 18-year career in the hospitality industry, as well as her time as an accountant, is the fact that she always looks out for others' well-being in their respective roles. "I believe it's very important to lift others as you climb. That's my philosophy. I must add value to everyone I touch," Brown explains. "Building positive relationships with others is very important in this aspect. As an individual grows in his or her profession, it

should not be about just taking for yourself. So I try to always ask myself, 'What can I leave for this person to bring out their absolute best?'"

One of the nuggets of wisdom that she passes on to those around her is the importance of being able to overcome the obstacles that are sure to come. "In our industry, there are a lot of walls to come up, but you've got to be able to find a way around them," she imparts. "This goes hand-in-hand with having people work with you. With the walls of challenges comes the opportunity to create new goals."

In addition to being a CPA, Brown received a degree in hospitality and tourism administration from the Centennial College of Applied Arts and Technology in Toronto, Ontario. She also completed the managerial accounting/finance program at Toronto's Ryerson Polytechnic University.

Born in Jamaica and raised in Canada, Brown is full of passion and laughter. She is further described as being one of commitment, integrity and a forgiving nature. Known to be conservative in her mode of corporate dress, she adds the fact that her shoes always stand out. "I'm generally simple, but my shoes are always popping," the cheerful Brown says.

Married to Otto and the proud mother of twins Sidney and Sebastian, the petite Brown enjoys working out and reading novels. "I really do work out each morning," she shares. And given her work ethic and solid reputation, it is obvious that the lifting helps her in more ways than one.

Photo by: DENISE GRAY

THE REAL MEANING OF SUCCESS

FRANK SKI
Host, Frank and Wanda Morning Show
V-103/WVEE FM

By Alonia Jernigan

Just as the masterful artist uses the stroke of his brush to create a fine work of art, so does Frank Ski use the platform of the media to touch and transform. From the outside looking in, it appears he is sitting on top of the world. After all, he has hosted and consistently kept Atlanta's V-103's *Frank and Wanda Morning Show* at the top of the charts for nearly a decade. He has also gained a reputation as one of the most beloved and sought-after media personalities, and his leadership and advice are all highly regarded. Yet, there is another facet to his life that makes it all worth it.

"Without a doubt, I love what I do. And like anybody else, I want to be remembered for being good in my profession," Frank shares. "But more than anything, I want my legacy to be that I have a strong family unit, that I've helped make the world a better place and that I'm a good friend."

With a persona that reflects the same sincere enthusiasm that is exuded over the airwaves, Frank goes on to say, "There are so many people who believe success is about the fancy cars, the beautiful homes and all the things that we can acquire. But I've personally learned that success is when you have a successful family unit. You have to ask yourself, 'Am I happy and at peace outside of my job?' If your job is still determining how successful you are, you haven't found it."

Married to Tanya for almost 15 years, Frank's love for family is a model for emulation. He excitedly says, "Monday is date night for me and Tanya, and we have lunch every Thursday. On Sundays after church, we go to brunch, then Sunday night we look forward to the movies and food." Fun, indeed, for the proud papa of four sons: Jarrett, Franklin, Harrison and Blake.

Still, the level of success Frank has achieved in his profession is undeniable. He is thankful to be a distinguished media mogul, having scored countless accomplishments across the country in radio, television, the recording industry and film. And while his visibility at the morning show provides a clear view of his commitment, love and compassion for the community, he makes his purpose clear when asked what his greatest success story is, "I've never really done anything for it to be a success. I've done it because it was the right thing to do. At the end of the day, my job is community service."

Frank's response is not merely a set of carefully crafted words. His actions speak much louder than his words ever could. Only he could express his desire to take a group of kids from his endeared Frank Ski Kids Foundation to the Galapagos Islands and watch it manifest itself. He reflects, "This was truly an accomplishment because it was a place I'd always dreamed about going to as a kid. When I finally went there, I was told they'd never had a U.S. student group come. That was probably one of the most amazing things we'd ever done."

Greater things are on the horizons. He has done a lot, and the best is yet to come.

"You'd rather talk about anything other than your retirement plan. I should know, I'm the 800lb gorilla in the room."

Don Smith
Vice President, Southern Division
Financial Professional

AXA Advisors, LLC
3348 Peachtree Road NE, Suite 800
Atlanta, GA 30326

Tel. (404) 760-2302 • Fax (404) 760-2390

donald.smith@axa-advisors.com
www.DonaldLSmith.com

Financial Professionals providing:

- Education Funding
- Financial Planning
- Mutual Funds

- Retirement Planning Strategies
- Wealth Preservation & Accumulation

AXA ADVISORS

redefining / standards

www.AXAonline.com

Dr. Carlton E. Brown
President of Clark Atlanta University

The Man with a Vision

When Clark Atlanta University appointed Dr. Carlton E. Brown to be Executive Vice President and Provost in July of 2007, the institution gained an experienced executive and visionary with passion for HBCUs and a reputation for inciting the kind of change that leads to excellence. On August 1, 2008, Brown became the third president of Clark Atlanta University (CAU), the largest institution in the Atlanta University Center.

Brown believes that by drawing upon its extraordinary roots – the individual attributes of Atlanta University (1865) and Clark College (1869) – Clark Atlanta University can achieve his vision of the university taking its rightful and pre-destined place of leadership in American higher education.

"We are unique and we have capabilities not represented by any other institution in the nation," said Brown.

There is a spirit of greatness within CAU, steeped in the rich heritage and legacies of its two parent institutions. Over the years, they attracted some of the nation's most notable educators, such as distinguished scholar and author W. E. B. DuBois, who joined Atlanta University in 1897, and long-serving Clark College President James P. Brawley, a leading academician. The two institutions helped to mold the minds of many leaders, such as author/composer James Weldon

Johnson, actor/producer/director Kenny Leon, Congressman Henry "Hank" Johnson, educator Marva Collins and many other notable alumni.

Clark Atlanta University is celebrating its 20th anniversary, having been formed in 1988 by the consolidation of Atlanta University and Clark College. CAU is the largest of the 39-member UNCF colleges and is the only private historically black institution classified by Carnegie as "Research University/High Research Activity."

For this Macon, Georgia native, who earned a bachelor's degree and a doctorate from the University of Massachusetts-Amherst in 1971 and 1979, respectively, ensuring that CAU fulfills the promise of the 1988 consolidation is an important goal in his presidency. Brown's belief is that CAU is uniquely positioned by its history, structure and capacity to re-achieve national leadership in higher education.

Brown, an educator, scholar, orator and longtime higher education executive, has distinguished himself by leading meaningful and transformative change at every institution for which he has held leadership roles. He was an executive at Hampton University and Old Dominion University and later served as president of Savannah State University from 1997 to 2006.

When the call came to join Clark Atlanta in 2007, the academician, multicultural education expert and self-described "music aficionado," left his appointed position with Georgia's Board of Regents to accept the newly created position of executive vice president and provost. He was elected president in May of 2008 by CAU's Board of Trustees.

On any given day, Brown can be found doing what he does best: steering the University-wide effort to implement his change management-strategy, which aims to result in a more powerful and more effective CAU.

Brown laid out his vision for CAU during his first address as president to administrators, faculty and staff in August of 2007: "We have much to do that will require the engagement of the entire university community to ensure that Clark Atlanta University achieves its rightful position in higher education," said Brown. "Together, we will make CAU better, stronger and greater for the future leaders being prepared at our institution."

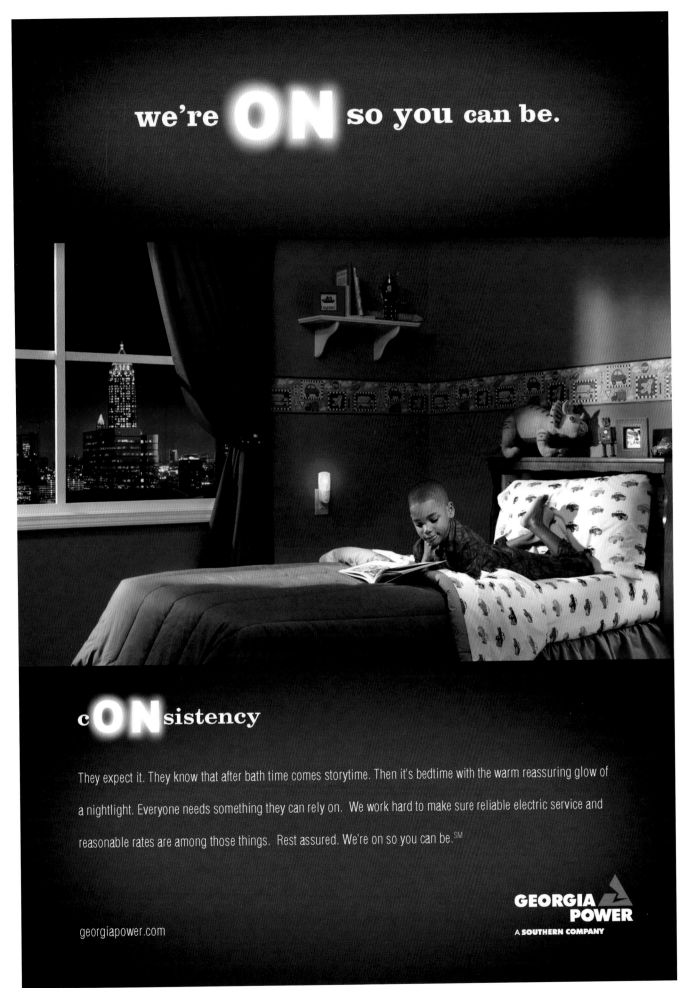

ATLANTA TECHNICAL COLLEGE

Named
AMERICA'S BEST COMMUNITY COLLEGE
by Washington Monthly

photo by Ron Witherspoon

DR. ALVETTA PETERMAN THOMAS, PRESIDENT

 ATLANTA TECHNICAL COLLEGE

404.225.4461 • atlantatech.edu

Tough Enough:

Troubled Times Present Great Opportunity for Continuing Education Programs

By Alonia Jernigan

It is no secret that America is facing tough economic times. The economic specialists have finally proclaimed the situation to be a recession. The sting of it all has been felt in massive layoffs, the forcing of individuals into early retirement and ultimately, government-initiated bailout plans and stimulus packages.

The state of Georgia fits into this equation. According to the Georgia Department of Labor (GDOL), as of March 25, 2009, the unemployment rate in the Metro Atlanta area rose to a preliminary unadjusted rate of 9.3 percent in February, up 4.1 percentage points throughout the year from February of 2008. The unemployment rate in Metro Atlanta rose seven-tenths of a percentage point from a revised 8.6 percent in January.

"The latest local unemployment rates reflect the severity of the ongoing recession in Georgia," says State Labor Commissioner Michael Thurmond. "In 87 of our state's 159 counties, double-digit unemployment is a sobering reality. A rising tide of joblessness is spreading across our state."

It is safe to say that the GDOL's findings substantiate the overwhelming outpour of individuals who attended a career expo and job fair organized by the GDOL in partnership with WSB-TV Channel 2 in mid-March. A reported 19,000 jobseekers were in attendance.

The need for so many people to find work could also signify that now is the time for jobseekers to be at the top of their game. In other words, one of the keys to success in these times is to assure that one's marketability is as strong as it can be. Therefore, now is the perfect time to identify ways in which to improve their level of attraction to potential employers like never before.

From an employer's perspective, some have resorted to sending current employees to school so they may be better equipped to fulfill the responsibilities of a job opening. This is their perceived best alternative to addressing the cost and process of hiring a new employee. Thus, jobseekers and current employees alike are finding themselves taking advantage of educational opportunities by either going back to school to gain a degree or an advanced degree, or by taking continuing education courses.

Dr. Alvetta Peterman Thomas, president of Atlanta Technical College, says, "The more varied your skill set, the greater chance you'll have to survive and, indeed, thrive in the current economy. Preparing people for strong careers during hard times – that is what we specialize in at Atlanta Technical College. And judging by our 98 percent job placement rate, I would say that we do a pretty good job of it."

Peterman Thomas goes on to say, "Atlanta Technical College offers a tremendous variety of continuing education classes for individuals as well as business. From American Heart Association training to online computer certifications – and even learning how to become a certified wedding planner – we have something for everyone. We also specialize in providing customized training for businesses and governmental organizations of all sizes."

A familiar adage says, "When life serves you lemons, make lemonade." Such could be the case when considering today's economic climate and when continuing education opportunities are valuable for improving a candidate's marketability. Additionally, there are other principles of professionalism that are necessary to follow, such as the proper preparation of a resumé, masterful interviewing skills and persistence. Being proactive with continuing education courses is a step toward embracing a positive, new outlook for a better future.

"When life serves you lemons, make lemonade."

THOMAS, KENNEDY, SAMPSON, & PATTERSON, LLP
ATTORNEYS AT LAW

 For over thirty-five years, perseverance has been the axiom of **Thomas, Kennedy, Sampson & Patterson, LLP.** Founded in 1971, the firm serves the legal needs of major corporations, governmental authorities, small businesses and individuals. The oldest minority-owned law firm in Georgia and among the largest minority-owned law firms in the southeastern United States, **Thomas, Kennedy, Sampson & Patterson, LLP** is rated a v by *Martindale-Hubbell* and is listed in the *Bar Register of Preeminent Lawyers*, published by *Martindale-Hubbell.*

In May of 2006, **Thomas, Kennedy Sampson and Patterson, LLP** was awarded The Coca-Cola Company's "Partner in the Promise" Award, as the minority business enterprise supplier of the year.

In another honor, the firm was recognized as one of the top "go to" companies in the country, as listed in the May 2007 *Fortune Magazine.* This places **Thomas, Kennedy, Sampson & Patterson, LLP** among the top 5 percent of law firms in the country.

"This recognition is a tremendous honor and an affirmation of the hard work we've invested over the years," says Managing Partner and co-founder Thomas G. Sampson. It is quite an honor, and a testament to the skills of everyone at the firm."

Thomas, Kennedy, Sampson, & Patterson, LLP is committed to excellence and is dedicated to meeting the needs of a broad-based practice.

Thomas, Kennedy, Sampson, & Patterson, LLP

3355 MAIN STREET

ATLANTA, GEORGIA 30337

404.688.4503 TEL

404.681.2950 CORPORATE FAX

404.684.9515 LITIGATION FAX

WWW.TKSP.COM

KISS 104.1

ATLANTA'S OLD SCHOOL R&B STATION

the TOM **JOYNER** morning show

Tom Joyner

Mornings 6 a.m. - 10 a.m.

Historic College Park's Newest Fine Dining Restaurant

Located minutes from airport area hotels, Hartsfield-Jackson International Airport, Georgia International Convention Center and Fort McPherson. The Pecan fuses Classic Southern Cuisine with modern eclectic influences. Visit us in Historic College Park and experience contemporary style and southern elegance.

Lunch	*Dinner*	*Brunch*
Tuesday-Friday	Tuesday-Saturday	Sunday
11:30 am - 2:30 pm	5:30 pm - 10:30 pm	11:00 am - 3:00 pm

3725 Main Street, College Park, GA 30337
(404) 762-8444 • www.thepecanonline.com

THIS GAME IS FOR EVERYONE

The Atlanta Braves proudly work with a number of minority and women owned businesses to help supply our success in Major League Baseball. Working with a vast network of diverse business partners ensures fair practices, greater perspectives and the truest community spirit.

For more information visit on supplier diversity visit **braves.com/supplierdiversity** or email us at supplierdiversity@braves.com.

TEAMING UP FOR DIVERSITY

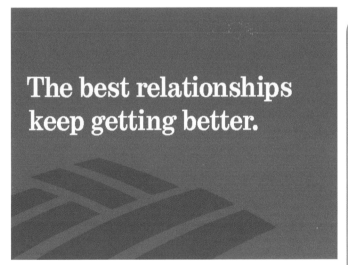

The best relationships keep getting better.

From your first checking account through retirement, you can always count on getting more with Bank of America. More financial choices. More security. More ways to access your money. That's our commitment to you, and to all our valued customers. To get more out of your banking relationship, call 1.800.432.1000 or visit www.bankofamerica.com today.

PHIPPS PLAZA
A SIMON® MALL

Luxury begins with Service

Mon to Sat
10:00am - 9:00pm
Sun
12:00pm - 5:30pm

3500 Peachtree Rd Ne   Atlanta, GA 30326
(404) 262-0992

News & Talk
1380 WAOK
The Voice of the Community

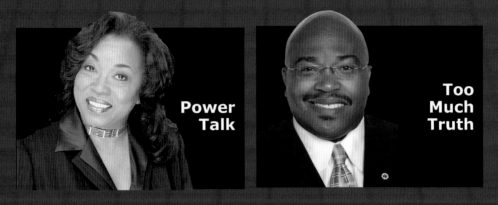

Power Talk

Too Much Truth

The Bev Smith Show

Sunday Morning Inspiration

Real Estate 101

SALUTES
WHO'S WHO
IN BLACK ATLANTA

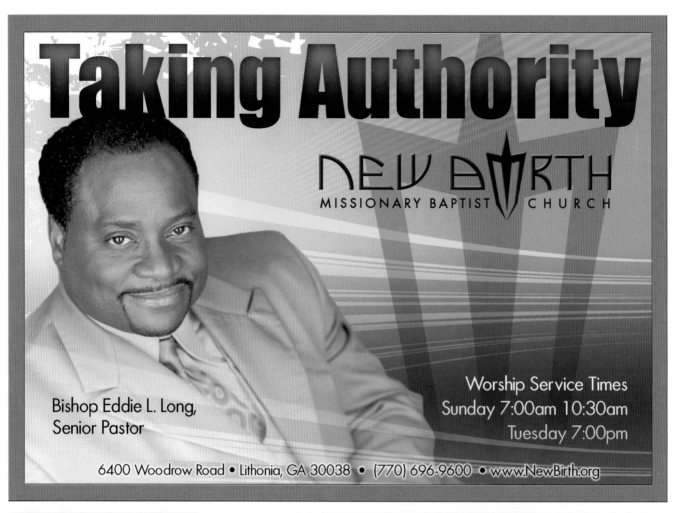

Taking Authority

NEW BIRTH
MISSIONARY BAPTIST CHURCH

Bishop Eddie L. Long,
Senior Pastor

Worship Service Times
Sunday 7:00am 10:30am
Tuesday 7:00pm

6400 Woodrow Road • Lithonia, GA 30038 • (770) 696-9600 • www.NewBirth.org

SAMSON'S
HEALTH & FITNESS CENTER

Making You & Your Staff Fit to Lead!

LET US SHOW YOU HOW TO DECREASE HEALTH INSURANCE COSTS AND ABSENTEEISM WHILE
INCREASING STAFF MORALE, TEAMWORK, AND PERFORMANCE!

> *The productivity of your company is first!*

We will custom design fitness and wellness programming
that educates & inspires, while getting results that contribute to your personal and corporate bottom line.
We create branded group fitness sessions, aerobics, and
personal training at your site or ours. *Free consultation!*

Private Studio
Personal Training

www.samsonsfitness.com

2451 Cumberland Parkway, Suite 3808, Atlanta Georgia 30339 > 1.877.600.2348

Atlanta's
CORPORATE SPOTLIGHT

INTEREST

LIMELIGHT

ATTENTION

JAZZ 91.9 FM
CLARK ATLANTA UNIVERSITY
THE JAZZ OF THE CITY WCLK.COM

PROMINENCE

HIGHLIGHT

CELEBRATE

HEADLINE

FOCUS

RECOGNITION

CORPORATE SPOTLIGHT

Wendy Williams

General Manager
Jazz 91.9 WCLK

Tammy Nobles

Assistant Station Manager
Jazz 91.9 WCLK

Wendy Williams serves as general manager of Jazz 91.9 WCLK, a professional public radio station licensed to Clark Atlanta University. Her career in broadcasting spans more than 20 years. For the past 16 years, Williams' leadership at WCLK has helped earn its reputation as a world-class radio station and as the 2007 Best of Atlanta in *Atlanta* magazine.

Williams currently serves on the board of Eastern Region Public Media. She is a founding member and chair of the African American Public Radio Consortium (AAPRC), Inc. The AAPRC has worked in partnership with NPR and the Corporation for Public Broadcasting to bring voices and programs of color to public radio such as *The Tavis Smiley Show* from NPR, *News & Notes* with Farai Chideya, and *Tell Me More* with Michel Martin. Additionally, she is a member of the Clark Atlanta University Guild.

A native of Pennsylvania, Williams received a communication degree from Bowling Green State University, and a Master of Business Administration degree in marketing from Clark Atlanta University. A member of Alpha Kappa Alpha Sorority, Inc., she loves traveling, cooking and meeting people.

Tammy Nobles serves as assistant station manager for Jazz 91.9 WCLK, a public radio station licensed to Clark Atlanta University in Atlanta. She is responsible for general supervision of the station's membership fundraising, community affairs, production and administrative support.

Prior to WCLK, Nobles served for 13 years as membership director for KLON FM 88.1, the country's largest jazz format public radio station, serving Los Angeles and Orange counties in California. She also served as foundation director for the Evander Holyfield Youth Foundation in Atlanta.

Nobles attended The Art Institute of Atlanta, where she studied in the culinary arts program. She also wrote, created and launched the business plan for Annie Laura's Kitchen Soul Food restaurant, now operating in its fifth year in Riverdale, Georgia.

Nobles received a Bachelor of Science degree in business administration and finance from California State University, Long Beach. She likes studying personalities and is a member of World Changers Church International.

Shed Jackson

Communications &
Marketing Director
Jazz 91.9 WCLK

Ray Cobb

Corporate Sales Underwriter
Jazz 91.9 WCLK

Shed Jackson is a seasoned communications management and media relations specialist with a solid foundation in planning, implementing and monitoring all channels of information exchange.

Shed's experience in media, communications, and entertainment includes serving as director of communications and marketing for Jazz 91.9 WCLK, a former public relations professional with an Atlanta-based PR firm, a publicity management expert, and a published author.

A trained pianist who has played professionally for more than 12 years, Shed served as the music director of numerous faith-based organizations. He is also a trained trumpeter who has played for more than six years, and has studied violin techniques, playing for nearly four years.

Shed is a second-year graduate student at Clark Atlanta University, completing a Master of Arts degree in teaching science education. He earned a Bachelor of Science degree in biology with a minor in chemistry from The University of Alabama at Birmingham. A member of numerous national and state education, civic and business associations, Shed serves on the boards of Jazz 91.9 WCLK, *Connect Magazine*, and the National Organization for Diversity in Sales and Marketing.

Ray C. Cobb, corporate sales underwriter for Clark Atlanta University, is responsible for identifying prospective clients and generating sales revenue for Jazz 91.9 WCLK and the Division of Communication Arts.

Ray entered the advertising industry as an intern for the Classified Advertising Department at *The Atlanta Journal-Constitution* (AJC) in the summer of 1997. After graduating college, he returned to the AJC where he served as an advertising assistant and inside sales representative from 1998 to 2002. In 2001 he was the recipient of the Inside Sales Person of the Year for Classified Advertising – Callbacks Division.

Ray holds a Bachelor of Arts degree in mass communication from the University of South Florida and lives in downtown Atlanta. In his spare time, he enjoys acting and the performing arts. One of Ray's greatest accomplishments was a 2001 trip to South Africa where he developed a passion for HIV/AIDS awareness and advocacy.

CORPORATE SPOTLIGHT

Rodney Evans

Host
Morning Gospel
Jazz 91.9 WCLK

Morris Baxter

Host
Morris In The Morning
Jazz 91.9 WCLK

Minister Rodney Evans' name evokes awe and wonder: awe that he has accomplished so much so early in life and wonder as to where he finds the energy. Though he knows it is not of himself, he never hesitates to give all praise, honor and glory to God. Evans accepted his call into the ministry in 2002 and preached his trial sermon on Sunday, May 4, 2003, titled "Whom He Calls He Qualifies." He was licensed by his pastor and godfather, the Reverend John Evans Butler Sr.

An associate minister at Faith Temple Missionary Baptist Church, Evans also serves as minister of music, praise and worship leader, church financial officer, and a Property Acquisition Committee member.

After working in so many different capacities with other nonprofit organizations, youth groups and churches, and experiencing the lack of enough organizations to handle the many issues and ills of the community concerning the children and young adults, Evans founded For The Children, Inc. in 2005.

He and his beautiful wife of 15 years, DeJerris, are the proud parents of Rodney Jr., Armeshia and Arkeria.

Originally from Detroit, Morris Baxter is a graduate of Norfolk State University. He started his career in radio at WOWI in Norfolk, Virginia, and worked at WMYK as the program director for ten years.

After several job opportunities at WNVZ, WPCE, WSVY and as a television entertainment reporter for WAVY (CBS), Baxter moved to Atlanta as a national promotions manager for Loud/Sony Records working projects for platinum-selling artists, including the Wu-Tang Clan, Three 6 Mafia, Mobb Deep, Xzibit and Big Pun. He also held the title of southeast regional director of promotions for Artist Direct/BMG. He later served as national director of promotions, working with such artists as Slum Village and 8Ball. His voice was featured on the multiplatinum-selling Blackstreet album, *Another Level*.

Through his words as a public speaker and over the airwaves, Baxter ignites his listeners with his "Morris Motivations" as the host of *Morris in the Mornings* on Jazz 91.9 WCLK. He is on the Community Advisory Board for Prostate Cancer. Morris and his wife, Erin, have one daughter, Madison.

Fonda Smith

Morning & Afternoon News Anchor
Jazz 91.9 WCLK

Esther Caspino

News & Traffic Anchor
Jazz 91.9 WCLK

Fonda Smith has worked in radio for more than 30 years. She is currently the morning and afternoon news anchor for Jazz 91.9 WCLK. Fonda enjoys doing the news and reporting on the latest events, both locally and nationally. During 9/11, she did live reports from the studios of Metro Networks for nine hours consecutively. She also did live reports for several radio stations in the Atlanta market, with at least two stations choosing to take her live reports over CNN's.

Fonda has worked as a sports anchor covering football and basketball during her 30 years in the broadcast field. She hails from Ohio, and was born and raised in Lima. Fonda received a Bachelor of Science degree in journalism from Bowling Green State University. She has several hours toward a master's degree in communications.

A faith-filled woman of God, Fonda is a Christian and a member of New Birth Missionary Baptist Church.

A native of Boston, Massachusetts, Esther Caspino attended California State University, Long Beach, obtaining a bachelor's degree in criminal justice. She also attended the University of Southern California School of Social Work certification program to treat psychiatric illnesses.

When Esther decided to explore the world of broadcast communications, she accepted her first position as a talk show producer and sports reporter with Clear Channel Broadcasting.

Esther volunteers with various battered women's shelters, senior citizens, Hosea Feed the Hungry, the Special Olympics and the Susan G. Koman Breast Cancer Foundation. She frequently visits area schools to speak to students.

For the past nine years, Esther has been one of the metro area's top news and traffic anchors for several stations, including the *Yolanda Adams Morning Show* on Praise 97.5, Smooth Jazz 107.5, *The Steve Harvey Morning Show* on Grown Folks Radio 102.5, Hot 107.9, WCLK 91.9, WXIA Channel 11, and PDS-TV 24, the DeKalb educational channel.

With a passion for cooking, her stellar cooking has afforded her the opportunity to provide services for the Screen Actors Guild and the Los Angeles Police Department.

Balance.

balancing your need for energy with a **BRIGHT** future

From lights to heating and cooling ... you need reliable electricity at an affordable price. At the same time, you want a future with clean air. That's why GreyStone Power works to balance the two.

The co-op sponsors the **Sun Power for Schools** project at a local high school to educate students about renewable energy and its impact on the environment. The solar energy they harness helps power your appliances. Learn more at **www.greenpoweremc.com**.

By working together, we can balance your need for energy with a bright future.

GreyStone
POWER CORPORATION
An Electric Membership Corporation

www.greystonepower.com

Atlanta's CORPORATE SPOTLIGHT

INTEREST

LIMELIGHT

ATTENTION

WELLPOINT℠

PROMINENCE

HIGHLIGHT

CELEBRATE

HEADLINE

FOCUS

RECOGNITION

Darlene Andrews

Director, Human Resources
BlueCross BlueShield of Georgia, Inc.
WellPoint, Inc.

Pamela Faison Bell

Staff Vice President
BlueCross BlueShield of Georgia Medicare
WellPoint, Inc.

Darlene Andrews is the current director of human resources for BlueCross BlueShield of Georgia, Inc. (BCBSGa). She supports Monye Connolly, president and general manager, and the senior leadership team on a variety of strategic and tactical initiatives. Andrews leads a team of HR professionals who support a client base consisting of 3,000 associates throughout Georgia, including Atlanta, Savannah, Macon and Columbus in multiple functions, such as sales, customer service operations, finance and information technology.

Prior to joining BCBSGa in 2001, she worked for Lucent Technologies, BOC Gases and Frito-Lay, Inc., where she held the positions of senior human resources business partner, regional manager of employee relations and human resources manager, respectively.

Active in community service, including minority health fairs, the March of Dimes and juvenile diabetes fundraisers, Andrews has also spearheaded a number of diversity and cultural training programs at BCBSGa, including women's panels on career development and formal mentoring programs. A graduate of Indiana University, she and her husband, Greg, reside in Marietta, Georgia, and have two children, Ryan and Chene.

In her role as staff vice president at WellPoint, Pamela Bell oversees BlueCross BlueShield of Georgia Medicare, a fiscal intermediary contractor to CMS (Medicare) for Georgia. She provides leadership for approximately 80 Georgia Medicare associates. Also serving as staff vice president for public affairs, Bell is the liaison between WellPoint's federal government solutions businesses, including National Government Services, the Federal Employee Program, TrustSolutions and WellPoint Public Affairs.

Throughout her career, Bell has successfully started programs, including a Medicare risk plan, a Medicare choice plan and a TRICARE managed care program. She is a registered records administrator and a certified managed care executive. She has also participated in WellPoint's Executive Experience and National Government Services' Senior Leadership programs.

Bell is a proud graduate of East Carolina University and was the first African American to successfully complete the university's Medical Records/Health Information Program. She also attended the University of Dallas. Bell enjoys traveling and spending time with her husband, Ron, daughter Candace and granddaughter Trinity.

Atlanta's
CORPORATE SPOTLIGHT

INTEREST

LIMELIGHT

ATTENTION

PROMINENCE

HIGHLIGHT

CELEBRATE

HEADLINE

FOCUS

RECOGNITION

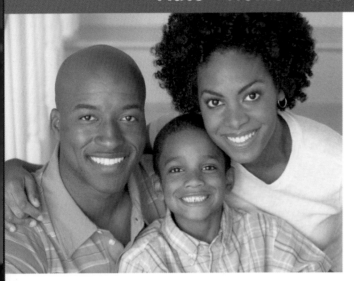

Michael R. Riggs

Director of Sales
American Family
Insurance Company

W ith a 13-year tenure with American Family Insurance Company, Michael R. Riggs is proud to have taken the lead role in making the company's expansion into Georgia a success. As the inaugural director of sales for American Family Insurance in Georgia, a regional leading Fortune 300 mutual insurance company, Michael is responsible for the overall sales and business operations within the state. He has hired six outstanding sales managers who have hired independent agents in the communities that provide quality service, and auto, home, commercial and life insurance products to meet the needs of the policy holders.

With a commitment to ensuring diversity and supporting programs to increase scholarship opportunities for African-American youth, he is proud to oversee corporate partnerships with more than 14 Metro Atlanta organizations.

Michael received a Bachelor of Engineering degree from the University of Missouri-Rolla. Currently, he is completing a Master of Business Administration degree.

A native of Kansas City, Missouri, Michael is married to Andrea Riggs. They have two beautiful children, 6-year-old Amani and 4-year-old Malcolm. Trustworthy and dependable, Michael enjoys traveling and spending time with family.

CORPORATE SPOTLIGHT

All your protection under one roof ®

CORPORATE SPOTLIGHT

Louis L. Besses IV

Multicultural Marketing Developer
American Family
Insurance Company

As multicultural marketing developer for American Family Insurance, Louis L. Besses IV plays an integral role in developing the company's marketing strategy that communicates brand and product awareness to the ethnic consumer base. This includes the African-American, Asian, Hispanic, and gay, lesbian, bisexual and transgender (GLBT) communities. Entrusted with the territories of Georgia and Ohio, Besses is also responsible for strategic planning of community-related initiatives such as financial education seminars, scholarships and partnership-sponsorship opportunities. He has been with the company since 2001.

Committed to the community, Besses serves on the board of directors for the Hispanic Chamber of Commerce for Ohio and several other community committees throughout Ohio and Georgia. He has been featured as one of the 40/40 Club Class of 2008 in *Kaleidoscope* magazine, and he is a recipient of the *Black Pages of Ohio*'s Corporate Leadership Award.

Armed with a bachelor's degree in sociology and minors in marketing and African-American studies from The Ohio State University, he also holds a master's degree in business administration. Besses and his wife, Valerie, are the proud parents of an infant daughter, Avery Gabriella.

Michael Fowler, LUTCF

District Sales Manager
American Family
Insurance Company

Michael Fowler is a district sales manager for American Family Insurance. Acting in this capacity gives him responsibility for managing sales plans for the company through a captive agent sales team. Michael also acts as a direct business partner to agents to ensure their individual business goals are met. He cites his inclusion in American Family's expansion into Georgia as one of his greatest professional accomplishments.

Prior to relocating to Atlanta in February of 2008, Michael was a sales agent for American Family in Chicago, Illinois. His tenure there earned him company honors to include recognition in the Life Diamond and All-American clubs. His agency was also recognized by J.D. Power and Associates for exceptional customer service.

Michael earned a bachelor's degree in communications from Eastern Illinois University (EIU). EIU is also where he became a noble member of Kappa Alpha Psi Fraternity, Inc.

Described as relentless, honest and genuine, the East St. Louis, Illinois, native enjoys working out. Michael clearly understands the importance of family. As such, he is happily married to Amber White-Fowler.

Lungen E. Howard is the district sales manager of District 323 with American Family Insurance in northeast Atlanta. In this position, he develops his sales district by providing support to agents pertaining to district growth, profit, agency development, product line consultation, company compliance and agency business operations management. His 22 years of insurance industry experience includes proficiency in the areas of claims, underwriting, insurance sales, sales training and sales management.

Lungen's expertise in the industry has not gone unnoticed. As such, he has earned American Family's AFLIC honors for five years and is a one-time recipient of All-American honors.

Lungen received a bachelor's degree in business administration and speech communication from the University of Minnesota. An avid sports fan, he was once recruited by coach Tony Dungy to play for the University of Minnesota, ultimately playing for head coach Lou Holtz of the same team.

A native of Detroit, Michigan, Lungen has been married to Shondale for 22 wonderful years. In his spare time, he enjoys watching college football, playing golf, reading spiritual literature, and enhancing both personal and professional development.

Lungen E. Howard

District Sales Manager
American Family
Insurance Company

Kye Wilson has used her "Let's get it done" attitude to propel her to levels of excellence in the insurance industry for more than ten years. Transitioning from an agent in Las Vegas to a district sales manager in Atlanta, the Evanston, Illinois, native has admirably remained a woman on the move in the industry.

Throughout the years, her focus on superior customer service has garnered her company and community awards, including the 2005 Woman Changing America Award from the National Action Network (NAN) and the 2006 J.D. Power and Associates Distinguished Agency recognition. *Rolling out* recognized Kye as one of Atlanta's 25 Women of Influence in 2008.

Her community service includes the Phenomenal Women Las Vegas Executive Advisory Committee, the UNCF, the Atlanta Urban League Young Professionals, the NAN and the Henry County Young Professionals. She also serves on the annual Girls Day Committee, a program of the Girls & Boys Clubs.

Kye enjoys attending empowerment conferences and speaking to youth about financial literacy and higher education. Leisurely, she enjoys traveling, making jewelry, bird watching and trying new foods.

Kye L. Wilson

District Sales Manager
American Family
Insurance Company

Atlanta's

MOST
INFLUENTIAL

POWERFUL

EFFECTIVE

GUIDING

PROMINENT

MOMENTOUS

SIGNIFICANT

AUTHORITATIVE

LEADING

MEANINGFUL

Hank Aaron

President
Henry Aaron, Inc.

Born in Mobile, Alabama, Henry "Hank" L. Aaron has been an active and influential leader in the business and civic communities for more than 23 years. Prior to joining Turner Broadcasting System, Inc., Aaron enjoyed a 23-year major league career, during which he rewrote baseball's hitting record book. Nicknamed "The Hammer," he holds more major league batting records than any other player in the game's history, including most runs batted in. Along with Frank Robinson, he was inducted into the Baseball Hall of Fame on August 1, 1982.

Aaron is senior vice president of the Atlanta National League Baseball Club, Inc., vice president of business development for the CNN Airport Network, and president of Henry Aaron, Inc. and the Henry Aaron Uniform Company. He is also a longtime Church's Chicken and Arby's restaurant franchisee, as well as former president and owner of Hank Aaron BMW.

In 1995 Aaron and his wife, Billye, established the Hank Aaron Chasing the Dream Foundation to give children with limited opportunities a chance to pursue their dreams.

The Honorable Roberta Abdul-Salaam

Representative, District 74
Georgia House of Representatives

The Honorable Roberta Abdul-Salaam, elected to the Georgia General Assembly in 2004, serves on the Judiciary Non-Civil, Economic Development and Tourism, and Transportation committees. Past president of the Houston County NAACP and chair of the Political Action Committee for the Clayton County NAACP, she has been involved with the Southern Christian Leadership Conference (SCLC) since age 13, serving on the national staff and as a consultant.

Roberta is founder and president of Vision Enterprises, Inc. She works to educate and empower Georgia's voters and trains numerous organizations, including the National Conference of Black Mayors and the National SCLC Convention. She was selected by Dr. Joseph E. Lowery as Region One director of the Georgia Coalition for the Peoples' Agenda's Voter Empowerment Crusade, which registered more than 50,000 Georgia voters.

The founder of the Riverdale Technical College Foundation, Inc. and the Clayton Village Anti-Violence Task Force, Roberta serves as vice chair of the Clayton County Legislative Delegation, secretary of the Georgia Legislative Black Caucus and state director of the Women Legislators' Lobby. She received the 2007 Hosea Williams Community Activist of the Year Award.

With advocacy for the African-American community as his cornerstone, George G. Andrews has built a solid professional career as a people's banker in the city of Atlanta and the state of Georgia. He is the founder/director of Capitol City Bank & Trust Company and currently serves as president and chief executive officer. Capitol City Bank has five branch offices in Atlanta, including Hartsfield-Jackson Atlanta International Airport, and three regional offices throughout Georgia.

Andrews was educated at Booker T. Washington High School and Morehouse College. After graduation, he entered the Trust Company Bank management training program.

Andrews is strongly committed to community involvement, serving on the boards of directors of the Urban Residential Development Corporation, the Urban Ministerial Alliance, the Atlanta Metropolitan College Foundation, the City of Atlanta Fulton County Recreation Authority and formerly, the Metropolitan Atlanta Rapid Transit Authority. Additionally, he served as secretary of the board of directors for the Independent Community Bankers of America and the Community Bankers Association.

Andrews is married to the former Janice Smith and they have two daughters, one son, three granddaughters and two grandsons.

George G. Andrews
President & Chief Executive Officer
Capitol City Bank & Trust Company

Since June of 1997, the Honorable Thurbert E. Baker has served as Georgia's 52nd attorney general. In 1988 Baker was elected to the Georgia House of Representatives, representing the 70th House District. After one term in the General Assembly, former Governor Zell Miller selected him to serve as his assistant administration floor leader, and later appointed him to the position of administration floor leader.

Baker is a trustee on the Ebenezer Baptist Church board and the National Medical Society, Emory University. He also serves on the board of governors of the State Bar of Georgia and as a member of the Judicial Nominating Commission. He has served as vice chairman of the National Association of Attorneys Generals' Conference on Violence Against Women in Washington, D.C.

Born in Rocky Mount, North Carolina, Baker received a bachelor's degree in political science from The University of North Carolina at Chapel Hill. He received a law degree from the Emory University School of Law in Atlanta.

He lives in Stone Mountain with his wife, Catherine, and has two daughters, Jocelyn and Chelsea.

The Honorable Thurbert E. Baker
Attorney General
State of Georgia

Gregory T. Baranco

President
Baranco Automotive Group

Gregory Baranco is president of Baranco Automotive Group, consisting of Baranco Acura, Baranco Lincoln and Baranco Pontiac GMC. A native of Baton Rouge, Louisiana, he graduated from Southern University with a Bachelor of Science degree in business administration.

In 1978 Baranco founded Baranco Pontiac, Inc., and he has since received numerous awards sponsored by General Motors, Ford and American Honda. Since 1990, his automotive group has remained one of *Black Enterprise*'s top 100 businesses, and he has received the coveted *Time* magazine Quality Dealer Award.

As chairman of the board of the First Southern Bank of Lithonia, Baranco negotiated a merger with the Citizens Trust Bank of Atlanta, making the new Citizens Trust Bank the third-largest minority bank in the United States. He serves on several other boards and is an active member of 100 Black Men of DeKalb County, Inc., the Maynard Jackson Youth Foundation, Arrive Alive and the United Way, among others.

Baranco is married to Juanita Powell Baranco. Together, they have four children.

Juanita Powell Baranco

Co-Owner &
Executive Vice President
Baranco Automotive Group

Juanita Baranco, along with her husband, Gregory, co-owns Baranco Automotive Group. Born in Washington, D.C., she was raised in Shreveport, Louisiana, where she earned Bachelor of Science and juris doctorate degrees from Louisiana State University. She holds memberships with the American Bar Association, the State Bar of Georgia and the Louisiana State Bar Association.

A community servant, Baranco actively supports the Scottsdale Child Development Center, and has served on the board of directors for Georgia Power Company, the Federal Reserve Bank of Atlanta and the John H. Harland Company. A member of Delta Sigma Theta Sorority, Inc., she is also a board member of the Sickle Cell Foundation of Georgia and the current chairman of the Clark Atlanta University trustee board. She has served on the University System of Georgia board of regents, serving as board chair and vice chair. Additionally, she is a member of Saints Peter and Paul Church, where she sings in the choir.

A sought-after speaker, Baranco has received numerous awards, including election into the YWCA Academy of Women Achievers. She and husband Gregory have four children.

The Honorable Eldrin A. Bell was elected in 2004 as chairman of the Clayton County Board of Commissioners. His election was historic in that he is the first African American in this position. Bell also served as the first African-American chief of police for the City of Atlanta to hold every rank from patrolman to chief.

Bell is a member of many civic and professional organizations, including the Gate City Bar Association, the National Organization of Black Law Enforcement Officers, the Georgia International Law Enforcement Exchange, the Governor's Martin Luther King Holiday Commission and the National Academy of Recording Arts & Sciences.

Bell received his education in Atlanta Public Schools. He completed undergraduate studies at Morris Brown College and Georgia State University. Additionally, Bell completed graduate studies at Harvard University Law School, the Northwestern University Traffic Institute and Atlanta University. He also received training at the FBI Academy and the National Executive Institute, and he is a Secret Service Academy graduate.

A member and minister at Salem Bible Church, Bell is the proud father of 12 children, eight of whom are adopted.

The Honorable Eldrin A. Bell

Chairman
Clayton County
Board of Commissioners

Justice Robert Benham is a cum laude graduate of Tuskegee University. He received a juris doctorate degree from The University of Georgia and a Master of Laws degree from the University of Virginia. Additionally, he has received honorary Doctor of Law degrees from The John Marshall Law School and Tuskegee University.

Benham served as a judge on the Georgia Court of Appeals for six years, until his appointment to the Supreme Court of Georgia, where he previously served as chief justice. To his credit, his court was listed as one of the most progressive supreme courts in the nation by the American Bar Association. He is a master in the Bleckley Inn of Court, and served as the late Chief Justice Rehnquist's appointee to the Federal-State Jurisdiction Committee.

Benham holds membership in numerous local, state and national professional organizations, and he serves on the boards of many civic, fraternal, business and religious organizations. A recipient of many distinguished awards, he is married to the former Nell Dodson, and they have two sons, Corey Brevard Benham and Austin Tyler Benham.

The Honorable Robert Benham

Justice
Supreme Court of Georgia

Ernestine Bennett

President & Chief Executive Officer
E B Enterprise Unlimited, Inc.
dba Wendy's

E rnestine Bennett owns and operates five Wendy's Old Fashioned Hamburgers restaurants in the Metro Atlanta area. She is also president of Alpharetta Medical, LLC and Shops at Panola, LLC.

Ernestine was named the Atlanta Business League's Woman of the Year; honored as one of the Top 100 Black Women of Influence; and profiled by Atlanta's WSB-TV, Channel 2 for Black History Month.

Ernestine is a longtime member of the board of directors of Bridgebuilders, Inc.; has served as an advisory board member, minority recruitment, for the Southern Region of the American Red Cross; and served on her church's board of trustees. She is a longtime member of the Atlanta Chamber of Commerce, the Henry County Chamber of Commerce and the Atlanta Suburban Chapter of Delta Sigma Theta Sorority, Inc., and a past member of the board of directors for the Metropolitan Atlanta Chapter of the National Coalition of 100 Black Women.

Ernestine received a Bachelor of Science degree in business education from North Carolina Agricultural and Technical State University, and a master's degree in public administration from The George Washington University.

Kathleen Jackson Bertrand

Senior Vice President
Community & Governmental Affairs
Atlanta Convention & Visitors Bureau

W ith the Atlanta Convention & Visitors Bureau (ACVB) since 1983, Kathleen Jackson Bertrand serves as senior vice president of community and governmental affairs. Bertrand has been instrumental in the ACVB's development of diversity marketing programs and its governmental relations. She is the highest-ranking woman or African-American staff member in the history of the organization.

Serving on numerous boards, Bertrand has been recognized by the *Atlanta Business Chronicle* as one of Atlanta's Top Hospitality Industry Leaders, by *Black Meetings and Tourism Magazine* as one of the Most Influential African-Americans in the Meetings/Tourism Industry, and by the Atlanta Business League as one of Atlanta's Top 100 Black Women of Influence. Under her direction, the ACVB publishes its African-American visitor publication, *Atlanta Heritage Guide*, which will see its 19th printing in 2009.

Bertrand is a well-known and honored jazz recording artist/writer, with performances ranging from two Olympic Games to performances before two presidents and jazz concerts worldwide. A three-time Montreux Jazz Festival performer, her discography includes four CDs, with her newest CD release and DVD scheduled for summer of 2009.

Committed to helping people live healthier and longer lives, Pfizer, Inc. was named the *Forbes* magazine Company of the Year in January of 1999. Communicating the message that everyone should have equal access to medicine is important to Melissa Bishop-Murphy, who is the southeastern director of government relations for Pfizer.

Prior to joining Pfizer, she worked as general counsel and a legislative liaison for the Georgia Department of Medical Assistance.

Melissa received a Bachelor of Arts degree in English/pre-law, summa cum laude, from Stillman College. She also received a Doctor of Jurisprudence degree from Georgetown University.

Melissa is a member of the National Coalition of 100 Black Women Decatur-DeKalb Chapter, Inc., a board member of the Georgia Partnership for Caring and was previously named to the 100s List of Georgia's Most Powerful Women by *Women Looking Ahead*. She received the National Organization of Black Elected Legislative Women's Shining Star Award. She has also served as a board member for the Stillman College National Alumni Association and has received its Distinguished Alumni Award.

Melissa Bishop-Murphy

Southeastern Director
Government Relations
Pfizer, Inc.

Johnnie B. Booker was named director of supplier diversity for The Coca-Cola Company in April of 2001. In this position, she is responsible for developing and implementing initiatives that ensure equal contracting opportunities for minority- and women-owned businesses. During her tenure, contracts with minority- and women-owned businesses have increased substantially.

Previously, Booker served as director of the Office of Equal Opportunity with the Federal Deposit Insurance Corporation, vice president of the Resolution Trust Corporation and as a member of its executive committee. She also served as deputy assistant secretary of fair housing and equal opportunity with the U.S. Department of Housing and Urban Development.

Booker received a Bachelor of Science degree from Hampton University and a Master of Social Work degree from the Atlanta University School of Social Work. She is an active board member of the National Minority Supplier Development Council, the Women's Business Enterprise National Council and several other organizations.

Her son, S. Courtney Booker III, daughter-in-law, Nissa, and two wonderful grandchildren, Dalyn and Aiden, bring her special joy.

Johnnie B. Booker

Global Director, Supplier Diversity
The Coca-Cola Company

The Honorable Tyrone Brooks

Representative, District 63
Georgia House of Representatives

T he Honorable Tyrone Brooks is a 29-year member of the Georgia House of Representatives, representing District 63. He serves on the Economic Development and Tourism, Governmental Affairs and Retirement committees.

His career in public service began as a 15-year-old civil rights activist and volunteer with the Southern Christian Leadership Conference. In 1967 Brooks became a full-time staffer and has been jailed 65 times for civil rights work.

Brooks led the movement to reactivate the town of Keysville, and helped to pass an anti-terrorism law, the Max Black Reapportionment Plan, and repeal the Jim Crow laws. He helped pass a law to bring African-American law enforcement officers into the Peace Officers Benefit Annuity Retirement Fund, denied because of race prior to 1976. His House Bill 16 resulted in winning an almost 20-year battle to change the Georgia state flag, and he is now known as "the man who changed the Georgia flag."

Brooks is a member of the Georgia Legislative Black Caucus, president of the Georgia Association of Black Elected Officials and co-founder of the Coalition for the Peoples' Agenda.

Marjorie M. Brown

Postmaster, Atlanta
United States Postal Service

A native of Jacksonville, Florida, Marjorie Brown began her postal career as a distribution clerk. Appointed the first female postmaster of Atlanta in 1996, she is responsible for an annual revenue exceeding $614 million, and she directs delivery to more than 421,000 addresses in Atlanta.

Previously, Marjorie served as district manager for the Westchester District in White Plains, New York. She held executive positions as director of marketing and communications, manager of retail sales and service, and manager of station/branch operations in Miami, Orlando and Jacksonville.

In 2003 Marjorie received the Vice President's Award for Leadership at the National Executives Conference and the Vice President's Team Award. She has been selected as one of Atlanta's Top 100 Black Women of Influence for five years and is an active member of Atlanta's Chamber of Commerce.

Marjorie attended Edward Waters College and completed studies at Duke University, Emory University and the University of Virginia. Additionally, she is a 2001 graduate of Leadership Atlanta. She is the very proud mother of five adult children and a grandmother of seven.

T arlee W. Brown is chairman and chief executive officer of the Brown Design Group, Inc., which he founded in 1975. For more than 33 years, he has led the company, which provides professional services in architecture, urban planning, engineering and project management.

Licensed and registered as an architect, Brown holds national certification from the National Council of Architectural Registration Boards and the American Institute of Certified Planners. He has practiced professionally in a number of states including Alabama, Georgia, Colorado, Florida, Ohio, Massachusetts, North Carolina, South Carolina, Texas, Washington and others.

Married to Grace Brown, he enjoys spending time with their three children, Audra, Gayle and Robert Jr.

Tarlee W. Brown
Chairman & Chief Executive Officer
Brown Design Group, Inc.

A udra Brown-Cooper is senior principal of the Brown Group companies, which collectively perform architecture, engineering, property management, development, construction and energy-efficient consulting. Her responsibilities include operations management and business development. Audra is also responsible for the expansion of services including development, construction and property management from the firm's initial core business of commercial architecture.

A certified State of Georgia erosion control inspector, Audra received an MBA degree in finance from Georgia State University, and a Bachelor of Science degree from Tuskegee University.

Audra is an active member of various community groups and provides continuous support to community schools. She is affiliated with the Atlanta Business League, Alpha Kappa Alpha Sorority, Inc., the National Association of Women in Construction as a board member, the East Point Business Association, the South Fulton Revitalization, Inc., the South Fulton Parkway Alliance, Inc., and Saint Stephens Missionary Baptist Church. She serves as a business partner for the Tri-Cities High School, Woodland Middle School and Mount Olive Elementary PTSAs.

She is the mother of three sons, Vincent, Johnathan and Coy, and the wife of Coy L. Cooper Jr.

Audra Brown-Cooper
President
Brown Group of Companies

Rick Caffey

Senior Vice President &
Market Manager
CBS Radio–Atlanta

Rick Caffey began his career at 1380 WAOK AM/WVEE V-103 FM as vice president and general manager on October 1, 1995. Named senior vice president and market manager of CBS Radio–Atlanta, he currently oversees a four-station cluster, including urban giant WVEE, WAOK, dave fm and Falcons Radio.

Prior to joining WAOK/WVEE, Caffey was station manager of WALR and general manager of the Atlanta Urban Radio Alliance. Prior to coming to Atlanta, he ran the No. 1 and No. 2 stations in Memphis, WHRK-FM and WDIA-AM, for US Radio. He was previously general sales manager for Bonneville's WTMX-FM in Chicago. The recipient of numerous community service awards, Caffey has been named to *Radio Ink magazine*'s 25 Most Successful African-Americans in Radio for six consecutive years.

Caffey is a graduate of Northern Illinois University with a Bachelor of Science degree in advertising and marketing. Married to Jacqui Caffey, he is the proud father of a son, Parris, and a daughter, Ciara.

Ryan Cameron

Host, *The Ryan Cameron Show*
WVEE V-103 FM

Ryan Cameron is afternoon drive host on WVEE V-103 FM in Atlanta. With a 20-plus-year career in media, he is one of the most talented personalities in the entertainment industry.

Cameron also hosts *Ryan Cameron Uncensored* on the Starz InBlack Television Network and is the first African-American public address announcer in the history of the Atlanta Hawks (NBA) franchise.

Cameron began his radio career at WVEE V-103 FM in Atlanta in 1991. In 1995 he moved to WKYS in Washington, D.C. After a year in Washington D.C., Cameron earned his own morning show for a new station in Atlanta, WHAT. In July of 2005, he returned to WVEE as host of *The Ryan Cameron Show*, which currently airs Monday through Friday from 2 to 6 p.m.

The Ryan Cameron Foundation was established to provide Atlanta's youth with the tools needed to empower them for their future leadership roles. A broadcasting major at the University of West Georgia, Cameron resides in Atlanta with his wife, Kysha, who helps oversee his foundation, and their children, Ryan Megan, Kai and Cayden.

Cris Carter, chairman of Carter Brothers, LLC, develops corporate vision, drives strategic growth, provides access to key contacts in the business community, supports public relations initiatives and directs relationship development.

Prior to entering the security industry, Cris' 16-year NFL career established him as one of the greatest wide receivers of all time, playing in eight pro bowls and becoming one of four players in NFL history to catch 1,000 or more receptions. In 2001 he founded Carter Brothers in Atlanta, Georgia, with his brother, John. Since its inception, Carter Brothers has achieved national success by bringing innovation to the security industry through its unique process-driven delivery of design, installation and maintenance of electronic security, fire and life safety systems.

Cris attended The Ohio State University, where he studied communications. He serves on the board of directors of Builders on Dreams for Youths and is an international ambassador for the Starlight Foundation.

In addition to his business enterprises, Cris is an NFL football analyst for ESPN, hosts a show on SIRIUS Satellite Radio and is a national columnist for YahooSports.com.

Cris Carter

Chairman
Carter Brothers, LLC

As president and chief executive officer for Carter Brothers, LLC, John Carter leads one of the nation's top electronic security, fire and life safety firms. He founded Carter Brothers in 2001 with his brother, Cris Carter.

In 2007 Carter Brothers received the inaugural Entrepreneurship of the Year Award from the National Urban League. Additionally, the National Minority Supplier Development Council named Carter Brothers the Regional Supplier of the Year. In 2006 Carter Brothers was featured in *Fortune* magazine's Top 500 list and *Black Enterprise*'s Top 100 issue.

John attended West Liberty State College, where he studied business management. He is a graduate of the Advanced Management Education Program at Northwestern University's Kellogg School of Business.

John is a member of the boards of directors for the YMCA and the National Minority Supplier Development Council, and a founding member of Carter Brothers Charities. He is also active in the community, supporting the Boys & Girls Clubs of America, Hosea Feed The Hungry and Homeless and the National Urban League.

John Carter

President & Chief Executive Officer
Carter Brothers, LLC

Xernona Clayton

Founder & President
Trumpet Awards Foundation, Inc.

Xernona Clayton was employed at Turner Broadcasting System for 31 years. She joined TBS SuperStation in 1979 as a documentary specials producer, and served TBS in a number of capacities through the years.

She is founder, president and chief executive officer of the Trumpet Awards Foundation, Inc. A recipient of numerous media awards, Xernona began her broadcast career in 1967, becoming the south's first African American to have her own television show.

After moving to Atlanta in 1965, Xernona accepted a position with the Southern Christian Leadership Conference, and worked closely with Dr. Martin Luther King Jr. She also traveled extensively with Mrs. Coretta Scott King on her nationwide concert tours. *The Peaceful Warrior*, a biography of Dr. King authored by her late husband, Ed Clayton, and co-authored by Xernona in the revised editions, has been published in several languages. Xernona's autobiography, *I've Been Marching All the Time*, was published in 1991.

A member of Alpha Kappa Alpha Sorority, Inc., she is married to Judge Paul L. Brady, and is a member of Ebenezer Baptist Church.

William A. Clement Jr.

Chairman & Chief Executive Officer
DOBBS, RAM & Company

William "Bill" Clement Jr. is chairman and chief executive officer of DOBBS, RAM & Company. DOBBS, RAM & Company is the primary contractor engaged by the Internal Revenue Service (IRS) to maintain the IRS E-Filing system, the national system used to electronically receive federal income tax returns.

Appointed by President Carter, Bill served as associate administrator of the U.S. Small Business Administration in Washington, D.C., during the Carter Administration. He also served as vice president and senior loan officer of Citizens Trust Bank.

Bill is president and chief executive officer of Atlanta Life Financial Group, Inc. and chairman of Jackson Securities. He is also a board member of Radiant Systems, Inc. and The Commerce Club. He is former co-chairman of the Atlanta Action Forum, a trustee of the Maynard Jackson Youth Foundation and a charter member of the 100 Black Men of Atlanta.

Born in Atlanta, Bill received a Bachelor of Arts degree from Morehouse College and a Master of Business Administration degree from the Wharton Business School at the University of Pennsylvania.

As fire chief for the City of East Point, Rosemary Roberts Cloud is the first African-American female fire chief in the United States. In her position, she is responsible for managing five fire stations and 120 employees in a city with 40,000 residents. She began her career in the fire service 29 years ago with the City of Atlanta Fire Department, and worked her way up the ranks from firefighter to chief officer.

Cloud has a Bachelor of Science degree in applied behavioral science from National-Louis University. She received additional training from the Harvard University School of Government, Dillard University and the National Fire Academy. She also attended the Naval Postgraduate School.

A recipient of many awards for her outstanding work in the community, Cloud's professional affiliations include the International Association of Fire Chiefs, Women Chief Fire Officers and the International Association of Black Professional Fire Fighters. The youngest of 14 children, she was born and raised in Atlanta, and has one daughter and one granddaughter.

Rosemary Roberts Cloud

Fire Chief
City of East Point

The Honorable Kecia A. Cunningham is a three-term commissioner for the City of Decatur, where she sets policy and enacts legislation for the city's 18,000 residents. She is active with the Georgia Municipal Association (GMA) and serves on its Legislative Policy Committee, crafting the legislative agenda and priorities for GMA's 500 member cities.

Cunningham is active with numerous community groups. She graduated from Leadership Georgia, Leadership Atlanta and the Regional Leadership Institute. Cunningham has been recognized by *Who's Who In Black Atlanta®*, *The Atlanta Journal-Constitution* and *Women Looking Ahead* magazine. Her honors include receiving the Human Rights Campaign Community Leadership Award and being named an Agnes Scott College Outstanding Young Alumna.

Cunningham received a Bachelor of Arts degree in psychology from Agnes Scott College. She resides in Decatur, Georgia.

**The Honorable
Kecia A. Cunningham**

Commissioner, District 2
City of Decatur

Amanda Davis

Co-Anchor
WAGA-TV/FOX 5

A manda Davis is an Emmy-winning co-anchor for the top-rated *FOX5 News* at 6 and 10 p.m. Davis came to FOX5 in 1986 from WSB-TV Atlanta, where she was an anchor and reporter.

At FOX 5, Davis has reported on various issues and served as anchor of the noon news. She launched the highly successful *Good Day Atlanta* before taking over the main anchor chair.

Throughout her career, Davis has received numerous honors and awards, including five Emmys from the National Academy of Television Arts & Sciences, and also the Best Newscast honors for anchoring *FOX5 News* in 1999 and 2000. Likewise, she has received five awards from the Atlanta Association of Black Journalists, including Best Anchor in 2000.

Davis' work to place Georgia's children in permanent homes is truly her labor of love. She began this project in 1997 with a series of stories called "A Place to Call Home." The Freddie Mac Foundation then came to FOX 5 with the idea of presenting weekly profiles of children available for adoption, and "Wednesday's Child" was launched in November of 2000.

Benjamin R. DeCosta

Chief Executive Officer
Hartsfield-Jackson Atlanta
International Airport

B en DeCosta is aviation general manager of the City of Atlanta Department of Aviation, and he functions as chief executive officer of Hartsfield-Jackson Atlanta International Airport. A national leader in aviation, he serves on the boards of directors for Airports Council International, one of the world's largest airport organizations, and the American Association of Airport Executives, the largest professional organization for airport executives in the world.

During DeCosta's tenure, Hartsfield-Jackson has received numerous accolades from industry experts. In 2008 the Air Transport Research Society announced the selection of the facility as the most efficient airport among all major airports worldwide. He was also honored in 2007 as Best Airport Director of the Year by *Airport Revenue News* magazine.

Prior to becoming general manager, DeCosta worked for the Port Authority of New York and New Jersey, and served as general manager of Newark International Airport. A native New Yorker, he received a Bachelor of Arts degree in physics at Queens College in 1968 before earning a juris doctorate degree from New York Law School in 1975.

The Honorable Myra H. Dixon has been a judge on the Fulton County State Court bench since 1998. Dixon presides over civil and criminal misdemeanor cases. Her career has been distinctive and diverse. She was a partner at Thomas, Kennedy, Sampson & Patterson, assistant U.S. attorney for the Northern District of Georgia, assistant public defender in Fulton County and associate to general counsel of the U.S. Navy.

As chair of the judicial section of the Gate City Bar, Dixon developed a program to improve the reading skills of 3rd grade males. She was honored by *Black Judges In America*®, *Women Looking Ahead* magazine, and received the Pinnacle Leadership Award from Delta Sigma Theta Sorority, Inc.

Dixon received a Bachelor of Science degree in political science from Tennessee State University and a juris doctorate, cum laude, from the Howard University School of Law.

She is married to attorney Pat D. Dixon Jr. and they have two children: Kyra, a graduate of Howard University, and Pat, a graduate of Morehouse College and presently a law student at the Howard University School of Law.

The Honorable Myra H. Dixon

Judge
Fulton Country State Court

Thomas W. Dortch Jr. is president and chief executive officer of TWD, Inc., a consulting firm with emphasis on business development, public relations and fundraising. He is also chairman emeritus of 100 Black Men of America's national board of directors. Under his guidance, the 100 expanded to include 102 chapters throughout the United States, Africa, England and the West Indies. The author of *The Miracles of Mentoring: The Joy of Investing in Our Future*, Dortch is also the voice of the 100's *Four for the Future*.

Dortch is the recipient of numerous awards and honors, including a U.S. Presidential Citation for Volunteerism and the Martin Luther King Jr. Distinguished Service Award. He was among *Ebony* and the *Atlanta Business Chronicle*'s 100 Most Influential Black Leaders in 2004.

Dortch earned a bachelor's degree in sociology and pre-professional social work from Fort Valley State University, and a Master of Arts degree in criminal justice administration from Clark Atlanta University. He also attended Georgia State University as a Ford fellow in the urban administration program, and he holds two honorary doctorate degrees.

Thomas W. Dortch Jr.

President & Chief Executive Officer
TWD, Inc.

Curley M. Dossman Jr.

President
Georgia-Pacific Foundation

Curley Dossman is responsible for community relations program development for plant communities and administration of the Georgia-Pacific Foundation and its community programs department. Dossman works closely with executive leadership on Atlanta- and Georgia-focused programs important to the company. In directing the activities of the Georgia-Pacific Foundation, he is responsible for developing and implementing the company's overall philanthropic strategies.

A member of numerous boards of directors, Dossman's board memberships include the Metro Atlanta YMCA, the National Black Arts Festival, the Professional Association of Georgia Educators, the High Museum of Art, Leadership Atlanta and the Atlanta Downtown Improvement District (chairman). Likewise, he is treasurer for Great Schools Atlanta, vice chairman of operations for 100 Black Men of America, chairman of the Metro Atlanta Chamber of Commerce education committee and an Atlanta Rotary member.

Curley received a bachelor's degree from Morehouse College in 1973, and a law degree from Washington University School of Law in 1976.

A native of Louisiana, Curley's wife, Jennifer, is an honors graduate of Spelman College, and their son, Jonathan, attended Morehouse College.

The Honorable William "Bill" Edwards

Commissioner, District 7
Fulton County

The Honorable William "Bill" Edwards has served the citizens of Fulton County as their District 7 commissioner since November of 2000, representing the residents of unincorporated south Fulton and the cities of Chattahoochee Hill, College Park, East Point, Fairburn, Hapeville, Union City, Palmetto and a portion of southwest Atlanta. He is currently serving as vice chairman of the Fulton County Commission for the fifth time. Edwards also served as interim chair of the Board of Commissioners from August through November of 2003.

During his eight years on the Board of Commissioners, Edwards has brought more than $2.5 billion into south Fulton County. Under his leadership, south Fulton has benefited from business and residential growth, improvements in infrastructure, and numerous quality of life, community and arts initiatives.

A resident of unincorporated south Fulton for more than 30 years, Edwards is the owner of the William Edwards Allstate Insurance Agency. He graduated from Morehouse College and the Atlanta School of Law. Edwards is a family man with two adult children and three grandchildren, and he is a member of Cascade United Methodist Church.

Sidmel Estes has taken more than three decades of journalism experience, primarily in television news, and transformed it into a dynamic media consulting and production company, BreakThrough Inc. Sidmel helped create and build *Good Day Atlanta* on WAGA-TV FOX 5, where she worked for 27 years. She made history in 1991 when elected first woman president of the National Association of Black Journalists.

Sidmel was listed in *Ebony*'s 100 Most Influential Black Americans and Organizations. She also received the Academy of Television Arts & Sciences' highest honor, the Silver Circle Award, which celebrates 25 years of service to the television industry.

An honors graduate, Sidmel received bachelor's and master's degrees from Northwestern University's Medill School of Journalism, where she was inducted as a charter member of the Hall of Achievement. She still serves on the school's board of advisors and on the board of the Northwestern Alumni Association.

A fellow of the McCormick Tribune Foundation, sponsored by the National Association of Broadcasters, Sidmel remains the No. 1 fan of sons Joshua and Sidney, who are now in college and high school, respectively.

Sidmel K. Estes

Founder & Chief Executive Officer
BreakThrough Inc.

Isaac Newton Farris Jr., nephew of Dr. Martin Luther King Jr., is president and chief executive officer of The Martin Luther King, Jr. Center for Nonviolent Social Change, an organization that educates the public about Dr. King's life, work and teachings. As the Center's primary spokesman, he oversees its programs and confers with political, business, religious, academic and grassroots leaders.

After serving as the Georgia field coordinator of Walter Mondale's presidential campaign, Farris went on to serve as deputy manager for the re-election of Atlanta Mayor Andrew Young. He acted as campaign manager for Martin Luther King III in his successful election as Fulton County commissioner. He has also held executive posts in government and industries.

Farris majored in political science at his uncle's alma mater, Morehouse College. His background and extensive experiences in public speaking about the life, leadership and legacy of Dr. Martin Luther King Jr. provides a unique perspective on the critical issues of our times.

Isaac Newton Farris Jr.

President & Chief Executive Officer
The King Center

MOST INFLUENTIAL

Gwendolyn Keyes Fleming

District Attorney
DeKalb County

When Gwen Keyes Fleming was sworn into office in December of 2005, she became the first African-American and first female district attorney in DeKalb County, Georgia. A native of New Jersey, Fleming graduated from Douglass College of Rutgers University with a Bachelor of Science degree in finance, and the Emory University School of Law.

Her prosecutorial career spans more than 13 years at both the misdemeanor and felony level, including a six-year stint as DeKalb's youngest elected solicitor general. The District Attorney's Office handles more than 9,000 felony cases a year. As district attorney, Fleming is responsible for supervising and training a staff of approximately 50 attorneys and 100-plus support personnel while administering an $11 million annual budget. She has expanded services by launching Animal Cruelty, Gang, Domestic Violence/Sexual Assault and High-Intensity Drug Trafficking Areas units, along with Elderly Abuse and Pre-Trial Diversion programs to focus on nonviolent first-time offenders.

Fleming has received numerous honors and recognitions. She is married to Randal Fleming and is a proud mother of two children.

Darryl Ford

Owner
Stone Mountain Chrysler Jeep Dodge

As its owner, Darryl Ford has redefined success for Stone Mountain Chrysler Jeep Dodge. Darryl's achievements have afforded him features in leading publications and bestowed honors for his accomplishments.

Recognized as one of America's Most Successful African-American Companies by *Black Enterprise*, Darryl was named a Man of Distinction and one of Atlanta's Most Influential in *Who's Who In Black Atlanta*®. In 2008 he was awarded Retailer of the Year by the U.S. Department of Commerce. Darryl has developed a Partners Program that pours money back into the community and was saluted with a resolution by the Georgia State Senate for his contributions to the citizens of Georgia.

Darryl is a proud member of the National Automobile Dealer, Chrysler Minority Dealer and Georgia Automobile Dealers associations; the National Association of Minority Automotive Dealers; the Atlanta Business League; and the Gwinnett Chamber of Commerce. He is vice chair for the DeKalb Chamber of Commerce and on the board of directors for the DeKalb Chapter of 100 Black Men.

T he Honorable Shirley Franklin became the 58th mayor of Atlanta in November of 2001, and redefined history by being elected the city's first woman mayor and the first African-American woman to serve as mayor of a major southern city. She offered the residents of Atlanta a vision and passion for making Atlanta a safer, cleaner city; a better city for families, seniors and children; and providing a more open, responsive and effective city government.

During the course of her outstanding career, Shirley has received numerous awards and has been featured in many publications, such as *Business to Business*, *The New York Times*, *The Wall Street Journal*, *Ebony*, *Jet* and *Women Looking Ahead*.

Shirley earned a Bachelor of Arts degree from Howard University and a Master of Arts degree from the University of Pennsylvania. In May of 2002 she was awarded an honorary Doctor of Laws degree from Howard University.

Shirley has tackled the tough challenges in city government and lived up to her campaign slogan, "If you make me mayor, I'll make you proud."

The Honorable Shirley Franklin

Mayor
City of Atlanta

J udge Ural D. Glanville has spent his life in public service – not only as a jurist, but also as a commissioned officer in the U.S. Army Reserve Judge Advocate General Corps (JAG). He is currently a colonel and commander of the 213th Legal Support Organization. On August 10, 2004, Glanville was elected to the Fulton County Superior Court, and serves as one of 19 superior court judges for Fulton County.

Glanville studied at Brevard College in North Carolina and the University of Georgia, where he earned a law degree. In the private sector, his work as an advocate spanned the spectrum from prosecution to criminal defense to civil litigation. Glanville also spent several years teaching at Georgia State University College of Law. Additionally, he spent nine years as a magistrate judge in the Fulton County State Court.

A member of 100 Black Men of Atlanta, Glanville is a 2005 graduate of Leadership Atlanta. He is married to the former Lisa Butts. They live with their two children, Evan and Leslie, in southwest Atlanta, and are active members of St. Paul's Episcopal Church.

The Honorable Ural D. Glanville

Judge
Fulton County Superior Court

Renée Lewis Glover

President & Chief Executive Officer
Atlanta Housing Authority

Renée Lewis Glover is president and chief executive officer of the Atlanta Housing Authority (AHA). She has been acknowledged nationally for her business leadership and strategic approach to community redevelopment. At AHA, Glover pioneered master-planned, mixed-finance and mixed-income residential development, where families of all socioeconomic profiles live next to each other in the same amenity-rich community. She has improved housing, as well as public schools, transit access and employment opportunities. The model she created at AHA is currently used by HUD as its redevelopment blueprint.

Glover has been recognized by the Atlanta History Center as one of Atlanta's Defining Women. She was named the 2002 Public Official of the Year by *GOVERNING* magazine. A collaboration among the Center for American Women and Politics, the Ford Foundation and the Council for Excellence in Government recognized her as one of the top ten American women in government.

Prior to AHA, Glover was a highly praised corporate finance attorney in Atlanta and New York City. She received a juris doctorate degree from Boston University, a master's degree from Yale University and a baccalaureate degree from Fisk University.

John Thomas Grant Jr.

Chief Executive Officer
100 Black Men of Atlanta, Inc.

John Thomas Grant Jr. is chief executive officer of 100 Black Men of Atlanta, Inc., and has been a member of the organization for almost 20 years. In his position, he is responsible for managing the organization's day-to-day growth and direction. He has garnered a reputation among his colleagues for his ability to obtain "blue-chip" corporate sponsors and successfully manage their investments in the organization.

Prior to 100 Black Men, Grant joined Airborne Express in 1979. Just two years later, he was promoted to area operations manager in Greenville, South Carolina. In 1984 he was relocated to Atlanta, where he served in several areas, including leading the customer service and sales organizations.

Grant's personal achievements led to numerous company awards, including the company's first and only Humanitarian Award in 1997. He currently serves on several boards, including the Alliance Theatre, the American Red Cross Southern Region, True Colors Theatre Company and the Atlanta Convention & Visitors Bureau. He also serves on the boards of the National Wildlife Federation, and the Metro Atlanta Chamber of Commerce and its Education Committee.

D r. Beverly L. Hall is superintendent of Atlanta Public Schools. She has implemented several nationally successful, comprehensive school reform models to improve student performance and encourage higher levels of achievement at all grade levels.

Hall is the advisory board chair of the Harvard Urban Superintendents Program, serving as a mentor superintendent to participants in the doctoral program. She is also a member of The Commission on Teaching, which develops specific policy recommendations to deal with the teaching crisis in America.

Before working in Atlanta, Hall was the state district superintendent of the Newark Public Schools, the largest school district in New Jersey. She was also the deputy chancellor for instruction in the New York City School System. Hall was honored by the Congressional Black Caucus in its 1998 tribute to the Most Challenged School Superintendents in America.

A native of Jamaica, West Indies, Hall received a Bachelor of Arts degree in English and a Master of Science degree in guidance and counseling from The City University of New York. She also received a doctorate degree in education from Fordham University.

Dr. Beverly L. Hall
Superintendent
Atlanta Public Schools

J ohn B. Hammond III is chief executive officer of the 100 Black Men of America, Inc. In this capacity, John is responsible for implementing the strategic imperatives of the board of directors and offering recommendations regarding strategy and policy for the organization's 106 chapters around the world. The 100 is known for its impactful programs that touch the lives of more than 125,000 children each year.

John is an educator, business leader and scholar. He conducted organizational research at Harvard Business School and taught organizational development and strategic communication courses at the MIT Sloan School of Management, the Harvard University Kennedy School of Government and the Emory University Goizueta Business School. Additionally, he is a published author in the area of diversity management and employee retention.

John received a Bachelor of Science degree from MIT and a Master of Business Administration degree from Emory University. He is currently working toward a Doctor of Philosophy degree at the MIT Sloan School of Management.

A native of Baton Rouge, John is married to Yoko (Kusumoto) Hammond and has three children, Therese, John and Yoji.

John B. Hammond III
Chief Executive Officer
100 Black Men of America, Inc.

The Honorable Barbara A. Harris

Judge
Municipal Court of Atlanta

The Honorable Barbara A. Harris serves as a judge in the Municipal Court of Atlanta Specialty Division. Previously, she was appointed chief judge on June 18, 1992, the first woman to serve in that capacity. During her tenure as chief judge, she established the Probation Department and the Domestic Violence, Environmental and Community Court divisions of the Atlanta Municipal Court.

A graduate of the University of Michigan Law School, Harris also earned a bachelor's degree, cum laude, from Harvard University. She has enhanced her judicial studies at The National Judicial College.

An active member of the Gate City Bar Association, Harris is co-founder of the Georgia Association of Black Women Attorneys. She has chaired and served on various committees for the Georgia Supreme Court, the State Bar of Georgia, the American Bar Association and the National Bar Association Judicial Council.

Harris has received the 2006 Georgia Association of Black Women Attorneys' creation of the Barbara A. Harris Founders Award for exemplary community service, the Gate City Bar Association's Thelma Wyatt Cummings Moore Legacy Award and the Now Black Women Award.

Judge Glenda A. Hatchett

Syndicated Television Host
Sony Pictures Television

Judge Glenda A. Hatchett is the jurist of the award-winning television series, *Judge Hatchett*. The author of *Say What You Mean and Mean What You Say*, she serves as the national spokesperson for CASA (Court Appointed Special Advocates).

After graduating from law school, Hatchett took a position at Delta Air Lines, where she was the highest-ranking African-American woman. She later accepted an appointment as chief presiding judge of the Fulton County Juvenile Court.

The local chapter of the National Bar Association selected Hatchett as Outstanding Jurist of the Year, and she won a Prism Award in 2003 for *Judge Hatchett*. The 100 Black Men of America named her Woman of the Year, and the Girl Scouts of America named her one of the Ten Women of Distinction.

Hatchett serves on the board of directors for the NFL's Atlanta Falcons and the Hospital Corporation of America. She graduated from Mount Holyoke College and Emory University Law School. Emory named her Outstanding Alumni of the Year, and presented her the Emory Medal. An Atlanta native, Hatchett resides in Atlanta with her two sons.

R ichard Holmes is senior vice president of the Metro Atlanta region for Georgia Power. He joined Georgia Power in 1974. In this role, he has operational responsibilities for Georgia Power's 1.2 million customers in the Metro Atlanta area.

Richard earned a bachelor's degree from Columbus State University and a Master of Business Administration degree from Clark Atlanta University. He also completed the Harvard University Business School Program for Management Development.

A member of 100 Black Men of Atlanta, Inc., Richard is chairman of the board of the Georgia State Department of Community Health. He serves on the boards of Literacy Action, the Kennesaw State University Foundation, the American Association of Blacks in Energy, the Atlanta Branch of the NAACP, the Atlanta BeltLine Partnership, the McPherson Planning Local Redevelopment Authority and the Atlanta Police Foundation. In 1999 he served as chairman of the Cobb Chamber of Commerce, becoming the first African American to lead the second-largest chamber of commerce in Georgia.

A native of Columbus, Georgia, Richard and his wife, Linda, reside in Peachtree City. They have two sons, Stephen and Mark.

Richard L. Holmes

Senior Vice President
Metro Atlanta Region
Georgia Power

C urrently serving his third term, the Honorable Paul Howard was first elected as district attorney of Fulton County in 1996, becoming the first African-American district attorney in Georgia history. He previously served as Fulton County solicitor general.

Howard's career began in 1976 as a City of Atlanta assistant solicitor. He left to join Fulton County as an assistant district attorney. Upon leaving the county, he joined the firm of Thomas, Kennedy, Sampson, Edward & Patterson.

Howard serves on the boards of directors for the Partnership Against Domestic Violence, the Fulton County Child Advocacy Center and Georgians for Children. He is a member of the Georgia Association of Black Elected Officials, the National Black Prosecutors Association and 100 Black Men of Atlanta, Inc. He has received numerous awards, including the Georgia Women's Political Caucus Good Guy Award and Gammon Theological Seminary's Outstanding Community Service Award.

Howard graduated, cum laude, from Morehouse College and earned a scholarship to Emory University's School of Law. While there, he served as president of the Black American Law Students Association and vice president of the Student Bar Association.

The Honorable
Paul L. Howard Jr.

District Attorney
Fulton County

Stephanie S. Hughley

Executive Producer
National Black Arts Festival

Stephanie S. Hughley is executive producer of the National Black Arts Festival (NBAF). She is responsible for artistic programming and programmatic policy, external and community relations, fund development, strategic planning and management.

As founding artistic director of NBAF, Hughley conceptualized and implemented the artistic content for each festival. She was the theatre and dance producer for the Atlanta Committee for the 1996 Olympic Games Cultural Olympiad.

Currently, Hughley serves on the Metro Atlanta Arts & Culture Coalition and the Atlanta Convention & Visitors Bureau boards. She is a member of the Association of Theatrical Press Agents & Managers, and serves as a consultant to many performing arts and cultural institutions.

Most recently, Hughley was inducted into the Atlanta Business League's Women's Hall of Fame and the Atlanta Convention and Business Bureau Hospitality Hall of Fame. She also received the Georgia Arts & Entertainment Legacy Award and the William Dawson Award from the Association of Performing Arts Presenters.

Hughley is a graduate of Kent State University (Bachelor of Science degree) and Antioch College (Master of Education degree) at Harvard University.

Bunnie Jackson-Ransom

President & Chief Executive Officer
First Class, Inc.

Bunnie Jackson-Ransom's professional career spans some 48 years, during which time she has been a college professor at Bennett College and Georgia State University, a governmental agency official during the days of "economic opportunity," a business consultant and an entrepreneur. Jackson-Ransom is the founder and chief executive officer of First Class, Inc., a 34-year-old marketing and public relations firm, and she has developed an unblemished reputation in her profession, excelling in the use of community relations as a marketing tool.

During the 1980s, she managed performing artists, assumed the reigns of Atlanta Artist Management as its president, and successfully handled the professional careers of The SOS Band and Cameo, carrying the recording artists to gold and platinum status.

A native of Louisburg, North Carolina, Jackson-Ransom is a graduate of North Carolina College in Durham. She received a Master of Business Administration degree from North Carolina Central University.

Jackson-Ransom has served her community in many capacities, and continues to receive many awards and honors for her work.

Maurice E. Jenkins Jr. was promoted to senior vice president of southern field operations for the United Negro College Fund, Inc. (UNCF) in 2006. He heads one of three regions overseeing fundraising activities of nine UNCF offices, covering 13 southern states with an annual goal of $21 million. In this position, he received the UNCF Region of the Year Award and the UNCF Award for Excellence.

Maurice is an active community leader and has served in many capacities, including as a member of the Leadership Atlanta Class of 2003; member of the Coca-Cola Scholars Foundation's National Scholarship Selection Committee; member of the Dr. Martin Luther King Jr. National Memorial Project in Washington, D.C.; and a graduate of the Diversity Leadership Academy.

For outstanding community service, Maurice has received numerous recognitions, including Outstanding Young People of Atlanta, the YMCA Partner with Youth Award, and a presidential citation from Alpha Phi Alpha Fraternity, Inc.

A native of Washington, D.C., Maurice is united in marriage to Gina Wessons, and enjoys being a father to son Maurice III and daughter Mia Elizabeth.

Maurice E. Jenkins Jr.

Senior Vice President
Southern Field Operations
United Negro College Fund, Inc.

A teacher by training, Ingrid Saunders Jones currently works for The Coca-Cola Company. A Detroit native, Jones earned a bachelor's degree from Michigan State University and a master's degree in education from Eastern Michigan University. She has held leadership positions in the educational, nonprofit, city, government and corporate sectors.

As director of corporate external affairs, Jones directs The Coca-Cola Company in community, humanitarian and civic affairs. As chair of The Coca-Cola Foundation, she leads the company's philanthropic commitment to education. Under her leadership, the foundation has contributed more than $256 million to education initiatives that increase access to higher education. Jones also serves on the boards of The Coca-Cola Scholars Foundation and Camp Coca-Cola.

Jones is a board member of Clark Atlanta University, The Carter Center, the Congressional Black Caucus Foundation, The Ohio State University President's Council on Women, and the Andrew Young School of Policy Studies at Georgia State University. She is also a member of the Rotary Club of Atlanta, Delta Sigma Theta Sorority, Inc. and the Society of International Business Fellows.

Jones received the National Urban League's 2004 Leadership Award.

Ingrid Saunders Jones

Senior Vice President
The Coca-Cola Company

Jonathan Jones

Chief Executive Officer
Housing Authority of
Fulton County

Jonathan Jones is chief executive officer of the Housing Authority of Fulton County. As such, Jones provides leadership to a staff of 40 and operates a public housing authority that owns and manages 109 public housing units, administers more than 2,200 rental assistance vouchers and has a consolidated budget exceeding $24 million. He also directs the activities of eight affiliate corporations, including Renaissance Realty, Renaissance Mortgage Lending and Renaissance Education and Counseling, creating a one-stop homeownership shop.

In the authority's role as a housing finance agency, Jones has coordinated financing for developers of affordable housing, including more than $500 million for nearly 9,000 elegantly styled, yet affordable, mixed-income housing units for families and seniors. He had a primary role in planning the $72 million U.S. Department of Housing and Urban Development HOPE VI redevelopment program, which includes a $17.2 million federal grant.

Jones received undergraduate and graduate education at Fisk University and Clark Atlanta University, respectively.

A native of Birmingham, Alabama, he is married to his wife of 31 years, Valerie, and has a daughter, Pedra, and two sons, Jelani and Jabari.

Nathan Lewis

President & Chief Executive Officer
Security Capital Brokerage, Inc.

A nationally recognized financial services expert, Nathan Lewis is president and chief executive officer of Security Capital Brokerage, Inc., an Atlanta-based investment bank. With responsibilities that include acquisitions and strategic planning, Lewis plays a vital role in assuring the company's stability and continued success. Previously, he worked at Jackson Securities under the tutelage of Maynard Jackson. Other corporations that have benefited from Lewis' financial management expertise are A.G. Edwards and Nestlé USA.

Lewis received a Bachelor of Business Administration degree from The University of Georgia and a Master of Business Administration degree from Clark Atlanta University. He studied marketing and investment management at the University of Pennsylvania's Wharton School of Business.

Lewis is registered with the Financial Industry Regulatory Authority as a general securities principal and qualified research analyst. He is board secretary for the Middle Georgia Center for Academic Excellence, a member of the National Association of Securities Professionals and the Association of Investment Management Sales Executives, and a board member of Cool Girls, Inc.

A Georgia native, Lewis enjoys reading, golf and spending time with wife Nicole and son Alex.

Milton J. Little Jr. became president of the United Way of Metropolitan Atlanta in July of 2007, after serving as president of the United Way of Massachusetts Bay and Merrimack Valley. Before joining the United Way, he served as interim president and chief executive officer of the National Urban League in New York, where he launched innovative partnerships with the Department of Housing and Urban Development, and the Labor and Commerce Departments, as well as with Verizon, Enterprise Rent-A-Car and Prudential.

A member of Phi Beta Kappa, Little graduated, magna cum laude, with a Bachelor of Arts degree in sociology from Morehouse College. He earned a Master of Arts degree in urban sociology and social policy from Columbia University.

Little currently chairs the Center for Assessment and Policy Development and co-chairs the Atlanta Regional Commission's Fifty Forward initiative. A member of 100 Black Men of Atlanta, Inc. and the Rotary Club of Atlanta, he also serves on the Georgia State University Nonprofit Studies Advisory Board. Married to Traci Gibson Little, he is the father of two sons, Milton and Taylor.

Milton J. Little Jr.

President
United Way of Metropolitan Atlanta

Evelyn Gibson Lowery has been a community and civil rights activist for many years. She has been founder and chair of SCLC/W.O.M.E.N. (Women's Organizational Movement for Equality Now), Inc. since 1979. Under her leadership, SCLC/W.O.M.E.N., Inc. made its mission the championing of the rights of women, children and families.

With her husband, Evelyn participated for years in demonstrations and marches, including marching in 1982 to extend the Voting Rights Act. Through the years, she was jailed three times regarding the issue of apartheid and shot at twice by the KKK.

In 2005 Evelyn unveiled The Freedom Wall in Selma, Alabama. She led the purchase and renovation of the historic Tabor Building at Auburn, and she has helped award more than $350,000 in scholarships to high school seniors.

The recipient of a myriad of awards and honors, Evelyn conducted her educational training at Clark Atlanta University and Youngstown University. She founded Jack and Jill of America in Mobile, Alabama, in 1958. The wife of Dr. Joseph Lowery, Evelyn is the mother of three daughters, Yvonne, Karen and Cheryl.

Evelyn Gibson Lowery

Founder & Chair
SCLC/W.O.M.E.N., Inc.

Rev. Dr. Joseph Echols Lowery

Co-Founder & President Emeritus
Southern Christian
Leadership Conference

L abeled as "dean of the civil rights movement" by the NAACP, the Reverend Dr. Joseph Lowery was named one of the nation's 15 greatest black preachers by *Ebony.*

Co-founder with Martin Luther King Jr. of the Southern Christian Leadership Conference, Lowery served as president and chief executive officer from 1977 to 1998. King named him chair of the delegation, delivering the demands of the 1965 Selma to Montgomery March to Governor Wallace. He is a founder of the National Black Leadership Forum and serves as chairman emeritus.

Lowery was one of the first five arrested at the South African Embassy in Washington, D.C., in the Free South Africa movement. Former pastor at Atlanta's oldest predominantly black United Methodist congregation for 18 years, Lowery added thousands of members and a 240-unit housing development. Likewise, he was pastor at Cascade United Methodist Church from 1986 to 1992. Upon retirement, he left ten acres of land, $1 million and plans for a new edifice.

Lowery is also credited with helping black farmers win a $2 billion federal court settlement against the U.S. Department of Agriculture.

The Honorable Joseph L. Macon

Mayor
City of East Point

T he Honorable Joseph L. Macon, in his first candidacy for public office, was elected mayor of the City of East Point, Georgia, on December 6, 2005. He is the 20th mayor of the City of East Point, and his historic election acknowledges him as the first African-American male elected since the city was incorporated in 1887.

Macon served three terms as an East Point planning and zoning commissioner, completing his service as a member of the commission upon his mayoral election. During his tenure as a member of the commission, he was an outspoken advocate for the rights of citizens and property owners. He also encourages the development of a diverse economic base through investment by business, industrial and commercial interests.

His leadership style is to build coalitions with the city's residents and business owners. Macon works closely with each member of the East Point City Council and the city manager to collectively build a vision of excellence for the City of East Point.

The Honorable Jim Maddox was elected to the Atlanta City Council in 1977 and is serving his eighth consecutive term. A graduate of Morehouse College and the Atlanta University School of Business Administration, Maddox is a retired contract administrator for Lockheed Martin Aeronautical Systems Corporation, where he worked for 34 years. He was also the campaign public affairs director for the United Way of Metropolitan Atlanta until he retired in 1999.

Maddox currently serves on the Atlanta Fire Fighters Pension Fund board of trustees and the boards of the Atlanta-Fulton County Public Library, the Atlanta Development Authority, the Atlanta BeltLine and the Center for Civil and Human Rights, among others.

Sponsor of the annual Toys for Kids Campaign at the Andrew & Walter Young Family YMCA, he was recently honored as Father of the Year by the Father's Day Council and the American Diabetes Association. Additionally, he received a Silver Beaver Award from The Boy Scouts of America.

An Atlanta native, Maddox is married to the former Alice J. Wise and is the proud father of Sheila, James Jr., Zachary and Sonya.

The Honorable Jim Maddox

Council Member, District 11
Atlanta City Council

An Atlanta native, the Honorable Clarence Terrell "C. T." Martin received a presidential appointment to the White House Office of Domestic Affairs in 1972, and was elected to the Atlanta City Council in a 1990 special election. His career includes tireless activism and advocacy for civil rights, higher education, civic citizenship development for African-American youth, equal opportunity for economic development in the disenfranchised small business entrepreneurial community, adequate family recreation opportunities, and public safety as key budget, policy and program priorities.

A graduate of Leadership Atlanta, Martin holds a master's degree from Atlanta University and a bachelor's degree from Shaw University.

Some of Martin's career highlights include founding Youthfest, an annual civic leadership development event for 3,000-plus youth; and securing design and construction funding for the $20 million Adamsville Natatorium. Additionally, he impacted college minority recruitment policy nationwide for 20 years by serving in leadership capacities for NSSFNS.

A recipient of some 150 community service awards, Martin is a board member of the Southwest Hospital Medical Center Foundation, the West End Medical Center and Another Way Out, Inc.

The Honorable Clarence Terrell Martin

Council Member, District 10
Atlanta City Council

Dr. Gary A. McGaha

President
Atlanta Metropolitan College

D r. Gary A. McGaha is president of Atlanta Metropolitan College (AMC). He has developed, and is implementing a comprehensive plan for AMC that focuses on academic excellence, enrollment growth, retention, graduation, expansion and collaborative relationships.

Under his leadership, the student enrollment has increased 30 percent since fall of 2006 and AMC now has the largest enrollment in the history of the institution. A new site for the college opened on Peachtree Street in downtown Atlanta in January. McGaha envisions and is planning for the college to open two additional sites.

Gary entered Mississippi Valley State University and graduated magna cum laude in 1972. He received a Master of Arts degree from Bowling Green State University in 1973 and a Doctor of Philosophy degree from the University of Mississippi in 1976. He is the first African American to receive a Ph.D. in political science from the University of Mississippi.

A native of Rienzi, Mississippi, Gary is married to Juliette Wilkinson McGaha and they have two daughters and two sons.

Miranda Mack McKenzie

Community Affairs Director
Anheuser-Busch Companies

M iranda Mack McKenzie is community affairs director for Anheuser-Busch Companies. She is responsible for representing the company's community affairs programming. Previously, she served as director of corporate affairs for Anheuser-Busch. She was responsible for implementing the company's ongoing community outreach programs in Georgia, Florida, Alabama and Mississippi.

Prior to her appointment with Anheuser-Busch, Miranda held positions with the Atlanta Committee for the Olympic Games and the Atlanta Centennial Olympic Properties.

Miranda has received numerous honors, including the National Association of Market Developers Marketer of the Year Award. *Dollars & Sense* magazine designated her as one of the Top African American Business and Professional Women. Other honors include *Ebony*'s 100 Best and Brightest Black Women in Corporate America, and the Atlanta Business League's 100 Women of Influence.

Miranda is an Atlanta native and an alumna of Morris Brown College, where she graduated, magna cum laude, and earned a Bachelor of Arts degree in English. She also attended The University of Georgia Graduate School and Georgia State University. Miranda has a son, Terrence Denard McKenzie, and three stepchildren, Therman Jr., Carmisha and Christopher McKenzie.

In January of 2009, the Honorable M. Yvette Miller became the first African-American woman to serve as chief judge of the Georgia Court of Appeals. When initially appointed in 1999, she became the first African-American female to serve on the court, and has been re-elected statewide to two six-year terms.

Miller serves on the executive committee of the National Council of Chief Judges of the State Courts of Appeals and the advisory board of the Girl Scout Council of Northwest Georgia. She has served as chair of the Georgia Student Finance Commission, a trustee of Leadership Georgia and vice president of the Georgia Association of Black Women Attorneys. Miller was inducted into the Gate City Bar Hall of Fame in October of 2008. She is a member of the Azalea City Chapter of The Links, Inc. and Delta Sigma Theta Sorority, Inc.

Miller is a member of Cascade United Methodist Church and a lifelong member of Steward Chapel AME. She is the daughter of Mr. and Mrs. Conrad Miller, and has one sibling, Dr. Conrad Miller Jr., all of Macon.

The Honorable M. Yvette Miller

Chief Judge
Court of Appeals of Georgia

With more than 20 years of experience, Mercedes Miller is a true veteran of the hospitality industry. She is currently the assistant executive director for the second-largest convention center in the state of Georgia, the Georgia International Convention Center (GICC).

An Atlanta native, Mercedes began her hospitality career in sales, working for The Stouffer Waverly Hotel. She later became part of the opening team for The Stouffer Concourse Hotel at the Hartsfield-Jackson Atlanta International Airport. Her career path led her to current employer, GICC, as a national sales manager, where she advanced to director of sales and eventually assistant executive director.

Mercedes attributes her success in large part to her community involvement. She is the past president of the Draper Boys & Girls Club of Metro Atlanta, serves on the board of directors for the Georgia American Red Cross Minority Recruitment Board and is a member of the American Society of Association Executives. She has been honored as one of Atlanta's most interesting personalities and a leader in her community by her inclusion in *Who's Who In Black Atlanta®*.

Mercedes Miller

Assistant Executive Director
Georgia International Convention Center

The Honorable Billy Mitchell

Representative, District 88
Georgia House of Representatives

The Honorable Billy Mitchell, formerly vice mayor of Stone Mountain, authored the legislation permitting the city's erection of the Freedom Bell, commemorating Martin Luther King Jr.'s exhortation to "let freedom ring, even from Stone Mountain of Georgia!" in the immortal "I Have a Dream" speech.

Overwhelmingly elected in November of 2002 to the Georgia General Assembly, Billy's constituents reside in most of Stone Mountain and other parts of DeKalb and Gwinnett counties.

He presently serves on the powerful Health and Human Services Committee and the Metropolitan Atlanta Rapid Transit Authority Oversight Committee. He has also been appointed by the Democratic Caucus to serve as deputy whip. The author of legislation signed into law every year he has served, he was selected to receive the prestigious Georgia Legislative Black Caucus Legislator of the Year Award after only his second term.

A frequent public speaker and writer, Billy is a contributor to the best-selling book, *Keeping the Faith*, by popular media personality, Tavis Smiley. The book was recognized as the Best Literary Work for Non-Fiction at the nationally televised NAACP Image Awards.

The Honorable Ceasar C. Mitchell

Council Member, Post 1 At-Large
Atlanta City Council

Atlanta City Council member Ceasar C. Mitchell practices real estate with the law firm of Epstein Becker & Green, P.C. On the Atlanta City Council, Ceasar has chaired the influential Public Safety and Community Development committees. He serves as chair of the City Utilities Committee and sits on the Budget Commission, which sets the city's annual revenue levels. In 2004 he served as acting president of the city council during a vacancy in the position.

Ceasar is actively engaged in civic, legal and community affairs, having served as board chair of Hands On Atlanta and a past president of the Gate City Bar Association. In 2003 he became the inaugural recipient of Leadership Atlanta's Rising Star Award, and he is a graduate of its 2005 class. He has been named one of the state's best and brightest in *Georgia Trend* magazine's 2005 Forty Under 40 feature.

Ceasar is an Atlanta native and a product of its public schools. He received a bachelor's degree in economics and English from Morehouse College, and a law degree from The University of Georgia.

Shirley Mitchell is a senior vice president of Bank of America's Georgia Market Development. She is responsible for strategic market planning; coordinating and leveraging the bank's local philanthropic contributions and sponsorships; and facilitating relationships with community leaders for the Metro Atlanta area and the state of Georgia.

Previously, Shirley was regional corporate relations director for AT&T. She succeeded at several positions at AT&T, including marketing program analysis director, strategic planner and senior project manager. A native of the Washington, D.C., area, she graduated from Howard University and obtained a Master of Business Administration degree from the University of Pittsburgh.

Shirley holds several leadership roles with civic and philanthropic organizations. She serves on the boards of directors for Leadership Atlanta, Midtown Alliance, the Committee for a Better Atlanta, The Atlanta Women's Foundation, the Metropolitan Atlanta Arts Fund and the Metro Atlanta Arts & Culture Coalition.

Shirley was named an Outstanding Citizen of Georgia by former Secretary of State Cathy Cox, and inducted into the 2007 YWCA Academy of Women Achievers. She recently received the Hispanic Leadership Award from the Hispanic Marketing Group.

Shirley Mitchell

Senior Vice President
Georgia Market Development
Bank of America

The Honorable Felicia A. Moore was elected to the Atlanta City Council in 1997. Now in her third term, she serves as chair of the Committee on Council, and sits on the Finance/Executive and Transportation committees. During her tenure on the council, she has served as chair of the Community Development/Human Resources Committee, the Finance/Executive Committee and the Transportation Committee.

In December of 2005, Moore was sworn in as president of the National Black Caucus of Local Elected Officials. As an active National League of Cities member, she serves on several committees, and is the vice chair of the Finance Administration and the Intergovernmental Relations Committee. She is also an active member of the Georgia Association of Black Elected Officials and the Georgia Municipal Association.

A licensed real estate broker with Keller Williams Realty, Moore is a member of the Atlanta and National boards of Realtors. She graduated, cum laude, from Central State University in Wilberforce, Ohio, with a Bachelor of Arts degree in communications.

The Honorable
Felicia A. Moore

Council Member, District 9
Atlanta City Council

Tony Morrow

Founder & Chief Executive Officer
The Pecan, Inc.

Award-winning chef Tony Morrow is founder, chief executive officer and executive chef of The Pecan, Inc. and Flavours Gourmet Catering, Inc. Born in St. Albans, New York, he was raised in southwest Atlanta.

Morrow earned a Bachelor of Science degree in marketing from Tuskegee University. He was then commissioned into the Air Force as a second lieutenant. During his eight-year tour of duty, Morrow was promoted to the rank of captain and served as chief financial officer for the Titan Missile System. He received a Master of Business Administration degree in management from The University of South Dakota in Vermillion in 1991. He also graduated, cum laude, from The Art Institute of Atlanta School of Culinary Arts.

Morrow is a member of Kappa Alpha Psi Fraternity, Inc. and Elizabeth Baptist Church. He has been a resident of southwest Atlanta for more than 25 years. He and his wife, Caiphia, have one son, DeVaughn.

Ericka D. Newsome-Hill

Director, Community Affairs
Atlanta Braves

Ericka D. Newsome-Hill is director of community affairs for the Atlanta Braves and executive director of the Atlanta Braves Foundation. In this capacity, she directs the many corporate relations and community service initiatives of the Atlanta Braves and implements the philanthropic programs of the Atlanta Braves Foundation. Dedicated to strengthening communities and brightening the futures of children, Newsome-Hill is instrumental in furthering the Braves' long-standing commitment of being a strong community partner and giving back to organizations in need.

A native of Toledo, Ohio, she earned a Bachelor of Science degree in exceptional education from the University of Central Florida and a Master of Science degree in sports marketing from St. Thomas University in Miami, Florida.

Active in the community, Newsome-Hill currently serves on the board of the Andrew & Walter Young Family YMCA. In addition, she is a member of the Atlanta Partners For Education Advisory Council, the Atlanta Corporate Donors Forum and Delta Sigma Theta Sorority, Inc.

Born in Atlanta, Dorothy Norwood began singing and touring with her family at the age of 8. In 1956 she moved to Chicago, Illinois, and was soon singing with such notables as the great Mahalia Jackson, the world-renowned Caravans and the incomparable Reverend James Cleveland.

Norwood launched her solo career in 1964 and recorded her first album *Johnny and Jesus* on Savoy Records. Today, with more than 50 years in the gospel music industry, she has recorded more than 49 albums. Believing that "if the mountains won't come to you, then you must go to the mountains," Norwood agreed to do a 30-state American and European tour with Mick Jagger and The Rolling Stones in 1972. She was able to spread the gospel to an audience that was virtually closed to gospel artists.

To date, Norwood has received five Gold Records, six Grammy nominations, one Stellar Award, eight Stellar nominations, a Soul Train Award and numerous citations for her contributions to the field of gospel music. Her latest release is entitled, *Fifty Years, It's Been Worth It All.*

Dorothy Norwood
National Gospel Recording Artist

Martin Olagbegi is founder and president of Nile, Inc., a design, construction and environmental-management firm located in Jonesboro, Georgia. Nile is responsible for employing numerous workers, subcontractors and suppliers throughout the north and southeast. As president and chief executive officer, Martin oversees the overall direction of the organization, including program and construction administration, marketing and other company initiatives.

A member of the NAACP, the Society of American Military Engineers, the National Action Network and the Colorful Arts Society, Inc., Martin also serves either as chairman or on the board of directors for numerous organizations, including the Atlanta City Employees Credit Union, Mount Nebo Baptist Church and Life Center and the Ondo State Association of Atlanta. He is a founding member of Nigerian Professionals and a life member of Alpha Phi Alpha Fraternity, Inc.

Martin is a trained architect from Prairie View A&M University in Texas. He is the husband of Julia Hampton Olagbegi, and together they are the proud parents of two children, Niran and Rolani.

Martin Olagbegi
President
Nile, Inc.

Vicki R. Palmer

Executive Vice President
Financial Services & Administration
Coca-Cola Enterprises

Vicki R. Palmer is executive vice president of financial services and administration for Coca-Cola Enterprises, the world's largest bottler of soft drink products of The Coca-Cola Company with worldwide revenues totaling approximately $20 billion. She is responsible for overseeing internal audit, risk management, diversity, the Ombuds Office and the Treasury Department, which manages the company's $10 billion debt portfolio, $5 billion pension plan and 401(k) plan investments. She also serves as a member of the company's Executive Leadership Team.

Palmer is an active member of Cascade United Methodist Church and serves on the boards of Spelman College, Woodward Academy, First Horizon National Corporation and Havertys Furniture Company. She is also a member of the Executive Leadership Council. In 2006 she was named one of the Top 50 Women in Corporate America by *Black Enterprise*.

Palmer is the wife of Kansas City businessman John E. Palmer and the proud mother of Alexandria, who is a student at the University of Pennsylvania.

Jackie Parker

Vice President
Global Inclusion & Diversity
Newell Rubbermaid, Inc.

Jackie Parker joined Newell Rubbermaid in 2006 as the company's first director of inclusion and diversity, and was promoted to vice president of inclusion and diversity. She is responsible for leading the strategic planning, development and implementation of inclusion and diversity initiatives within Newell Rubbermaid, Inc. In this role, she manages the daily operations of the Corporate Diversity departments.

In less than a year with the company, Jackie launched several key initiatives, including global inclusion training for executives and employees, integration of diversity and inclusion into recruiting and human resources processes, mentoring for women and people of color, the addition of domestic partner benefits, and the incorporation of diversity principles into product development and marketing.

She serves as a member of the Executive Diversity Council for the Conference Board, Workforce Opportunity Network, Diversity Best Practices and the Atlanta Diversity Managers Affinity Group. Jackie holds a Master of Business Administration degree in marketing from Johns Hopkins University, and a Bachelor of Science degree in marketing from Hampton University. She currently resides in Roswell, Georgia, with her husband and two children.

Richard J. Pennington became the 22nd chief of the Atlanta Police Department in 2002. His law enforcement career began with the Metropolitan Police Department in Washington, D.C., where he rose through the ranks to become assistant chief. In 1994 he became chief of the New Orleans Police Department.

Pennington is a graduate of American University, the University of the District of Columbia, the FBI Academy National Executive Institute, the George Washington University Executive Development Program, and the Harvard University Program for Senior Executives.

Pennington is a past president of the National Organization of Black Law Enforcement Executives, and is a board member of the American Red Cross-Metropolitan Atlanta Chapter and the Brady Campaign to Prevent Gun Violence. He is a member of numerous organizations, including the International Association of Chiefs of Police, the Major City Police Chiefs Association, the Georgia Association of Chiefs of Police, 100 Black Men of Atlanta, Inc., Alpha Kappa Psi Fraternity, Inc. and Cascade United Methodist Church.

He was listed in *Ebony* as one of the 100 Most Influential and in Governing as Public Official of the Year.

Richard J. Pennington
Chief of Police
Atlanta Police Department

Dottie Peoples, a three-time Grammy nominee, multiple Stellar Award winner and recipient of more than 50 prestigious awards, nominations and recognitions, is founder and chief executive officer of new label DP Muzik. She has also released a new CD, *Do It!*, which heralds some significant and exciting changes in Dottie's musical career.

Her new CD signifies the realization of God's hand in guiding this dream to reality. At the helm of the production, as with all her CDs, is Dottie herself. Equipped with a varied cache of material and a group of dedicated musicians, a refreshingly new Dottie has emerged. With a blueprint from her previous successes, she brought forth not just that traditional "Dottie" style which earned her the title, "Songbird of The South," but also with a fresh, new inspirational take on her classic sound that broadens the scope of this multitalented singer.

Dottie's purpose in her endeavors is to bless the people of God. As if running her own label does not keep her busy enough, she currently serves as national spokeswoman for Speaking of Women's Health and Universal Sisters.

Dottie Peoples
President & Chief Executive Officer
DP Muzik

Tyler Perry

President &
Chief Executive Officer
The Tyler Perry Company

Tyler Perry and his talents as a playwright, director, producer and actor have taken urban theater to another level. This New Orleans native has had a stellar decade and shows no signs of letting up.

In 1992 Tyler wrote a series of letters to himself in an effort to find catharsis for his own childhood pain. Those letters became his first hit musical, *I Know I've Been Changed*. He collaborated with Bishop T.D. Jakes to produce *Woman Thou Art Loosed* and *Behind Closed Doors*. He then brought to life a portrayal of a 78-year-old grandmother, Mabel "Madea" Simmons, and the following productions made history.

Tyler received the 2004 Black Business Professionals Entrepreneur of the Year award. In 2001 he received the prestigious Helen Hayes Award for Outstanding Lead Actor. Tyler has appeared on the covers of *Jet* and *Essence* and been featured in numerous other magazines.

Tyler released his first major motion picture, *Diary of a Mad Black Woman*, in 2005. His latest film, *Madea Goes to Jail*, opened No. 1 at the box office in February of 2009.

The Honorable Patsy Y. Porter

Judge
Fulton County State Court

A native Atlantan, the Honorable Patsy Y. Porter is a Fulton County State Court judge. She presides over cases involving medical malpractice, wrongful death, automobile accidents and criminal misdemeanor offenses.

Committed to the Atlanta community, Porter is a member and past president of the Georgia Association of Black Women Attorneys (GABWA), a member of the Gate City Bar Association and a member of the board of trustees for the Georgia Bar Foundation. Likewise, she is past president of the Atlanta Legal Aid Society, co-chair of the board of directors for the Andrew and Walter Young YMCA, a member of the Board to Determine Fitness of Bar Applicants and a Leadership Atlanta Alumna.

Porter has received numerous awards, including the Leah Ward Sears Award for Distinction in the Profession, the Jurist of the Year Award, the Spirit of GABWA Award, the Judge With A Heart Award and the Millennium Award of Excellence in Law.

She received an undergraduate degree from Georgia State University and a law degree from Woodrow Wilson College of Law.

Porter is married and has two sons.

Erica Qualls is general manager for the Atlanta Marriott Marquis. Qualls is responsible for guest and associate satisfaction, managing the hotel's finances and assets, owner relations, and fostering business alliances that promote Marriott International. The Atlanta Marriott Marquis is Marriott International's third-largest hotel with 1,675 hotel rooms, and more than 120,000 square feet of meeting and convention space.

Throughout her employment with Marriott International, Qualls has held a variety of key positions. Previously, she was hotel manager for the Atlanta Marriott Marquis, and director of human resources and general manager in Sunnyvale, California.

Qualls is involved in national and local community organizations, including the Children's Miracle Network, Hands On Atlanta and the United Way. She is a member of the boards of the Atlanta Business League and the UNCF Atlanta Corporate Campaign.

Qualls is listed as one of Atlanta's Top 100 Black Women of Influence by the Atlanta Business League, and the Atlanta Business League presented her with its prestigious League Leadership Award for outstanding volunteerism. Married to David Bascoe for 24 years, Qualls is the proud mother of four.

Erica Qualls

General Manager
Atlanta Marriot Marquis

The Honorable M. Kasim Reed is a partner with Holland & Knight, LLP and a member of the Georgia General Assembly. He was elected to the Georgia State Senate after two terms as state representative for District 52 of the Georgia House of Representatives.

In January of 2003, Reed became one of the youngest members of the Georgia State Senate. He currently serves on the Senate Judiciary, Special Judiciary, Ethics, Transportation, Urban Affairs, and State and Local Government Operations committees. Reed is a member of the American Bar Association, the National Bar Association and the State Bar of Georgia. Additionally, he was campaign manager for Mayor Shirley Franklin's successful effort to become Atlanta's first female mayor.

Reed's civic and professional leadership has been nationally recognized in *The New York Times*, *The Washington Post*, *Black Enterprise* and *Ebony*. He was also the youngest elected general trustee of the Howard University board, and the first member to serve the university's board as both an undergraduate and a graduate student.

Reed received Bachelor of Arts and law degrees from Howard University in Washington, D.C.

The Honorable M. Kasim Reed

Senator, District 35
Georgia State Senate

Brenda Reid

Media &
Community Relations Manager
Publix Super Markets, Inc.

B renda Reid is media and community relations manager for Publix Super Markets, Inc. She is responsible for media relations, corporate giving and public relations, and she has served as the company spokesperson since 2000. Previously, she served as public relations and communications manager for *The Atlanta Journal-Constitution*, where she spent 20 years in the newspaper business.

A graduate of Leadership Atlanta's class of 2003, Reid is a member of the YWCA of Greater Atlanta, an advisory board member of Toys For Tots of Metro Atlanta, an Education Committee member of the Metro Atlanta Chamber of Commerce, a Chairman's Club member of the Gwinnett Chamber of Commerce and a Chairman's Club member of the Birmingham Area Chamber of Commerce. She has received several awards, including the Russell Athletic Woman of Distinction Award and the Atlanta Business League's Top 100 Business Women of the Year.

Reid holds a Bachelor of Arts degree in mass communications and journalism from Clark Atlanta University. A Lithonia resident, she has two sons, Horace Jr. (15) and Brendan (10). They are members of St. Philip AME Church in Decatur.

Lee Rhyant

Executive Vice President &
General Manager
Lockheed Martin
Aeronautics Company

L ee Rhyant is executive vice president and general manager of the Lockheed Martin Aeronautics Company in Marietta, Georgia. He has more than 35 years of aerospace and automotive industry experience, having also worked for Rolls-Royce Aerospace and General Motors.

Recognized as the 2008 Cobb County Citizen of the Year, Rhyant received the Justice Robert Benham Award from Blacks United for Youth-Cobb, Inc. He was honored for superior leadership by Bethune-Cookman College, the Georgia Minority Supplier Development Council and 100 Black Men of America, Inc. He was named the Atlanta Urban League's 2007 Man of Influence and *Atlanta Tribune: The Magazine*'s 2008 Inaugural Man of the Year.

Rhyant serves on numerous boards, including Bethune-Cookman College, SafeAmerica and the Cobb Chamber of Commerce. He graduated from Bethune-Cookman College and received a Master of Business Administration degree from Indiana University. He studied at the London School of Business, the Massachusetts Institute of Technology, Harvard University, the General Motors Institute and the University of Michigan.

Rhyant and wife Evelyn have twin sons, Roderick and Broderick. They live in Roswell and attend Zion Baptist Church in Marietta.

Charles Robinson Jr. is president and chief executive officer of Sadie G. Mays Health and Rehabilitation Center. Accredited by the Joint Commission on the Accreditation of Healthcare Organizations, he manages and operates a long-term health care facility and directs a staff of more than 225. His drive, tenacity and compassion have helped him sustain, revive and cement Sadie G. Mays' place in the community.

With more than 20 years of proven success and recognition by his peers as an innovative leader, Robinson was the first African American certified by the American College of Healthcare Administrators, the first African-American chairman of the Georgia Health Care Association and the first African-American president of the Georgia chapter of the American College of Healthcare Administrators.

Robinson received a Master of Business Administration degree from Brenau University and a Bachelor of Arts degree in business administration from Fort Valley State University. Not only has he served Fort Valley State University in many aspects, but also is well respected in the business and professional world, as well as his church and civic organizations throughout the state and metropolitan communities.

Charles Robinson Jr.

President & Chief Executive Officer
Sadie G. Mays Health and
Rehabilitation Center

Simon Robinson is founder and president of Simon Sign Systems, an Atlanta-based manufacturer of commercial signs and graphics. In 2006 he also founded Corporate Concepts & Design, a specialty advertising, promotions and team apparel company.

Created in 1989, Simon Signs Systems began as a small, home-based business, but has evolved into a thriving enterprise with several high-profile clients, such as The Coca-Cola Company, Anheuser-Busch, the UNCF and Morehouse College. His professional affiliations include the United States Sign Council, the International Sign Association, and the Georgia Chamber of Commerce.

Robinson holds a Bachelor of Arts degree in health and psychology from Stillman College in Tuscaloosa, Alabama. Prior to forming Simon Sign Systems, he held a variety of sales and key account positions in Fortune 500 companies.

Possessing a staunch commitment to community service, Robinson has donated his time, talent and services to numerous organizations. He is also an active member of Omega Psi Phi Fraternity, Inc., the On the Move Ministry at Word of Faith Family Worship Center and the NAACP.

Robinson and his wife, Gwendolyn, reside in East Point, Georgia.

Simon Robinson

Founder & President
Simon Sign Systems

H. Jerome Russell

President
Russell New Urban Development
H.J. Russell & Company

H. Jerome Russell is a native of Atlanta, Georgia. In 1995 he became president and chief operating officer of the newly reorganized and consolidated H.J. Russell & Company, a fully integrated construction and real estate company. He is currently president of Russell New Urban Development, a division of the company.

Under Russell's leadership, H.J. Russell & Company's annual revenue now exceeds $150 million. The company's involvement in construction extends into major cities and states such as Atlanta, Richmond, Washington, Dallas and New York. In addition, the Property Management Division has increased its portfolio from managing 4,000 to more than 11,000 units in Georgia, Florida and Illinois.

Russell serves on the boards of several organizations, including Citizens Trust Bank, Concessions International, the YMCA of Metropolitan Atlanta, Central Atlanta Progress and H.J. Russell & Company. He is a member of the Urban Land Institute, the Rotary Club of Atlanta, the Metro Atlanta Chamber of Commerce and 100 Black Men of Atlanta, Inc.

Russell is married and has four children. In his spare time, he enjoys basketball, tennis, golf, travel and occasionally, a good book.

Herman J. Russell

Chairman
H.J. Russell & Company

Beginning in the early civil rights movement, Herman J. Russell has built one of the greatest success stories in America. H.J. Russell & Company is the fourth-largest minority industrial service company in the United States. Russell's portfolio includes construction, construction management, real estate development and property management.

A quiet but influential civic leader, Russell worked closely with Dr. Martin Luther King Jr. in the 1960s. He became the first black member and president of the Atlanta Chamber of Commerce. He has served as a board member for several civic and business organizations.

Russell has received many awards, including the Dow Jones Entrepreneurial Excellence Award, the National and Georgia Black MBA Association, Inc.'s Entrepreneur of the Year Awards, and Ernst & Young's 2001 Entrepreneur of the Year Lifetime Achievement Award.

A graduate of Tuskegee University, Russell holds honorary degrees from Morehouse College, Georgia State University and Morris Brown College. He resides in Atlanta with his wife, Sylvia E. Russell. His children, Donata Russell Major, H. Jerome Russell and Michael Russell, are all executives in the Russell companies.

Michael Russell became chief executive officer of H.J. Russell & Company in October of 2003. He succeeds his father, Herman Russell, who founded the company in 1952 and led it for 50 years. A 19-year veteran of the construction and real estate development industry, Michael is charged with leading the company as it embarks on another 50 years. He also serves as chief executive officer of Concessions International, another Russell company.

Active in the community, Michael serves as chairman of the Atlanta Business League, on the executive committee of the Metro Atlanta Chamber of Commerce and on the boards of directors for The Commerce Club, the Grady Memorial Hospital Corporation and the Children's Healthcare of Atlanta Foundation. A member of the Georgia State University Robinson College board of advisors, he was previously president of the Georgia Chapter of Associated Builders and Contractors, Inc.

Michael received a Bachelor of Science degree in civil engineering from the University of Virginia and a Master of Business Administration degree from Georgia State University. An Atlanta native, he and wife Lovette have two sons, Michael Jr. and Benjamin.

Michael Russell
Chief Executive Officer
H.J. Russell & Company

A native of Deland, Florida, Carrie Salone is president of Salone Enterprises, Inc. and the owner and operator of two McDonald's restaurants in the Buckhead and downtown Decatur areas. Prior to becoming an entrepreneur, she worked in the health care industry, where she held numerous positions with the Centers for Disease Control.

President of the McDonald's Women's Operators' Network, Inc., Carrie also serves on the boards of directors for the Buckhead Business Association and the Black McDonald's Operators Association in the Atlanta region. An active member of the community, she is a mentor for the PowerGirls Network Institute and high school students in DeKalb County, and belongs to several organizations, including Jack and Jill of America, Inc. and the DeKalb County Business Association.

Carrie graduated from Florida State University with a Bachelor of Science degree, and received a master's degree in public health from the Morehouse School of Medicine in 1997, graduating summa cum laude.

As a woman of faith, she is an active member of New Birth Missionary Baptist Church. She is also the mother of two beautiful daughters, Alleah and Ayana.

Carrie Salone
Owner/Operator
McDonald's

Thomas G. Sampson

Managing Partner
Thomas, Kennedy,
Sampson & Patterson

Thomas G. Sampson is managing partner at Thomas, Kennedy, Sampson & Patterson, Atlanta's oldest minority-owned law firm. Like his father, Sampson graduated from Morehouse College. He earned a juris doctorate degree from The University of North Carolina at Chapel Hill.

Former Governor Roy Barnes appointed Sampson vice chairman on the State Judicial Nominating Commission. He has served as president of the Gate City Bar Association and the Atlanta Legal Aid Society. A member of the board of governors of the State Bar of Georgia, he was appointed by Mayor Shirley Franklin to a special panel to evaluate the Municipal Court of Atlanta and the City Court of Atlanta.

Sampson was an adjunct professor of law at Georgia State University for eight years. A mentor and trailblazer, he is the first African American to be inducted into the Georgia Chapter of the American Board of Trial Advocates.

Sampson has been married to his college sweetheart, Dr. Jacquelyn Sampson, for 39 years. His son is a partner with his firm, and his daughter is a medical student at Meharry Medical College.

**David Satcher,
M.D., Ph.D.**

Director
The Satcher Health Leadership Institute &
Center of Excellence on Health Disparities

Dr. David Satcher is director of The Satcher Health Leadership Institute, which was established in 2006 at the Morehouse School of Medicine in Atlanta, Georgia. The mission of the Institute is to develop a diverse group of public health leaders, foster and support leadership strategies, and influence policies toward the reduction and ultimate elimination of disparities in health.

Satcher was sworn in as the 16th surgeon general of the United States in 1998. He also served as assistant secretary for health in the Department of Health and Human Services from February of 1998 to January of 2001, making him the second person in history to have held both positions simultaneously.

Satcher graduated from Morehouse College in Atlanta, Georgia, in 1963. He holds Doctor of Medicine and Doctor of Philosophy degrees from Case Western Reserve University in Ohio.

A proponent of healthy lifestyles through physical activity and good nutrition, Satcher is an avid runner, rower and gardener.

D r. Beverly Scott is general manager and chief executive officer for the Metropolitan Atlanta Rapid Transit Authority (MARTA). In this position, she is responsible for overseeing the day-to-day operations of the authority. Prior to accepting this post for MARTA, she served as general manager and chief executive officer for the Sacramento Regional Transit District.

Scott has received numerous national and local awards, including citations from the U.S. Department of Transportation, the American Public Transportation Association, the National Business League, the Women's Transportation Seminar, the Rhode Island Professional Engineers Society, the Sierra Club, the Conference of Minority Transportation Officials, the National Forum for Black Public Administrators, the Urban League and City Year.

She holds a doctorate degree in political science, with specialization in public administration, from Howard University and a Bachelor of Arts degree in political science from Fisk University, where she graduated magna cum laude and Phi Beta Kappa.

Dr. Beverly A. Scott

General Manager &
Chief Executive Officer
Metropolitan Atlanta
Rapid Transit Authority

M . Alexis Scott is publisher and chief executive officer of the *Atlanta Daily World*, founded by her grandfather in 1928. In 1932 the paper became the nation's first black-owned daily newspaper in the 20th century. The paper now publishes once a week and is online.

Alexis joined the paper in 1997, following a 22-year career with *The Atlanta Journal-Constitution* and Cox Enterprises, Inc. She was a reporter, editor and vice president of community affairs before becoming Cox's director of diversity.

Alexis is a panelist on WAGA-TV FOX 5's politics show, *The Georgia Gang*. On the board of the Atlanta Life Financial Group, she is active in several nonprofits, and has numerous honors. In 2009 she received the Promenade of Distinction Award from the Trumpet Awards Foundation and the Pioneer Award from the Black Women Film Preservation Project. She has an honorary degree from Argosy University, and attended Barnard College and Spelman College.

Alexis is a member of First Congregational Church, United Church of Christ, where she was president for ten years and Sunday school teacher for 30. She has two adult sons.

M. Alexis Scott

Publisher & Chief Executive Officer
Atlanta Daily World

The Honorable Leah Ward Sears

Chief Justice
Georgia Supreme Court

Chief Justice Leah Ward Sears has achieved a distinguished position in Georgia's history. She is the youngest person and black woman to serve as a Superior Court judge in Georgia and to be appointed to the Georgia Supreme Court. She also retained her appointed position as a Supreme Court justice, thus becoming the first woman to win a contested statewide election in Georgia.

Before joining the Georgia Supreme Court, Sears was an attorney with the law firm of Alston & Bird, and was a trial judge on the Superior Court of Fulton County.

Sears received an undergraduate degree from Cornell University, and then graduated from Emory University School of Law. She earned a master's degree in appellate judicial process from the University of Virginia.

In addition to her participation in a wide variety of professional and civic affiliations, Sears is the proud mother of Addison and Brennan, and the wife of Haskell Sears Ward.

Rhonda Mims Simpson

President
ING Foundation

Rhonda Mims is president of the ING Foundation and head of community relations. In this role, she is responsible for creating a uniform community relations platform focusing on financial literacy and education.

Mims also serves as ING US PAC treasurer, and conducts government affairs for some of the southeastern states. Prior to that role, she was counsel with the ING U.S. Financial Services litigation team overseeing the management of outside counsel of litigation matters, and was a territorial sales manager for ING, based in Fairfax, Virginia.

Previously, Mims was a civil litigation attorney with the U.S. Department of Justice and a senior attorney with the National District Attorney Association's American Prosecutor's Research Institute.

She was named 2005 Woman of the Year by *Women Looking Ahead* and one of the Top 25 Women Leaders by *Atlanta Woman*. Additionally, Mims served on the boards of directors of the Atlanta YWCA and the Georgia chapter of Junior Achievement.

Mims received a Bachelor of Science degree and a juris doctorate degree from the University of South Carolina. She holds NASD Series 7 and 66 designations.

The Honorable Sonna Singleton is District 1 commissioner in Clayton County. She represents nearly 70,000 citizens living in the unincorporated areas of Rex, Ellenwood, Lake City, portions of Morrow, Forest Park, Conley and Jonesboro. In this position, she provides policy direction to employees, department heads and elected officials, and is responsible for a $200 million county budget. Sonna is known for her focus on community associations and her ability to get citizens involved in the community.

As commissioner, one of Sonna's main focuses is public safety and quality of life community issues. She is co-founder and co-sponsor of the annual East Clayton Community Day Festival, a day-long vendor-entertainment and community fair that attracts more than 10,000 residents to east Clayton.

Sonna received a Bachelor of Science degree from Tennessee State University and is currently enrolled in a master's teacher education program at Clayton State University. A native of Snow Hill, North Carolina, she is divorced and is the proud mother of Jordyn.

The Honorable Sonna Singleton

Commissioner, District 1
Clayton County
Board of Commissioners

John B. Smith Sr. is publisher and chief executive officer of *The Atlanta Inquirer* newspaper in Atlanta, Georgia. Smith has guided and inspired each employee to create more vividly while they are working to produce a good and meaningful newspaper.

He has been named Young Man of the Year in business and selected as one of 25 City Shapers in *Atlanta* magazine. He has been the recipient of the Morehouse College Alumni Award in the area of business and the Georgia Department of Labor Black History Achievers Award in journalism.

Additionally, Smith is chair of the National Newspaper Publishers Association (NNPA), also known as The Black Press of America, which is a 69-year-old federation of more than 200 African-American newspapers from across the United States, read by more than 15 million people weekly. He has been active in NNPA since he was advertising manager for *The Atlanta Inquirer* back in the 1960s.

Active with Omega Psi Phi Fraternity, Inc., Smith is married to the former Frances Evans, also of LaGrange, Georgia. They have three adult children and five grandchildren.

John B. Smith Sr.

Publisher & Chief Executive Officer
The Atlanta Inquirer

Wanda Smith

Host
The Frank & Wanda Morning Show
WVEE V-103 FM

Comedienne Wanda Smith is the morning drive co-host on WVEE V-103 FM's *The Frank & Wanda Morning Show*. A native of Miami, Florida, she has made people laugh for years. Her style of comedy is up-front, honest and never inhibited. She is a staple on the comedy circuit, hosting some of Atlanta's largest local, regional and national comedy events.

Smith has also performed on BET's *Comic View* and *Def Comedy Jam*. She joined *The Frank Ski Morning Show* in November of 1998, and is now the most recognized woman on drive-time radio. Causing drivers to laugh uncontrollably, she is credited for several early morning traffic accidents.

Not only does Smith enjoy making people laugh, but she is also very concerned about her Atlanta community and is never too busy to devote time for those in need. As a humanitarian, Smith is involved with children, teens, the elderly and single mothers. With a laugh, smile or just a shoulder to cry on, she believes she is the mother everyone wishes they had.

The Honorable Calvin Smyre

Representative, District 132
Georgia House of Representatives

State Representative Calvin Smyre earned a Bachelor of Science degree from Fort Valley State University, majoring in business administration with a minor in accounting.

His career path has taken him from being a community organizer and director of the War on Poverty Program in Columbus, Georgia, to executive vice president of corporate external affairs for Synovus Financial Corp. and president of the Synovus Foundation. Synovus Financial Corp. is a financial services holding company with more than $34 billion in assets, based in Columbus, Georgia.

Smyre was elected to the Georgia House of Representatives in 1974, as its youngest member at 26 years of age. As a 34-year legislative veteran and one of the deans, he serves on the most important panels of the house. In the state's budgetary process, he serves on the Appropriations Committee, responsible for allocating the $20 billion state budget.

Smyre is president of the National Black Caucus of State Legislators, a member of the Assembly on State Issues of the National Conference of State Legislators, and he represents Synovus on the Financial Services Roundtable.

D r. Louis W. Sullivan returned to Morehouse School of Medicine (MSM) in 1993 after serving as secretary of the U.S. Department of Health and Human Services (HHS) in the Bush administration. He served one of the longest tenures, 47 months, of any HHS secretary in history. At HHS, Sullivan was responsible for the major health, welfare, food and drug safety, medical research and income security programs serving Americans.

Sullivan became the founding dean and director of the Medical Education Program at Morehouse College in 1975. On July 1, 1981, MSM became independent from Morehouse College with Sullivan as its dean and first president.

Sullivan graduated, magna cum laude, from Morehouse College, and earned a medical degree, cum laude, from the Boston University School of Medicine. He is a member of Phi Beta Kappa Society and Alpha Omega Alpha Medical Honor Society.

In addition, Sullivan is the chairman of the board for BioSante Pharmaceuticals, Inc. and serves on the board of directors for Emergent BioSolutions, Inc., Henry Schein, Inc. and United Therapeutics. He also serves on the editorial board of *Minority Health Today*.

Louis W. Sullivan, M.D.
President Emeritus
Morehouse School of Medicine

D r. Earl Suttle is the founder and chairman of Leadership Success International, LLC, an international training and consulting company based in Atlanta, Georgia, that specializes in working with organizations to increase their profits and productivity through developing their people.

He has produced numerous CDs and DVDs on leadership and personal development, and is the co-author of four books with Dr. John Hubbard: *Earl's Pearls on Enjoying Excellence, Preparing for and Managing High-Risk Situations in the Lives of College Athletes (An Athlete's Guide), Preparing for and Managing High-Risk Situations in the Lives of Professional Athletes (A Player's Guide)*, and *Great Life Choices for Teens (Who Want to Make a Difference)*.

As a business consultant and dynamic professional speaker, Suttle delivers several keynote addresses and presentations throughout the year nationally and internationally to a wide range of organizations including AFLAC Insurance, AT&T Corporation, Delta Airlines and many more. Suttle is a consultant to the NBA and the NFL, where he works directly with players. He is also a faculty member of the prestigious Success University.

Earl Suttle, Ph.D.
Founder & Chairman
Leadership Success International, LLC

Felicia Mabuza Suttle, Ph.D.

President & Chief Executive Officer
Experience South Africa

Dr. Felicia Mabuza Suttle is an international, award-winning entrepreneur, highly acclaimed talk show host, sought-after public speaker, author and role model. She served as president of South African Tourism USA, where she was responsible for overseeing tourism for South Africa in America.

As president and chief executive officer of Experience South Africa, Suttle continues her passion, giving Americans, especially African Americans, a personalized experience of South African culture, heritage and Ubuntu (humanity and warmth of the people). Through her talk show, *Conversations with Felicia* on The Africa Channel, she attempts to change misperceptions about Africa and South Africa in the international media, and encourages investors to do business in South Africa. She is also a founding member of a multimillion-dollar company, Pamodzi Investment Holdings.

In a South African Broadcasting Corporation survey, Suttle was named among the 100 Great South Africans. She was also mentioned as one of the country's top ten most popular personalities by the *Sunday Times* newspaper. Suttle received bachelor's and master's degrees from Marquette University, and a Doctor of Philosophy degree in communications from the University of Berkley.

Beverly Daniel Tatum, Ph.D.

President
Spelman College

The board of trustees of Spelman College appointed Dr. Beverly Daniel Tatum as the institution's ninth president. Tatum, a scholar, teacher, author and administrator, assumed her duties at Spelman in August of 2002.

Raised in Bridgewater, Massachusetts, Tatum earned a Bachelor of Arts degree from Wesleyan University in psychology. She earned a Master of Arts degree and a Doctor of Philosophy degree in clinical psychology from the University of Michigan, Ann Arbor.

Tatum came to Spelman following a 13-year career at Mount Holyoke College, where she was acting president and dean. Before joining Mount Holyoke, she was an associate professor and assistant professor at Westfield State College in Westfield, Massachusetts.

Her noted book, *Why Are All The Black Kids Sitting Together in the Cafeteria?: And Other Conversations About Race*, exploded on the national scene in 1997. Tatum has been a featured lecturer on the subject of race relations, appearing on several panels around the country, including President Clinton's Initiative on Race.

Beverly is married to Travis Tatum, a professor of education at Westfield State College. They have two sons.

D r. Alvetta Peterman Thomas is president of Atlanta Technical College, named America's Best Community College by *Washington Monthly* magazine. A veteran educator with more than 20 years of experience in education, she is the only African-American woman to lead a technical college in Georgia.

Alvetta has been honored by the National Science Foundation; the U.S. House of Representatives; and the DTAE/UGA Community and Technical College Leadership Initiative, of which she was a first-cohort graduate. In 2007 she was named one of Atlanta's Twenty-Five Most Influential Women by *rolling out* magazine.

Alvetta is a member of the Atlanta Workforce Development Board, the Metro Atlanta Chamber of Commerce, Civitan International, the Atlanta Education Committee and Leadership Atlanta 2009. She received a bachelor's degree from Alabama State University, a master's degree from Clark Atlanta University and a doctorate degree from The University of Georgia.

Not just focused on her career, Alvetta and her husband, AJ, are the proud parents of two and grandparents of three.

Dr. Alvetta Peterman Thomas

President
Atlanta Technical College

A tlanta native "Able" Mable Thomas is actively involved in the community. Currently, Thomas owns Master Communications, Inc., a communications and leadership business that seeks to empower individuals and organizations with the ability to create and control their own unique vision. She also founded the Greater Vine City Opportunities Program, Inc., which provides youth and family educational enrichment opportunities for at-risk, inner-city youth.

Thomas served as a state representative in Georgia and as a member of the Atlanta City Council, Post 1, citywide. During her tenure, she was a tireless advocate for elderly, economic development, women and family issues.

Her memberships include the Atlanta Business League, the National Congress of Black Women, Leadership Atlanta, the Regional Leadership Institute and the Center for Women Policy Studies - Foreign Policy Institute. She was named one of the 50 Most Influential Women in Georgia by *The Georgia Informer* and was inducted into the Boys and Girls Club of America Hall of Fame in 2002. In addition, "Able" Mable was voted one of the 100 Most Influential Georgians by *Georgia Trend* in January of 2008.

"Able" Mable Thomas

Owner
Master Communications, Inc.

Jannet Thoms

Principal
Booz Allen Hamilton

Jannet Thoms is a principal for Booz Allen Hamilton and leads the Southeast state/local and West Coast civil-transportation markets. She is the former deputy general manager for MARTA and the previous chief information officer/assistant general manger of technology, where she provided leadership over some of MARTA's most forward-thinking technology initiatives.

Thoms' background includes more than 20 years of consulting, leadership and technology experience. She obtained a master's degree in business, a bachelor's degree in management information systems and has completed significant coursework toward a doctorate in information systems.

Named one of the 50 Most Powerful African-Americans in Business by the *Atlanta Business Journal*, Thoms was awarded Woman of the Year by Georgia's Women in Technology and the National Black MBA Association's Outstanding MBA of the Year. Who's Who Publishing Co., LLC and the *Atlanta Business Journal* have also recognized her as one of Atlanta's Most Influential African-American leaders.

Thoms serves on the Women in Technology Foundation and the Children's Healthcare Sports Network boards. She is a former president of the Atlanta Chapter of the National Black MBA Association.

**The Honorable
Michael Thurmond**

Commissioner
Georgia Department of Labor

In 1986 the Honorable Michael Thurmond became the first African American elected to the Georgia General Assembly from Clarke County since Reconstruction. Following his tenure in the General Assembly, Thurmond was called upon to direct Georgia's historic transition from welfare to work. He created the Workfirst program, which helped more than 90,000 welfare-dependent Georgia families into the workforce.

In 1997 Thurmond became a distinguished practitioner at the University of Georgia's Carl Vinson Institute of Government, and soon after was elected Georgia labor commissioner. Under his leadership, the Department of Labor saw the transformation of unemployment offices into state-of-the-art Career Centers, and Georgia was recognized as being No. 1 in the nation in helping unemployed residents find jobs.

Thurmond graduated from Paine College and earned a juris doctorate degree from the University of South Carolina School of Law. In 1991 he completed the political executives program at the John F. Kennedy School of Government at Harvard University. He is the author of *Freedom: Georgia's Antislavery Heritage, 1733-1865*.

Thurmond and his wife, Zola, are the proud parents of a daughter, Mikaya.

Since 1992, Pat Upshaw-Monteith has gone from co-executive director to executive director, and was promoted to president and chief executive officer of Leadership Atlanta in 2005. Prior to Leadership Atlanta, Upshaw-Monteith was assistant general manager of the Atlanta Symphony Orchestra for 13 years, where she produced the orchestra's successful *Pops* series at Chastain Park and directed the symphony's educational programs.

A member of the Rotary Club of Atlanta, she served on the MARTA board for two-and-a-half years under her appointment with the board of commissioners of DeKalb County, and currently serves on the board of Oglethorpe University. Other board appointments include DeKalb County Department of Family and Children Services, The Salvation Army, the Ron Clark Academy, St. Pius X Catholic High School and the Metro Atlanta Chamber of Commerce. She recently received the *Business to Business* 2008 Women of Excellence Award.

Upshaw-Monteith earned a master's degree from Bowling Green State University and a bachelor's degree from Albany State University. She has also acted in several national television commercials, industrial films and the well-noted TV series, *In the Heat of the Night*.

Pat Upshaw-Monteith
President & Chief Executive Officer
Leadership Atlanta

Janis L. Ware has practical, hands-on, demonstrated expertise as a publisher, community development practitioner, real estate broker, housing expert, employer, businesswoman, community activist, entrepreneur and more. A native Atlantan, Janis is a graduate of Washington High School and the prestigious University of Georgia School of Business.

She has worn many hats in her professional and civic career, including that of current chair of the Southside Medical Center. Janis' board memberships have included the Atlanta Housing Authority, Habitat for Humanity, the Empire Real Estate Board, The Atlanta Business League and the National Newspaper Publishers Association.

Janis is an alumna of Leadership Atlanta, and has been recognized by *Who's Who In Black Atlanta®* and *Atlanta* magazine as one of its Women Making a Mark Award recipients.

She is the president and chief executive officer of Essence Unlimited, her real estate corporation. Janis is the second-generation owner of *The Atlanta Voice* newspaper, which is celebrating its 42nd-year anniversary, and she serves as executive director of SUMMECH Community Development Corporation.

Janis L. Ware
President & Chief Executive Officer
Essence Unlimited

Willie A. Watkins

Proprietor
Willie A. Watkins Funeral Home, Inc.

For 26 years, the signature style of Willie A. Watkins has allowed Georgians to bid farewell to their loved ones in a way that only he can provide. As proprietor of the funeral home that bears his name, Watkins has set the standard for excellence in his industry. Honing his skills since childhood, Watkins currently has establishments in Atlanta's historic West End community and Douglasville. He looks forward to opening the highly anticipated location in Stone Mountain in 2009.

In appreciation for the community's patronage, Watkins hosts an Annual Community Day on Memorial Day, feeding more than 3,000 people. He is a board member of the Southern Christian Leadership Conference, the West End Medical Center and the Atlanta Business League. He is also an executive board member for the NAACP.

Watkins is also a member of several professional organizations, including the West End Merchants Association, 100 Black Men of Atlanta, the Butler Street YMCA, the Concerned Black Clergy and the Phi Sigma Eta Mortuary Fraternity. Watkins attended Morehouse College and Gupton-Jones College of Funeral Service.

The Honorable Al Williams

Representative, District 165
Georgia House of Representatives

The Honorable Al Williams, state representative of District 165, is former chairman of the Georgia Legislative Black Caucus, the largest state black legislative caucus in the nation. His committee appointments include Economic Development and Tourism, State Institutions and Property, and Game, Fish and Parks.

His memberships include the Liberty County Democratic Committee, the Liberty County Chamber of Commerce, the National Association of State Legislators, the National Association of Black State Legislators, the Georgia Association of Black Elected Officials and the NAACP. A recipient of a 2008 Trumpet Award, Al has been recognized by *Black Enterprise*, as well as *Atlanta Tribune: The Magazine*.

A Vietnam War veteran, Al attended Saint Leo University and the John Marshall School of Law. He was bestowed an honorary Doctor of Humanities degree from Trinity Bible College.

Al is chairman of the deacon board at Calvary Baptist Church of Richmond Hill. He considers his pilgrimage to the Holy Land in 2000 as one of the most rewarding experiences in his life. Al and his wife, Olivia, are the parents of five sons.

James E. Williams is president of Williams Communications System, a communications consulting firm specializing in sales, marketing and management. His current clients include the Atlanta Braves, Fred Williams' Trucking and Atlanta Peach Movers.

Williams began as a radio announcer at WABQ in Cleveland, then transitioned to photojournalism and reporting at WAGA-TV in Atlanta. He moved into the business end of television with a sales career at WTBS and was promoted through the years, retiring in 2005 as executive vice president of Turner Broadcasting System, Inc.

His primary responsibilities included domestic sales oversight for WTBS, Turner South, Direct Response and The Turner Trade Group, and international responsibilities for all sales of Time Warner assets throughout Asia, Europe and Latin America.

He received a bachelor's degree in urban studies from Georgia State University. Williams' civic interests include various positions on the boards of Meharry Medical College, Atlanta Technical College, the Atlanta Tipoff Club, the Atlanta Sports Council and the Georgia Alliance for Children. He is also a member of the Kappa Boulé, Leadership Atlanta, Greenforest Baptist Church and the Atlanta Guardsmen (past president).

James E. Williams

President
Williams Communications System

Chris Womack, a senior vice president, is responsible for Georgia Power Company's coal- and gas-fired generating facilities. He is also an officer with Southern Company Generation and Energy Marketing, which manages and generates electricity for the company's retail markets. The company also sells energy in the competitive wholesale business.

Joining Alabama Power in 1988, he held positions including assistant to the vice president of public affairs, director of community relations and vice president of public relations. He also served as senior vice president of public relations and corporate services, senior vice president of human resources and chief people officer of Southern Company. Previously, Womack was a congressional legislative aide and a subcommittee staff director.

Womack is on the boards of A.G. Gaston Enterprises, the Boy Scouts of America — Southern Regional Council and INROADS, a member of 100 Black Men of Atlanta and a national trustee for the Boys & Girls Clubs of America.

A native of Greenville, Alabama, Womack holds a bachelor's degree from Western Michigan University and a master's degree from American University. He also attended the Stanford Executive Program.

Christopher C. Womack

Senior Vice President
Georgia Power Company

Brenda Wood

Anchor
11 Alive News, WXIA-TV

B renda Wood joined the 11Alive News team in September of 1997 as a weekday anchor, airing at 6, 7 and 11 p.m. As a journalist, she has gained the respect and trust of news viewers throughout Atlanta.

Brenda has received numerous honors and awards, including 15 Emmy's from the National Academy of Television Arts and Sciences, seven awards from the Atlanta Association of Black Journalists, two awards from the Georgia Association of Broadcasters for News Personality of the Year and two for her prime time newsmagazine show, *Minute by Minute*. She was also co-producer and host of 11Alive's Emmy Award-winning prime time magazine, *Journeys with Brenda Wood*.

Brenda is a member of the National Academy of Television Arts and Sciences, the National Association of Black Journalists and the Atlanta Association of Black Journalists. She graduated, summa cum laude, with a bachelor's degree in speech communication and mass media from Loma Linda University in California.

A devoted member of her church, Brenda's faith plays a large role in her life. She and her husband, Keith, have two daughters, Kristen and Kandis.

The Honorable Andrew Young

Principal & Chairman
GoodWorks International, LLC

T hrough the Honorable Andrew Young's involvement with GoodWorks International, he is able to execute his lifelong mission of energizing the private sector to advance economic development in Africa and the Caribbean. He puts corporate executives in contact with leaders and key players in these markets to form successful business partnerships. He also offers strategic advice to corporations on doing business successfully in those markets, and advises the governments on economic policy issues.

Young has served as U.S. ambassador to the United Nations and as co-chair of the Atlanta Committee for the Centennial Olympic Games. He served two terms as mayor of Atlanta, was elected three times as a congressman and is a leading figure in the civil rights movement. He currently serves on the board of several Fortune 500 companies, and was appointed by President Clinton to chair the $100 million Southern Africa Enterprise Development Fund.

GoodWorks International, LLC, also known as GWI Consulting, is a global business advisory firm that links forward-thinking global companies with fast-growing countries in Africa and the Caribbean to create significant, profitable business opportunities.

Carolyn Young joined her husband, Ambassador Andrew Young, at GoodWorks International, LLC after 30 years of teaching in Atlanta Public Schools. She is a graduate of Clark College and Georgia State University, where she earned a Master of Education degree.

Presently, Carolyn sits on the boards of Clark Atlanta University, Atlanta Area Technical College, Rabun Gap Nacoochee School, the Starlight Foundation, the Andrew Young School of Public Policy at Georgia State University and Literacy Action, Inc. She also co-sponsored the Bethesda House Orphanage in Soweto for children with AIDS. Formerly, she served as co-chair of G-Capp with Jane Fonda and as vice president of Sophisticates.

Carolyn has received many honors, including the Teacher Incentive Award, the Southern Bell Black History Calendar Teacher of Excellence Award, the Atlanta Area II Teacher of the Year Award and the Outstanding UNCF Volunteer Award. She also received the Faithful Servant Award from the Southern Christian Leadership Conference Women, of which she is a founding member.

Carolyn is a former Sunday school superintendent and director of Vacation Bible School at Union Baptist Church.

Carolyn Young

Executive
GoodWorks International, Inc.

James E. Young began Citizens Trust Bank of Atlanta on February 2, 1998 as president and chief executive officer. Previously, under his leadership, First Southern Bank grew from $22 million in assets to $58 million in assets at the time of the merger. The merger created a financial services company with $184 million in assets and 11 metropolitan Atlanta banking locations. It is one of the top five African-American-owned commercial banks in the country.

Young is a member of the boards of the National Bankers Association, the Atlanta Chamber of Commerce, the Atlanta Action Forum and Central Atlanta Progress. He also serves the DeKalb Convention and Visitors Bureau, the DeKalb County Pension Board, DeKalb Medical Center and the Atlanta Neighborhood Development Partnership. Additionally, Young is a board member for the Metro Atlanta YMCA and the Boys & Girls Club of Metro Atlanta.

A Cleveland, Tennessee native, Young received a bachelor's degree from Tennessee State University in 1971. He is married to Rebecca Young, a DeKalb County Public Schools teacher, and they have three sons and a daughter.

James E. Young

President & Chief Executive Officer
Citizens Trust Bank

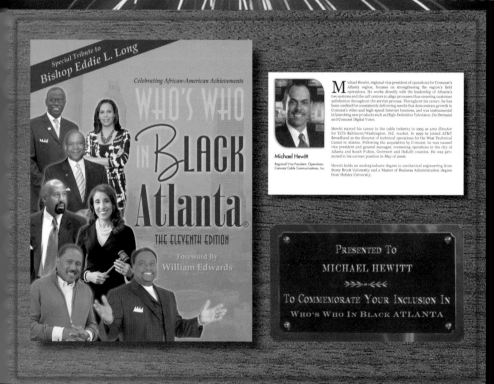

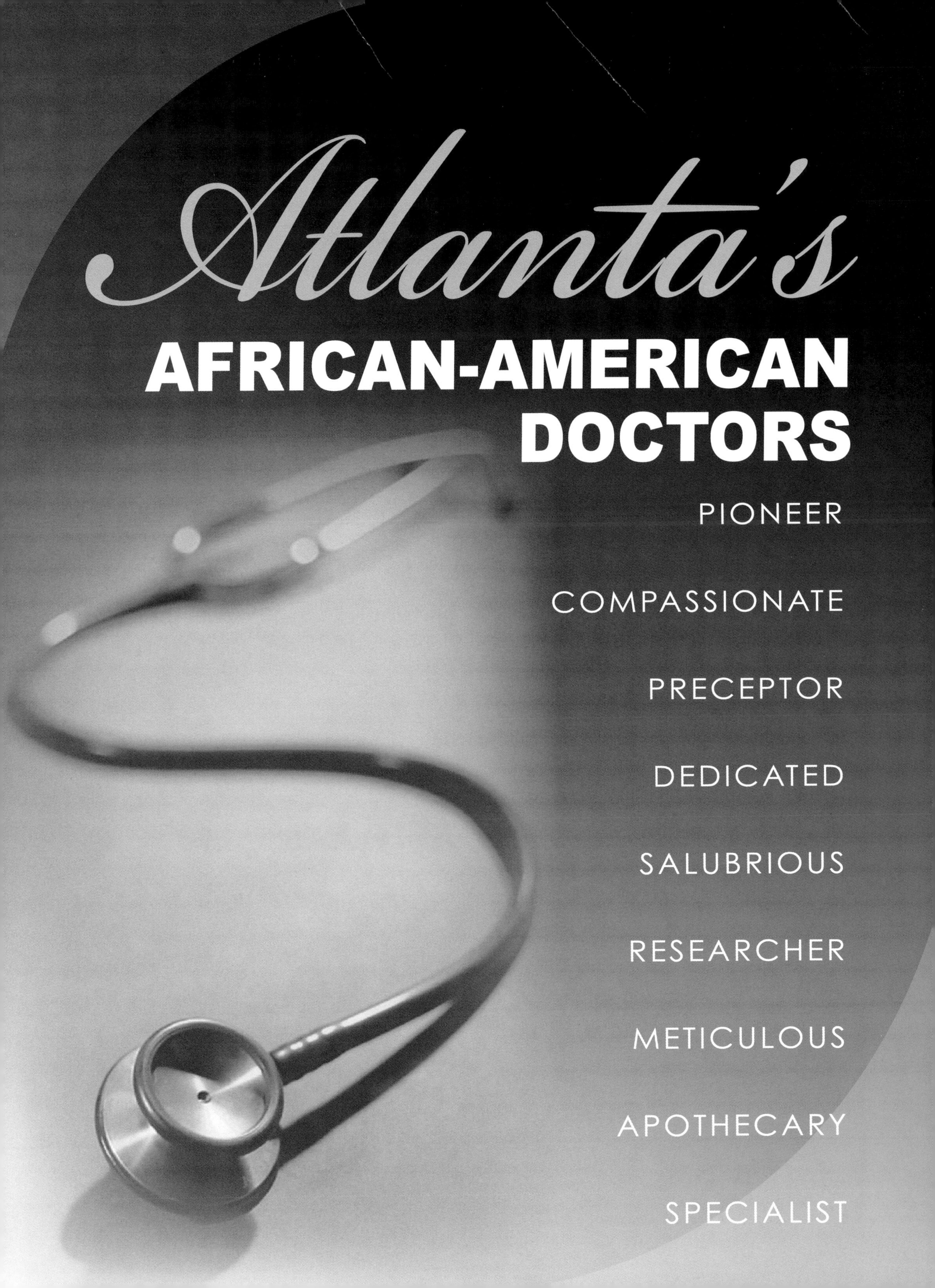

Atlanta's

AFRICAN-AMERICAN DOCTORS

PIONEER

COMPASSIONATE

PRECEPTOR

DEDICATED

SALUBRIOUS

RESEARCHER

METICULOUS

APOTHECARY

SPECIALIST

Marco Antonio Belizaire, D.C.

Sports & Family Chiropractor
AGAPE Chiropractic &
Wellness Center, Inc.

Dr. Robin T. Bingham

General Dentist
Bingham Dental Group, LLC

Dr. Marco Belizaire has practiced chiropractic medicine for more than 16 years in Atlanta and in Panama City, Panama. He and his wife, Virginia, a licensed medical aesthetician and student naturopath, are the owners of AGAPE Chiropractic & Wellness Center. This center encompasses corrective chiropractic care, sports peak performance, nutrition and detoxification with spa services. Their goal is to educate, encourage and empower their practice members to make wise health choices.

As a former Olympian, Marco utilizes his background, along with postgraduate training in sports chiropractic, to work with elite track athletes and several Olympic teams. His contributions were instrumental in several high performances in the Beijing Olympics, including double Olympic gold medals and a silver medal. In addition, his bilingual background allows him to reach different population groups.

He received a Bachelor of Science degree from Fairleigh Dickinson University in New Jersey and a Doctor of Chiropractic degree from Life University.

Marco and Virginia are the parents of Stephen, Sterling and twins, Marquis and Miranda. He is a member of Faith Christian Center in Smyrna and enjoys salsa dancing.

St. Louis native Dr. Robin T. Bingham currently practices general dentistry in Conyers, Georgia. She attended Tennessee State University and graduated from Meharry Medical College. Bingham moved to Conyers in 2002 after serving her country as a U.S. Naval dental officer. After 12 years of practicing dentistry, she owns and operates Bingham Dental Group, LLC, a state-of-the-art facility offering general and cosmetic dentistry for the entire family.

Her ongoing commitment to continued education allows Bingham to remain current with the most recent cutting-edge dental procedures and techniques, demonstrated by recently passing the American Academy of Cosmetic Dentistry accreditation written exam. She remains driven by her goal of becoming an outstanding dentist and providing quality dental care to her patients.

Bingham is a member of Alpha Kappa Alpha Sorority, Inc. and the Order of the Eastern Star. Her professional affiliations include the American and Georgia dental associations, the Georgia Dental Society, the American Association of Women Dentists and the American Academy of Cosmetic Dentistry. In addition, she is a life member of the Meharry Medical College Alumni Association.

Vera E. Burns, O.D.

Optometrist

William A. Cooper, M.D.

Medical Director of the
Cardiovascular Surgery Service
WellStar Kennestone Hospital

Dr. Vera E. Burns is a native of Savannah, Georgia. She provides eye care services in a three-doctor practice in Tucker, Georgia. Burns graduated with honors from Savannah State University, receiving a Bachelor of Science degree. She received an optometric degree from the Indiana University School of Optometry.

Burns was the first African-American female optometrist in Atlanta, and the first woman appointed by the Georgia Board of Optometry by Governor Joe Frank Harris, with re-appointments by Governors Miller and Barnes. She was recognized in 1998 as a Georgia Woman Pioneer in Healthcare.

Burns provided community service as a member of the 1996 Summer Olympic Games Eyecare Team. From 1997 to 2007, she was the first optometrist to provide the Georgia Institute of Technology with eye/vision care services and sport optometry to its athletic association. She provides mentoring to the Spelman College Health Careers Club and is a member of Cascade United Methodist Church.

Burns is grateful for the opportunity to provide the gift of eyesight to a 20-year loyal following of children, adults and geriatrics.

A native of Hayti, Missouri, Dr. William Cooper graduated, with honors, from the University of Missouri-Kansas City in the combined Bachelor of Arts/Medical Degree Program. He was recognized as a University of Missouri chancellor's scholar, and a member of the Alpha Omega Alpha Honor Medical Society and the Mortar Board National College Senior Honor Society.

Cooper completed five years of general surgery and two years of cardiothoracic research in the Emory University General Surgery Residency Program. He served as chief resident in cardiothoracic surgery from 2000 to 2001. After completing postgraduate training, he joined the faculty in the Division of Cardiothoracic Surgery at Emory University. In 2004 Cooper was selected as medical director of the cardiovascular surgery service of the new Cardiac Surgery Program at WellStar Kennestone Hospital in Marietta.

He is a member of the Society of Thoracic Surgeons, and the Southern Thoracic Surgical, Atlanta Medical and Georgia State Medical associations. Serving 23 years in the U.S. Army Reserve, Cooper completed two tours of duty in 2004 and 2008. He and Sandi have three children, Sydney, Cameron and William Jr.

AFRICAN-AMERICAN DOCTORS

William Kevin Dancy, D.D.S.

Family & Cosmetic Dentist
Nanston Dental Group

Valda O. Gibson, M.D.

Hospitalist & Physician
Northside Hospital

Dr. Kevin Dancy practices general, restorative cosmetic dentistry in southwest Atlanta. He believes that esthetic dentistry gives him the opportunity to provide patients with the beautiful smiles they have always desired. He enjoys seeing patients of all ages and building professional, confident and long-lasting relationships with them and their families.

Dancy was awarded fellowship into the Academy of General Dentistry in 2006 and is anticipating the Mastership Award soon. He has been featured in several publications and honored by many organizations as one of Atlanta's leading dentists.

Dancy received a Bachelor of Science degree in biology from Morehouse College, a Doctor of Dental Surgery degree from Meharry Medical College and a master's degree in restorative dentistry from the University of Michigan. A member of Friendship Baptist Church, his affiliations include Omega Psi Phi Fraternity, Inc., 100 Black Men of South Metro, Inc., the National Dental Association and the American Dental Association.

A native of Atlanta, Dancy is married to Dr. Measha Peterson Dancy, an internist, and they have one daughter, Ryli McKinna. He enjoys golf, racquetball and jazz.

Dr. Valda Gibson is a physician in internal medicine at Northside Hospital. She has served as a hospitalist with Northside's internal medicine service for 13 years. In this position, she delivers care to patients as an attending and consulting physician, and has served on multiple committees within the hospital.

A member of many civic organizations including the Metro Atlanta Chapter of 100 Black Women, Inc., Alpha Kappa Alpha Sorority, Inc. and the Atlanta Chapter of Jack and Jill of America, Valda is an active member of Zion Hill Baptist Church. Currently, she is involved with the Atlanta Medical Society and the Medical Association of Atlanta. Previously, she was involved with the Rebecca Lee Medical Society.

Valda graduated from Howard University, cum laude, with a Bachelor of Science degree in zoology. She attended The University of North Carolina at Chapel Hill and received a Doctor of Medicine degree, followed by an internship and residency through the Emory University/Grady Hospital Residency Programs.

The proud mother of Bethany Gibson, Valda is a native of Fayetteville, North Carolina, who has held residence in Atlanta since 1995.

Leon L. Haley Jr., M.D.

Deputy Senior Vice President,
Medical Affairs &
Chief of Emergency Medicine
Grady Health System

Angela Johnson, D.D.S.

Owner
J & J Family Dentistry

Dr. Leon L. Haley Jr. is deputy senior vice president of medical affairs and chief of emergency medicine for the Grady Health System. He is also vice chairman for Grady Clinical Affairs and an associate professor of emergency medicine at Emory University.

A Pittsburgh native, Haley holds degrees from Brown University, the University of Pittsburgh and the University of Michigan. He is board-certified in emergency medicine and a fellow of the American College of Emergency Physicians. A member of the American College of Emergency Physicians, the American College of Healthcare Executives and the American College of Physician Executives, Haley is also a member of the IOM Committee on Health and Insurance Status.

He received the *Atlanta Business Chronicle* Healthcare Heroes and Up and Comers awards, and the Georgia Association of Physician Assistants Physician of the Year Award. In addition, *Georgia Trend* magazine named him one of 40 Leaders Under 40.

Haley is a member of Omega Psi Phi and Sigma Pi Phi fraternities. He is married to Dr. Carla Y. Neal-Haley and they have three children, Grant, Wesley and Nichelle.

Dr. Angela Johnson has been practicing general dentistry in the Atlanta area for more than 15 years. Currently practicing at J & J Family Dentistry, she graduated, cum laude, from Tougaloo College in Mississippi, receiving a bachelor's degree in biology. She received a Doctor of Dental Surgery degree in 1993 from the Meharry Medical College School of Dentistry.

Johnson is a member of the American Dental Association and the National Dental Association, where she has served as local and national chair of the Women Dentist Health Symposium. She is also a member of the Georgia Dental Association, the Northern District Dental Society and the North Georgia Dental Society, where she has served as treasurer. Additionally, she was a part of the 1996 Olympic Games dental team, providing dental care to many athletes from around the world.

A native of Jackson, Mississippi, Johnson developed a passion for people and community service, which is exemplified daily in her patient care, and her memberships in many community and civic organizations. She is married to Dr. Gary Johnson, and they have two sons, Evan and Dylan.

Gary L. Johnson, D.D.S.

Owner
J & J Family Dentistry

Paul King, M.D.

Neurosurgeon
Metro Atlanta Neurosurgery, PC

Dr. Gary L. Johnson always had a desire to help people. He assuages this desire daily by eliminating people's pain and giving them beautiful smiles. He and his wife, Dr. Angela Jamison Johnson, own and operate J & J Family Dentistry, located in southwest Atlanta.

After graduating from Terrell High School in Texas, Johnson made a conscious decision to enroll in a historically black college, which led him to graduate, cum laude, from Grambling State University in Louisiana with a Bachelor of Science degree in biology. He then pursued and earned a Doctor of Dental Surgery degree from the Meharry Medical College School of Dentistry in Nashville, Tennessee.

Johnson is a member of Elizabeth Baptist Church, where he works in the entrepreneurial ministry. He is a member of the North Georgia Dental Society and the American Dental Association. He also serves on the boards of Atlanta's Laffapalooza and Advanced Career Training of Riverdale.

Johnson enjoys visiting schools and educating young people about dental health, as well as emphasizing their unlimited possibilities for a successful future. He is the father of Evan and Dylan.

Dr. Paul King is a board-certified neurosurgeon. He received an undergraduate degree from Fisk University and a medical degree from Michigan State University. King completed his residency at Henry Ford Hospital in Detroit, Michigan.

He moved to Atlanta in 1999 to start a private practice, Metro Atlanta Neurosurgery, PC. King is the current president and Legislative Committee co-chair of the Atlanta Medical Association, Inc., the oldest African-American medical association in the world. He also serves as a board member of the Medical Association of Atlanta.

King founded the Metro Atlanta Neurosurgery Foundation in 2000. The mission of the foundation's Adopt-A-Village Program is to provide medical services and essential medicines to people living in rural communities in developing nations. To date, King has led six medical missions to Ghana and has taken medications and supplies worth thousands of dollars. The next mission is scheduled for August of this year.

King and his wife, Monica, have been married for 36 years. Their family includes children Paul II, Kimani (Adrienne) and Aaron.

Melody T. McCloud, M.D.

President & Medical Director
Atlanta Women's Health Care

Dr. Monica Denise McIntyre

Pediatric Dentist
Kids Dental

Dr. Melody T. McCloud is an obstetrician-gynecologist who established her practice in 1985. She is founder and medical director of Atlanta Women's Health Care, and founder of The McCloud Renaissance, LLC. She lectures nationwide on women's health, the benefits of sex, black women's imagery and social issues.

McCloud serves on the advisory council to the Centers for Disease Control and Prevention, and is a member of the American College of Obstetricians and Gynecologists, Leadership Atlanta, the Atlanta Regional Commission and the YWCA Academy of Women Achievers. A recipient of numerous community awards, she is a graduate of the Boston University School of Medicine and Emory University hospitals.

Called a trailblazing Renaissance woman since the 1970s, McCloud is a media consultant who has had interviews on CNN, ABC, NBC and FOX affiliates. Her articles have been printed in *PARADE*, *Essence* and *Family Circle* magazines, and in *USA Today* and *The Atlanta Journal-Constitution*.

An award-winning poet and occasional voice-over talent, McCloud has another national publication pending. She is author of *Blessed Health: The African-American Woman's Guide to Physical and Spiritual Well-Being.*

Dr. Monica Denise McIntyre is a pediatric dentist in Riverdale, Georgia. She attended Tennessee State University and Meharry Medical College in Nashville, Tennessee. Both the University Medical Center in Jackson, Mississippi, and Howard University provided her postgraduate and specialty training.

McIntyre moved to the Atlanta area in 2001 and practiced as an associate dentist at the Dentistry for Children pediatric dental offices in southeast Atlanta. In 2007 she ventured out and started her own practice, Kids Dental, located in Riverdale. McIntyre enjoys providing quality dental care to children in a caring, fun and friendly manner. Her practice motto is, "Each Child is our Treasure, Every Smile is our Pleasure."

McIntyre's professional affiliations include the American Dental Association, the American Academy of Pediatric Dentistry, the Georgia Dental Association, and the Georgia Dental Society. A member of Delta Sigma Theta Sorority, Inc., she is an active member of Knights Monumental AME Church and serves as the minister of music.

She is a native of Memphis, Tennessee, and is the proud mother of twin toddlers, Evan William and Erin Renee McIntyre.

Sherrie Smith-Scott, D.D.S.

Senior Dentist
Dental Health Associates

Estonna Patrese Wells-Jarrett, M.D.

Partner
Sandy Springs Pediatrics &
Adolescent Medicine, P.C.

Dr. Sherrie Smith-Scott is a practicing dentist with Dental Health Associates. She has been the senior dentist to supervise and provide dental care for more than ten years at the Morrow, Georgia, location.

A native of Los Angeles, California, Smith-Scott graduated from the Lynwood Adventist Academy with honors and received the Bank of America Laboratory Science Award. Upon graduation, she enrolled at Fisk University as a chemistry major. After her junior year, she was accepted to Meharry Medical College as an early admission candidate.

In 1991 Smith-Scott earned a Doctor of Dental Surgery degree and was the recipient of the Black Women's Dentist Association Award. She furthered her dental education at the University of Rochester Medical Center Eastman Dental Center in Rochester, New York, where she graduated with a postdoctoral degree in general dentistry.

Sensitive to the apprehension most patients initially experience concerning dental treatment, Smith-Scott makes it a priority to ease the dental tension. She is the wife of Dr. Edgar L. Scott III, an internist, and the mother of two handsome sons, Edgar IV and Bradley.

Dr. Estonna Wells-Jarrett is a partner in her practice, Sandy Springs Pediatrics and Adolescent Medicine, P.C. She provides general pediatric care for infants, children, adolescents and young adults up to 21 years of age and has a special interest in aiding families with special needs children.

Wells-Jarrett is a diplomate of the American Board of Pediatrics and an American Academy of Pediatrics fellow. She was the first African-American physician hired by her practice and was offered full partnership within a year of service. An active participant of Alpha Kappa Alpha Sorority, Inc., she serves as a mentor to an undergraduate student at Kennesaw State University.

Wells-Jarrett received a Bachelor of Science degree, with honors, from the College of Charleston. She received a medical degree from the Emory University School of Medicine and completed a pediatric internship and residency at The University of Texas Southwestern Medical Center at Dallas and the Children's Medical Center of Dallas.

A South Carolina native, Wells-Jarrett is the wife of Anthony Jarrett and the mother of a lovely daughter, Alexis Nicole.

Atlanta's
ENTREPRENEURS

EXPLORER

INDUSTRIALIST

PIONEER

CAPITALIST

TYCOON

HEROIC

PHILANTHROPIC

HUMANITARIAN

ALTRUISTIC

Evelyn Arnette

President & Chief Executive Officer
A Customer's Point of View, Inc.

Evelyn Arnette is president and chief executive officer of A Customer's Point of View, Inc., a firm she founded in 1997. A Customer's Point of View, Inc. specializes in mystery shopping services.

Arnette has been featured in *Black Enterprise* and *The Atlanta Journal-Constitution*, and on the *Good Day Atlanta* morning television show and various radio programs, where she has provided advice to business owners on customer service. She has been nominated for the U.S. Small Business Administration's Small Business Person of the Year. A Customer's Point of View, Inc. was selected for the Georgia 2003-2004 Governor's Mentor Protégé Program. It has also been awarded the Creative Style Award by the Atlanta Business League.

Arnette has served as a contributing writer for *Atlanta Tribune: The Magazine*. She has instructed and developed training sessions on mystery shopping, customer service and sales. In addition, she has provided consulting services to existing mystery shopping companies.

Arnette has a Bachelor of Arts degree and a Master of Business Administration degree in marketing. She is a member of Delta Sigma Theta Sorority, Inc.

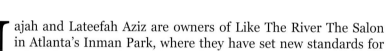

**Lateefah Aziz &
Najah Aziz**

Owners
Like The River The Salon

Najah and Lateefah Aziz are owners of Like The River The Salon in Atlanta's Inman Park, where they have set new standards for salons in community service work.

The sisters resigned their corporate careers to start their business, and since have led charitable efforts. Lateefah and Najah provided 20 women at the Atlanta Day Shelter for Women and Children with A Day of Pampering, which included a limousine ride to and from Like The River, lunch and complimentary hair care services that bolstered the ladies' self-esteem. The event was featured in *The Atlanta Journal-Constitution*, FOX 5 News and *The Chronicles of Philanthropy*.

The sisters also hosted A Clothes Encounter at Like The River, an event that raised money for Dress For Success Atlanta and Pets Are Loving Support. Najah and Lateefah also donated Christmas toys for the youths of the shelter. Additionally, they and their staff participated in the My Day of Beauty, providing complimentary hair care services to special education students of DeKalb County.

Originally from Chicago, the Aziz sisters have planned events for cancer survivors, Cool Girls, Inc. and other organizations.

Allison Babb is recognized as a leading expert on self-employment success for solo entrepreneurs. After many years in senior management in corporate America, Allison successfully transitioned to self-employment. She is founder and chief executive officer of GreatSmallBusinessAdvice.com. As an author, speaker and small business coach, she reveals easy, yet lucrative strategies to small business owners.

Allison has been featured on radio shows, including *Entrepreneurs On Call*, a niche television show, and in news articles and other publications discussing her book, *7 Biggest Mistakes Small Business Owners Make*, and sharing her valuable insights on small business success.

With her gift for coaching and teaching, Allison has been a featured speaker at many entrepreneurial groups. She also brings it to her personal life by leading a single parent support group at her church, which she has done for many years.

Allison received a Bachelor of Arts degree in business administration from Eastern Nazarene College, and is a graduate of Coach University. A native of Trinidad and Tobago, she resides in Kennesaw, Georgia, where she is a single mom to her two sons, CJ and AJ.

Allison Babb

Founder & Chief Executive Officer
Allison Babb International, LLC

Vince Bailey is a 26-year media veteran who began his career as a United Way volunteer reader for the blind in his hometown of Gary, Indiana.

For the past 12 years, Vince has operated Vince Bailey Productions, a full-service audio video production and consulting company based in Lawrenceville, Georgia. Past clients include the National Forest Service, the Centers for Medicare & Medicaid Services, UnitedHealthcare, the SCLC and Job Corps centers around the country. He is a professional announcer for college and professional sporting events and broadcasts (now for the Atlanta Dream), and continues to provide voice talent for commercial clients nationwide.

Vince has served on many boards and committees, including the Fulton County Workforce Investment Board (Youth Council chair and vice chair), the Georgia Black United Fund, the Atlanta Business League board of directors, the Atlanta Job Corps Community Advisory Council, and the Fulton County Schools Career and Technical Education Advisory Council. He is also a member of the DeKalb Chamber of Commerce, the Georgia Black Chamber of Commerce and the South DeKalb Business Association.

Vince Bailey

Chief Executive Officer
Vince Bailey Productions

Courtland C. Bivens III

Ret. Colonel, U.S. Army Reserve
Ret. Flight Directorate
U.S. Government

Courtland C. Bivens III attended the U.S. Military Academy at West Point, New York, where he acquired a Bachelor of Science degree in mechanical engineering. Following a four-year stint in the U.S. Army, he obtained a master's degree in aerospace engineering from the U.S. Naval Postgraduate School. Bivens then completed training at the U.S. Naval Test Pilot School at Patuxent River, Maryland. Being accepted into the U.S. Army War College at historic Carlisle Barracks, Pennsylvania, was a capstone in Biven's career.

During 18 years at the NASA Ames Research Center, Bivens obtained patents on two aeronautical inventions. In 2001 he retired as chief engineer of flight testing at U.S. Army Aviation Technical Test Center in Fort Rucker, Alabama. In 2003 he retired as a colonel in the U.S. Army Reserve.

Bivens' hobbies include creating elaborate ceilings and wood millwork. He and his wife, publicist Regina Lynch-Hudson, have been featured on six episodes on HGTV. A history buff and pilot, Bivens is shopping a historical film project to television networks. An avid fencer, he is a member of the Atlanta Fencing Club.

Robert H. Bolton

President & Chief Executive Officer
R.H. Bolton, Inc.

Atlanta-native Robert H. Bolton is founder of R.H. Bolton, Inc., an innovative event-management firm specializing in planning and executing conventions, convocations, nuptials, fundraisers and other signature events.

For more than a decade, premier institutions, organizations and corporations including Harvard and Dillard universities, Morehouse and Spelman colleges, the Centers for Disease Control, the UNCF and Coca-Cola have sought Bolton's talents, whose professional experience spans more than 20 years. Recently, he assisted the star-studded 75th birthday celebration for baseball legend Hank Aaron, featuring former President Clinton as guest speaker.

The Morehouse graduate is best lauded for the "A Candle in the Dark" gala he created for his alma mater in 1989, which has grossed more than $9 million and honored 145 achievers including Sidney Poitier, Oprah Winfrey, Ray Charles, Muhammad Ali and Denzel Washington.

Bolton is a three-time recipient of the Georgia Public Relations Society of America Phoenix Award. He was included in the July 2007 issue of *Black Enterprise* and was the only event planner featured on WATL-TV's 2006 *Atlanta Bridal Guide Show*. Bolton resides in Atlanta with wife Tammy and daughter, Micah.

Zee Bradford is president and chief executive officer of TBG Worldwide, a full-service public relations firm. Zee has served as one of the city's spokespersons during her tenure with both the City of Atlanta, as press secretary, and with the City of East Point, as chief public information officer, where she also managed a 24-hour municipal television station. She has also served as public relations director with Infinity Broadcasting and national public relations director for The King Center.

A member of Delta Sigma Theta Sorority, Inc. and Pine Street Missionary Baptist Church, Zee is also a board member of the National Black College Alumni Hall of Fame and the University Community Academy. She is a former board chairwoman of Outstanding Atlanta, a former board member of Leadership Atlanta and also The Junior League of Atlanta.

Zee has been recognized by the Atlanta Business League as one of Atlanta's Top 100 Black Women of Influence. She is a graduate of Morris Brown College and the prestigious Coca-Cola Diversity Leadership Academy. Zee is the mother of two and has one grandson.

Zee Bradford
President & Chief Executive Officer
TBG Worldwide

Riki Brooks used her professional experience from the stages of *Dreamgirls*, *Ain't Misbehavin'* and *A Chorus Line* to develop a positive, creative and professional environment for young women and teens to spread their wings through professional theater. She received numerous citations and awards from Mayor Shirley Franklin and Roswell Mayor Jere Wood for producing *Satin Dolls*, *In My Father's House* and *Walking in the Spirit*.

Reaching the top 100 in the gospel charts for her CDs *I'm Ready For Jesus* and *Rejoice*, and hosting T.D. Jakes' 2005 MegaFest Family Expo led Riki to produce Gospel Fest in 2007. Gospel Fest hosts seminars, workshops and panel discussions that assist upcoming artists in their pursuit of a gospel music career. She received a proclamation from Duluth Mayor Nancy Harris for Gospel Fest 2008 at the Gwinnett Convention Center.

Riki earned a Bachelor of Science degree in performing arts and drama from Bowie State College. A native of Baltimore, Maryland, she is the wife of Tony Collins, former musician of the renowned group the Whispers. She is also the mother of two, Tony Jr. and Shykeria.

Riki Brooks
Founder
Leading Women's Repertory Theatre
Atlanta Gospel Fest Conference

Curtis Bunn

Founder & President
National Book Club Conference, Inc.

Curtis Bunn is founder and president of the National Book Club Conference, Inc., an organization that hosts the premier annual literary event for black authors and readers. The conference has featured such authors as Terry McMillan, Walter Mosley, Tavis Smiley, Iyanla Vanzant, Eric Jerome Dickey, E. Lynn Harris, J. California Cooper, Pearl Cleage and many others.

Bunn, who had an award-winning and distinguished 25-year career as a sports journalist in Washington, D.C., New York and Atlanta, wrote an *Essence* No. 1 bestselling novel, *Baggage Check*. Additionally, he is the host of *Author Spotlight with Curtis Bunn*, an Internet literary talk show that exposes readers to their favorite authors.

Last year, Bunn became an adjunct professor of sports reporting at Morehouse College. Months before, he opened his boutique marketing firm, The Bunn Group, Inc.

Anthony M. Davis

Owner, Couturier & Stylist
Anthony Davis Designs

Anthony M. Davis is owner of Anthony Davis Designs, a couture fashion design and image consulting service. As an architect of style and taste, he is dedicated to offering his clients the best in personal service. Being committed to helping each client maintain an impressionable image, his mission is to become an indispensable source and guide through everything from couture fashion design, image consulting and wardrobe styling.

Because of his attention to detail and diligence to stay ahead of the trend, his services have been requested to orchestrate numerous fashion images. Along with a list of individual clients, he has worked with such clients as Parisian/Saks as a freelance stylist for their Pink Ribbon Fashion Show, and the Georgia Breast Cancer Coalition Fund and Susan G. Komen for the Cure with Tea at the Ritz, also hosted by Parisian.

Other projects include designing costumes for Clark Atlanta University's theater productions, The American Heart Association 2009 Wear Red for Women fashion campaign and becoming the official designer and wardrobe stylist to Yolanda Reynolds, publisher of *Who's Who In Black Atlanta*®.

Alexis Day, the quintessential realtor, breathes fresh energy into the real estate business. Founder and managing partner of Dynasty Real Estate Group at Keller Williams Realty in Buckhead, Alexis' savvy blend of instinct, timing, dedication and professionalism is what has spawned the surge of her unique clientele base.

Although raised in Palos Verdes Estates, California, she enjoys the personalities, communities and culture that are the pinnacle of the city of Atlanta. Her ever-flowing entrepreneurial spirit and unique value proposition, coupled with the essence of Atlanta, has collectively positioned Alexis as an emerging leader in the luxury homes and lifestyle market.

Alexis serves on the board of Keller Williams Realty's Homes of Distinction, an invitation-only organization for marketing upper-tier homes, and is a member of the Institute of Luxury Home Marketing, providing exceptional service in the fine homes and estates market.

Having owned three successful retail businesses and earning a degree in visual communications while studying abroad, Alexis attributes her business exposure and more than 14 years of marketing experience to her burgeoning results-oriented real estate career.

Alexis Day

Founder & Managing Partner
Dynasty Real Estate Group
Keller Williams Realty-Buckhead

Michelle Elliott DeShields is founder of Consult With ME! Educational Consulting, and has more than 14 years of experience in the field of education as a teacher, counselor and private tutor in the entertainment industry. As an education project manager with Georgia Public Broadcasting, Michelle worked closely with the Georgia Department of Education and traveled throughout the state providing training for educators on effectively integrating technology into the classroom curriculum.

Michelle donates her time and energy. She is professionally associated with Alpha Kappa Alpha Sorority, Inc., the Professional Sport Wives Association, the Baseball Wives Charitable Foundation, the Atlanta Business League, Ladies Who Launch, the American School Counselor Association and the Professional Association of Georgia Educators.

Michelle received a Bachelor of Science degree in education from Alabama A&M University and the University of West Georgia awarded her a Master of Education degree in guidance and counseling.

A native of Huntsville, Alabama, Michelle is the wife of Delino DeShields, a former MLB player and current coach in the Cincinnati Reds organization, and mother of Delaney.

Michelle Elliott DeShields

Founder
Consult With ME!
Educational Consulting

Peggy Duncan

Personal Productivity Expert
PSC Press

Peggy Duncan is a personal productivity expert and travels internationally, speaking to audiences on organization, time management and technology tips, tricks, and strategies. She is also a consultant and helps her clients develop faster, smarter ways to work. Formally trained at IBM, she was recognized by the chairman for streamlining processes that saved the company close to $1 million a year.

An award-winning technology blogger, Peggy is author of several books, *Conquer Email Overload with Better Habits, Etiquette, and Outlook; The Time Management Memory Jogger*™; *Just Show Me Which Button to Click! in PowerPoint 2003*; and an E-book, *Shameless Self-Promotion: Do-It-Yourself PR – Get Found Online*. She has appeared on *Today, Black Enterprise Business Report* and the U.S. Virgin Islands PBS affiliate. In addition, her expertise has been cited in publications such as *Self, Essence, O, The Oprah Magazine, Black Enterprise, The New York Times* and *The Wall Street Journal*.

Peggy received a Bachelor of Business Administration degree in marketing and train-the-trainer certification from Georgia State University. Additionally, she received a distinguished service award as a SCORE volunteer.

Sonja Ebron

Chief Executive Officer
blackEnergy, LLC

Sonja Ebron is a social entrepreneur and blackEnergy's chief executive officer. A national distributor of energy conservation products, blackEnergy is an organizer of energy buying groups that help people use their utility bills to support black communities.

Ms. Magazine recently labeled Sonja a change agent for "the belief that environmental and social consciousness can create satisfaction in the soul and the wallet." She is the recipient of the Atlanta Business League's 2007 Super Tuesday Award for Non-Traditional Business, and she was named a 2008 SuperWoman by *Atlanta Tribune: The Magazine*.

Sonja is a Ph.D. electrical engineer and former college professor with a background in utilities. She is a senior fellow of the Environmental Leadership Program and a member of Engineers Without Borders.

Damali Edwards founded Edwards Consulting Firm, Inc. (ECF), a retained search practice, in 2002 and serves as chief executive officer. In this role, she is responsible for business development, operations and search execution. Her experience and passion for her work inspired her to create the Conscious RecruitingSM model that centers on the trilogy relationship between search firm, hiring authority and candidate. ECF provides expert recruiting counsel and acts as a strategic business partner to ensure that client companies are prepared for the next generation of hiring.

Edwards graduated from the University of Virginia, earning a Bachelor of Arts degree. Certified as a job and career transition and development coach and entrepreneurship coach by the Career Planning and Adult Development Network, in 2008 she launched a private practice coaching company to assist individuals in career transition looking for their next-level jobs or to start their own businesses.

Edwards is a member of the International Association for Corporate & Professional Recruitment and Delta Sigma Theta Sorority, Inc.

Damali Edwards

Chief Executive Officer
Edwards Consulting Firm, Inc.

Marshawn Evans is founder of ME Unlimited, a corporate life-enrichment consulting firm. Author of *SKIRTS in the Boardroom: A Woman's Survival Guide to Success in Business & Life* (Wiley 2008), she is president of EDGE 3M Sports & Entertainment, a full-service brand management agency, and founder and executive producer of The Caring EDGE Awards.

Handpicked by Donald Trump for *The Apprentice*, Marshawn was the only person to lead the all-women team to victory as project manager. As Miss District of Columbia, she finished third runner-up at the Miss America Competition. Marshawn, a Harry S. Truman scholar and a former U.S. ambassador to the International Summit of Achievement in Ireland, received more than $200,000 in scholarships and graduated, magna cum laude, from Texas Christian University.

A graduate of Georgetown University Law Center, Marshawn practiced as a commercial litigator and employment lawyer for one of Atlanta's most prestigious law firms. Recently named one of Atlanta's Power 30 Under 30, she has been featured by *Glamour Magazine, Upscale, Monarch, Diversity Business Magazine, USA Today, The Big Idea with Donny Deutsch*, ABC, FOX News, MTV and NBC.

Marshawn Evans

Founder
ME Unlimited

Art Franklin

Chief Executive Officer
Franklin Media Group

Art Franklin is chief executive officer of Franklin Media Group, an Atlanta-based media and public relations firm. Specializing in crisis management, the former broadcast journalist's career spanned 27 years, and earned him more than 100 journalism and community awards, including two coveted Emmy Awards.

The University of Michigan graduate and Detroit native is also an author, screenwriter and former record company chief executive officer. *Atlanta Tribune: The Magazine* named Art a Man of Distinction in the April 2008 issue. He has been honored by 100 Black Men of South Metro Atlanta, the Concerned Black Clergy, the *Birmingham Business Journal's* Top 40 Under Forty, *The Birmingham News* as a top nine next generation black leader, local NAACP chapters, and various other organizations including his fraternity, Omega Psi Phi Fraternity, Inc. Art was Birmingham's first African-American male to anchor news in primetime and the first African-American male to anchor a regularly broadcast newscast in Lansing, Michigan.

Art is a proud father of one son and two grandchildren.

Heidi B. Fuller

Founder
Complete Balance

A native of Atlanta, Heidi B. Fuller is a public relations and marketing professional with more than 20 years of experience in providing consultation and support to corporations, small businesses and local municipalities. She is founder of Complete Balance, a self-empowerment company that conducts seminars and workshops to promote professional growth and personnel development. Her clients have included such companies as the Environmental Protection Agency and Hallmark Greeting Cards.

Heidi is founder and former chief executive officer of Service With Elan', a self-started marketing and promotions company that provided talent for companies at various industry-specific conventions and tradeshows. Her client list included Coors Brewing and the Coca-Cola Company.

A former talk show host and program director for *In His Presence*, a nationally syndicated gospel radio show, Heidi currently works with On Common Ground News and hosts an online gospel-talk entertainment show, *The Fuller View*.

Heidi is a lifetime member and mentor for Campfire USA, a national civic organization for youth, and a member of New Birth Missionary Baptist Church. She is a mother of two, Hunter age 12 and Madison age 9.

Bobby L. Gardner is the founder, president and chief executive officer of B&G Security International, LLC and B&G Security International Training Academy. With offices located in Anchorage, Alaska, and Columbus, Georgia, corporate headquarters are located in Rex, Georgia. In May of 1998 Gardner was inspired to open the first African-American-owned security guard agency in the state of Alaska.

Some of B&G Security's clients include subcontracting with Cardillo and Sons Security Inc. on the Transportation Security Administration project for assessment center testing, Waste Management, Barnes & Noble, Georgia Military College and Bantec affiliates of AFLAC. B&G Security Alaska has also assisted in the executive protection of such high-profile clients as Destiny's Child, James Brown, Bill Cosby, Gladys Knight, OutKast, Kenny G, Musiq Soulchild, BB King and more.

B&G Security International Training Academy is a Workforce Investment Act-approved training provider for the state of Georgia. Gardner is a Georgia Board of Private Detectives and Security Agencies certified instructor. He resides in South Atlanta with his wife, Angela, and their four children.

Bobby L. Gardner

Founder & President
B&G Security International, LLC.

Angelia Gay-Bankston is founder of the Angel's Paradise Higher Learning Academy I and II. Her academies have received the highest national accreditation from The National Association for the Education of Young Children. The academy offers specialized learning programs designed to give children a balance of activities that will help them achieve goals for social, emotional, physical, intellectual and creative development.

A Georgia State University graduate, Angelia holds a Bachelor of Arts degree in public relations and journalism. She is a member of the Georgia Child Care Association, the National Black Child Development Institute, the American Red Cross Minority Recruitment Advisory Board, and the Atlanta Business League. She served as vice president for Georgia United Child Care Consortium and Associates.

Angelia won the Atlanta Business League's Success Against the Odds Award, Georgia Minority Business Neophyte Award, and was recognized as one of the Top 100 Black Women of Influence by *Women Looking Ahead* and 100 Most Influential Women by the Atlanta Business League. In addition to being a successful entrepreneur, she is a devoted wife to Reginald and loving mother of three children.

Angelia Gay-Bankston

Founder
Angel's Paradise Higher
Learning Academy

ENTREPRENEURS

Nena Gilreath

Co-Founder & Co-Artistic Director
Ballethnic Dance Company

Nena Gilreath serves as co-founder and co-artistic director of Ballethnic Dance Company and the Ballethnic Academy of Dance. This professional ballet company was founded in 1990 by Gilreath and her husband, co-founder Waverly Lucas. Her roles within the company include mentoring young dancers, assisting Lucas in creating Ballethnic's unique style and implementing outreach programs, including the BUDDY Project.

Gilreath is a recipient of the Atlanta NAACP 2008 President's Award for her positive influence on today's youth. Her other awards and recognitions include *Atlanta Tribune: The Magazine*'s Power Couples (2009), the Charles Loridan Award, Lexus Leaders of the Arts, the Pinnacle Leadership Award, the Global Diversity Business Exchange Atlanta Entrepreneur Award and the Atlanta Business League's Success Against The Odds Award.

Gilreath received a Bachelor of Fine Arts degree in dance from the North Carolina School of the Arts. She began her career with Ruth Mitchell Dance Theatre, toured nationally and internationally with the Dance Theatre of Harlem, and returned to Atlanta in 1988 to dance with the Atlanta Ballet.

Lisa Marie Glover

Owner
Ivy Vining Consulting, LLC

Lisa Marie Glover has more than 20 years of experience in the field of transportation planning. Her transportation consultancy offers a full array of quality services in transportation planning.

Lisa is recognized for her accomplishments in the transportation planning industry. She was selected to participate in the Women's Transportation Seminar's Leadership Institute, the Atlanta Regional Commission's Regional Leadership Institute and the Georgia Academy for Economic Development. Currently, she serves as a member of the Transportation Research Board's International Committee on Women's Issues in Transportation.

Lisa received a Bachelor of Science degree in construction science and management from Tuskegee University, and Morgan State University awarded her a Master of Science degree in transportation science. From 2004 to 2006, she served as the first African-American female transportation planning manager for Henry County, then the third fastest-growing county in the United States.

Her past professional experience includes the City of Detroit Department of Transportation, the Atlanta Committee for the Olympic Games Main Press Center, the Metropolitan Atlanta Rapid Transit Authority, DeKalb County government and the Henry County Board of Commissioners.

If a thing of beauty is a joy forever, then the works of art created by photographer Denise Gray will never become extinct. As one of Atlanta's most highly esteemed photographers, Denise's business focuses on location photography and specializes in event services such as corporate, portraiture and special events. Her clients include Fortune 500 companies and businesses throughout metropolitan Atlanta.

Formally trained at the Southeastern Center of Arts, there were few female role models for the Chicago native to emulate. Nonetheless, after sharpening her skills for the past 30 years, Denise created a path of her own, and was eventually selected as the official photographer of *Who's Who In Black Atlanta®* and the Gate City Bar Association, among others.

Denise enjoys mentoring up-and-coming photographers. She also spent six years as a mentor with Big Brothers Big Sisters. Denise has been a member of Sistagraphy, an organization of her professional peers, since 1993. A community activist, Denise is a member of the American Red Cross Minority Recruitment Advisory Board, Integrity Networking Group and the Sisters Empowerment Network.

Denise Gray

Owner
Denise Gray Photography

Tracy I. Gray Jr. is president and chief executive officer of Gray & Associates Diversity Advertising and Public Relations, Inc., a strategic branding practice. Gray & Associates provides innovative program design and project management to increase awareness and revenue. Tracy has provided his services to numerous clients including the Black McDonald's Operator Association, the Wheels of Dreams Youth Foundation, the Organization of Black Airline Pilots, the national office of the Arthritis Foundation, Delta Air Lines, The Coca-Cola Company, WSB-TV, Turner Entertainment and the U.S. Army.

Tracy is also a compelling diversity, marketing and human resources speaker. He has the ability to build trust and initiate programs that resonate with all stakeholders. He received a Bachelor of Science degree in journalism from Northern Illinois University, and attended the Northwestern University Medill School of Journalism for a Master of Journalism degree in communications management.

A native of Evanston, Illinois, Tracy is an award-winning communicator, author and active community volunteer. He is a member of the Public Relations Society of America, the American Marketing Association and the National Association for Multi-Ethnicity in Communications.

Tracy I. Gray Jr.

President & Chief Executive Officer
Gray & Associates Diversity
Advertising & Public Relations, Inc.

David Greene Sr.

Owner
Jireh Custom Framing, LLC

I nspirational businessman, devoted family man and committed man of faith are only a few of the descriptions that are appropriately attributed to David Greene Sr. As owner of Jireh Custom Framing, LLC, he is entrusted with and has gained a distinct reputation for encasing art treasures in an awe-inspiring manner. He is also a member of Professional Picture Framers of America.

A native of Poulan, Georgia, Greene and his family have resided in Atlanta, Georgia, since 2007. A 20-year veteran of the U.S. Army, he has received postsecondary education at Bishop College in Dallas, Texas, and Savannah State College in Savannah, Georgia. Prior to becoming an entrepreneur, Greene worked as a corrections deputy with the Broward Sheriff's Office in Fort Lauderdale, Florida.

Greene is proud to serve as a deacon at J.A.M. Worldwide Ministries Christian Church. In his spare time, he enjoys woodwork, fishing, listening to jazz and gospel, reading, and spending time with family. He has been married to his high school sweetheart, Esther, for 35 years. They are the parents of four adult children and grandparents of seven.

Herbert Greene Jr.

Chief Executive Officer
Americollect, LLC &
Urban Suburban, Inc. & Subsidiaries

H erbert Greene is chief executive officer of Americollect, LLC, one of the fastest-growing African-American-owned collection agencies in the country. Recognizing Americollect's growth potential in catering to a largely untapped financial niche, Greene bought the upstart company in 2006 and doubled its growth in less than two years.

With nearly $100 million under management in its collection portfolio, Americollect is positioned to receive its ISO certification, a high-level, internationally recognized auditing standard and security-related designation that certifies that a company's security policies and procedures comply with applicable laws and regulations. It is one of the few minority-owned collection agencies holding the industry's standard.

Greene launched Americollect as an affiliate of Urban Suburban, Inc. & Subsidiaries, a multifaceted real estate development company he founded more than 20 years ago. A stalwart development company in the Metro Atlanta area, Urban Suburban's portfolio is currently worth more than $20 million, and it has been a staunch investor and partner in the success of the redevelopment of some of Atlanta's formerly blighted communities.

An Atlanta native, Greene holds a degree in finance from Morehouse College.

John S. Hall is owner of Hall's Of Fine Wines, located in the revitalized Inman Park Historic District. In each year of operation, Hall's has been nominated as one of the best wine shops in Atlanta by various publications and Web sites. Hall's offers various opportunities for customers to acquaint themselves with the world of wine, such as hosting award-winning winemakers, presenting full-course wine dinners at local restaurants and offering onsite wine tastings and classes.

Previously, his career spanned several industries and organizations, including Georgia-Pacific, Alumax, Pepsi and Bristol-Myers/Squibb. He is a founding member of the Society of Competitive Intelligence Professionals and the Clark Atlanta University Alumni Association. In addition, John served on the Woodward Academy Standing Committee.

He holds a Bachelor of Science degree from the University of Arkansas at Pine Bluff, a Master of Arts degree from the University of Northern Iowa and a Master of Business Administration degree from Clark Atlanta University.

John and his spouse, Tina Capers-Hall, are the proud parents of Ian, a junior at Hampton University, and Gabrielle, a freshman at Woodward Academy.

John S. Hall

Entrepreneur & Proprietor
Hall's Of Fine Wines

Deanna L. Hamilton is managing partner and chief financial officer of Think Retail Solutions, a consumer product marketing and specialty printing company. In this role, she is responsible for the overall strategic planning, growth and financial practices of the corporation, which include the treasury, accounting, budget, and tax and audit activities.

Hamilton believes to whom much is given, much is required. She volunteers time as immediate past president of the Atlanta Chapter of the National Black MBA Association and board chair of Why Not Sports. Hamilton has received countless honors and was named one of the Top 50 Under 50 Corporate Executives by *Diversity MBA Magazine*, one of the Top 25 Women of Influence by *rolling out* and one of the 100 Women of Influence by the Atlanta Business League. In addition, she was named the National Black MBA Association Atlanta Chapter MBA of the Year.

A native of Detroit, Michigan, Hamilton received a Master of Science degree in finance and management and a Bachelor of Business Administration degree in finance from Walsh College.

Deanna L. Hamilton

Chief Financial Officer
Think Retail Solutions

Virginia W. Harris

President & Chief Executive Officer
The Harris Group LLP

Virginia W. Harris is president and chief executive officer of The Harris Group, a full-service consulting firm offering project management, quality management, procurement management, contract management and personal development. She is a dynamic, highly respected public servant and community leader.

Virginia serves on the board of directors as the immediate past president of the Metropolitan Atlanta Chapter of the National Coalition of 100 Black Women, Inc., president of the Albany State University Foundation, chair of the Georgia Department of Labor statewide Youth Motivational Task Force Program and vice president of the Gwinnett-Rockdale-Newton community service board. She is an active member of Alpha Kappa Alpha Sorority, Inc. and regularly participates in the National Urban League BEEP-Program, lecturing at historically black colleges and universities.

Virginia resides in Stone Mountain with her husband, Keith. They have two adult children, Mark and Veketa, and two grandsons, Joshua and Andrew. Her educational accomplishments include a bachelor's degree in business administration and a Master of Public Administration degree. In addition, she is a member of NBFG Baptist Church and an avid tennis player.

Angela J. Henry

President & Chief Executive Officer
The Alegna Group, Inc.

Angela J. Henry is chief executive officer of The Alegna Group, Inc., an Atlanta-based accounting firm specializing in entertainment and service industries. She ensures the business and financial success of her clients.

Angela has appeared in film and performed with top artists. Her combination of experience as a creative professional and financial strategist helps her to deliver a strong, yet unique approach in providing services to her entertainment clients. A greenbelt trained in Six Sigma methodology, she was recognized by ING for automating the disbursement function, and she received the Platinum Award of Distinction in her financial leadership role at ING.

Angela holds Bachelor of Business Administration and Master of Business Administration degrees, with honors, in accounting and finance. A licensed certified public accountant, she is a member of The American Institute of Certified Public Accountants and the Georgia Society of CPAs. She is also a member of the National Academy of Recording Arts & Sciences, and the National Association of Black Female Executives in Music & Entertainment.

A native of The Bronx, New York, Angela loves foreign travel and snorkeling.

ichael Hightower is founder and manager of The Collaborative Firm, LLC. He has more than 25 years of experience in the public, private and educational arenas and provides a wealth of experience in public policy, with an emphasis on planning, economic development and local governance issues. His strengths are evident in his wealth of experience in building public and private partnerships in many communities throughout metropolitan Atlanta.

In addition to running The Collaborative Firm, LLC for almost five years, Michael serves on numerous boards and commissions for local, state and national governmental entities. Some of his involvements include serving as past president of the National Association of Counties, the National League of Cities, the Georgia Municipal Association and the Association of Counties Commissioners of Georgia. He is currently active with the Urban Land Institute and the Georgia, Clayton, Airport Area and South Fulton chambers of commerce.

Michael is founder and manager of the South Metro Development Outlook Forum and founder of the Old National Merchants Association (College Park), an organization of business and governmental leaders in the airport area.

Michael Hightower

Managing Partner
The Collaborative Firm, LLC

arren A. Huntley is founder and chief executive officer of Atlanta-based special events planning and event design firm Warren Huntley Presents, Inc., which specializes in event production, design and logistic services specifically for the entertainment, retail, sports and marketing industries in addition to high-end weddings and social events.

Warren graduated from The Art Institute of Atlanta with a degree in business in 1982 and from New York University with a Bachelor of Arts degree in marketing in 1984.

Born in Brooklyn, Warren is an avid art collector and published writer of both nonfiction and poetry. His professional and volunteer affiliations include The Boys and Girls Clubs of America, March of Dimes, ISES (International Special Events Society), Childkind, The Children's Wish Foundation, Men Against Violence, and AID Atlanta. In addition, he sits on the board of directors of Open Hand/Atlanta.

The Warren Huntley Presents, Inc. client list reads like a who's who, and includes *Essence*, BET, *Billboard*, The Coca-Cola Company, Rolls Royce, Rain Forest Films, Ford Motor Company and the National Urban League.

Warren A. Huntley

President & Chief Executive Officer
Warren Huntley Presents, Inc.

Melvin "M.J." Hutchens Jr.

Originator
Sarah's Garden

Full of innovation and originality, Melvin "M.J." Hutchens Jr. has created a brand that is sure to take the world by storm, especially parents and children. Built upon the premise that love is a universal and essential element that can transform any situation, Sarah's Garden is a vibrant approach to instilling self-esteem in children through the use of a unique product line. The *Sarah's Garden* coloring book is fully developed while additional items such as more books, toys, T-shirts, a children's clothing line, school materials, room décor, party favors, and others are on the way.

The Winter Park, Florida, native has always had a love for children, and is the loving and supportive single father of three. He has also spent the last 20 years as a professionally trained stylist.

An active member of Higher Living Ministries, M.J. faithfully works with youth in juvenile detention centers. He is passionate about teaching others the hidden potential in all God's creations. In his spare time, he enjoys playing racquetball. His life's motto is, "Love life, but it's up to you to love."

Alonia Jernigan

President & Chief Executive Officer
The Effective Communicator

As president and chief executive officer of The Effective Communicator, a full-service corporate communications and professional development company, Jernigan is known as an excellent writer, captivating and witty speaker, and challenging teacher and trainer.

A native Atlantan, Jernigan is a product of the Atlanta Public Schools system and Spelman College. She founded and published the award-winning *IMANI Magazine* in 1997, publishing until 2004. The publication gained tremendous acclaim, including a letter of commendation from the White House. Jernigan has written feature articles on many notable personalities from across the country, and was recently nominated as Most Outstanding Journalist by the *Electronic Urban Report*. She created The Dream Institute, Inc. to help youth bring their visions to life through the enhancement of their writing and public speaking skills.

Jernigan is an author in her own right, and looks forward to releasing her autobiography, "The Pursuit of Destiny," in spring of 2009. A licensed and ordained minister of the gospel, she is married to Elder James Jernigan and is the mother of three children and a young adult niece.

James (Jamie) P. Jernigan Sr. is a shrewd and honest businessman, and a dedicated family man. As chief executive officer for the Jernigan Financial Group, he is responsible for working with families and individuals to help secure their financial futures. He does so through the sale of an array of insurance and financial educational products. Jernigan is also a certified debt consultant. His mantra is: "Secure your family with a deed, not a debt." A native of Greensboro, Georgia, he is a product of the Atlanta Public Schools system.

Jernigan is a licensed and ordained minister of the gospel, and he works closely with the men's ministry at Greater Bethany Baptist Church. He is especially concerned about the well-being of the elderly. In an effort to hone his ministerial skills, he began studies in leadership development at Beulah Heights Bible College.

Jernigan has been married to Alonia Jernigan since 1991. They are the proud parents of James Jernigan Jr. (16), Kori Alexis (13) and Emmanuel Alonzo (4). In his spare time, Jernigan enjoys reading, traveling and spending time with family.

James P. Jernigan Sr.
President & Chief Executive Officer
Jernigan Financial Group

Carol Johnson is president and chief executive officer of Pink Platinum Marketing, a marketing firm that specializes in customized campaigns for small- to medium-sized businesses, nonprofit organizations and foundations looking to enhance their visibility while increasing their revenue base. Carol helps clients achieve an exponential marketing reach with measurable results. She is known as an innovative marketing catalyst because of her abilities to strategically combine technical expertise with her gift of creativity.

After completing a Bachelor of Science degree in engineering from Southern Polytechnic State University in Marietta, Georgia, Carol spent five years as marketing manager for InterServ, Inc., handling marketing initiatives for Fortune 500 companies. Following InterServ, she served as systems manager for Wachovia.

A proponent of volunteerism, Carol currently serves on the advisory board of the One Economy Corporation and is a member of the board of directors for the Ryan Cameron Foundation. Additionally, she is past vice president of the Stewart Foundation.

A native of Jacksonville, Florida, Carol resides in Henry County with her husband of 15 years, Kelvin, and two daughters. They attend Ray of Hope Christian Church.

Carol S. Johnson
President & Chief Executive Officer
Pink Platinum Marketing

Yvonne Bryant Johnson

President & Chief Executive Officer
Bryant & Associates, LLC

Yvonne Bryant Johnson is president and chief executive officer of Bryant & Associates, LLC, an executive coaching, facilitation services and training company located in Atlanta. Named one of Atlanta's Top 100 Black Women of Influence from 2007 to 2009, she is also an executive coach for the Executive Master of Business Administration Program at the Kennesaw State University Coles College of Business.

A graduate of Leadership Atlanta, Leadership America and the inaugural class of the Greater Atlanta Economic Alliance Academy, Johnson is the 2009 board chair of the Georgia Center for Child Advocacy. She has served as board chair of the Youth Ensemble of Atlanta, the Partnership Against Domestic Violence and Sickle Cell Empowerment for a Liberated Life. Additionally, she serves on the board of the Atlanta Business League.

Johnson's educational accomplishments include earning a Master of Business Administration degree from Emory University and attending The Johns Hopkins University, the University of London and the University of Ghana. She graduated with honors from Spelman College, and she was one of the first Spelman graduates to receive the Alumnae Achievement Award in business.

Warren R. Jones

President & Chief Executive Officer
Ever-Redi Enterprises Inc./
Ever-Redi Exterminating Co.

Warren R. Jones is president and chief executive officer of Ever-Redi Enterprises Inc./Ever-Redi Exterminating Co. In this position, he directs the corporation, and oversees the daily management and marketing activities of Ever-Redi Exterminating Co.

Warren founded Ever-Redi Exterminating Co. to be a viable termite and pest control alternative, serving both the residential and commercial markets, offering quality service at affordable prices, while simultaneously enhancing the community spiritually, economically, environmentally and educationally. Ever-Redi Exterminating has kept with its motto, "Ever-Redi to Exceed Your Needs," where it has experienced phenomenal growth in propelling the company to be one of the largest minority pest control companies in the country.

Warren graduated from the University of Maryland with a Bachelor of Science degree in business management, and a Master of Business Administration degree in marketing and international trade. He has participated in several trade missions and is listed in *Who's Who Among U.S. Executives.*

A Christian, Warren pledged Alpha Phi Alpha Fraternity, Inc. He is married to Margrie Lovette Jones and has a son, Warren Jared Jones, who is a student at Morehouse College.

Jamahl L. King, founder and chief executive officer of S.T.E.P.S. (Striving Towards Excellence with Perfection in Sight) Event Planning Firm, has established a solid reputation for conceptualizing and actualizing events with a profound level of quality. King graduated from Morehouse College in 1993, with a degree in mass communications, and launched S.T.E.P.S. in 1996.

Ne-Yo, Bronner Bros., Groundrush Media, Keith Sweat, Infiniti Broadcasting Corporation – WVEE Radio, The Cochran Firm of Atlanta, Time Warner, BET, Rainforest Films and Sony Urban Music are among those who repeatedly seek his services. The Atlanta-based S.T.E.P.S. firm has been featured in *Upscale, Sister 2 Sister, Atlanta Tribune: The Magazine* and *The Atlanta Journal-Constitution*. In addition, he received the notable Dream Catchers Award from the Atlanta Urban League Young Professionals.

A native of Hammond, Indiana, King is on the boards of directors of the Compound Foundation, the University of West Georgia Black Men With Initiative program and the Miss/Ms. Black Georgia USA Foundation. He is also a founding member of the Frank Ski Kids Foundation Inc. and a member of Victory Church in Stone Mountain, Georgia.

Jamahl L. King
Founder & Chief Executive Officer
S.T.E.P.S. Event Planning Firm

Robert E. Leach, president and founder of RELM Group, is the driving force behind maximizing advertising budgets out of south Atlanta. This native New Yorker has more than 20 years' experience in sales and marketing and is a two-time graduate of Syracuse University.

Leveraging his professional experience with Viacom, Entercom and Cox Radio has given Robert a chance to help thousands of businesses in different industries increase sales. His company has developed successful advertising campaigns and/or developed Web sites for the 21 Steps to Homeownership Program with Dominique Wilkins, 1Source Financial Solutions, Dozier Homes and Energizer.

Robert's work was recognized as one of the Georgia Black Chamber of Commerce and Wal-Mart JOZ Business Spotlight Winners in 2008, and by the South Fulton Chamber of Commerce as the Small Business of the Year in 2006. Additionally, he is active in his community, serving as a board member of the South Fulton Chamber of Commerce, a member of Phi Beta Sigma Fraternity, Inc. and by speaking and facilitating workshops for students and organizations based on his book, *A Game Plan To Advertising in a Down Economy*.

Robert E. Leach
President
RELM Group

Nancy J. Lewis

President
Progressive Techniques, Inc.

Nancy J. Lewis is a leading motivational and inspirational keynote speaker, trainer, author and registered corporate coach. She is the president of Progressive Techniques, Inc., based in Fayetteville, Georgia, where the motto of her organization is "Developing a Better YOU!" Nancy conducts dynamic keynotes and seminars on customer service, leadership, diversity, human resources and personal enrichment. She delivers customized, energizing, interactive and content-rich presentations that provide strategies for everyday living.

She has been featured regularly on local radio and television broadcasts. Currently, Nancy hosts a monthly radio broadcast, entitled *The Coaches Corner* on KISS 104.1 FM, and is a contributing writer for several publications.

She is a member of the National Speakers Association, the Society for Human Resource Management, and many other community and civic organizations. Nancy has worked with Fortune 100 and 500 organizations, government agencies and academia, and is called "The Speaker Who Keeps It Real."

Nancy is married to the Reverend Kevin E. Lewis and they have three sons.

Edward C. London

Board Chairman
National Association of
Real Estate Brokers, Inc.

Edward C. London is chairman of the board and served as the 22nd president of the National Association of Real Estate Brokers, Inc. He is also chief executive officer and chairman of EC London & Associates, Inc., an Atlanta-based residential real estate developer and builder. The firm also markets and manages properties for its corporate clients, while providing facilities services for government agencies throughout the United States.

London has earned numerous professional awards and designations, and holds a bachelor's degree in economics, a Master of Business Administration degree and a law degree. He is married to Nell London, founder of First Step Outreach, Inc., a nonprofit, community-based organization located in Atlanta, Georgia.

Waverly T. Lucas II is co-founder and co-artistic director of Ballethnic Dance Company and Ballethnic Academy of Dance, which he founded in 1990 with his wife, Nena Gilreath. As a choreographer, he created more than 30 ballets, including *Urban Nutcracker* and *The Leopard Tale*. Lucas established the Danseur Development Project, offering athletic discipline and mentoring to young males.

His choreography has been featured at the Olympic Arts and National Black Arts festivals, the Lincoln Center and in the Atlanta Opera's *Aida*. A Recipient of the Princess Grace Scholarship, his honors include recognition as one of Atlanta's Community Leaders and one of the Lexus Leaders of the Arts. *Atlanta Tribune: The Magazine* recognized Lucas and Nena as a power couple, and he received a National Choreographers Award, the Charles Loridan Award and the Atlanta Branch NAACP President's Award.

Lucas attended Marygrove College in Detroit, where he conceived the concept and name for Ballethnic. He toured with the Dance Theatre of Harlem and danced with the Atlanta Ballet. Lucas has studied West African dance and drumming in Senegal, and conducted dance workshops nationally and internationally.

Waverly T. Lucas II

Co-Founder, Co-Artistic Director &
Choreographer
Ballethnic Dance Company, Inc.

Dr. Bessie Ludd is founder and chief executive officer of Bess Productions, an entertainment company that molds and develops talent, and provides a venue for upcoming and established artists. Naturally gifted in the arts, she has been producing and directing theater for 17 years, and has produced more than 100 successful shows.

Ludd has been called upon by various corporations, including The Children's Hospital in Seattle, Washington, and the Mary Bridge Children's Hospital & Health Center in Tacoma, Washington. Her ability to use her gifting has raised $37 million for the Boeing Corporation in Seattle, Washington.

Ludd's cast and choirs have performed for many charitable events throughout the Pacific Northwest, including performances for Danny Glover, Tony Estella and the Make-A-Wish Foundation. Her youth-based programs have transformed numerous young lives, leading them to high self-esteem, Ivy League college education and professional entertainment jobs.

Ludd has a degree in business administration and a Doctor of Divinity degree. A native of Shreveport, Louisiana, she now resides in Marietta with her husband, Dr. Adolph Ludd Sr.

Dr. Bessie Ludd

Founder & Chief Executive Officer
Bess Productions

Jill Strickland Luse

President
J. Strickland Communications Co.

Jill Strickland Luse is president of J. Strickland Communications Co. in Atlanta. Her company delivers professional public relations, media relations and community engagement services to some of the nation's most respected and valued organizations.

Prior to starting her firm, Jill was the deputy communications director/press secretary for the City of Atlanta. She has also provided communications services to the 2000 Gore/Lieberman presidential campaign, Mayor Shirley Franklin's 2006 inauguration and U.S. Senator Hillary Rodham Clinton's Atlanta visit in October of 2005.

Jill started her career as a news reporter/anchor in Huntsville, Alabama, and at 640 WGST, and as an assignment editor at CBS Atlanta. She has received journalism awards from the AP Broadcast Association, the Atlanta Association of Black Journalists and the Huntsville Press Club.

Jill earned a Bachelor of Journalism degree in broadcast news from The University of Georgia. Her board appointments include the United Way of Metropolitan Atlanta Fulton County advisory board, Communities In Schools of Atlanta, The Names Project Foundation and the Grant Park Conservancy.

A native of Atlanta, Jill is married to Keith R. Luse and they have one daughter.

Regina Lynch-Hudson

Owner
The Write Publicist & Co.

Regina Lynch-Hudson of The Write Publicist & Co. maintains an exclusive clientele that includes primarily travel and business accounts, and representation of high-net-worth individuals in various specialties. More than 80 percent of her clients are out of state.

A branding mastermind, Regina self-syndicated "Regina's PR Remedies," a column sponsored by computer giant Gateway, which appeared in newspapers nationwide. She syndicated "Regina Roams," a column first published by AirTran Airways' in-flight magazine, garnering a readership of 3 million-plus. Today, Regina pens the AirTran Airways-sponsored business travel column "Doing Biz In." In regional *Season* magazine, she conceptualized "Regina's A-List Abodes," a décor feature that highlighted homes of high-profile Atlantans. Next, the six-time guest of HGTV elevated to home review placements in national magazines such as *Ebony*.

In addition to her columns, Regina has reaped repeat coverage in publications such as *Black Enterprise*, *Essence* and *The Atlanta Journal-Constitution*. Today, she operates on cruise control, enjoying the luxury of only accepting select projects.

The former Bennett College belle is married to West Point graduate Courtland C. Bivens III, a pilot, retired colonel and aerospace engineer.

Tandy Mackey is owner of a Kumon Math & Reading Center franchise, which offers services in math and reading to young children. Consistently a top-performing franchise, Kumon is ranked No. 1 in the tutoring category. Tandy received awards for becoming one of the fastest growing centers in the first year of opening, completing higher levels of mathematics and reading.

A native of Indianapolis, Indiana, Tandy earned a Bachelor of Science degree in English education from Central State University and a reading certification from the University of West Georgia. She received a Master of Business Administration degree with a major in marketing from Indiana Wesleyan University, where she developed a passion for becoming an entrepreneur.

Tandy spends most of her time educating youth and adults in becoming productive citizens in society. She is active in numerous local community organizations such as Our House, a center for young girls, and TC&C Enterprises Inc., where she lectures to young adults on how to become entrepreneurs.

Tandy is a member of Elizabeth Baptist Church in Atlanta and a lifelong member of Eastern Star Baptist Church in Indianapolis.

Tandy E. Mackey

Owner
Kumon Math & Reading Center

President of Sheila Maddox, Inc. and associate broker with Coldwell Banker Residential Brokerage, Sheila Maddox has been a leader in the Atlanta business and real estate communities for 25 years. She is widely recognized and highly respected for her business acumen and civic involvement.

Sheila received several coveted honors, including the International President's Elite, the International President's Circle, the Coldwell Banker Hall of Fame and the Atlanta Board of Realtors Phoenix Award. A member of the Empire Board of Realtists, Inc. Million Dollar Club and the Atlanta Board of Realtors Million Dollar Club, she was founding president of the Southwest Atlanta Real Estate Focus Group.

An Atlanta native, Shelia graduated, magna cum laude, from Howard University. She served on the Howard University board of trustees and is past president of the Howard University Alumni Club of Atlanta.

An actress, voice-over talent and member of the American Federation of Television & Radio Artists, Sheila serves on the Screen Actors Guild (Georgia Branch) executive board. She is the daughter of Atlanta City Councilman Jim Maddox and retired Atlanta Public Schools teacher Alice Wise Maddox.

Sheila Maddox

President
Sheila Maddox, Inc.

Joseph Malbrough

President
Parkland Place Associates

Joseph Malbrough is president of Parkland Place Associates and Parkland Place & Company, LLC. Parkland Place Associates own and operate The UPS Store #0328, a packing, shipping and postal franchise store in Smyrna, Georgia, while Parkland Place & Company is a real estate investment and management company.

Prior to starting Parkland Place Associates, Malbrough served as assistant vice president of new business development for the United Way of Metropolitan Atlanta and was the top revenue producer for the Metro Atlanta Chamber of Commerce for ten years. He served on the board of the Southeast Chapter of UNICEF from 2001 to 2007, and is an active member of Antioch Baptist Church North.

Malbrough received a Bachelor of Communications degree from Lamar University in Beaumont, Texas.

A native of Beaumont, Malbrough and his wife, Cara, are the proud parents of Evan and Jared. They currently reside in Smyrna.

Y. Dyan Matthews

Owner & Project Manager
Media Events Link

Y. Dyan Matthews owns and operates Media Events Link, a public relations and special events firm specializing in public and government relations, special events and television production.

A graduate of Morris Brown College, Dyan earned a Bachelor of Arts degree in journalism and English. She also received a fellowship in English from the University of Michigan.

Dyan recently retired as chief of staff to Fulton County Commission vice chairman William "Bill" Edwards. She is currently active in several community and nonprofit organizations, including chairman of the South Fulton Chapter of the Southern Crescent Alzheimer's Memory Walk, co-chair of the Political Awareness & Economic Development Committee for the MECCA Chapter of the National Coalition of 100 Black Women and a member of the East Point/College Park Chapter of Delta Sigma Theta Sorority, Inc. and the South Fulton Chamber of Commerce.

Residents of Fairburn, Dyan and her husband, Bill, have three children and seven grandchildren.

Reco McDaniel is the founder and chief executive officer of C.O.D.E. R.E.D. Marketing, LLC, a marketing and training company comprised of a team of like-minded individuals focused on personal growth, spiritual fulfillment and financial stability.

While in college and working full time, he saw that he was getting no closer to accomplishing his goals so he started a business part time. Within a short period, Reco was able to leave his job and pursue his dreams.

Since paying off debts, changing his lifestyle and achieving many goals, he has coached and mentored thousands of people nationwide while building a personal business that exceeds annual revenues of more than $6 million. These accomplishments have allowed him to become financially free in his mid-20s. His objective is to train, educate and create wealth in every interested person he comes in contact with. His teachings, focusing on personal growth, spiritual fulfillment and financial stability, are unparalleled, transcending cultural and age barriers.

A native of Atlanta, Georgia, Reco is happily married to his best friend, Shaneé, and is the father of a son, Reco Jr.

Reco T. McDaniel

President & Chief Executive Officer
C.O.D.E. R.E.D. Marketing, LLC

Marchia Mickens is founder and owner of the U.S. United Pageant System, which recognizes outstanding women for outstanding achievements in the community, in addition to their professional and personal lives. She emphasizes that the U.S. United Pageant is not a beauty pageant. The U.S. United Pageant looks for women who can think on their feet, are personable and articulate, and want to use the crown and title to make a difference in the community.

Marchia believes that pageants offer many opportunities and benefits for women of all ages, shapes, sizes and backgrounds. She brings more than ten years of experience to the pageant world and has held several national and international pageant titles. Marchia has used her titles to promote her platform, "Are you aware...mammograms can save lives."

A native of Harrisburg, Pennsylvania, she received a Bachelor of Science degree in education from Indiana University of Pennsylvania and a master's degree in instructional technology from American Intercontinental University.

Marchia Mickens

Founder
U.S. United Pageant

India Miller

Event Planner

I ndia Miller began her career as an event planner in 2000 after attending Clayton State College, where she majored in communication. She specializes in social events in Atlanta, with movers and shakers from Chris Tucker to Jermaine Dupree. She eventually joined radio personalities Ryan and Kysha Cameron in planning events for their foundation, which is the source for a great deal of charitable work.

Miller joined Martin, Yolanda and Bernice King in the remembrance of their mother, the late Coretta Scott King, on her birthday at The King Center, where she was interviewed about Mrs. King's legacy. Currently, she is an active member of the RainbowPUSH Coalition, where she marched for voters' rights in Atlanta beside the Reverend Jesse Jackson, Mayor Shirley Franklin, actor Harry Belafonte and singer Willie Nelson.

Miller currently resides in Atlanta with her children, Clairissia, Diamond and Reginald. A favorite quote by her late mother and grandmother (Willie Mae and Clara Miller Perdue) is, "Always strive to be someone of importance."

Joel Miller

Chief Executive Officer &
Chief Strategist
Wall Street Capital Funding, Inc.

J oel Miller's specialty is mortgage financing, from residential mortgages to providing investment banking services for the placement of $7 billion from a select group of private equity funds. At the age of 28, Miller became one of the youngest chief executive officer mortgage bankers in U.S. history. Today, he continues to expand his scope of influence in the world of finance as an investor, real estate developer, public speaker, writer and author.

Miller has served as a marketing and strategic advisor to one of the nation's top ten wholesale banks and as a consultant on financial institution mergers, most recently for the Greenpoint Mortgage/Capital One Bank merger. Currently, he serves as a regular lecturer of economics at the Clayton State University School of Business.

In late 2008, Miller received the privilege of serving as a secondary advisor to President Barack Obama's transition team on the topics of housing and the economy. In addition, he authors a column, "The Wealth Zone," in *Atlanta Tribune: The Magazine* and hosts a radio show on Newstalk 1160 WCFO-AM.

Tiffany Harris Moore, a native Atlantan, was crowned Mrs. Georgia Plus America in October of 2008. She became an author in March of 2006 with the publication of her first book, *Here Comes The Bling: The Sponsored Wedding Guide*. Shortly thereafter, Tiffany began hosting "How-To" seminars on cost-effective living and accepting motivational speaking engagements. She later published a Christian children's book, *If I Believe I Can Do Anything*.

Tiffany has focused her philanthropic efforts by volunteering with Habitat for Humanity and the DeShawn Snow Foundation, Inc. She has been featured on *The Clark Howard Show* and in *Atlanta Wedding Ideas Magazine, The Sunday Paper, rolling out, The Atlanta Journal-Constitution, The Southside Insider* and *The South Fulton Neighbor*. She also writes a monthly column in *Consumer Issues Magazine*.

A member of Alpha Phi Omega, a national service fraternity, Tiffany received an associate degree from Atlanta Metropolitan College and a Bachelor of Arts degree from Georgia State University. She also holds certifications in a wide range of areas. She is the wife of Lawrence J. Moore Jr. and mother of one daughter, Taylor Louise.

Tiffany Harris Moore

Mrs. Georgia Plus America
Author & Motivational Speaker

Kendra Norman-Bellamy is an eight-time national best-selling author and founder of KNB Publications, LLC. Her award-winning Christian fiction titles are currently made available through the publishers of Harlequin Books, Moody Publishers and Urban Books. She and her novels have been featured in *Essence, Upscale, Precious Times, HOPE for Women* and *E.K.G. Literary* magazines.

Kendra is a motivational speaker and the mastermind behind The Writer's Hut, an online support group for creators of literary works. Furthermore, she is founder of The Writer's Cocoon, a national focus group for aspiring and published writers, and Cruisin' For Christ, a groundbreaking cruise that celebrates Christian writing, gospel music and other artistries that glorify God.

Among her most recent literary recognitions, Kendra was presented with the 2008 Best Christian Fiction Award and the 2008 Best Anthology Award by the African American Literary Awards Show in New York. A graduate of Valdosta Technical College, she is a member of Iota Phi Lambda Sorority, Inc. and resides in Stone Mountain, Georgia, with her family.

Kendra Norman-Bellamy

National Best-Selling
Author & Publisher
KNB Publications, LLC

Mary H. Parker

President & Chief Executive Officer
ALL(n)1 Security Services, Inc.

Mary Parker is president and chief executive officer of ALL(n)1 Security Services, Inc., a full-service security company. She is responsible for developing new business relationships for strategic alliance and joint venture opportunities and increasing the company's visibility in national and global markets.

Mary received the City of Atlanta Female Business Enterprise Phoenix Trailblazer Award in 2008, the Women Flying High Award in 2006 and the Atlanta Area Council of the Boy Scouts of America Silver Beaver Award. She was named the U.S. Department of Commerce Atlanta Regional Entrepreneur of the Year and one of the 100 Most Influential Black Women of Atlanta. In addition, her company was named the U.S. Atlanta Region Business Firm of the Year and the Atlanta Business League Non-Traditional Business of the Year in 2005.

A member of Vistage International, Mary serves on the board of the Georgia Women's Business Council. She earned a Bachelor of Science degree in criminology and a master's degree in security management from Stafford University.

Mary resides in Atlanta with her daughter, Chana (Greg), and three granddaughters, Amber, Essence and Jada.

Donna Permell

Chief Executive Officer
Prime Phocus, LLC

Donna Permell is chief executive officer of Prime Phocus, LLC. With more than 25 years of experience and dedication in photography, her work has been featured in many publications, including *ELLE* magazine (United Kingdom), *Essence* and *Glamour* magazines.

Donna is a member of Professional Photography of America, Advertising Photographers of America, the National PhotoShop Group, and Wedding and Portrait Photographers International. She is also a member of The Associated Press, the Georgia Production Partnership and Women & Film.

Passionate about teaching, Donna is committed to sharing her knowledge with the next generation of photographers.

Vickley Raeford is president of Raeford Land Clearing, Inc. The company is responsible for the vegetation and waste management of more than 400 Georgia Power Company electrical substations and more than 100 miles of right-of-ways. In addition, demolition, metal gate fabrication and storm damage clearing are services the company provides to the U.S. Forest and National Park services.

Raeford received a 2009 Trumpet Award, a 2008 Minority Business Owners Award and a 2007 Micro-Entrepreneur Award for the Edge Connection, SBA. Featured in national advertisements for Southern Company, she is the founder of Business Leaders on the Move and president of the Business and Professional Federation of Women for Western Georgia, COGIC.

Raeford received a Bachelor of Science degree in criminal justice from Jackson State University and a Master of Business Administration degree from Central Michigan University. She received the Bellsouth Fast-Trac scholarship and a Thomas Edison Electric Grant and graduated from the Amos Tuck School of Business Administration at Dartmouth College.

A native of Forest, Mississippi, Raeford is the wife of Maurice and the loving mother of Jonathan and Phillip.

Vickley L. Raeford
President
Raeford Land Clearing, Inc.

Discriminating sophistication, awe-inspiring creativity and exhilarating passion are the by-products of creations produced by Cheryl Ragland, owner of Exquisite Interior Design, Inc., a rapidly growing Atlanta enterprise.

An Arkansas native, Ragland has, for the past nine years, integrated the expertise gained from her corporate career, followed her dream of working for herself, and emerged as one of Atlanta's most promising entrepreneurs. Catering to residential and commercial clientele, Exquisite Interior Design, Inc., provides a broad array of services and deliverables to include custom draperies, redecorating and furniture and accessory selection.

She has been acknowledged by Urban Professionals as an Entrepreneur on the Move, and she looks forward to launching Uplifting Hands, a nonprofit initiative that will allow her to personally transform the homes of the less fortunate. Ragland attributes much of her success to strong family support, particularly that which has been rendered by her sister, Felicia.

In her spare time, Ragland enjoys the theater, trips to the spa, and spending time with family and friends. She is the proud mother of Tremayne and Brittany.

Cheryl Ragland
Owner
Exquisite Interior Design, Inc.

Jamarr Rawlinson & Monica Coleman

Co-Owners
Creative Connections
Mobile Barbershop

Jamarr Rawlinson and Monica Coleman are co-owners of Creative Connections Mobile Barbershop, a fully mobile barber and beauty service that brings the salon experience to facilities that provide residential or recreational accommodations to senior citizens and youth.

Established in 2006, Creative Connections has grown to form partnerships with Humana Healthcare, the mayor's Golden Age Clubs and the Clayton County Office of Senior Services. The company has been profiled by *The Atlanta Journal-Constitution*, *Black Enterprise*, *Sophisticate's Black Hair Styles and Care Guide* and WAOK AM. In addition, Creative Connections won the grand prize of $35,000 in the Miller Brewing Co. Urban Entrepreneurs Series National Business Plan Competition.

Rawlinson is a graduate of the Master Barber Program at Atlanta Technical College and enjoyed a successful career as a barber in traditional shops for eight years prior to starting the company. Coleman graduated, summa cum laude, from Hampton University and previously worked for the City of Atlanta, the Apollo Theater and the National Basketball Association in integrated marketing communications. The couple resides in Austell, Georgia.

Shiwana Reed

Principal Partner & Managing Broker
Allure Realty Group

Shiwana Reed is principal partner and managing broker of Allure Realty Group, Atlanta's premier luxury real estate firm. Shiwana has lead responsibility in planning, organizing, and directing the company's real estate operations. She departed from the Williams Academy of Real Estate as a distinguished graduate and began her career in 2001, quickly inheriting a reputation as a master negotiator and skilled professional.

Inducted as a lifetime member of the Million Dollar Club and awarded some of the industry's most prestigious designations, Shiwana values relationships and consistently brings to life "the Allure Experience," providing unsurpassed service to the world's top professionals and entertainers.

Shiwana is also co-owner and founding partner of S&G Property Management, LLC, which provides real estate management and portfolio services to investors around the world. A native of Warner Robins, Georgia, Shiwana now resides in North Atlanta and is the mother of two, Joshua and Haley.

Veteran broadcast journalist Angela Robinson is president and chief executive officer of ARC Media, LLC, a full-service media company. She is also host and executive producer of *IN CONTACT*, an award-winning news and public affairs talk show produced by the Atlanta Association of Black Journalists. Angela was the primary news anchor for the NBC affiliate in Atlanta, an anchor/reporter at WTTG FOX 5 in Washington, D.C., and an editor/reporter for the former CBS affiliate in Atlanta.

Angela has won multiple Emmy awards, National Association of Black Journalists and Atlanta Association of Black Journalists awards, the Telly Award, the Absolute Africa Award and RainbowPUSH Coalition's 2005 Journalist of the Year Award. Recognized as one of Atlanta's Top 100 Black Women of Influence, she was named a Pioneer Journalist by the Atlanta Association of Black Journalists. In addition, she is a member of the National Association of Black Journalists' Regional Hall of Fame.

Angela graduated from Syracuse University and was awarded the Chancellor's Citation for distinguished achievement in journalism. An Atlanta native, she holds membership and affiliation with several professional and community organizations.

Angela Robinson

President & Chief Executive Officer
ARC Media, LLC

Ronnie Robinson is founder and chief executive officer of BlackMercedesClub.com, a membership-supported online club specifically designed to uplift and support black businesses nationwide. The hub will be located in Atlanta.

An entrepreneur for more than 13 years, Robinson understands the need to help revitalize and support black businesses. His site has been recognized by the Columbus Black Chamber of Commerce for filling a void when it comes to providing knowledge about black businesses, professionals and resources. His vision is that black people all over America will commit to financially supporting black businesses and professionals, thereby lifting up the businessmen and women and redefining our communities.

Robinson is a native of Mississippi, having been born in Yazoo City but raised in Greenville, Mississippi. He is the husband of Donna Robinson and father of six children: three sons, Ronnie Jr., Lavor and Stephen; and three daughters, Demarra, Bryana and Kayla.

Ronnie Robinson

Founder & Chief Executive Officer
BlackMercedesClub.com

Earnestine Shuemake

Owner
OBA's Atlanta
E. Shuemake Stokes Decors

E arnestine Shuemake, a decorator, consultant and visual artist, uses her God-inspired ideas to be out-of-the-box in her craft. She has won awards for her unique style and credits her father, Ernest, and mother, Mary, for her passion, heart and creative wisdom.

Along with decorations for events, weddings and other gatherings, Earnestine creates decors for home and office. The owner of OBA's Atlanta and E. Shuemake Stokes Decors, creations have been featured in such publications as *Newsweek, Onyx Woman, Essence by Mail, Women's Wear Daily, The South Fulton Neighbor*, and *The Atlanta Journal- Constitution*.

Earnestine, founder of Camp Girlfriend, an organization for spiritually motivated sisters inspired the "Girls with Pearls" for Michelle Obama on Inaugural Day. She is a member of the Decorators Alliance of North America, Rakes and Hoes Gardening Club, SCLC, East Point Southern Zodiacs of the Red Hat Society, and the High Museum of Art. Additionally, she serves as a board member of the East Point Business and Industrial Development Authority.

She is happily married to Robert Wayne Stokes and has a young adult son, Oba, the parent company's namesake.

Jacqui Steele

Founder & President
Steele Program Managers, LLC.

J acqui Steele is founder and president of Steele Program Managers, LLC. in Stone Mountain, Georgia. She started the construction management firm in 2005 and is now managing more than $70 million in projects.

With more than 18 years of experience in the construction industry, Jacqui has worked on projects for MARTA, Spelman College, the Georgia Board of Regents, Hartsfield-Jackson Atlanta International Airport, the DeKalb County Board of Education and DeKalb County, among others. Having managed more than $1.2 billion of projects in her career, she has truly been part of Atlanta's growth over the years.

Jacqui has been a member of and serves in various community and professional organizations. She serves on the board of directors of the Construction Management Association of America (Atlanta) and volunteers her time as a business mentor.

With a passion for life and a drive to challenge herself beyond what others believe possible, Jacqui sets high standards for all that she does. A native of Atlanta, she has three children, Martez, Joseph and Amber. She is married to the love of her life, Larry.

Teague Stradford-Dow is president and designer of Teague Stradford Enterprises. Since 1994, the firm has manufactured custom-designed academic, choir, judicial and pulpit robes, as well as prom and wedding clothing.

As a designer, Teague has been recognized with feature stories in *The Atlanta Journal-Constitution* and *The Korea Times*, and designs shown in AirTran Airways' magazine. She has also been recognized in Revlon advertisement, *The New York Times* and *Women's Wear Daily* in New York.

Teague is also a professor and mentor at the American InterContinental University (AIU) and The Art Institute of Atlanta. Currently, her artistic works, including photographs of murals, other paintings and wall art, are frequently displayed in AIU Buckhead's gallery and New Orleans/French Quarters' home gallery. A *Women Looking Ahead* magazine honoree, Teague is a member of the Fashion Group International and is listed in several *Who's Who* publications.

Teague holds a Bachelor of Arts degree from Parson's School of Design and a Master of Arts degree from Goddard College, both in fashion design. She is the grandmother of Jhania, mother of Diane and wife of Danny Dow.

Teague Stradford-Dow
President & Designer
Teague Stradford Enterprises

Sonja Strayhand is an award-winning interior designer for residential and commercial design. President of Sonja Strayhand Interiors, she operates a full-service interior design firm that handles every aspect of a design project from concept to final installation. Utilizing her knowledge of interior design history, her years of experience, along with the client's personal style, Sonja showcases contemporary, transitional, eclectic and classic design concepts.

Her designs have gained her wide recognition. Sonja received the 2009 Georgia Minority Business Award, the Atlanta Business League's 2005 Outstanding Achievements in Creative Style, and the 2004 Best Interior Design Award at the Street of Dreams, a luxury homes tour. She was also listed as one of the *Atlanta Woman* magazine's Top 25 Power Women to Watch of 2006. The Atlanta College of Art graduate is one of the premier showcase designers for the exclusive Brian Jordan Le Jardin community of south Fulton.

Sonja stays abreast of industry trends through professional affiliations, including the American Society of Interior Designers and the International Interior Design Association. A native of Philadelphia, Pennsylvania, she is the proud mother of 7-year-old Ronald Jr.

Sonja Strayhand
President
Sonja Strayhand Interior Design, Inc.

Belinda C. Stubblefield

Owner
WineStyles Cascade

B elinda Stubblefield joined the entrepreneurial ranks in 2006, when she and her husband opened WineStyles Cascade, a neighborhood wine store offering wonderful wines from around the world at very affordable prices, as well as educational wine tastings twice weekly.

In 2007 Stubblefield became a joint venture partner with The Paradies Shops, Inc. The following year, the partnership was awarded the rights to operate 13 retail stores at Atlanta Hartsfield-Jackson International Airport, including *New York Times* Booksellers, Brighton and Brooks Brothers clothier.

Prior to her entrepreneurial endeavors, Stubblefield held leadership roles at Delta Air Lines, Inc., Nestlé, Procter & Gamble and IBM. Her career has spanned sales, marketing, strategic planning, customer service and global diversity. Stubblefield was the first African-American female officer of Delta Air Lines.

Stubblefield holds a bachelor's degree in mathematics/applied science from UCLA and an MBA from Harvard Business School. She serves on the boards of The Herndon Foundation, Consumer Credit Counseling Service of Greater Atlanta and *Women Looking Ahead*.

She is married to Ronald Frieson and has two wonderful stepchildren, Ron Jr. and Robin.

Ken R. Taunton

Managing Director
The Royster Group

K en Taunton is a managing director with The Royster Group, a premier executive search firm committed to diversity, seamless execution and excellent service. Previously, Taunton was a senior associate with Korn/Ferry International, specializing in the general and health care practices. He also worked for Merck & Company in various positions and received the distinguished Vice President's Award for Merck's strategic recruitment planning and diversity initiatives.

Taunton has been a member of several boards, ranging from the Georgia Minority Supplier Development Council to nonprofit organizations. He was quoted in *The Wall Street Journal* and featured in an *Atlanta Tribune: The Magazine* article, "Corporate Headhunter Finds the Perfect Fit for Top Executives."

Recently, the U.S. Small Business Administration honored Taunton in its Emerging 200 Initiative, which identified 200 businesses across the nation that demonstrated a high potential for growth. He was one of only 16 other business owners selected.

Taunton received a Master of Business Administration degree from the Eugene W. Stetson School of Business and Economics at Mercer University and a Bachelor of Science degree in marketing from The University of Alabama at Birmingham.

C.T. Taylor is a media innovator with a career that spans more than 42 years, beginning with his own teen show at WMBM radio while in high school in Miami, Florida. Taylor launched a career in television broadcasting at Miami's leading television station, WTVJ, where he was a pioneer in black television programming while hosting and producing the award-winning show *Black Is*. He was also acclaimed as a top local and CBS news network correspondent, covering the bloody Liberty City riots of the 1960s and 1970s, and various Caribbean stories.

After relocating to Atlanta, Georgia, in 1986, Taylor was offered the opportunity to perform in his first love: radio. Within two years, he was honored as Announcer of the Year at 1380 WAOK AM.

Taylor is executive producer of "Your Daily Dose," an informative one-minute health awareness segment that airs on local radio stations. Additionally, he serves as a board member for the American Red Cross and is a member of the South Fulton Chamber of Commerce, the East Point Business Association and Siloam Church International.

C.T. Taylor

Executive Producer
"Your Daily Dose"

Since 2006, Sheila Tenney has sat at the helm of The Media Savvy Group, Inc. The company specializes in media, event management, marketing communication strategies and documentary production.

Sheila received numerous awards in radio, television and film, and was a production assistant for School Daze Picture Company, where she made her big screen debut. She also hosted a television show, *Inside CAU*, and served as the promotions, marketing and membership director for Jazz 91.9 WCLK.

A committed community servant, Sheila holds memberships in several organizations, including The Junior League of Atlanta, the Atlanta Association of Black Journalists, Alpha Kappa Alpha Sorority, Inc., The Pierians, Inc., and the Clark Atlanta University (CAU) African American Alumni Association. She is also a former board member of the National Coalition of 100 Black Women – Metropolitan Atlanta Chapter. A member of the CAU Fundraising Guild, she assisted with raising $1 million to assist students in the arts. Furthermore, Sheila is a Coca-Cola Diversity Academy fellow.

She received a bachelor's degree in radio, television and film from Clark College, and a master's degree in international affairs/marketing from CAU.

Sheila Tenney

Chief Executive Officer
The Media Savvy Group, Inc.

Frankie Thompson

President & Chief Executive Officer
Frankie Thompson Enterprises, Inc.

Frankie Thompson Enterprises, Inc. was founded by Frankie Thompson in 1982. His emerging company has international contracts specifically in industrial supplies of pipes, pumps, valves, generators, HVAC systems and lighting systems.

His company is certified as an 8(a) minority-owned business with the U.S. Small Business Administration, the Georgia Department of Administrative Services and the Georgia Department of Transportation. It is also recognized for exports by the U.S. Department of Commerce.

Frankie is a 1974 graduate of Savannah State College with a degree in business administration, and a graduate of the Georgia Governor's Mentor Protégé Program. He is active in community affairs, which is showcased in his membership to the Georgia Utility Contractors Association, where he serves on the Legislative Committee and the Community Services Committee. Moreover, he is a member of Mount Vernon Baptist Church, where he served as vice chairman of the trustee board.

Ed Ukaonu

President & Chief Executive Officer
ViXio Technology, LLC

Ed Ukaonu is president and chief executive officer of ViXio Technology, LLC, an information technology (IT) firm that provides IT solutions to government agencies and businesses.

A consummate entrepreneur, Ed has invested 100 percent ownership in a WineStyles franchise. His passion for wine and ability to create relationship synergies between WineStyles and ViXio Technology resulted in great value for both companies. He recently bought the state of Georgia's master licensing rights from Global NES, Inc., the premier provider of renewable energy sources, and is now managing director of Global NES-GA, Inc.

Previously, Ed was a senior level executive at Siebel Systems, a customer relationship management system provider, and worked for PriceWaterhouseCoopers as a senior level manager. This wealth of experience has provided Ed access to many business models, relationships and an understanding of leveraging the knowledge and relationships to provide value for his clients.

Ed is a Gwinnett County Chamber of Commerce board member and president of the Embassy International Chamber of Commerce. Ed has an MBA from The State University of New York and is married with two children.

Lila Vaughn is a native of Chicago, Illinois. For the past 20 years, she has worked professionally as a certified nail technician and an educator of total body waxing.

In 1994 Lila married Paul Vaughn, a business executive, and moved to Atlanta, Georgia. She is the proud owner of Lila's Hands Spa, a nail spa that she has owned and operated for 11 years. Lila has served noted celebrities such as Hank Aaron, the late Johnnie Cochran, Sugar Ray Leonard, Robin Roberts, Reggie Miller, Grant Hill and Les Brown, among others. She currently serves Ambassador Andrew Young and Carolyn Young. Lila's nail spa has been featured in prominent publications, including *UPSCALE* Magazine and *The Atlanta Journal-Constitution*.

Lila is president of the Mecca Chapter of the National Coalition of 100 Black Women, Inc. She is former chaplain of Les Gemmes, Inc. and is currently treasurer for the women's usher board at her church.

Lila and her husband, Paul, reside in Atlanta. She lives with her personal motto: "I can do all things through Christ, who strengthens me."

Lila Vaughn

Owner
Lila's Hands Spa

Kevin L. Waller Sr., chief executive officer of Ubiquity Enterprises, LLC, has developed a national distribution network providing proprietary, innovative, first-to-market health and wellness products targeted to support specific body systems. In addition to his entrepreneurial endeavors, he serves as manager of the Administrative Service Team (Atlanta) for the Federal Highway Administration, supporting 28 states.

Kevin is a retired lieutenant colonel who served for 21 years as an Army finance officer. He is a member of Kappa Alpha Psi Fraternity, Inc., Rotary International, Toastmasters International and the Shiloh Baptist Church music ministry.

In 1982 Kevin received a Bachelor of Arts degree from Lincoln University (Missouri) and was recognized by *Who's Who Among Students in American Universities and Colleges*. In 1984 he earned a Master of Business Administration degree from The Ohio State University. In 2001 he was awarded a Master of Information Systems degree from Webster University. He was inducted into the Lincoln University Army ROTC Hall of Fame in 2006.

Born in Chicago, Kevin is the husband of Priscilla Waller and proud father of three children, Christina, Kevin Jr. and Chrystle.

Kevin L. Waller Sr.

Chief Executive Officer
Ubiquity Enterprises, LLC

Telain Ware

President & Chief Executive Officer
Marketing Consultants of Atlanta

Telain Ware is president and chief executive officer of Marketing Consultants of Atlanta, Inc., and has been providing marketing and public relations consulting services across many industries since 2000. Her professional background spans more than 20 years and includes positions with many leading corporations, such as AT&T, the former BellSouth Mobility, The Coca-Cola Company, 100 Black Men of America, Inc. and Multicast Media Technology's faith property, StreamingFaith.com.

Her community involvement includes the development of literacy and mentoring programs, tutoring at Bethune Elementary in Atlanta, managing voter registration drives and volunteering with Hosea Feed The Hungry and Homeless, the American Cancer Society and New Birth Missionary Baptist Church.

Ware earned a Bachelor of Arts degree from Bowling Green State University with a major in interpersonal and public communication and a minor in marketing and advertising. Additionally, she received a master's degree in human resource management and development from National-Louis University.

In addition to adjunct teaching, Ware conducts seminars on marketing and public relations strategies. She currently serves as a marketing and public relations consultant for 100 Black Men of Atlanta, Inc.

Everett Washington

Founder & Chief Executive Officer
PedigreeVisions
Executive Consulting Group

Everett Washington is founder and chief executive officer of the PedigreeVisions Executive Consulting Group. In this position, he has consulted senior executives and small business owners on corporate operations and customer relations management, along with facilitating roundtable sessions for the purpose of resolving executive level concerns. Some of Everett's clientele include several doctors and lawyers to Fortune 500 corporations such as Bellsouth, AT&T and Ford.

Everett is one of the founding executive board members of the Embassy International Chamber of Commerce. His promotion to performance manager at BellSouth was considered one of the fastest in company history before the merger with AT&T. He also served in the Army as a military intelligence analyst.

Everett received a Bachelor of Arts degree in business management and a Master of Business Administration degree from the University of Maryland. He was awarded a project management professional designation from Boston University.

A native of Jacksonville, Florida, Everett is married to Bridget and has two children, Danielle and Christian. He attends New Birth Cathedral in Lithonia, Georgia, and serves in several ministries, including the New Birth Knights motorcycle ministry.

Carolyn Wilbourn is owner and international designer of Wilbourn Sisters Designs, Inc. She creates "designs to soothe the soul" for ladies, men and children. Carolyn provides fashion show entertainment and modeling for elite profit and nonprofit organizations. She speaks publicly to young, eager minds on entrepreneurship and design, and she teaches modeling and etiquette workshops.

A member of the Atlanta Business League and Delta Sigma Theta Sorority, Inc., Carolyn supports the UNCF. She is the recipient of many awards for her gifts and talents. She has been in business with her sister, Janice, for 24 years. They are two of the seven designing women who learned their trade from their mother, Elizabeth.

The Wilbourn sisters' designs are featured at Macy's/Greenbriar Mall for special holidays throughout the year. Their merchandise is featured in boutiques in many cites throughout the United States and abroad.

Carolyn resides in Los Angeles, California, where she caters to the high-profile entertainment industry. She loves to travel and enjoys decorating homes, boutiques and galleries. She also enjoys set-designing for special events.

Carolyn Wilbourn

Owner, Stylist &
International Fashion Designer
Wilbourn Sisters Designs, Inc.

Janice Wilbourn-Woods is a witness for her personal Lord and savior, Jesus Christ. She was born and raised in Jackson, Tennessee. Her mother, Elizabeth, an entrepreneur herself, taught her seven daughters to sew, design and be independent women.

Janice has resided in Atlanta for 17 years, working in a successful business with her sister, Carolyn Wilbourn. She is owner, designer, seamstress, stylist and business manager for the Soul Soothing Exclusive Design Corporation, specializing in ladies designer fashions and accessories for all occasions, and producing fashion show entertainment.

Janice's professional affiliations include the Atlanta Business League, the UNCF and *Cambridge International Who's Who*. She lends guidance to the spiritual needs of the community, mentoring youth and students from Spread the Word Church of Atlanta, Bauder College, Clark Atlanta University and Georgia Southern University in the Fashion Design Intern Program and other private organizations.

Janice is the recipient of many awards for great accomplishments throughout her career. She is happily married to Erroll Woods.

Janice Wilbourn-Woods

Owner, Designer & Manager
Wilbourn Sisters Designs, Inc.

Elizabeth Wilson

Chief Executive Officer
EW & Associates, Inc.

Elizabeth Wilson is chief executive officer of EW & Associates, Inc. and senior director for the Association for Enterprise Opportunity, a national trade association for small- and micro-business training programs in the United States. She has provided professional leadership and training in the development of nonprofit services and management, including program design, project planning, development budgeting, staff recruitment, marketing and fundraising in her various positions.

Wilson developed the first micro-enterprise program for women in Atlanta, BusinessNOW, and was instrumental in founding and organizing the Georgia Micro Enterprise Network. Through these and other endeavors, she has assisted hundreds of low- and moderate-income individuals throughout Atlanta in developing small businesses and reaching self-sufficiency.

Wilson has written several books, including *When Life Gives You Lemons, Open a Lemonade Stand.* She continues to be actively involved in the community and beyond by making presentations to community organizations, coalitions, churches and associations, and providing consulting services to several women's international economic development organizations.

She is married to IBM systems analyst C.W. Wilson.

Joseph L. Wilson

Chief Executive Officer
J.L. Wilson Bookkeeping &
Tax Service

Joseph L. Wilson is chief executive officer of J.L. Wilson Bookkeeping and Tax Service. In addition to managing the day-to-day operations of the company, his professional license permits him to represent clients before the Internal Revenue Service.

Previously, Wilson worked with Westinghouse Credit Corporation, a Fortune 100 company based in Pittsburgh, Pennsylvania. He served Westinghouse in six different professional commercial financial positions.

His community service achievements include coaching and winning an Olympic-style youth basketball league tournament in 1995. In addition, he is a member of Cascade United Methodist Church.

After self-publishing his first book in the health and fitness field, Wilson is seeking the services of a major publisher for his next. His two children, Kevin and Tiffany, continue looking forward to expanding his tracks.

Yvonne J. Wiltz is president and chief executive officer of VonCreations, Inc., a full-service event management and marketing company that offers services for meetings, conferences and special events. Founded in 1989, VonCreations, Inc. has an impressive list of past and current clients that includes The Home Depot, Cubic Transportation Systems, MARTA, the Hammonds House Museum, the U.S. Department of Labor, the Women's Bureau and the Gate City Bar Association, to name a few.

VonCreations prides itself in offering creative and innovative approaches to events and meetings. Attention to detail, professionalism and outstanding company service is the VonCreations motto, and the creation of themed events, complete with staging and room décor, provides a "wow" factor to attendees.

The recipient of numerous performance awards, Yvonne has also served as president of the Metropolitan Atlanta Chapter of the National Coalition of 100 Black Women, Inc. and as 1st and 2nd vice president of the National Coalition of 100 Black Women, Inc.

Yvonne J. Wiltz

President & Chief Executive Officer
VonCreations, Inc.

After developing a strong interest in the printing industry while in high school, Jeanette Khalilah Zakkee founded Zakkee and Associates. Her 30 years of experience enhances her ability to fulfill the needs of businesses in the private and public sectors.

Named among the 100 Most Influential and Powerful Women in Georgia by *Women Looking Ahead*, Jeanette was also named Businesswoman of the Year by the Concerned Black Clergy (CBC). She received the President's and Service awards from the National Coalition of 100 Black Women (NCBM) – MECCA Chapter and has been featured in *rolling out*, *Atlanta Daily World*, *Crossroads*, *Booking Matters* and *Who's Who In Black Atlanta®*. The Trumpet Foundation presented her with a High Heels in High Places Award during the Trumpet Awards weekend.

Jeanette is a member of the Atlanta Business League, the Georgia Chamber of Commerce, the NCBM – MECCA Chapter and the CBC. She holds board positions with the Atlanta Business League Foundation, YES, Inc. and Human Rediscovery.

A California native, Jeanette is married to Daleel and has two daughters, Angelina and Daaimah, and five grandchildren.

Jeanette Khalilah Zakkee

Founder & President
Zakkee and Associates

Atlanta's
CORPORATE BRASS

PROFICIENT

EXCEL

OUTSHINE

SURPASS

TRANSCEND

ENHANCE

SURMOUNT

MASTER

TRIUMPH

Caleb Adebiyi

Senior Vice President &
Market Manager
Premier Banking & Investments
Bank of America

Nikki Barjon

Chief Operating Officer &
Vice President
The R Agency

Caleb Adebiyi is senior vice president and market manager for Premier Banking & Investments, a Wealth Management Division of Bank of America in Atlanta, with his office based in Alpharetta. In this capacity, he manages teams of professional advisors dedicated to providing tailored financial solutions to select affluent clients. His territory extends to points northeast of Atlanta, including Athens and Augusta.

Caleb was named winner of Bank of America's Customer Experience Leadership Award. He was a member of the Southeast Executive Council for Premier Banking & Investments for 2006. In 2007 he was elected as a board member of the Bank of America Gasparilla Distance Classic in Tampa, Florida. In 2005 Caleb was the recipient of the Bank of America Spirit Award of Excellence. He was also the recipient of the Bank of America Partnership for Growth Partner Award in 2005.

Passionate about running, Caleb and his wife, Fereshteh, recently completed their 11th marathon in Rome, Italy.

Nikki Barjon is chief operating officer and vice president of a leading branding and public relations firm, The R Agency, known for its reputation of high-profile clients in business, entertainment and sports. She currently spearheads the daily operations of the agency alongside Michael Roberts, who operates one of the largest privately held companies in St. Louis with 2007 revenues of $980 million. She has a stellar reputation and track record for shaping some of the largest brands in the world, including Lifetime Television, BET, former Olympian Marion Jones and television syndicate, Kingworld.

Long considered one of the most powerful women in branding and publicity, Nikki is credited with driving some of the most dominant brands in sports and entertainment, including Atlanta Braves all-star Brian Jordan, top-rated syndicated radio host Warren Ballentine, NFL star Ray Buchanan, legendary comedian John Witherspoon, and corporate clients such as Ford Motors, Crowne Plaza, Metro Sports and Winsonic.

Nikki was educated at the University of Pennsylvania and Temple University, where she received a bachelor's degree in psychology and a full scholarship as captain of the women's track team.

Charles E. Bell

Budget Management Chief
Hartsfield-Jackson Atlanta
International Airport

Luther Bellinger

Sales Manager
Silestone of Atlanta

Charles Bell is budget management chief of Hartsfield-Jackson Atlanta International Airport. He is responsible for overseeing the development of the budget for the City of Atlanta Department of Aviation. He and his staff, the Office of Management & Budget, monitor the department's budget and are responsible for airport management and performance analysis.

Bell is active in the community. He has served the past nine years on the board of directors for the Atlanta City Employees Credit Union and is chair of its Supervisory Committee. Additionally, he is a devoted member of the Atlanta Alumni Chapter of Kappa Alpha Psi Fraternity, Inc. Bell's fraternal contributions include being a past chapter president, treasurer and secretary. Additionally, he serves as chair of the chapter's youth mentoring program and the fraternity's regional (Georgia and South Carolina) treasurer.

Bell holds a Bachelor of Arts degree from Morehouse College and a Master of Business Administration degree from Atlanta University. As a budget manager, he loves to say, "If you have no one to count the beans, you'll soon have no beans to count."

Luther Bellinger is the sales manager at Silestone of Atlanta, the region's leading innovator in stone surfaces. Having been in the kitchen and bath business for more than 15 years, the chances are great that the countertop you are using came out of his facility.

From granite to limestone, plastic products to green surfaces, Luther is recognized in the industry as an expert consultant on residential and commercial surfaces. As such, he has the distinct pleasure of working with Metro Atlanta's premier designers and architects to determine the most beneficial surface options to meet their clients' needs.

With a career background in customer service, and the mindset that every home and business needs a countertop and a committed professional to serve them, Luther has cultivated a growing client list that includes Hartsfield-Jackson International Airport, Cartier, D.R. Horton and Philips Arena, to name a few.

Luther is a member of the American Society of Interior Designers, the National Kitchen and Bath Association, the National Association of The Remodeling Industry and The Luxury Marketing Council.

Lori George Billingsley

Director, Community &
Multicultural Communications
Coca-Cola North America

Delroy Bowen

Executive Chef
Proof of the Pudding
Georgia International Convention Center

Lori George Billingsley is director of community and multicultural communications for Coca-Cola North America (CCNA). In her position, she manages public and media relations for all community outreach, multicultural marketing and diversity as business for the company's North America operating unit. Lori has been with The Coca-Cola Company (TCCC) for seven years in a variety of positions, including director of regional communications for CCNA, director of issues communications and director of shareowner affairs for TCCC.

Her career, spanning more than 23 years, includes owning a public relations consultancy, serving as a vice president for a leading public relations firm and working for the District of Columbia government. Lori has taught communications courses at three colleges and universities, including her undergraduate alma mater, Howard University. She received a Master of Arts degree from American University and is currently seeking a Master of Divinity degree from Gordon Conwell Theological Seminary. Lori is a married, ordained minister and published writer.

Delroy Bowen is the executive chef of the Georgia International Convention Center (GICC), and a two-year employee of the Southeast's largest catering company, Proof of the Pudding. In this position he manages the culinary staff, creates menus, refines recipes and completes all purchasing for events at the GICC, some as large as 20,000 people.

Delroy began his career in the country's culinary capital, New York City. He became one of the city's most applauded chefs, first as chef at Robert De Niro's Tribeca Grill, then moving on to open 2Seven7, rated one of New York's very best restaurants.

Delroy is a culinary graduate and nominated alumnus of the year at The French Culinary Institute in New York City. He has been favorably reviewed in *The New York Times*, the *New York Post, Zagat New York City Restaurants, Paper Magazine, Time Out New York*, the *Naples Daily News, The Atlanta Journal-Constitution* and the *Southeast National Restaurant Association Magazine*.

A native of Jamaica, Delroy now resides in Atlanta with his wife, who is also a chef, and their two sons.

Larry A. Bowman

Senior Director
Stadium Operations & Security
Atlanta Braves

D. Jean Brannan

President & Chief Operating Officer
Sickle Cell Foundation of Georgia, Inc.

Larry A. Bowman is senior director of stadium operations and security for the Atlanta Braves. In this position he oversees multimillion-dollar games, ballpark expenses and parking budgets, supervision of employees and major contractors, major game and service-related contracts, site and player security, game operations, logistics, life safety and support services, crisis communication, and management and implementation of MLB policies and procedures.

Prior to the Braves, Larry served as operations manager at the Greensboro Coliseum, where he oversaw critical portions of the facility's renovation and expansion. He also worked in the Office of the City Manager where he developed and managed the City of Greensboro's Minority and Women Business Enterprise Program.

Larry received a bachelor's degree, magna cum laude, from North Carolina A&T State University in political science. As a CIC fellow, he matriculated through the political science/public policy doctorate program of The Ohio State University.

Born in the Bronx, Larry has served on several professional and/or civic boards and commissions. His interests include Bible study fellowship, physical fitness and creative writing. Larry and his wife, Claudia, reside in Alpharetta.

D. Jean Brannan is president and chief operating officer of the Sickle Cell Foundation of Georgia, Inc. In this position, she manages the daily activities of the foundation throughout the state of Georgia.

Jean is an active member of the community, serving as a member of the Atlanta Newborn Screening Advisory Council, the advisory board of the American Red Cross and the Atlanta Public Schools Adult Education Advisory Committee. Additionally, she is an active member of St. Anthony Catholic Church.

Jean has received numerous honors and awards, including the Atlanta Medical Association's Pillar of Strength Award and the National Coalition of 100 Black Women's Unsung Heroine Award. To her credit, she also received one of the Intergenerational Resource Center's 2005 Portraits of Sweet Success.

She received a Bachelor of Arts degree in business administration from Morris Brown College. A native of Miami, Florida, Jean is the wife of Solomon Brannan, the mother of two sons and one daughter, and the grandmother of two.

Moses Brown Jr.

Vice President
Reed Elsevier Inc.
LexisNexis

Wendell H. Brown

Senior Electrical Engineering Inspector
MHR International

Moses Brown Jr. is vice president and director of supplier diversity for Reed Elsevier's global procurement organization. Prior to joining Reed Elsevier Inc., he served as an executive with ChoicePoint Inc., a recent acquisition of LexisNexis, a Reed Elsevier Company.

Brown earned a degree in business administration from Morehouse College and is a graduate of Leadership Atlanta. He serves on the boards of directors for Zoo Atlanta, Excel Federal Credit Union, the Atlanta Sports Council, the North Fulton CID, the Windward Business Association and the Greater North Fulton Chamber of Commerce. In addition, he serves on the boards of advisors for the Metro Atlanta Chamber of Commerce and the Center for Puppetry Arts.

Brown is a mentor with the Morehouse College Executive Mentoring Program and a member of 100 Black Men of America, Inc. A two-time recipient of the Equifax W. Lee Burge Community Service Award, he served as a venue technology manager at the Georgia Dome during the 1996 Olympics.

A resident of Alpharetta, Brown is the proud father of a daughter, Maranie, and son, Harrison.

Wendell Brown serves as senior electrical engineering inspector for MHR International, the primary team for the Hartsfield-Jackson Atlanta International Airport Development Program (CONRAC) project.

Previously, Brown spent three years with the Delon Hampton project management team for the City of Atlanta Combined Sewer Overflow, and 20 years with MARTA as a chief inspector and quality assurance engineer. He received Occupational Safety & Health Administration safety certification from the Georgia Institute of Technology and construction management certification from the University of Wisconsin.

Brown returned from the U.S. Navy in 1974. He later entered the International Brotherhood of Electrical Workers and earned a journeyman's electrical license, and a master electrical license with the State of Georgia.

A member of 100 Black Men of Atlanta, Brown received both Man of the Year and the Outstanding Community Service Award. He also received the Outstanding Georgia Citizen Award from the secretary of state. He and his wife, Scarlet, were featured in *Atlanta Tribune: The Magazine* as one of Atlanta's Power Couples. The couple also received the Atlanta Urban League's Excellence in Transportation and Leadership Award.

Katherine Bryant

Vice President of Consumer Advocacy
LexisNexis

Lori Burden

Senior Sales Manager
The Ritz-Carlton Hotels

Katherine Bryant is the vice president of consumer advocacy for LexisNexis. There, Katherine is responsible for the company's consumer outreach, affected consumer and consumer advocacy functions. Previously, she served as assistant vice president and general counsel with ChoicePoint Inc.

Katherine currently provides leadership related to consumer outreach, consumer advocacy and consumer policy. In this capacity, she must build and maintain relationships with consumer advocates to create awareness of LexisNexis consumer policies and practices, lead the operations teams that are responsible for assisting affected and curious consumers and develop and evaluate policies regarding curious and affected customers.

Before LexisNexis, Katherine was an associate with Morris, Manning and Martin, LLP in Atlanta and Rothgerber Johnson & Lyons LLP in Denver. Her practice consisted of mergers and acquisitions, employment law and general corporate matters.

Katherine is a former board member of the National Association of Professional Background Screeners. She graduated from Boston University with a Bachelor of Arts degree in history and has a Doctor of Jurisprudence degree from the University of Denver. Currently, Katherine lives in Atlanta, Georgia.

Lori Burden is a senior sales manager concentrating on corporate and association business in the Midwestern and mid-Atlantic markets for The Ritz-Carlton, Atlanta (Downtown) and The Ritz-Carlton, Buckhead. She began her career with Marriott International in 1994 and joined The Ritz-Carlton in 1998.

A recipient of The Ritz-Carlton Golden Circle and President's awards, Lori received a Women of Business Achievement Award from the Trumpet Awards Foundation in 2006. In addition, she holds a degree in business administration from Georgia State University.

Actively involved with the PTA, Lori enjoys reading, traveling and spending time with her family. She is married to Preston and has two sons, Reese and Dean.

Reginald Carson

Lead Public Health Analyst
Centers for Disease
Control and Prevention

Charmaine Caruth

Land Analyst
Georgia Power Company

Reginald Carson is a lead public health analyst for the Centers for Disease Control and Prevention (CDC), working for the National Center for HIV/AIDS, Viral Hepatitis, STD, and TB Prevention in the Office of the Director, with the centers' $2 billion grant and cooperative agreement funding opportunities initiative. He assists with the development and implementation of public health strategies through non-research proposals and funding opportunities to achieve the goals of global HIV, and domestically with HIV, STDs, tuberculosis and viral hepatitis.

Reginald has been an employee with CDC since 1992, and has received several promotions and outstanding yearly evaluations/awards for his work with public health projects. He is a life member of Omega Psi Phi, Fraternity, Inc., Big Brothers Big Sisters of America and the National Urban League. He is also a charter member of both Atlanta's Highland Cigar Co. and the Buckhead Cigar clubs.

Reginald received a Bachelor of Science degree from Elizabeth City State University. The husband of Simone Silva-Carson, he is the proud father of one daughter, Phoenix.

Charmaine Caruth is a land analyst for the Land Department at the Georgia Power Company in Atlanta. She is responsible for estimating land costs, managing the banking system and a host of other related tasks.

Charmaine is also the fundraising chair for the American Association of Blacks in Energy. She is scheduled to chair the first Sweet Auburn Golf Tournament being held in Atlanta this spring.

During her spare time, she focuses her creative skills towards her blue jean company for women, S.P.R.E.A.D Jeans (Simply, Perfect, Representing, Every-Woman's, Amazing, Dimension). Charmaine is the co-owner of Spread Jeans along with her business partner, Sam Norris.

In 2008 Charmaine was featured as Solo Woman of the Month for her creative force in her business. She has also been featured on Power Talk FM Radio with Michael Ray. Charmaine received a Bachelor of Arts degree in criminal justice from Saint Leo University. Her hobbies include traveling and reading.

Janice Clark

Director of Purchasing
The Ritz-Carlton, Buckhead

Tanya M. Coleman

Marketing Advertising Manager
Publix Super Markets, Inc.

As purchasing director for The Ritz-Carlton, Buckhead, Janice Clark manages the highly logistical process of securing resources and monitoring compliance with purchasing standards while controlling acquisition costs for the 517-room hotel.

She is the corporate environmental conservation leader for the hotel and holds certifications in customer service excellence and total quality management programs, as well as Steven Covey's Principles of Leadership. Janice is proud of her work to increase spending with minority companies through a program created by The Ritz-Carlton Hotel Company, L.L.C. This is especially significant to her since her late mother, Jimmie Garnes, was active in the civil rights movement.

During her 23-year tenure with The Ritz-Carlton, Buckhead, Janice has received numerous accolades, including 2002 Leader of the Year. She consistently volunteers for the hotel's Community Footprints Program, AIDS Walk of Atlanta, Hospice Care and the Atlanta Community Food Bank.

A native of Hazlehurst, Georgia, Janice is a positive and empowering role model. She credits her mother with teaching her to how to survive, not only in business, but also in life.

Tanya M. Coleman, the marketing advertising manager for Publix Super Markets, Inc., oversees the creative development of advertising for billboards, radio, newspaper, direct mail pieces and in-store point-of-purchase materials for Atlanta division stores. An integral part of her work includes positioning retail operations to align community and marketing sponsorships with the overall Publix brand and mission, thus maximizing advertising strategies for more than 178 stores in Georgia, Alabama, South Carolina and Tennessee.

Tanya is a member of Friendship Baptist Church, the Atlanta Junior League, the Inquirers Literary Club and the Dogwood City Chapter of The Links, Inc., where she is vice president. An advocate for the arts and adult literacy programs, she serves on the board of directors for the Atlanta College of Art and as co-chair of the Spelman College Museum Advisory Committee.

Tanya received a Bachelor of Arts degree from Spelman College, and she is a member of Delta Sigma Theta Sorority, Inc.

Tanya was born in Atlanta and she has one daughter, Kafi Bethea, and two granddaughters, Ariana and Kyla.

Shan Carr Cooper

Senior Manager
Diversity Workforce Management
Lockheed Martin Corporation

Keith L. Durden

Manager
Network Customer Service Centers
AT&T

Shan Cooper joined the Lockheed Martin Corporation in 2002 as senior manager of diversity workforce management. She developed a comprehensive, corporatewide diversity and EOP strategy, resulting in major initiatives and policies that enhanced Lockheed Martin's core business units worldwide.

Cooper joined the Lockheed Martin Aeronautics Company as vice president and deputy of human resources, having responsibility for human resource operations across the company. Previously, she held leadership roles at Fortune 500 companies, most recently at Lucent Technologies. She also consulted at BellSouth, The Southern Company and Georgia-Pacific.

Cooper received the 2006 Women of Color in Technology Corporate Responsibility Award and a 2007 YWCA Tribute to Women of Achievement nomination. She sits on the board of Girls Inc. and is executive advisor to the National Management Association chapter in Marietta. Cooper is a member of the Society for Human Resource Management and the Lockheed Martin Leadership Association. She is vice chair of the YWCA of Northwest Georgia board of directors.

Cooper received a Master of Business Administration degree from the Emory University Goizueta Business School. She and husband Eddie reside in Brookhaven, Georgia.

Keith Durden is manager of network customer service centers for AT&T. He is a 27-year veteran of the company. Additionally, Keith is membership director of the Community Network of AT&T – Atlanta Chapter, and is southeast regional director-elect. The Community Network is AT&T's African-American employee resource group and has chapters in 22 states.

A native of Birmingham, Alabama, Keith received an associate degree from Booker T. Washington Business College. He later became an entrepreneur and owns Keith Travel Store. He has written fundraising proposals for The Stewart Foundation and UNCF that illustrate how $50,000 and $250,000, respectively, could be raised for their initiatives.

Keith volunteers annually for the Mayor's Masked Ball, UNCF's biggest fundraiser, and has also volunteered for the Atlanta Community Food Bank. He serves as the local volunteer coordinator of the Tavis Smiley Group and sits on the board of The Stewart Foundation. Keith is also establishing a Metro Atlanta chapter of C.W. Hayes High School of Birmingham, Alabama. More than 50 former Pacesetters have been located in the metro area.

Nedra Farrar-Luten

Director, Human Resources &
Organizational Development
Hartsfield-Jackson Atlanta
International Airport

Morgan A. Garriss

Programs & Communications
South Fulton Chamber of Commerce

Nedra Farrar-Luten is director of human resources and organizational development at Hartsfield-Jackson Atlanta International Airport. An expert at airport and public personnel management, she spent 14 years with the Raleigh-Durham Airport Authority in North Carolina. She recently chaired the Airport Minority Advisory Council, where she advocated the inclusion of minorities and women in airport contracting and employment opportunities.

Nedra regularly met with members of Congress and officials with the Federal Aviation Administration to ensure that the disadvantaged business enterprises regulation is strengthened and its associated policies are fair. She served on Governor Sonny Perdue's Task Force for a New Georgia, creating a leadership development model for state employees. She was named one of the 100 Most Influential Women in Government by *Women Looking Ahead* magazine.

Nedra has a communications degree from North Carolina State University and obtained certification in public personnel administration from The University of North Carolina Institute of Government. She is certified as a human resource professional by the International Public Management Association for Human Resources. The Brooklyn native is the proud mother of two sons, Christian and Thomas David.

Morgan A. Garriss is a public relations professional in the Metro Atlanta area. In addition to freelance writing and public relations, Morgan is head of programs and communications for the South Fulton Chamber of Commerce (SFCOC). She reports directly to the chief executive officer and serves as liaison between the SFCOC, its board of directors, its members and the local media, promoting the mission of the organization. She also manages the administrative responsibilities of the office, coordinates special events and interfaces with county and state officials.

A graduate of Hampton University in Virginia, Morgan was awarded an academic scholarship from the National Association of Black Journalists and the Hampton Roads Black Media Professionals. While in Virginia, Morgan was an active volunteer and a mentor to at-risk youth. Recently, Morgan received the 2008 Georgia Association of Chamber of Commerce Executives Annual Conference Scholarship in Jekyll Island.

Morgan is a native of Oakland, California, but has been a Metro Atlanta resident most of her life. She is a proud member of Saint Philip A.M.E Church in East Atlanta and an active community volunteer.

Ronnie Glover

Sales Manager
Swank Audio Visuals

Wayne Glover

Director, Commercial Marketing
GreyStone Power Corporation

Ronnie Glover is a sales manager for Swank Audio Visuals, a contract audio visual firm with the Hyatt Regency Atlanta. He has served in this role for three years. During the past ten years, he has advanced from technician to assistant director. Prior to his work experience at Swank, Ronnie was employed with Presentation Services, another Hyatt Regency Atlanta contractor.

Complementing his growth has been a driving passion to help those within the community, churches and organizations, such as the Atlanta Business League, 100 Black Women, 100 Black Men, RainbowPUSH, the SCLC, Concerned Black Clergy and various other nonprofit groups. Ronnie has a deep desire to plan and hold successful events and meetings at the Hyatt Regency Atlanta, setting a trend for affordable events. He is thankful to God for allowing him to be a vessel of hope and understanding, as well as to assist organizations with presenting their messages to the Metro Atlanta area.

Ronnie holds an associate degree in business management from Monroe Community College in The Bronx, New York. He has four children, Sheniequa, Qiyamah, Yasmeen and Qiydar.

A graduate of the Georgia Institute of Technology, with a Bachelor of Science degree in electrical engineering, Wayne Glover directs industrial and commercial GreyStone members in energy conservation and power quality enhancement. He credits his success to his firm belief in the three E's: excellence, always do it to the best of your abilities; enthusiasm, do not moan and groan; and ethics, always be truthful and honest.

A native of Warner Robins, Georgia, Glover attends Simpson Street Church of Christ. He has served as past president of the PTC at Southwest Atlanta Christian Academy, the August Jaycees and the Atlanta Chapter of the American Association of Blacks in Energy. Glover served as a board member of the Butler Street YMCA (Northwest Branch) and on the board of directors of the Upward Bound Program at Paine College, the South Fulton Chamber of Commerce and 100 Black Men of DeKalb, Inc.

Glover and his wife, Bridgette, live in Cobb. They have two children, Zachary, 14, and Kathryn Jacobie, 11.

Todd Gray

Assistant Vice President &
Associate Business Manager
Corporate Supplier Diversity
Wachovia

Barbara Greene

Director of Housekeeping
The Ritz-Carlton, Buckhead

Todd Gray is responsible for the implementation of processes, procedures and tools that support enterprise-wide supplier diversity initiatives. He promotes and encourages the success and inclusion of minority- and women-owned business enterprises as they seek supplier partnership opportunities with Wachovia.

Gray represents Wachovia as a mentor through the Georgia Governor's Mentor Protégé Program for small businesses. He also supports youth minority entrepreneurship through his partnership with the Greater Atlanta Economic Alliance Construction Skills Development Institute. He serves on the South Regions Minority Supplier Development Council board of directors, and is a member of the Anneewakee Trails Homeowners Association, the Atlanta MABL Men's Baseball League, the Atlanta Urban League and Berean Church board. Additionally, Gray is founder and director of P.O.L.I.S.H.E.D. Mentoring Program for young men ages 13 to 18.

Gray was recognized in the *Atlanta Business Chronicle*'s diversity profile as one of Atlanta's Top 50 Rising Stars and featured in the *Business Leaders in Atlanta* publication.

He earned a bachelor's degree in network and communications management and a Master of Business Administration degree in finance and marketing from DeVry University.

Barbara Greene manages one of the largest departments at the hotel, with 65 ladies and gentlemen under her leadership, preparing 517 guestrooms and suites every day, in addition to keeping the hotel's public spaces squeaky clean. With polished wood paneled walls, custom furnishings, fine fabrics and literally tons of marble and granite throughout the hotel, housekeeping at The Ritz-Carlton, Buckhead is a role of finesse as much as it is deep cleaning.

A 25-year veteran of The Ritz-Carlton, Barbara was director of housekeeping at The Ritz-Carlton, Atlanta (Downtown) prior to her appointment to The Ritz-Carlton, Buckhead. She holds certifications in various programs, including crisis management and talent plus.

Barbara is a generous volunteer for many community service activities, including The Ritz-Carlton Community Footprints Program, the Atlanta Community Food Bank and AIDS Walk.

An Atlanta native, she is married to Alvin Cotson and is the proud mother of two sons, Josephious and Jarivas, and a daughter, Tarlisha. Barbara fondly recalls her days at East Atlanta High School, where she participated in numerous fashion shows and won an award for Best Dressed.

Carmalitha L. Gumbs

Marketing Support Sales Specialist
Humana MarketPOINT
Humana Inc.

Vicki Hamilton

Senior Vice President of
Enterprise Performance
Turner Broadcasting System, Inc.

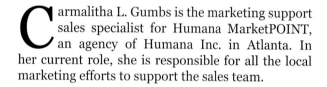

Carmalitha L. Gumbs is the marketing support sales specialist for Humana MarketPOINT, an agency of Humana Inc. in Atlanta. In her current role, she is responsible for all the local marketing efforts to support the sales team.

Carmalitha graduated, magna cum laude, from Norfolk State University in Norfolk, Virginia, with a Bachelor of Science degree in social work. Additionally, she received a Master of Business Administration degree from Strayer University in Glen Allen, Virginia.

A Virginia native, Carmalitha is very much a community advocate and has made her mark here in Atlanta in a short time. She is an active member of Alpha Kappa Alpha Sorority, Inc. (Tau Epsilon Omega Chapter), the National Black MBA Association, the Atlanta Urban League Young Professionals and the American Marketing Association. In her spare time, she enjoys reading, shopping, meeting new people and event planning.

A member of Fellowship of Love Church in Fayetteville, Carmalitha serves on the community relations, children and youth ministries. She is the proud mother of a beautiful daughter, Kerrington. They reside in Atlanta.

Vicki Hamilton is senior vice president of enterprise performance in the Strategy and Operations Group at Turner Broadcasting System, Inc. She is responsible for ensuring that infrastructure and processes are in place to support the company's business activity on emerging consumer platforms.

Previously, Hamilton served as chief operating officer for Cinema Screen Media, overseeing sales, business and IT operations. Earlier, she worked at The Weather Channel in operations, technology and general management roles.

Hamilton is active in the National Association for Multi-Ethnicity in Communications, GlobalEXECWomen, Synchronicity, Women in Technology, Women in Cable Telecommunications and the Society of Cable Telecommunications Engineers. She is a Betsy Magness Leadership Institute fellow and a volunteer mentor in programs sponsored by 100 Black Men of North Metro, Inc.

Hamilton earned a Bachelor of Science degree in business administration from the University of Dayton and a Master of Business Administration degree from Saint Louis University.

Preston L. Harden

Services Executive
Communications Sector
Microsoft Corporation

Moses A. Hardie Jr.

Senior Director, Human Resources
Insurance Services
LexisNexis

Preston L. Harden serves as services executive of the Communications Sector for Microsoft Corporation. In this position, he is responsible for cultivating, executing and managing Microsoft Dynamics opportunities. He is responsible for major strategic national and international accounts, including Cox Communications, Showtime, Omnicom, Comcast and McGraw-Hill.

Preston has a passion for enabling youth, and as a result, was instrumental in establishing Blacks at Microsoft Minority Student Day for the Atlanta-based location. The goal of the event is to provide area minority high school students with information about the exciting tools, resources and career opportunities available. Throughout the day, Microsoft employees guide students through hands-on technology labs and information sessions. In addition, Preston also finds time to participate with local career day programs evangelizing the passion for technology and education.

Preston received a Bachelor of Business Management degree with a concentration in human resource from Clayton State University, with such affiliations as Toastmasters International, PMI and Big Brothers of America. A native of Atlanta, he is the proud son of Charles Harden and the late beloved Sarah F. Harden.

Moses A. Hardie Jr. serves as senior director of human resources in the insurance division for LexisNexis in Alpharetta, Georgia. Previously, he served as chief people officer, where he was responsible for all strategic, advisory and operational human resources services for the company's flagship operation. There are locations in Alpharetta, Georgia; Hartford, Connecticut; Orem, Utah; Dallas, Texas; San Ramon, California; and Chicago, Illinois.

Prior to his appointment at LexisNexis, Moses was assistant vice president of human resources shared services for Allstate Insurance Company in Northbrook, Illinois. A member of Kappa Alpha Psi Fraternity, Inc., he has served on the board of directors for the Hampton University School of Business, as well as several charitable organizations.

Moses received an undergraduate degree from Hampton University and a Master of Business Administration degree from the University of Illinois at Chicago.

Moses and his wife, Joanne, have two adult children.

Sandra Harris

Director, Account Management
Humana Inc.

Phillip Head

Garde Manger Chef
The Ritz-Carlton, Buckhead

Sandra Harris serves as director of account management for Humana Inc. She works in Humana's Atlanta/Dunwoody office and is responsible for managing a portfolio of major clients. She is responsible for the overall profitability and growth of the portfolio throughout the state of Georgia. Her current portfolio includes approximately 80 accounts that generate more than $80 million in annual premiums.

Harris has been in the health care industry for 15 years, and joined the Humana family in July of 2000 as a senior account executive. She steadily worked her way up the ranks and has served as director of account management for the past five years.

Harris earned a Bachelor of Science degree in business administration from Paine College in Augusta, Georgia; a Master of Business Administration degree from the University of Kentucky; and a Master of Health Services Administration degree from Barry University in Miami, Florida. She is also a member of Delta Sigma Theta Sorority, Inc.

Harris and her husband, Vernon, reside in Buford, Georgia. They enjoy spending quality time with family and traveling to tropical destinations.

Phillip Head is garde manger chef at The Ritz-Carlton, Buckhead, responsible for supervising the preparation of salads, cold entrees and more for The Café, as well as wedding receptions, social galas, parties and banquets. His salad dressings are so popular that guests of the hotel frequently request to take some home with them!

A 23-year veteran of The Ritz-Carlton, Phillip believes in mentoring the ladies and gentlemen working with him, encouraging them to reach for greatness and take the initiative to constantly improve and grow.

He began cooking alongside his grandmother, Idea Mae Head, at the age of 6. She passed along her mother's recipes to Phillip and he has given his children, LaShannon, Jamie and Cedric, the same gift, spending time in the kitchen together and learning about family traditions.

An Atlanta native, Phillip is a true family man. He is happiest in his role as a father and enjoys the simple things, such as teaching his children how to drive.

James Hutchinson

Vice President of Marketing
Georgia Lottery Corporation

Mychal Jackson

Solution Sales Professional
Microsoft Corporation

As vice president of marketing, James Hutchinson stewards the Georgia Lottery Corporation brand, creating innovative advertising and marketing programs that engage players and non-players. He is responsible for the marketing launches of more than ten new products per year while maintaining the brand and marketing communications for dozens of existing products.

James was recently named Marketer of the Year by the American Marketing Association. Last year, under his leadership, the Georgia Lottery produced three exclusive television shows for primetime viewing and launched a multilevel, 12-month 25th anniversary celebration.

As a member of the executive team for the Georgia Lottery, James plays an integral role in product development and the long-term strategic direction of the business. He has also served in senior management marketing positions with Walt Disney World and The Athlete's Foot. Prior to joining the Georgia Lottery, he served as the chief marketing officer for the Florida Lottery.

A native of Houston, Texas, James graduated from The University of Texas with a Bachelor of Science degree in advertising.

Mychal Jackson is a solutions sales professional for Microsoft's communication sector. In this position, he is responsible for sales of the Information Worker Solutions in the telco and cable markets. Prior to Microsoft, Mychal excelled as partner and service account manager at Cisco Systems and consulting principal at Silicon Graphics.

Mychal is a Microsoft Gold Star Award winner and serves as diversity chair for Microsoft's Alpharetta City Council. He is the recipient of outstanding leadership recognition as an industry mentor for Leaders of Tomorrow and Boy Scouts of America.

Mychal received a Bachelor of Science degree in computer science from San Jose State University and a Master of Science degree in business management of technology from Georgia Tech. He is a member of the National Black MBA Association and Alpha Phi Alpha Fraternity, Inc.

Born in Chicago, Mychal owns a real estate investment company and resides in Roswell with his wife, Angela, and three children, Jasmyne, Jamehl and Jamahrae. In his leisure time, Mychal enjoys golfing, motorcycling, snowboarding and traveling.

Sabrina Jenkins

Special Events Director
Atlanta Braves/Turner Field

T. Anthony (Tony) Jones

Business Travel Manager
The Ritz-Carlton, Buckhead

Sabrina Jenkins is director of special events for the Atlanta Braves/Turner Field. Her duties include negotiating contracts, managing budgets and overall marketing strategies, while supervising and executing event logistics. Sabrina also oversees the Atlanta Braves Supplier Diversity Program.

Since beginning with the Braves in 1992, Sabrina has worked in the ticket sales and special events departments. However, her knowledge of the organization is vast. In 2008 and 2009 the Atlanta Business League named Sabrina as one of Atlanta's 100 Top Black Women of Influence. In October of 2006 *rolling out* magazine nominated her as one of the Top 25 Most Influential Women in Atlanta. Sabrina is currently the president of the National Association of Black Sports Professionals – Atlanta Chapter and is also a two-time nominee for the Georgia Minority Supplier Development Council Advocate of the Year.

After receiving a full scholarship, Sabrina graduated from Augusta State University with a bachelor's degree in marketing. A native of Atlanta, she is a member of Salem Bible Church in Lithonia, Georgia, and serves on the Coinonia Ministry. Sabrina currently resides in Atlanta.

The Ritz-Carlton, Buckhead celebrates its 25th anniversary this year as the preferred hotel for corporate executives from around the country traveling to Atlanta to conduct business. As a business travel manager for The Ritz-Carlton, Buckhead, Tony Jones manages the health and welfare of the hotel's corporate accounts; businesses with negotiated contracts for their executives and road warriors. In addition, he maintains sound relationships with high-level corporate decision makers.

In this role, Tony keeps up with business trends, market analysis and the performance of a number of industries, as well as gauges the potential for business from new and relocating companies. He networks constantly, thinks competitively and brings solid value to his clients.

Tony earned a Bachelor of Science degree from Temple University in Philadelphia, Pennsylvania. He is a member of Rotary Club International and BPOE (Elks). Tony is a certified SCUBA instructor and enjoys boating, camping and playing golf.

He is married to Cheryl Jones and has a son, Thomas A. Jones III.

Christopher Kunney

Chief Information Officer &
Vice President, Information Services
Piedmont HealthCare

Rodney Lawson

Assistant Vice President &
General Manager
LexisNexis

Christopher Kunney currently serves as chief information officer and vice president of information services for Piedmont HealthCare. His responsibilities include planning and directing information services, and developing long-term strategies and resource requirements across the health system.

Christopher earned a Bachelor of Science degree in computer science/mathematics from Fort Valley State University and an executive Master of Science degree in management of technology from the Georgia Institute of Technology. He has also earned various certifications in the areas of health care information technology, customer relationship management, technical management, total quality control and project management.

Christopher has served as an adjunct professor for DeVry University and sits on DeVry's Industry Advisory Roundtable. His memberships include the Georgia Association of Healthcare Executives, the College of Healthcare Information Management Executives, the American College of Healthcare Executives, the National Black MBA Association, Inc., Kappa Alpha Psi Fraternity, Inc. and New Birth Missionary Baptist Church.

Christopher received the CIO Boot Camp Minority Scholarship from the College of Healthcare Information Management Executives. He was honored in *Black Enterprise*'s "People on the Move" and *Atlanta Hospital News*' "Minorities in Healthcare."

Rodney Lawson is general manager of the Breckinridge Work Place Solution Facility for LexisNexis in Duluth, Georgia. Responsible for a $40 million operation with LexisNexis, he has repeatedly maximized profitability and delivered sustainable improvements.

An expert at communicating vision, aligning cultural change efforts and igniting competitive spirits, Rodney has earned a reputation for building high-performance sales and service organizations that increase revenues through the development and leadership of people. He has managed multiple cultures in the U.S. and internationally, steering the performance for a South American company.

Rodney holds a Bachelor of Science degree, with honors, in management from the University of Phoenix and a Master of Business Administration degree, with honors, in international business from the Nova Southeastern University H. Wayne Huizenga School of Business and Entrepreneurship. In addition, he attended field seminars at the University of Chile and the University of South Africa while pursuing an international Master of Business Administration degree.

Rodney is a member of the Beta Gamma Sigma, Inc. international honor society, recognized by the educational and corporate world as an honor society recognizing excellence.

Kimberly Little

Assistant Vice President
Product Management
Risk & Information Analytics Group
LexisNexis

Lisa Longino

Sales Manager
The Ritz-Carlton Hotels

Kimberly Little is assistant vice president of product management for the LexisNexis Risk & Information Analytics Group. In this position, she oversees product strategy and planning, and guides product innovation efforts for solutions designed to manage the identity risk of individuals and businesses.

For more than 16 years, Kimberly has been focused on driving business strategy and the development, execution and promotion of innovative technology products and services in the global marketplace. She has lead high-performance teams in a variety of industries, ranging from communications (Lucent Technologies and its spin off, Avaya Inc.) to hospitality (Cendant Inc.).

Kimberly holds a Master of Business Administration degree from Otterbein College in Ohio, with an emphasis on innovation, intellectual property and technology management. She is also a graduate of Vanderbilt University, completing a doctoral program in policy development and program evaluation, and receiving a Master of Public Policy degree and a Bachelor of Science degree in human and organizational development.

A native of Louisville, Kentucky, Kimberly is the wife of Dr. Luther Little Jr. and the proud daughter of Peggy A. Vaden.

Lisa Longino is a sales manager working with customers from the social, nonprofit and government sectors, as well as construction, architecture, real estate, aerospace and engineering companies in the state of Georgia. When these industries gather for meetings, she manages the process to set up successful programs at The Ritz-Carlton, Atlanta (Downtown) or The Ritz-Carlton, Buckhead.

Lisa is passionately involved in two outreach ministries at her church; Christ Kids, supporting underprivileged children in Capetown, South Africa; and Hands of Love Food Ministries, which assists individuals in low-income areas of the city.

An Atlanta native, Lisa enjoys spending time with her close-knit family. This month her brother will be deployed to Afghanistan with the U.S. Army National Guard. She greatly admires her parents, and looks to Oprah Winfrey and Tyra Banks for inspiration about exploring business ventures to thrive in activities she finds enjoyable.

Lisa will obtain a Bachelor of Business Administration degree in marketing from Troy University this year. Additionally, she enjoys traveling, shopping, going to concerts and watching football.

LeRon McKendrick

Senior Brand Manager
Newell Rubbermaid

Chanda Hurt Moran

Senior Vice President
Atlanta Business Banking
Wachovia Bank, N.A.

L eRon McKendrick is senior brand manager for the Beauty & Style global business unit of Newell Rubbermaid. During her tenure with the organization, she launched Goody® Mosaic, a complete styling tools and hair accessories line celebrating diverse hair textures. She currently oversees strategic marketing initiatives for the salon professional hair care division.

Her award-winning advertisement campaigns have received recognition by *Advertising Age*, and she is a recipient of the Kinship in Business Award from *Sister 2 Sister* magazine. LeRon has more than ten years of brand management and new product development with global beauty care brands, such as Dark & Lovely®, Ultra Sheen® and Neutrogena®.

A native of Atlanta, LeRon holds a Master of Business Administration degree from Georgia Southern University and a Bachelor of Business Administration degree in marketing from Savannah State University. She is an active member of Alpha Kappa Alpha Sorority, Inc. and a life member of the Savannah State University National Alumni Association.

A s senior vice president in Wachovia's Business Banking Group, Chanda Hurt Moran works diligently leading a team of banking specialists who are committed to meeting and exceeding the customer's financial needs.

Chanda has worked as a business consultant for more than 18 years. She began her career with Exxon Company, U.S.A., now ExxonMobil, where she advised independent dealers on the operations of their businesses. In 1994 she began her banking career in Atlanta, transitioning her experience with Exxon into advising entrepreneurs across various industries.

She holds a Master of Science degree in general administration from Central Michigan University and a Bachelor of Science degree in industrial administration from Mercer University.

Chanda is a board member of the National Black Arts Festival and the South Fulton Chamber of Commerce. She is a member of Delta Sigma Theta Sorority, Inc. and serves in various capacities at Andrews Chapel United Methodist Church. She and her husband, Jason, are the proud parents of Keyra Jai and Jason II.

Gwendolyn Motley

Director of Marketing
Greenbriar Mall

Regina Murray

Vice President
Banking Center Manager
Bank of America

Gwendolyn Motley is the director of marketing for Greenbriar Mall, the oldest enclosed mall in Atlanta, Georgia. She is responsible for the development and implementation of the center's marketing plan, and the daily administration and operation of the marketing program. Her position requires an extraordinary sense and appreciation of the arts, science and culture to help develop and maintain a strategic marketing plan and to oversee its implementation from beginning to end.

Gwendolyn has been very instrumental in launching and organizing key events at the center, including the National Black Arts Festival, the Delta Sigma Theta Sorority, Inc. Health Fair and most recently, Just Churchin' A Gospel Series™.

A native Georgian, Gwendolyn obtained a Bachelor of Business Administration degree in marketing from the University of West Georgia. She has been a member of numerous boards, including the American Red Cross Minority Recruitment Board, and serves her church as secretary.

The wife of Leonard Motley Jr., she is the proud mother of a son, Jacob.

Regina Murray is vice president, banking center manager for Bank of America in Atlanta. In this role, Regina provides management, organization and leadership to a diverse sales team in Atlanta's metropolitan areas.

Regina's primary focus and motivation is to daily educate and empower the families in the community where her branch is located. During her career in the financial services industry, Regina has been a licensed real estate broker in both California and Georgia.

With a career that spans 27 years in the banking industry, the heart of the community embodies everything in which Regina is involved. By partnering with Atlanta's nonprofit groups, she is able to assist many and has been recognized for her leadership, as well as her performance.

A native of California, Regina recently earned a Doctor of Ministry degree in the field of Christian education from Jacksonville Theological Seminary. Her hobbies include traveling, reading and cooking.

Donna Northington

Senior Vice President of
Strategic Planning
Turner Network Sales
Turner Broadcasting System, Inc.

Linda Odom-Vega

Executive Chief of Staff
New Birth Missionary Baptist Church

Donna Northington is senior vice president of strategic planning for Turner Network Sales (TNS), the domestic distribution, sales and marketing arm of Turner Broadcasting System, Inc. She leads a group that translates TNS strategic initiatives into financial and operating plans. She also assesses the economic impact of various business decisions and acquisition targets.

Previously, Northington was senior vice president of finance and business integration for Covad Communications, Inc., and Eastern Group controller for Coca-Cola Enterprises Inc. She is a member of Women in Cable Telecommunications, a Betsy Magness Leadership Institute fellow and a member of the National Association for Multi-Ethnicity in Communications. She also serves on the advisory board for the Cable & Telecommunications Association for Marketing.

CableFAX: The Magazine named Northington one of the Most Influential Minorities in Cable for 2006, 2007 and 2008. She earned a Bachelor of Fine Arts degree from the University of Massachusetts and a Master of Business Administration degree in finance from Columbia University.

Linda Odom-Vega is a seasoned executive and community leader in Atlanta. As executive chief of staff, Vega oversees the administration and external business affairs of New Birth Missionary Baptist Church under the leadership of chief executive officer and senior pastor, Bishop Eddie L. Long. Vega was previously senior vice president in the Wachovia Bank Georgia Banking Division for 20 years in various leadership roles.

Linda's passion for community service is displayed by serving on boards as the advisory chair for One Economy Corporation, The Embassy International Chamber of Commerce, the Southern Regional Medical Center Foundation Development Committee, the Latin American Association and *Women Looking Ahead.*

Her awards and recognitions include the Atlanta Business League's 100 Most Influential Women, *WLA* Georgia's 100 Most Influential Women and recognition as a 2003 Leadership Atlanta alumna. Linda has been acknowledged in numerous magazine articles regarding her accomplishments and commitment to community service.

Linda's philosophy on life is that people who are prospering are truly prosperous when they reach back and empower those who have lost hope or need direction to increase their quality of life.

T. Phillips

Vice President, Quality Assurance
Insurance Technology Solutions
LexisNexis

Na'eema Rashad

Senior Coordinator
Trumpet Awards Foundation, Inc.

T. Phillips joined LexisNexis in March of 2007 and is directly responsible for the development, strategy, oversight and direction of the LexisNexis RIAG insurance technology quality assurance organization. Supported by a team of 40-plus, which includes software testing engineers, a configuration management team and a Quality Assurance Center of Excellence, T. partners closely with the project management and development organizations.

Some of her key accomplishments include implementing industry-best practices, procedures and methodologies; establishing a Quality Assurance Center of Excellence; and establishing an enterprise-wide quality council.

Prior to LexisNexis, T. founded and managed her own software testing and quality assurance consulting firm for 13 years, where she supported clients such as AT&T, Merrill Lynch, Prudential and AIG. Her career also includes ten years of experience in program/project management and seven years of experience in business analysis.

T. earned a double major Bachelor of Arts degree in economics and political science at Wellesley College and Master of Arts and Master of Business Administration degrees from Georgia State University. She is also a certified project management professional through the Project Management Institute.

Na'eema Rashad is a senior coordinator for the Trumpet Awards Foundation, Inc. In addition to executive responsibilities and administrative duties, she assists in all phases of execution for the annual Trumpet Awards. The Trumpet Awards is a prestigious event heralding the accomplishments of African Americans and others who have helped enrich the greatness of society.

The planning of the event, including the presence of approximately 4,000 people from around the world, is extensive and requires endless hours of detail inclusion, necessitating skill and fortitude. Rashad possesses the titillating combination of leadership and follow-through, which are prerequisites for success and excellence. Her professional assignments offer an opportunity to define and refine her best leadership skills.

An excellent leader who demonstrates those qualities throughout her career tasks, Rashad has an excellent talent for finding talent. She is sincerely dedicated to her tasks and never fails to execute timely and proficiently. She keeps her goals in focus while being a single mother to Justice Ali.

Melanie J. Richburg, Ph.D.

Southeast Human Resources Manager
Johnson Controls, Inc.

John Ripoll

Senior Vice President
Private Client Advisor
U.S. Trust, Bank of America
Private Wealth Management

D r. Melanie Richburg is the southeast regional human resources manager for the service and systems businesses of Johnson Controls, Inc.–Building Efficiency Group. Johnson Controls, Inc. is a leading supplier of building management systems and controls for quality building environments.

A native of Montgomery, Alabama, Melanie is a licensed professional counselor, a national certified counselor and certified sports counselor. She received a Doctor of Philosophy degree in counseling and human development from Clark Atlanta University. Melanie has published several articles and served as a presenter and facilitator at conferences, workshops and seminars on the local, state and national levels.

Her service efforts have included marathon participation and mentoring with The American Stroke Association Train to End Stroke Program, volunteering and participating with AIDS Walk Atlanta, volunteering for the Hosea Williams Feed the Hungry and Homeless Program, pacesetter status with the American Cancer Society Making Strides Against Breast Cancer and JCI community service coordinator for The Drake House.

Melanie is a member of Antioch Baptist Church-North and Alpha Kappa Alpha Sorority, Inc.

J ohn Ripoll is senior vice president, private client advisor for U.S. Trust, Bank of America Private Wealth Management. In this position, he is responsible for coordinating the delivery of wealth management solutions to ultra high-net-worth clients and prospects in the Atlanta market. During his 20-year career, John has consistently been a top performer in the industry.

Active in the community, John serves on the board of directors for the Piedmont Park Conservancy. He is also a supporter of Cool Girls, an award-winning early intervention after-school program dedicated to the empowerment of low-income girls. His professional memberships include the Association for Corporate Growth, The Bond Club of New York and the National Association of Securities Professionals.

John received dual degrees from Tulane University, a Bachelor of Science degree in management with a concentration in finance and a Bachelor of Science degree with a concentration in economics.

A native of New Orleans, Louisiana, John is the husband of Lisa Nicholls and has twin daughters, Claire and Sophia.

Irvin Royer

In-Room Dining Manager
The Ritz-Carlton, Buckhead

Franklin Rucker, P.E.

Director, Engineering
Department of Aviation
Hartsfield-Jackson Atlanta
International Airport

Irvin Royer, in-room dining manager of The Ritz-Carlton, Buckhead, is charged with organizing the timely delivery of perfectly prepared meals to guests of the 517-room hotel. In-room dining operates 24/7 and functions similarly to a restaurant, with the difference that all meals are "home delivery." Each order is presented on a crisp, white tablecloth, with fresh flowers, and brought to the guestroom within minutes of preparation by a knowledgeable server who will open a bottle of wine and set the stage to enhance the dining experience.

Irvin is an expert in planning, organizing, multitasking and problem solving, supervising staff and providing superior customer service. He is certified in total quality management, safety, food handling and preservation, restaurant management, customer service and effective leadership programs.

Irvin is a native of Dominica, a small island in the Caribbean, but he grew up in the U.S. Virgin Islands. He enjoys cooking foods with the tastes of the islands, and especially with jerk seasoning. Irvin is a single father of two teenage daughters, DeMytrke and AaLiyah.

As director of engineering, Franklin Rucker is responsible for the implementation of design and construction projects developed by the Department of Aviation and the Hartsfield-Jackson Development Program. He displayed exceptional leadership in overseeing the construction of the airport's new automated Hold Baggage Screening System. During this massive project, he managed construction of three separate systems that are among the largest in the world and serve as a model for many other airports throughout the country.

Prior to joining the Department of Aviation, Rucker served as project manager/project engineer for numerous civil projects in the public and private sectors. Some of his major accomplishments include participation in the construction of several Metropolitan Atlanta Rapid Transit Authority stations and the Georgia Dome.

Rucker earned a bachelor's degree in civil engineering from the Georgia Institute of Technology and is a registered professional engineer in the state of Georgia. Married and the father of four, he resides in Fayetteville, Georgia, where he is a member of New Hope Baptist Church.

Alana Sanders

Vice President
Marketing Communications
MarketingPros, LLC

Woquita D. Scandrick

Executive Steward
The Ritz-Carlton, Buckhead

Alana Sanders is the vice president of marketing communications for MarketingPros, LLC, a full-service marketing and advertising firm. In this position, she oversees all operations of the Marketing and Advertising Department for small businesses and major corporations across the United States, helping businesses reach minority markets. Sanders has worked with companies such as Verizon Wireless, Goody Hair Products, Paul Mitchell, E&J Gallo and many more. Additionally, she has helped many businesses become international through her effective marketing skills in Internet marketing.

Alana teaches the art of marketing and advertising at various universities, providing aspiring marketers with updated information about the marketing world. Additionally, she has been featured in publications and was nominated for numerous awards for her success within the industry.

A native of Louisiana, Alana holds a bachelor's degree in mass communications and a Master of Business Administration degree. She is currently pursuing a Doctor of Philosophy degree in leadership and organizational change.

The Ritz-Carlton, Buckhead celebrates its 25th anniversary this year as the social center of the city and the scene of the most elegant weddings, galas, social events and banquets. As executive steward, Woquita Scandrick is responsible for providing the serving equipment, on time and in perfect condition, for the hotel's restaurants and the hundreds of social and business functions that take place annually.

Woquita is a master of organizing complex tasks. She oversees the Silver-Polishing Department, where a gleaming finish is maintained on the silverware, serving dishes, coffee urns, bowls and platters used throughout the hotel. She monitors the hotel's business levels to be sure the right equipment is always ready when needed, sets the budget to replenish supplies and ensures the seamless flow of materials so that all hotel departments can deliver flawless events, for which the hotel is renowned.

Woquita served five years in the U.S. Navy, graduating from the U. S. Navy Apprenticeship Training Program and working as an aviation storekeeper.

A native of Atlanta, she celebrates her ninth wedding anniversary this year and has four children.

Mona Singleton

Marketing Manager
Associated Construction Publications

Donald L. Smith

Field Vice President &
Financial Advisor
AXA Advisors, LLC

Mona Singleton is marketing manager for Associated Construction Publications (ACP), a division of Reed Elsevier. An icon in the industry, ACP is comprised of 14 regional magazines devoted to the heavy highway construction industry, with most publications dating back to the early 1900s.

Singleton is responsible for developing marketing strategies and creating the necessary marketing tools to support the sales force and editorial staff on a regional and national level. She has taken the marketing component to the next level with her unique style and high-energy campaigns. In 2006 she received the Superstar Award for her commitment to excellence in innovation, customer service, valuing people, working across divisions and having a passion for winning.

An enterprising professional with more than 22 years' experience, Singleton has worked directly with company chief executive officers to foster growth and expand the presence of businesses, including Holsted Marketing, *Upscale* magazine, Bronner Brothers, Who's Who Publishing and Images USA.

Singleton is the parent of one son, Justin. She volunteers with Banking on Our Future, a program dedicated to empowering youths ages 9 to 18 through financial literacy.

Donald (Don) Smith is a field vice president and financial advisor with AXA Advisors, LLC. In his current role, he is responsible for supporting business development for the Southeast Marketing Center. For the past 17 years, Smith has worked with thousands of clients and hundreds of financial advisors and managers. He is a member of the National Association of Insurance and Financial Advisors and the General Agents and Managers Association.

Through his affiliation with AXA, Smith has served as a dedicated supporter and contributor to a multitude of civic organizations, including the National Association of Black Accountants, the National Urban League, the UNCF, the French American Chamber of Commerce, Junior Achievement and a host of others.

Smith is frequently asked to speak, write, or contribute on the subjects of financial planning, insurance, investments, leadership and diversity, and has done so for a long list of publications.

A graduate of Louisiana State University, Smith is married to his beautiful wife of 18 years, artist Vonda Smith. Together, they are the proud parents of son Julien, 13, and daughter Jhenna, 9.

Anthony Taylor Jr.

Vice President & Sector Manager
Parsons Water & Infrastructure

Loretta Young Walker

Senior Vice President &
Chief Human Resources Officer
Turner Broadcasting System, Inc.

Anthony Taylor Jr. is vice president and sector manager for Parsons Water & Infrastructure for Georgia and the Carolinas. He has worked for Parsons Water & Infrastructure for 13 years, where he has profit and loss responsibilities for engineering and program management services in the water and wastewater industry.

Taylor was listed in several publications, including *Who's Who in Science and Engineering* and *Who's Who of Emerging Leaders*. Recipient of the 2008 Black Engineer of the Year Special Recognition Award, he has published technical articles on public private partnerships for physical infrastructure development.

Taylor attended North Carolina State University, where he received a Bachelor of Science degree in civil engineering. He also holds a Master of Science degree in management and a Doctor of Philosophy degree in engineering management. Additionally, Taylor completed the executive management program at the MIT Sloan School of Management in 2008.

A native of Nassau, Bahamas, he is the son of Ruth Inez Taylor, who resides in Nassau, the husband of Kaaryn and the very proud father of Anthony III, Andrew and Ann.

Loretta Young Walker is senior vice president and chief human resources officer for Turner Broadcasting System, Inc. (TBS, Inc.), where she oversees recruitment, compensation, training and development, performance-management, and succession-planning within the respective Turner domestic networks and businesses, as well as the human resources specialists and shared-services areas. She also has executive oversight of the company's coordinated diversity efforts and talent-management strategies.

Walker joined TBS, Inc. in 1999 from BellSouth, where she was director of human resources for the Long Distance Division. She earned a Bachelor of Science degree in computer information systems from Auburn University at Montgomery and a Master of Business Administration degree at Samford University.

Walker is a Betsy Magness Leadership Institute fellow. She is also president of the board of directors of the Warren/Holyfield Boys & Girls Club, a member of the boards of the Emma L. Bowen Foundation and the National Association for Multi-Ethnicity in Communications (NAMIC), and a graduate of the NAMIC Executive Leadership Development Program.

W. Denise Ware

Area Director, Sales & Marketing
Noble Investment Group

Myrna White

Director of Public Affairs
Hartsfield-Jackson Atlanta
International Airport

Flanked by determination, dedication and diligence, W. Denise Ware is one of the most profound professionals in the hospitality industry. As an executive with Noble Investment Group, she has responsibility for two of Metro Atlanta's newest and most distinguished hotels, the Courtyard Atlanta Airport West and the Hampton Inn & Suites Atlanta (Camp Creek Parkway). Her career in the industry spans a solid 18 years.

A native of Washington, D.C., Ware graduated, summa cum laude, from Sojourner-Douglass College. Her work in the industry has produced such honors as Employee of the Year and Top Producer. She holds memberships with the National Coalition of Black Meeting Planners, the Religious Conference Management Association, the Society of Government Planners and the National Travel Association.

Very active in her church, Open Word Christian Ministries, Ware serves as a cheerleading coach for Upward Bound and a member of Tayo Reed's International Academy of Dance. With a profound faith in God, she is a proud cancer survivor. She is single and enjoys cheerleading, playing softball and reading.

Myrna White manages the Office of Public Affairs for the Department of Aviation at the world's busiest airport. The diverse business unit is comprised of intergovernmental affairs, media/public relations, community relations, the Office of Protocol, special events, graphics and Web content.

With an aviation career spanning more than 17 years, White began her tenure conducting public information workshops to educate the community and gain acceptance of the airport's fifth runway. The $1.2 billion runway, dubbed "the most important runway in America," opened in 2006.

White was honored to receive the 2009 Pinnacle Leadership Award from the East Point/College Park Alumnae Chapter of Delta Sigma Theta Sorority, Inc. Additionally, both the Georgia State Senate and the Georgia House of Representatives passed resolutions in 2006, commending White for her professional leadership and service to the community.

She currently serves on the boards of directors for the Fayette County Chamber of Commerce, Arts Clayton and *Women Looking Ahead* magazine, and she is on the American Red Cross Minority Recruitment advisory board. White is a graduate of The University of Georgia School of Journalism.

Fred Williams

Assistant Coach
Atlanta Dream

Jan J. Williams

Financial Advisor
AXA Advisors, LLC

Atlanta Dream assistant coach Fred Williams brings more than 20 years of coaching and scouting experience to the team. Most recently, he served as head coach of the San Diego Siege, a National Women's Basketball League (NWBL) team. In 2006 he was named NWBL Coach of the Year, and he led the Siege to a 15-5 record and a championship appearance.

Prior to coaching with the now defunct NWBL, Williams was the head coach of the Utah Starzz. He led the team from a 13-15 season in 1999 to back-to-back playoff appearances in 2000 and 2001. He was also an assistant coach with the Charlotte Sting from 2003 until 2004.

In addition to his WNBA experience, Williams spent ten years coaching at the University of Southern California (USC) as an assistant coach under Cheryl Miller and as head coach. He helped guide USC to a national championship, and led USC to a 20-9 record and a trip to the NCAA tournament. A Boise State University graduate, Williams has also served as an advance scout for the NBA's Sacramento Kings and Utah Jazz.

Jan Williams is a financial advisor with AXA Advisors, LLC, in the Atlanta office. He is a credentialed qualified plans specialist, executive benefit specialist, estate planning specialist, certified senior advisor, and received a retirement planning specialist certification from The Wharton School at the University of Pennsylvania. A member of the NFL Players Association's Financial Advisory Network, he is a long-standing member of the Million Dollar Round Table, AllianceBerstein's Elite Advisor Team and AXA's Sterling Group.

Previously, Jan served 20 years as a military officer in the U.S. Marine Corps, where he served as the controller for Marine Forces Pacific.

He earned dual degrees in finance and engineering from North Carolina A&T State University, a Master of Business degree in finance from Pepperdine University, and a Master of Science degree in computer science from the Naval Postgraduate School.

Jan is the lead volunteer instructor for Good Choice Inc.; treasurer of the West End Medical Center's board of directors; and a member of 100 Black Men of America, Inc., the National Black MBA Association, and Cascade United Methodist Church.

Travell Williams

Senior Sales Manager
Hilton Atlanta Airport Hotel

Winford Williams

Vice President
Insurance Services Division
LexisNexis Group

Travell Williams is a role model of excellence, whether in business, academia, religion or public service. He exemplifies the wealth of talent and leadership for which Atlanta is known, and it is fitting that his accomplishments would be recognized by induction into *Who's Who In Black Atlanta®*.

Travell is currently a senior sales manager at the Hilton Atlanta Airport Hotel. His fantastic personality, client dedication and wealth of experience leave his clients feeling comfortable, knowing that their expectations will be exceeded when planning corporate meetings, parties or social events. It is not surprising that Travell has significantly exceeded all of the hotel's goals during the years. He is often singled out within the hotel for advice and direction on sales and operational opportunities, as he has earned the respect of every team member in the building.

Travell serves, not only as a resource, but also as a means to educate and understand the younger generation in addition to being a servant to the community and a business leader in the field of hospitality.

Winford Williams is a vice president within the Insurance Services Division for LexisNexis Group, responsible for developing information products that serve the personal auto and property insurance markets. He has extensive experience in the insurance industry, beginning in 1985 as an application developer at Policy Management Systems in Columbia, South Carolina.

For the past 20 years, Winford has contributed to the phenomenal growth of the Insurance Services Division that is now part of LexisNexis Group. He led the construction of online systems that facilitate the underwriting experience for insurance carriers and large data-warehousing applications. Currently, he is responsible for a motor vehicle reporting application that interfaces with various departments of motor vehicles throughout the United States and the ministries of Canada.

In addition to his responsibilities at LexisNexis, Winford impacts the community, serving as an elder at Salem Bible Church of Lithonia, Georgia. He is married and has two sons and a daughter. He helps couples address the challenges of marriage through mentoring and counseling.

Winford holds a Bachelor of Science degree in computer information systems from DeVry University in Atlanta.

Atlanta's
ACADEMIA

PERFORM

ELEVATE

PHENOM

SCHOLAR

PRODIGY

MENTOR

MERIT

VALUE

ATTAIN

Tonya Cook

Program Specialist
Georgia State University

Harold Craig

Vice President
Economic Development
Atlanta Technical College

Tonya Cook is a program specialist for Georgia State University's student life and leadership/ intercultural relations. She plans a diverse range of cultural and educational programs for the university. Tonya is the event chairperson for the annual Martin Luther King Jr. Convocation, which pays homage to the life and legacy of Dr. King.

She is an alumna of the Atlanta Women Foundation's Destiny Fund (2008) and the United Way V.I.P. Program (2008). Tonya is an inductee of the Zeta Phi Beta Sorority, Inc. Hall of Fame and was included among the *Women Looking Ahead* list of Georgia's 100 powerful and influential women (nonprofit and diversity). Additionally, she is the concept creator of Zeta Phi Beta's annual Stork's Nest Blitz, which is a baby-item collection drive and health fair.

Tonya received a bachelor's degree in marketing (1994) and a Master of Science degree in human resource development (2005) from Georgia State University. A native of Atlanta, Georgia, she is a member of Providence Missionary Baptist Church.

Harold Craig is vice president of economic development for Atlanta Technical College, named America's Best Community College by *Washington Monthly* magazine. He is responsible for managing the college's business and industry services, including customized contract training, workforce assessments, administration of the Georgia Work Ready Program, and the Georgia Retraining Tax Credit Program. His division also includes the Continuing Education Department, the Professional Assessment and Certification Center, the American Heart Association Training Center, the Georgia Fatherhood Program and other local and state-funded programs and services.

Harold serves on the boards for the Atlanta Enterprise Center, Atlanta Metro Fair Housing Services and the South Metro Microenterprise Coalition, Inc. An alumnus of Leadership Atlanta, he holds memberships in Alpha Phi Alpha Fraternity, Inc. (life member), the NAACP and the Clark Atlanta University Alumni Association.

Harold is a graduate of Clark Atlanta University and has a certification in economic development from the Georgia Institute of Technology. He and his wife, Sandra, reside in Jonesboro, where they attend Atlanta Southside Seventh-day Adventist Church. They are the parents of three children, and they have four grandsons.

Rodney Ellis

Executive Vice President
Atlanta Technical College

Dr. Hazel Arnett Ervin

Director of General Education
Morehouse College

Rodney Ellis currently serves as executive vice president at Atlanta Technical College, named America's Best Community College by *Washington Monthly* magazine. He is responsible for overseeing the day-to-day operations of academic and student affairs. He also serves as the executive director for the Atlanta Technical College Foundation, Inc.

Rodney is certified by the Technical College System of Georgia as an economic developer trainer. He is also an active member of the Kiwanis Club of Atlanta.

Rodney is a graduate of The University of Alabama, where he majored in political science. He received a master's degree from Auburn University at Montgomery in Alabama. While matriculating at both schools, he was heavily involved in the Alabama political process at the local, state and federal levels.

An educator, editor, administrator, J. William Fulbright fellow, consultant and recipient of several faculty development grants, Dr. Hazel Arnett Ervin is an associate professor of English and director of general education at Morehouse College. Trained in the Teacher Preparation Program at Guilford College in the late 1970s and in African-American literature at Howard University in the early 1990s, she promotes higher education that is outcome-based and measurable.

At Morehouse, Ervin serves in the role of director, overseeing the redesign of the college's core curriculum. She is a consultant to national testing services and a member of numerous educational organizations. She is also editor of the best-selling *African American Literary Criticism, 1773 to 2000*; *The Handbook of African American Literature*; and *The Critical Response to Ann Petry*. Ervin speaks frequently at colleges, universities, churches and libraries on pedagogy and assessment, the acclaimed 1940s writer Ann Petry, and the African-American oral tradition.

Ervin's favorite quote is: "I am only one, but I am one. And I will not let what I cannot do prevent me from doing what I can."

Robert D. Flanigan Jr.

Vice President, Business and
Financial Affairs & Treasurer
Spelman College

John Holman

English Professor
Georgia State University

Robert D. Flanigan Jr. is the vice president for business and financial affairs and treasurer of Spelman College, presiding over the Division of Business and Financial Affairs and managing in excess of $500 million of the college's assets. He has served in this post since 1994; however, his tenure with the college spans 37 years, having joined in 1970 as assistant to the business manager.

Flanigan currently serves on several boards, including Tuition Plan, the Paideia School and the Children's School. He is past chairman of Leadership Atlanta and has served on the boards of the Commonfund, the Girl Scouts Council of Northwest Georgia, the Georgia Center for Children and the National Association of College and University Business Officers.

Flanigan holds a Bachelor of Arts degree in business administration from Clark College and a Master of Business Administration degree in finance and management from Emory University. In addition, he also attended the London School of Business.

John Holman is a professor of English at Georgia State University, where he directs the creative writing program. He is author of *Squabble and Other Stories*, and *Luminous Mysteries: A Novel*.

Holman received a Bachelor of Arts degree from The University of North Carolina at Chapel Hill, a Master of Arts degree from North Carolina Central University and a Doctor of Philosophy degree from The University of Southern Mississippi. He has taught as a professor or writer in residence at St. Augustine's College, the University of South Florida, the University of Florida, the University of Houston, North Carolina Central University and Colgate University.

Holman has given several workshops and readings of his fiction. His fiction has appeared in many anthologies and magazines, including *The New Yorker* and *THE OXFORD AMERICAN* magazine. He is also a recipient of the Whiting Writers' Award.

Joseph Jennings

Director, Jazz Ensemble
Coordinator, Jazz Studies Track
Spelman College

Mehari Kassa

Director of Development
The Ron Clark Academy

Joseph Jennings is director of the Jazz Ensemble and coordinator of the Jazz Studies Track at Spelman College. His teaching career spans an impressive 30 years, including time at Clark and Morehouse colleges. He has performed with Johnny Taylor, Duke Pearson, Cecil Bridgewater and Vanessa Ruben.

Previous to Spelman, Jennings was director of music at the Atlanta Center for Black Art and was artist-in-residence at the Neighborhood Arts Center. He is founder of the Neighborhood Arts Ensemble, a 22-piece big band, and co-founder of the recording group Life Force, which performed at the North Sea Jazz Festival in 1991. In 1994 he directed the Atlanta All Stars at the Olympic Winter Games in Lillehammer, Norway. Jennings' latest CD is *Life Force Speaks.*

His numerous awards include the Bronze Jubilee, the International Association of Jazz Educators Outstanding Service Award, the President's Outstanding Service Award from Spelman College and the African American Classical Music Award.

Jennings earned a Bachelor of Music degree from Southern University and a Master of Arts degree in music education from the University of Illinois.

Mehari Kassa is the director of development for The Ron Clark Academy (RCA). In this role, his primary focus is developing and implementing community-based fundraising programs that include identifying, cultivating, and soliciting major gift donors for both annual and capital contributions. RCA is challenged with raising $3 million annually for student scholarships; Mehari works with trustees and volunteers to fulfill these scholarships.

Led to RCA by his love for children, Mehari volunteered to help the two co-founders during the school's startup. He has always said when he retired he would either teach or start his own school, so when the co-founders asked him to join them full time in building RCA, Mehari decided to retire early.

The Atlanta native is a recipient of the 2008 Power 30 Under 30 Award for Community Service, and currently serves on the board of The Villages at Carver Family YMCA. Mehari received a Bachelor of Science degree in chemical engineering from Drexel University, and is a graduate of The Lovett School's class of 1997.

Basil G. Lee

Mathematics Instructor
Benjamin Banneker High School

Gary S. May, Ph.D.

Steve W. Chaddick School Chair of
Electrical & Computer Engineering
Georgia Institute of Technology

The Fulton County Teacher of the Year, Basil G. Lee is an exceptional educator who teaches at Benjamin Banneker High School. At Banneker, Basil is the National Honor Society adviser and the varsity math team coach, and has served as Banneker's athletic director, the cross country coach and a chess club sponsor.

Basil has received numerous awards for his diligent efforts. He was selected by *USA Today* for their All-USA Teacher Team. AT&T and the Atlanta Braves Foundation selected him as their Georgia Educator of Excellence. He spent two weeks in Japan with the International Educators to Japan. Additionally, his commitment to education is highlighted in the UNCF's annual report.

Basil earned a mechanical engineering degree from Cornell University and pledged with Alpha Phi Alpha Fraternity, Inc. He also earned a Master of Arts degree and an Educational Specialist degree in secondary mathematics from the University of West Georgia.

Basil is the husband of Debra and father of four – Bianca, Brianne, Brandi and Braxton.

Dr. Gary S. May, the Steve W. Chaddick School chair of Electrical and Computer Engineering at Georgia Tech, is that department's chief academic officer, providing leadership to 114 faculty members and 2,300 students in the nation's fifth-ranked program.

May performs research in semiconductor manufacturing and has authored 250 publications. He was Georgia Tech's Outstanding Young Alumnus (1993), and received Georgia Tech's Outstanding Service Award (1999), two Best Paper Awards from IEEE (1998, 2000), the NSBE Golden Torch Award (2006) and the AAAS Outstanding Mentor Award (2007). He has created programs to increase participation among underrepresented students in science and engineering. Since 1998, 211 minorities have received doctorates in such fields at Georgia Tech, the most in the nation.

A St. Louis native, May received a Bachelor of Science degree in electrical engineering from Georgia Tech in 1985, and Master of Science and Doctor of Philosophy degrees in electrical engineering and computer science from the University of California, Berkeley in 1988 and 1991, respectively.

May and his wife, LeShelle, have two daughters, Simone and Jordan. He is a member of Cascade United Methodist Church.

Bobby Olive Sr.

Vice President, Student Affairs
Atlanta Metropolitan College

Arlethia Perry-Johnson

Special Assistant
External Affairs
Kennesaw State University

Bobby Olive Sr. is vice president of student affairs at Atlanta Metropolitan College. Olive serves on the 100 Black Men of Atlanta, Inc.'s board of directors, and is a member of the National Junior College Athletic Association, the National Association of Collegiate Directors of Athletics and the European Access Network. He is past president of the Southeastern Association of Educational Opportunity of Program Personnel and the Georgia Association of Special Programs Personnel.

His honors include Outstanding Young Man in America, Civitan Club Sportsmanship, Kennesaw State University BSA Humanitarian and Georgia Association of Special Programs Personnel Outstanding Service awards. He was co-captain of the Tennessee State University (TSU) men's basketball team, received the Southeastern Association of Educational Opportunity Program Personnel Executive Committee and President's awards, was inducted into the Paris-Henry County Sports Hall of Fame and received a special Citation Award from Richard Riley, former secretary of the U.S. Department of Education.

Olive earned a bachelor's degree in biology from TSU and a master's degree in rehabilitation guidance and counseling from Georgia State University. Olive and wife Patsy have three children and nine grandchildren.

Arlethia Perry-Johnson is special assistant to the president of external affairs at Kennesaw State University (KSU), the state's third-largest university with more than 21,000 students. She is responsible for the administration of KSU's university relations department and legislative and community affairs.

Arlethia joined KSU in October of 2006, after serving 11 years as the chief communications officer for the Board of Regents of the University System of Georgia (USG), the state's system of 35 public colleges and universities. She also currently serves as director of the USG's African-American Male Initiative, aimed at increasing black male participation in college. Additional past appointments include key communications posts at Penn State, Rutgers, the Tennessee Valley Authority and Virginia Commonwealth University.

Arlethia's current civic engagements include serving on the executive committees of Communities In Schools of Georgia and the Georgia Council on Economic Education. She was selected for the 2003-04 Associates Program of the National Center for Public Policy and Higher Education, and is a graduate of Leadership Georgia.

Arlethia and her husband, Steven C. Johnson, are the proud parents of La'Nita M. Johnson.

Corey L. Posey

Director
Multicultural & International
Student Affairs
Berry College

David K. Price

Founder & President
BaSix Knowledge Academy

Corey L. Posey is director of multicultural and international student affairs at Berry College. He has earned a Bachelor of Science degree in sociology from the University of Maryland Eastern Shore, a Bachelor of Social Work degree from Salisbury University, and a master's degree in higher education and student affairs from The Ohio State University.

Additionally, Posey is a founding member of Team Invasion Midwest (TIM). TIM is a division of DJ Green Lantern's Team Invasion label, and a promotion company pioneering the resurgence of hip-hop music and culture.

Posey serves as the TIM sponsorship liaison and tour manager of the Invasion EDU program. He is originally from East Orange, New Jersey, and is a graduate of Arts High School in Newark, New Jersey.

Educator, entrepreneur, counselor, mentor, psalmist and minister are just a few words that describe headmaster David K. Price, founder and president of BaSix Knowledge Academy.

A native of Anniston, Alabama, Price is a Morehouse College graduate and earned a master's degree in education from Troy University. His experience spans more than 12 years in both high school and college arenas. Students in Fulton and DeKalb counties, along with those in the Anniston Public School System, have benefited from his expertise. Additionally, he taught in private institutions, including Clark Atlanta University, Georgia Perimeter and Morehouse College.

Price formed BaSix Knowledge Enrichment Center and Academy in 1997. Originally an after-school tutorial center out of his home, BaSix has emerged to a fully accredited K-12 private and adult independent study academy. BaSix also offers tutorials and educational consulting.

A sought-after teacher, consultant and motivational speaker, his passion for leadership development and desire to see the ultimate success of all of his students has positioned him as a leader among leaders, obedient to God's vision, compassionate towards God's people and efficient with God's work.

Dr. Jerome Ratchford

Interim Vice President
Student Success and Enrollment Services
Kennesaw State University

Dr. Jennifer A. Wade-Berg

Chief Diversity Officer
Assistant Professor
Kennesaw State University

Dr. Jerome Ratchford is interim vice president for Student Success and Enrollment Services at Kennesaw State University (KSU). He oversees a division wherein personnel interact directly with students to assure their success. Jerome also held academic and administrative positions at other institutions.

During his 20 years at KSU, Jerome has served as the head of a department and dean of Student Success. He has also served on several committees, including the Foundations of Excellence in the First Year of College Task Force and the Chancellor's Task Force on Pre-College Programs for Youth in At-Risk Situations.

The African American Student Alliance (AASA), an organization founded by Jerome, established the Dr. Jerome Ratchford Award of Excellence. The award recognizes a faculty, staff member or student honoree who continues Jerome's tradition of leadership and service in promoting pluralism and an Afrocentric presence on KSU's campus.

Jerome received a bachelor's degree in education from the University of Kentucky, a master's degree in counseling and guidance from Indiana University and a Doctor of Philosophy degree in educational leadership in higher education from Bowling Green State University in Ohio.

Dr. Jennifer A. Wade-Berg is the chief diversity officer at Kennesaw State University. She began at the university in August of 2008 after serving as the faculty fellow for inclusion with the Office of the Provost at the University of Colorado Denver. She is responsible for overseeing efforts to foster an environment that values diversity on campus.

She is also an assistant professor in the department of political science, where she will be teaching in the areas of public administration and nonprofit management. A native of Atlanta, Jennifer earned a Bachelor of Arts degree in government from Wesleyan University in Connecticut. She holds a master's and doctorate degrees in public administration from The University of Georgia's School of Public and International Affairs.

Jennifer volunteers in the community through her involvement with The Links, Inc. and Alpha Kappa Alpha Sorority, Inc. She is married to John Berg and they have one daughter, Skylar Alexandria Wade-Berg.

Natosha Reneé Willis

Teacher, Special Education
DeKalb County Schools

Born and raised in Columbus, Ohio, Natosha Reneé Willis serves as a special education teacher at Rock Chapel Elementary in the DeKalb County School System. Currently, Natosha is in her third year of teaching and has already touched the lives of many. Having worked with children since middle school, she has found a way to connect with students of all levels.

With a passion for working with children and youth, Natosha is committed to helping children achieve their goals. Not only is she interested in helping youth academically, but she is also committed to educating them on the widespread epidemic of HIV/AIDS and other sexually transmitted diseases. Her commitment and passion is evident through past volunteer work with the Columbus AIDS Task Force and Planned Parenthood.

Natosha received a Bachelor of Science degree and a Master of Education degree in special education from The Ohio State University. Before moving to the Atlanta area, she attended Mt. Olivet Baptist Church in Columbus, where she taught Sunday school and worked in children's church.

Natosha currently resides in Lithonia, Georgia.

Atlanta's
COUNSELORS

BENEVOLENT

PRINCIPLED

VESTED

DEMOCRATIC

ACCOMPLISHED

MEDIATOR

ADVOCATE

LITIGATOR

ARBITER

Precious Anderson

Managing Partner
The Anderson Firm, LLC

P recious Anderson is managing partner of The Anderson Firm, LLC, a legal and business boutique in downtown Atlanta. Prior to founding the firm, she worked at King & Spalding.

Precious advises clients on starting, protecting or dissolving business, entertainment and family law matters. Her representation includes contract drafting and negotiation, dispute resolution, facilitating business sales and acquisitions, and strategically pursuing the interests of those involved in severed familial relationships. Some of her representative clients include small- to mid-sized businesses, athletes, entertainers, high-net-worth investors, start-ups, nonprofits and companies in the energy, government contracting, real estate, technology, marketing and faith-based industries.

Precious received a juris doctorate degree from Harvard Law School. She also received Bachelor of Science and Bachelor of Arts degrees from Florida A&M University, where she graduated, double summa cum laude.

The Atlanta Community Food Bank and Investing In Our Youth are two nonprofits for which Precious holds board positions. A member of the Georgia Association of Women Attorneys' Leadership Academy and the United Way Volunteer Involvement Program, her other entrepreneurial pursuits include co-founding Women Talk Media and heading Prized Productions.

Hadiya C. J. Claxton

Senior Associate, Attorney at Law
King & Spalding LLP

H adiya C. J. Claxton is a senior associate in the Real Estate Practice Group of King & Spalding LLP's Atlanta office. She represents clients involved in a wide range of commercial real estate transactions, including acquisition, development and disposition of office buildings, industrial properties, apartment projects and other mixed-use developments. She has extensive experience in complex real estate transactions and related matters, becoming a key player in her field.

Hadiya currently serves on the Hiring Committee for King & Spalding and dedicates much effort to recruiting and training talented attorneys. She is an active member of the American Bar Association, the Atlanta Bar Association and the State Bar of Georgia.

Hadiya received a bachelor's degree, summa cum laude, from Spelman College in 1999 and a juris doctorate degree from Harvard Law School in 2002. During her academic career, she received numerous honors, including membership in Phi Beta Kappa and the Golden Key International Honour Society and listings on the National Dean's List.

The wife of Colin Taylor, Hadiya is the proud mother of two children, Caden and Courtney.

Thomas Cox is an experienced litigator who concentrates his practice in the areas of labor and employment, and litigation. He is rated AV, the highest rating attainable, by the *Martindale-Hubbell Law Directory*. He has also been named to the *Georgia Super Lawyers* list.

Thomas defends multiple private sector corporate clients in all types of employment-related litigation, arbitration and mediation. These include claims of discrimination and sexual harassment; claims under the Americans with Disabilities Act, the Family and Medical Leave Act and Title VII; and the intentional infliction of emotional distress.

Thomas has been a featured panelist in a *Daily Report* expert's roundtable involving age discrimination claim avoidance. His cases have also been featured in *Ohio Lawyers Weekly*. He graduated, cum laude, with a Bachelor of Arts degree from Morehouse College. He also received a juris doctorate degree from Boston College Law School.

An active member and officer of Cascade United Methodist Church, Thomas and his wife, Gwendolyn, are the proud parents of two children, Thomas Cox III and Taylor Cox.

Thomas A. Cox Jr.

Member, Attorney at Law
Miller & Martin PLLC

Thomas F. Cuffie founded The Cuffie Law Firm in 1981, specializing in serious injury and wrongful death claims. There are now two locations in Atlanta, one near Greenbriar Mall and the other in DeKalb County near Stonecrest Mall. Thomas has won more than 25 cases where the award exceeded $1 million.

For three consecutive terms he served as an Atlanta city councilman. He was chairman for the Atlanta Fulton County Stadium Authority, which coordinated construction of Olympic Stadium (now Turner Field). Since 1995, he has been the attorney for the Georgia Funeral Service Practitioners Association (GFPSA). Thomas founded the 100 Black Men of Atlanta, Inc. and has received numerous prestigious awards from GFPSA, the Gate City Bar Association and 100 Black Men of Atlanta.

Thomas, a Sylvester native, earned a political science degree from Morehouse College. During college, he became a policeman and was subsequently promoted to detective. Upon finishing North Carolina Central Law School, Thomas was appointed associate city attorney for the City of Atlanta. He is married to Dr. Kaneta Lott Cuffie and has two adult children, Kimberly and Thomas.

Thomas F. Cuffie, Esq.

Founder & Attorney at Law
The Cuffie Law Firm

Dr. Flora B. Devine

Special Assistant & Attorney at Law
Legal Affairs
Kennesaw State University

Dr. Flora B. Devine is a university attorney and special assistant to the president of legal affairs at Kennesaw State University, the state's third-largest university. As a member of university president Daniel S. Papp's cabinet, she is responsible for the division's handling of all legal matters for the institution.

Prior to her work at Kennesaw State, Flora served as legal counsel in a private practice and for the City of Atlanta, the U.S. Environmental Protection Agency and Georgia Perimeter College. She has also served as an adjunct professor at Clark College, Georgia State University and Kennesaw State, teaching communications law, higher education law, conflict resolution and multiculturalism in education.

Flora's recent community service includes serving as the past chair of the Georgia Indigent Defense Council and the Georgia Supreme Court Commission on Indigent Defense. She is a member of the Morehouse College Martin Luther King, Jr. International Chapel Colloquium of Scholars, a former board member of the National Association of College and University Attorneys, and a fellow of the American Council on Education.

Johnita P. Due

Assistant General Counsel &
Diversity Council Chair
CNN

Johnita P. Due is assistant general counsel and chair of CNN's 28-member Diversity Council. She advises on First Amendment, copyright and new media issues, and contributed to the development of CNN's *Black in America* series.

Named among the Top Black Voices in Network News by *Ebony* and a Diversity Champion by *Diversity Edge Magazine*, Due received a NAMIC Luminary Award and the Ida B. Wells Award from the National Association of Black Journalists and the National Conference of Editorial Writers. She has been a McCormick Tribune fellow, a term member of the Council on Foreign Relations and a member of Leadership Atlanta. Due is a board member of Vox Teen Communications and the national Lawyers' Committee for Civil Rights Under Law.

Before joining CNN, she was associate general counsel for The McGraw-Hill Companies, Inc., an adjunct professor at Cornell Law School and a litigation associate at Winthrop, Stimson, Putnam & Roberts.

Due holds an Artium Baccalaureatus degree in psychology from Harvard University, a Master of Arts degree in psychology from the University of Sussex and a Doctor of Jurisprudence degree from Cornell University.

Attorney Don Edwards is in private legal practice in his Atlanta law firm, the Law Office of Donald P. Edwards, specializing as a trial lawyer in the areas of personal injury, wrongful death and medical malpractice since 1973.

Don has pursued a successful legal practice while devoting a significant amount of time and energy to community service. Notably, he has been chair of the Fulton County Board of Ethics, the South Atlanta Sankofa District of the Boy Scouts of America and the Christian Council of Metropolitan Atlanta.

Don is a 2004 inductee to the Gate City Bar Association Hall of Fame, a past president of the Gate City Bar Association and a recipient of the Chief Justice Award for Community Service, the State Bar of Georgia's highest award for community service.

Don graduated, cum laude, from Morehouse College. He was awarded a juris doctorate degree from the Boston University School of Law. He is the husband of Jo Roberson Edwards and grateful father of Nia, Domia and Dawnalisa Edwards.

Donald P. Edwards

Attorney at Law
Law Office of Donald P. Edwards

Stanley E. Foster is the managing partner of Hollowell Foster & Gepp, P.C., one of the oldest and largest minority-owned law firms in the southeastern United States. Foster also leads the corporate and municipal finance practices of the firm. He has practiced law for more than 29 years, and has been named a Super Lawyer by *Atlanta* magazine three times.

Foster is a member of the National Association of Bond Lawyers, the National Association of Securities Professionals, and the Gate City, Atlanta and American bar associations. A graduate of Brown University, Foster received a juris doctorate degree from the University of Pennsylvania, where he served as an Arthur J. Littlejohn Legal Writing fellow.

A Georgia native, Foster is an active member of Big Bethel A.M.E. Church, and has served as counsel to the presiding prelate of both the AME and CME churches. He is married to Latiquia Foster, and he is the proud parent of three children, Joshua, Mathew and Epiphany.

Stanley E. Foster, Esq.

Managing Partner
Hollowell Foster & Gepp, P.C.

Harold E. Franklin Jr.

Partner, Attorney at Law
King & Spalding LLP

H arold E. Franklin Jr. is a partner in King & Spalding's Tort and Environmental Practice Group. Franklin's national practice focuses on complex and high-stakes product liability litigation. Fluent in Spanish, his practice has also included matters in Puerto Rico, Europe and South America.

Featured by *Georgia Trend* magazine as a Legal Elite, Franklin was listed as a Rising Star and a Super Lawyer. In 2007 he was featured by the *Fulton Daily Report* as one of the top 15 lawyers in Georgia under the age of 40.

His affiliations include the American Bar Association; the Atlanta Bar Association (2008 membership committee chair); the Gate City Bar Association (2007 president); the National Bar Association (2007 regional director, 2008 national chair); and the International Association of Defense Counsel and Lawyers Committee for Civil Rights Under Law (executive board). The Georgia Congressional Delegation to the Judicial Advisory Panel regarding presidential appointments appointed Franklin in 2009.

A 1990 Emory University graduate with bachelor's degrees in economics and Spanish, Franklin graduated in 1999 from the Georgia State University College of Law. He and wife Cynthia have three children.

Paula J. Frederick

Deputy General Counsel
State Bar of Georgia

P aula Frederick is deputy general counsel for the State Bar of Georgia, where she interprets and enforces the ethics rules for lawyers. She came to the bar in 1988 after working six years as a lawyer with the Atlanta Legal Aid Society, where she handled civil legal matters for poor people.

A native of Riverside, California, Paula attended Duke University in Durham, North Carolina, and earned a Bachelor of Arts degree in political science in May of 1979. She is a 1982 graduate of the Vanderbilt University School of Law.

Paula was the first African-American president of the Atlanta Bar Association. She was president of the Georgia Association of Black Women Attorneys in 1998, and is an active member of the American Bar Association, the Gate City Bar Association and the Georgia Association for Women Lawyers.

Paula has served on the boards of many local charitable organizations and bar foundations. She is the recipient of numerous awards for her service to the bar.

R onald J. Freeman Sr. is co-founder of Johnson & Freeman, LLC, located in midtown Atlanta and historic Union City, Georgia. In 1982 he graduated with high honors from Morehouse College with a Bachelor of Arts degree in political science. After receiving a Regents Scholarship from the State of Georgia, he received a juris doctorate degree in 1985 from the Georgia State University College of Law. His primary focus is in the areas of construction law and business litigation.

In 2004, 2006, 2007 and 2008, Ronald was recognized as one of the top lawyers in the state of Georgia by *Atlanta* and *Law & Politics* magazines. This recognition is awarded to the top 5 percent of lawyers in the state. Ronald was presented with the Alumni Career Achievement Award by his alma mater, the Georgia State University College of Law BLSA Chapter, and the Excellence in Law Award by the Judicial Section of the Gate City Bar Association.

Ronald remains active in his personal life and community, which fosters the development of mentor/protégé relationships in a number of nonprofit and community-oriented organizations.

Ronald J. Freeman Sr.

Co-Founder, Attorney at Law
Johnson & Freeman, LLC

K aren D. Fultz is a member of Cozen O'Connor. She focuses her practice on subrogation and recovery. Prior to joining the firm, Karen was an associate with Lackland & Associates in Atlanta, and she served as a judicial intern for the Honorable Denise Page Hood of the U.S. District Court for the Eastern District of Michigan. She received a Bachelor of Arts degree from Michigan State University in 1993, and a law degree, cum laude, in 1998 from Thomas M. Cooley Law School, where she served on Moot Court.

As a member of the Subrogation and Recovery Department, Karen handles product liability cases ranging from $100,000 to more than $1 million. She is admitted to practice in Georgia and Tennessee, and her practice also includes family law matters.

Karen served as president of the Gate City Bar Association (2005) and continues to serve as a member. She is also a member of the Atlanta Volunteer Lawyers Foundation, the Georgia Association of Black Women Attorneys, the Atlanta Bar Association and the American and National bar associations.

Karen D. Fultz

Member, Attorney At Law
Cozen O'Connor

Sheila M. Govan

Attorney at Law
Govan and Associates

Sheila Govan has been practicing bankruptcy law and personal injury law for more than 15 years. She has successfully represented thousands of clients. Govan and her support staff have been recognized as one of the largest minority firms to serve bankruptcy clients in the Atlanta area.

Govan continues to be instrumental in helping consumers understand bankruptcy. She has been featured on *The Reggie Gay Gospel Show*, the *Bobby Hurd Show* and *The Layman's Lawyer* as a person of expertise in bankruptcy law. She is a member of the State Bar of Georgia, the Atlanta Bar Association, the National Bar Association and the Georgia Association for Women Lawyers.

Govan received a Bachelor of Arts degree from The LeMoyne-Owen College in Memphis, Tennessee. She also received a Doctor of Jurisprudence degree from John Marshall Law School in Atlanta, Georgia.

A native of Memphis, Tennessee, Govan is the proud mother of one daughter, Crystal. She enjoys reading, movies and traveling.

H. Eric Hilton

Vice President, General Counsel &
Corporate Secretary
H.J. Russell & Company

H. Eric Hilton is vice president, general counsel and corporate secretary of H.J. Russell & Company, where he is responsible for managing and directing the company's legal affairs, and overseeing the company's human resources and risk management functions. Additionally, he manages legal affairs for the company's various affiliates, including Concessions International LLC, which operates airport concessions in nine major airports nationwide. He also serves on the executive committees for both companies.

Hilton holds memberships in a number of business and civic organizations, including the American Bar Association, the Association of Corporate Counsel, the Minority Corporate Counsel Association and Kappa Alpha Psi Fraternity, Inc. He continues to serve on legal panels and regularly contributes to various publications. In 2007 Hilton was recognized by the *Fulton County Daily Report* in its annual "On the Rise – 15 to Watch" segment.

He earned a Bachelor of Science degree in economics from Hampton University and a juris doctorate degree from the George Washington University Law School. A native of Washington, D.C., Hilton and his wife, Marla, are the parents of two children, Hunter and Juliana.

K ristal A. Holmes, an attorney licensed to practice law in the state of Georgia, is a founding partner of Holmes & Lekan, LLC. The firm specializes in criminal defense, family law, probate law, personal injury and medical malpractice and real estate law.

A member of the Georgia Association of Criminal Defense Lawyers and the Gwinnett County Bar Association, Kristal is a founding member of the Gwinnett County Minority Bar Association. She is admitted to practice in all Georgia State and Superior courts, the Georgia Court of Appeals, the Georgia Supreme Court and the U.S. District Court of the Northern District of Georgia.

Kristal received a Bachelor of Arts degree, magna cum laude, from Spelman College in 1995. In 1999 she received a law degree from the Emory University School of Law. While attending law school at Emory, she spent a semester studying international environmental law and comparative health law at Macquarie University in Sydney, Australia.

A native of Gary, Indiana, Kristal is an avid art collector and artist.

Kristal A. Holmes

Partner, Attorney at Law
Holmes & Lekan, LLC

A llegra Lawrence-Hardy is a litigation partner in the national law firm of Sutherland Asbill & Brennan LLP, focusing on labor and employment law. She has litigated cases in federal and state courts for Fortune 100 companies across the country. She regularly advises employers on compliance with the various employment laws and often speaks to management, lawyers and human resources professionals on labor and employment law issues.

Allegra has been recognized as one of the top litigators in the state by *Georgia Trend*, *Atlanta Magazine* and the *Fulton County Daily Report*. She chairs Sutherland's Diversity Committee and is a member of the firm's Hiring Committee. Allegra is also a founding member of the Atlanta Legal Diversity Consortium, a past president of the Georgia Association of Black Women Attorneys and a member of the board of directors for the Justice Center of Atlanta. Additionally, she chairs the State Bar of Georgia's Women and Minorities in the Profession Committee.

Allegra graduated, magna cum laude, from Spelman College and holds a law degree from Yale University. An Atlanta native, she is married to Timothy Hardy.

Allegra Lawrence-Hardy

Litigation Partner
Sutherland Asbill & Brennan LLP

Bernie Lawrence-Watkins

Attorney at Law
B. Lawrence Watkins & Associates, PC

Bernie Lawrence-Watkins is an experienced transactional attorney who practices in the areas of entertainment, intellectual property, business transactions and government contracting. She currently writes articles for *Production Market Place*, an online entertainment publication.

A devoted community attendant, in 2007 she received the Metro Atlanta Community Champion Award from MADD and was honored by *rolling out* magazine as one of Atlanta's 25 Most Influential Women. Since 2001, she has volunteered with the Minority Business Development Association and the MED Week Committee to bring local entrepreneurs to Atlanta Public Schools for Business in School Day.

A founding member of the BWEL Foundation, Lawrence-Watkins is also on the local advisory board for BB&T, the United Way AAP, the One Economy Corporation and the Smyrna Basketball Association. She is a member of the Black Entertainment and Sports Law Association, Alpha Kappa Alpha Sorority, Inc. and the Atlanta Chapter of Jack and Jill of America, Inc.

Lawrence-Watkins hold a degree in business administration from Howard University and a juris doctorate from the University of Baltimore School of Law. She is married and has two sons.

Corliss Scroggins Lawson

Founding Partner
Corliss & Associates, P.C.

Corliss Scroggins Lawson is founding partner of Corliss & Associates, P.C., located in the historic downtown district of Fayetteville, Georgia. Prior to opening her own firm on June 1, 2006, she was a complex commercial litigator and managing partner of the Atlanta office of Lord, Bissell & Brook, LLP.

Lawson's practice covers a broad array of legal areas, including products liability, environmental, construction defect, unfair and deceptive trade practices, toxic torts, complex insurance defense, premises liability, railroad and aviation defense, and other general tort and breach of contract cases. She is also experienced in handling employment discrimination and sexual harassment cases. A seasoned litigator, her experience includes trying cases, heavy motion practice, arbitration, mediation and administrative hearings.

Lawson has been selected as a Georgia Super Lawyer for the years 2005, 2006 and 2007. She also recently joined Henning Mediation and Arbitration Service as a mediator, and is a registered mediator with the Georgia Office of Dispute Resolution.

D avid Long-Daniels is a well-known trial lawyer and chair of Greenberg Traurig's Atlanta Labor and Employment Practice. He represents clients in all types of employment matters, including claims under the Fair Labor Standard Act, Title VII of the Civil Rights Act, Family and Medical Leave Act, Americans with Disabilities Act and other federal and state labor employment matters.

As an adjunct law professor, David has taught labor and employment at both the University of Alabama School of Law and the Walter F. George School of Law at Mercer University. He is the author of many articles and publications, and is a recognized speaker at numerous seminars.

David is listed in the 2007-2008 edition of the *Chambers & Partners USA Guide* and as one of *Georgia Trend*'s Georgia's Legal Elite in 2006 and 2008. He received a Bachelor of Science degree from The University of Alabama in 1982, a Master of Public Administration degree from Valdosta State University in 1985, and a juris doctorate degree, cum laude, from Mercer University in 1990.

David Long-Daniels

Shareholder, Attorney at Law
Greenberg Traurig, LLP

C urtis J. Martin II is a partner with Mozley, Finlayson & Loggins LLP. He practices in the areas of commercial litigation, automobile and trucking litigation, product liability, and premises liability. He is vice president of the Gate City Bar Association, the oldest African-American bar association in the state of Georgia.

He received a juris doctorate degree from Valparaiso University. During law school, he served as president of the Black Law Students Association and the Multicultural Law Students Association.

He has engaged in numerous pro bono and civic activities in his service to the community and the legal profession. These activities include providing pro bono legal representation on behalf of the victims of domestic violence, and serving as a speaker and mentor to high school students.

Martin serves on the board of directors of Horizons Atlanta, a nonprofit organization designed to provide an academic enrichment program to public school children from economically disadvantaged families. He is also a contributor to the *Atlanta Business Journal*, authoring a bi-monthly column focused on legal issues.

Curtis J. Martin II, Esq.

Partner, Attorney at Law
Mozley, Finlayson & Loggins LLP

Anne P. Maynard

Attorney at Law
King & Spalding LLP

Anne Maynard is an attorney at King & Spalding LLP. She is a member of the Tort Litigation Practice Group, which concentrates on complex litigation relating to toxic torts and product liability.

Anne has received numerous academic and community honors that reflect her outstanding abilities, including listings in *Who's Who Among Students in American Universities & Colleges*; the National Dean's List; the Wig and Gavel Award, which designated her as the most likely to succeed in the practice of law; the Phi Alpha Alpha Honor Society for Public Affairs and Administration; and the State Bar of Georgia Pro Bono Honor Roll.

Anne attributes her success to her community service. She is a volunteer with the Atlanta Legal Aid Society, the Atlanta Volunteer Lawyers Foundation and the DeKalb Volunteer Lawyers Foundation. She is also an advocate for the homeless and battered women.

Anne graduated, cum laude, with a Bachelor of Arts degree from the University of the Virgin Islands. She also received a law degree from The John Marshall Law School and a master's degree in public administration from Georgia State University.

Karen V. Mills

Partner, Attorney at Law
Arnall Golden Gregory LLP

Karen V. Mills is a partner in the Corporate Practice Group at the law firm of Arnall Golden Gregory LLP. In this position, she advises companies of all sizes on issues related to mergers and acquisitions, equity and debt financings, corporate governance, and technology-related matters such as privacy and data security.

Karen was named a Rising Star by *Atlanta* magazine in 2005. She was elected as the second African-American female partner at Arnall Golden Gregory in December of 2007.

Karen received a bachelor's degree, with honors, in electrical engineering from the Georgia Institute of Technology. She also received a juris doctorate degree from The University of North Carolina at Chapel Hill.

A native of Macon, Georgia, Karen is passionate about empowering girls and young women. She currently serves on the board of trustees of the Atlanta Girls' School and the executive board of the Georgia Association of Black Women Attorneys.

Clyde Mize Jr. is an associate in the Real Estate Group at Morris, Manning & Martin, LLP. He represents clients including nonprofit corporations, builders, developers, lending institutions and individuals regarding their various real estate endeavors.

A dedicated servant leader, Clyde has worked toward strengthening Metropolitan Atlanta. He has built homes with Atlanta Habitat for Humanity, organized events for law students, and taught seminars for homeowners and individuals in the financial and real estate industries. For six years, Clyde served in the Youth Ministry of Elizabeth Baptist Church. A member of Alpha Phi Alpha Fraternity, Inc., he is involved in various professional and civic organizations, including the State Bar of Georgia and the Gate City Bar Association. In 2007 he was recognized for his volunteerism during the National Philanthropy Day celebration at the Georgia World Congress Center.

Clyde received a Bachelor of Science degree from the University of Illinois at Urbana-Champaign in 1995, and a juris doctorate degree from The University of Iowa College of Law in 1998. He is married to Dr. Ida Rose-Mize, and they have one son, Noah.

Clyde E. Mize Jr.

Attorney at Law
Morris, Manning & Martin, LLP

Patrise Perkins-Hooker is a partner with the law firm of Hollowell Foster & Gepp, P.C., practicing in the areas of general corporate law, commercial real estate transactions and probate. She also represents municipalities with quiet title and condemnation proceedings.

Patrise received a Bachelor of Science degree in industrial management, with honors, from the Georgia Institute of Technology in 1980 and a joint Doctor of Jurisprudence and Master of Business Administration degree from Emory University in 1984.

She was admitted to practice law in Georgia and the Federal District Court for the Northern District of Georgia and Tax Courts in 1984 and in the Supreme Court of Georgia in 1989. Additionally, she serves on the board of governors of the State Bar of Georgia and is a member of its Finance Committee.

A member of Radcliffe Presbyterian Church, Patrise and her loving husband, Douglas Hooker, have been married for more than 30 years. She has two children and six grandchildren.

Patrise Perkins-Hooker

Partner & Attorney at Law
Hollowell Foster & Gepp, P.C.

Auma Ngesa Reggy

Partner, Attorney at Law
Adorno & Yoss LLC

Auma Reggy is a partner in the Intellectual Property Practice Group of Adorno & Yoss LLC. In this position, she advises and represents clients in actions and negotiations across the spectrum of intellectual property, including trademarks, copyrights, advertising, trade secrets, endorsements, the Internet and domain names.

Law & Politics and *Atlanta* Magazine named Auma a Georgia Rising Star in Intellectual Property Law in 2005, 2006 and 2007. She is a member of My Sister's Keeper Foundation for Women, Inc., the board of directors of The Kenya Project, Inc. and a member of the board of advisers of IMPACT360.

Auma received a Bachelor of Arts degree in economics and French from Eastern College. The Howard University School of Law awarded her a juris doctorate degree with honors.

A native of Nairobi, Kenya, Auma has studied in Kenya, Germany, France and the United States. She is the daughter of Dr. Mae Alice Reggy-Mamo and the late Dr. John Odhiambo Reggy. She is the sister of Dr. Atieno A. Reggy, Anyango E. Reggy and Achieng' A. Reggy.

Leron E. Rogers

Partner, Attorney at Law
Hewitt & Rogers

Leron E. Rogers is a partner in the law firm of Hewitt & Rogers in Atlanta. The firm's practice areas include business transactions, entertainment law and business litigation, among other services.

Leron heads up the firm's Entertainment, Technology and Media Law Practice Group, and is known throughout the country for representing high-profile entertainers and athletes in their professional and business ventures. He represents successful artists, management companies, record labels and publishing companies, as well as Grammy-nominated songwriters and producers. In addition to representing individual entertainers, he represents successful corporations that conduct significant business within the technology, media and entertainment industry, as well as professional athletes in their off-the-field business ventures.

A member of the National Academy of Recording Arts and Sciences, the Future of Music Coalition advisory board and Kappa Alpha Psi Fraternity, Inc., Leron is a frequent speaker and featured panelist at conferences and workshops. Additionally, he has been featured in local and national publications.

Leron received a Bachelor of Business Administration degree in finance from Southwest Texas State University, and obtained a juris doctorate degree from Florida State University's Law School.

T acita Scott is a partner with Adorno & Yoss LLC. She represents corporations and religious institutions in all areas of employment law and business litigation.

In addition to graduating from Leadership Atlanta in 2007, MADD honored Tacita with a 2007 Community Champion Award. Furthermore, *Atlanta Woman* magazine named her one of Atlanta's 25 Power Women to Watch in 2006, and *Atlanta* magazine has repeatedly named her a Georgia Rising Star Super Lawyer.

In addition to serving on the board of directors for Goodwill Industries of North Georgia, Tacita serves on the boards of trustees for the Lawyers' Committee for Civil Rights Under Law and on the advisory committee for CCLMI. An advocate for diversity, she serves on the advisory board for the Atlanta Large Law Firm Diversity Alliance and on the steering committee for the State Bar of Georgia's Diversity Program.

A graduate of Spelman College and Vanderbilt University Law School, Tacita is the wife of Thom Scott II.

Tacita A. Mikel Scott

Partner, Attorney at Law
Adorno & Yoss LLC

K en Southall is a seasoned intellectual property lawyer with more than 18 years of experience representing large corporations and individuals in patent, trademark and copyright matters. He has represented a diverse clientele, including the world's largest software maker, the world's largest semiconductor manufacturer, automobile manufacturers and suppliers, manufacturers of paper and packaging products, makers of hair care products, athletes, entertainers and the world's largest retailer. Prior to joining Adorno & Yoss, Ken served as chief intellectual property law counsel for a division of the General Electric Company.

He is a graduate of Virginia Tech, where he received a Bachelor of Science degree in electrical engineering, and the Georgia State University College of Law, where he served on the board of visitors. His awards include being recognized by *Diversity & The Bar* as one of the nation's Top Minority Intellectual Property Law Partners.

Ken is married to attorney Noni Ellison Southall. They have two children, Kenneth Jr. and Kourtney.

Ken Southall

Partner, Attorney at Law
Adorno & Yoss LLC

Noni Ellison Southall, Esq.

Senior Counsel
Turner Broadcasting System, Inc.

Noni Ellison Southall serves as senior counsel for Turner Broadcasting System, Inc. (TBS), the owner of Cartoon Network, CNN, TruTV, TCM and TNT cable networks and the head of TBS music group. Noni manages all substantive and administrative matters regarding music utilized by TBS, both domestic and international. In addition to negotiating music-related deals, she oversees administration of the TBS music publishing companies and the Williams Street record label.

Noni earned a Bachelor of Arts degree, magna cum laude, from Howard University and Doctor of Jurisprudence and Master of Business Administration degrees from the University of Chicago.

A board member of the Atlanta Urban League, BESLA and Corporate Counsel Women of Color, she is admitted to practice before the U.S. Supreme Court and is a founding member of the Black Professionals at Turner Business Resource Group. Noni also received the National Council of Negro Women Tribute to Black Women Community Leaders and the Trumpet Awards Foundation, Inc. High Heels in High Places awards.

A Louisiana native, she is the wife of attorney Kenneth Southall and the mother of two children.

Jesse Spikes

Senior Partner, Attorney at Law
McKenna Long & Aldridge, LLP

Jesse Spikes is a senior partner based in the Atlanta office of McKenna Long & Aldridge LLP. In this position, he focuses on corporate transactions, governance and compliance, internal investigations and audits, as well as special committee representations. He also works with businesses in the area of advertising and marketing law, including the negotiation of endorsements and the preparation of licensing agreements.

Currently serving as a director on the board of Atlanta Life Financial Group, Jesse has also advised corporate clients with respect to litigation strategy and has represented independent board committees of private companies.

His community activities include service as chairman of the Fulton County Board of Registration and Elections, and on the boards of the Children's Healthcare of Atlanta Foundation, the Metro Atlanta Chamber of Commerce, Agnes Scott College, the Atlanta Organizing Committee for the 1996 Olympic Games and many other organizations.

A McDonough native, Jesse received a bachelor's degree from Dartmouth College and a juris doctorate degree from Harvard Law School. He also attended Oxford University on a Rhodes Scholarship.

M ichael Tyler is a partner with Kilpatrick Stockton LLP, where he practices commercial litigation and land use law. He earned a juris doctorate degree from Harvard Law School. He also received a Master of Public Administration degree from Harvard University and a Bachelor of Arts degree from Morehouse College.

Tyler serves on the boards of the Metropolitan Atlanta Rapid Transit Authority, the Piedmont Park Conservancy, the National Black Arts Festival, Providence Missionary Baptist Church, the Lawyers' Committee for Civil Rights Under Law and the Georgia Supreme Court Committee on Civil Justice. He previously served on the boards of the Georgia Regional Transportation Authority, the State Bar of Georgia Disciplinary Board, the City of Atlanta Zoning Review Board, the Atlanta Urban League and the Gate City Bar Association.

Tyler has twice received the Gate City Bar Association's A.T. Walden Outstanding Lawyer Award. He has also been named to the *Atlanta Business Chronicle*'s Who's Who in Atlanta, *Georgia Trend* magazine's Legal Elite and *James* magazine's Super Lawyers. He is married to Cathy Clark Tyler and has three children, Michael, Malcolm and Matthew.

Michael Tyler

Partner, Attorney at Law
Kilpatrick Stockton LLP

L isa A. Wade is a partner with Swift, Currie, McGhee & Hiers, LLP. A member of the firm's Employment Practices Section, her practice also includes workers' compensation and insurance defense cases.

Wade has defended cases involving premises liability, automobile accidents, product liability, coverage issues, zoning, property damage, and slips and falls. In the area of workers' compensation, she represents companies that are both self-insured and commercially insured. Currently the lead defense counsel for the City of Atlanta's workers' compensation matters, she has handled various employment practice issues for employers.

She was chairwoman on the Board of Zoning Adjustment for the City of Atlanta and has served as the Atlanta Board of Education's Civil Service Commission legal adviser and as hearing officer for termination cases of certificated and non-certificated employees.

A member of the American, Gate City and Atlanta bar associations, the State Bar of Georgia, the Georgia Association of Black Women Attorneys, the Georgia Defense Lawyers Association and DRI, Wade received a bachelor's degree from Brown University and a juris doctorate degree from The University of Georgia School of Law.

Lisa A. Wade

Partner, Attorney at Law
Swift, Currie, McGhee & Hiers, LLP

Christopher L. Walker

Vice President & General Counsel
H.J. Russell & Company

Christopher L. Walker is vice president and general counsel of H.J. Russell & Company. He is responsible for providing legal support to all business units and company affiliates. These include Russell New Urban Development, LLC, which has several developments throughout Atlanta and nationally, and Concessions International LLC, which operates airport concessions in nine major airports nationwide.

Walker holds memberships in a number of business and civic organizations, including the American Bar Association, the Association of Corporate Counsel, the National Black MBA Association and Alpha Phi Alpha Fraternity, Inc. He also volunteers with the YMCA, and the Boys & Girls Clubs of America.

Walker earned a Bachelor of Business Administration degree in accounting and a Master of Business Administration degree in finance from Millsaps College. Additionally, he earned a juris doctorate degree from the University of Mississippi School of Law.

He and his wife, Kesha, are the parents of two children, Christopher and Kendall.

Gerald Wells

Partner
DLA Piper LLP

Gerald Wells is a partner in the franchise and distribution department of DLA Piper LLP. Wells counsels start-up and established franchisors, licensors and manufacturers, and his practice focuses in franchising, licensing, distribution, general corporate law and mergers and acquisitions. He also represents and advises businesses on a wide variety of corporate and transactional matters, including corporate organization, compliance and negotiation and the preparation of commercial, technology and employment contracts.

Wells earned a Bachelor of Arts degree from the University of Maryland and a Doctor of Jurisprudence degree from The College of William & Mary Law School, where he was an Earl Warren scholar and a Wilkens scholar.

Following graduation, he clerked for the Honorable Hart T. Mankin, U.S. Court of Appeals for Veterans Claims. Wells has also worked for the U.S. Office Products Company and the Hewlett-Packard Company. Prior to joining DLA Piper, he was a partner in the corporate section of Smith, Gambrell & Russell, LLP.

Wells is a member of the American and National bar associations and is admitted to the District of Columbia, Maryland and Georgia bars.

William K. Whitner, a partner in the Atlanta office of the international law firm of Paul, Hastings, Janofsky & Walker LLP, is a business lawyer whose focus is on complex civil corporate matters.

Whitner graduated, with honors, from Georgetown University and completed his law studies at Yale Law School. His legal experience includes business tort and intellectual property litigation and contract and franchise disputes. He represents large global, national and local companies in state and federal courts and arbitrations.

Active in the community, Whitner is a member of 100 Black Men of South Metro, Inc. and serves on the board of the Anti-Prejudice Consortium. He is a fellow of the Litigation Counsel of America and the Lawyers Foundation of Georgia. Whitner was appointed by the Georgia Supreme Court to serve on the Commission on Access and Fairness in the Courts, and also serves on the State Bar of Georgia Committee on Women and Minorities in the Profession.

William K. Whitner

Partner & Attorney at Law
Paul, Hastings, Janofsky & Walker LLP

Attorney Rita Tucker Williams is a native Atlantan. She is chief executive officer and managing attorney of the law firm of Williams & Associates. She has developed an outstanding reputation as a lawyer who stands for justice for all people.

Williams began her law firm in 1990 and has developed three specialty areas, representing people seriously injured in accidents, family law and criminal law. She began her legal career as an associate at the prestigious law firm of Alston & Bird LLP. She is comfortable working on complex litigation, such as product liability and wrongful death cases, and sentinel appellate briefs, due to her early legal training.

Williams has been honored in editions of *Who's Who In Black Atlanta*, *Who's Who in American Women*, *Who's Who in America*, *Who's Who in American Law* and *Who's Who in the World*. She is committed to a world of grace, justice and power for all people. Williams' unique background, commitment to excellence and accomplished staff are poised to place Williams & Associates on the world stage in the arena of injury law firms.

Rita Tucker Williams, Esq.

Attorney & Founder
Williams & Associates, P.C.

Brent L. Wilson

Partner, Attorney at Law
Elarbee, Thompson, Sapp & Wilson, LLP

B rent Wilson, a partner of Elarbee, Thompson, Sapp & Wilson, LLP, devotes his practice to the representation of management clients in labor and employment. He is also focused on proactively counseling and training employers regarding day-to-day employment decisions to avoid litigation.

A frequent speaker for various organizations and educational forums for attorneys and human resource professionals, Brent is active in numerous professional organizations, including the Minority Corporate Counsel Association, the National Association of African Americans in Human Resources and the Society for Human Resource Management. He is a founding member of the National Employment Law Council and the Georgia Diversity Program of the State Bar of Georgia, and serves on the board of directors for the Boys & Girls Clubs of Metro Atlanta.

Brent's awards and honors include being named one of America's Leading Black Lawyers by *Black Enterprise*, one of Georgia's Super Lawyers (2004-2008), a Top 100 Vote-Getter and one of *Georgia Trend*'s Legal Elite. He earned a Bachelor of Arts degree, cum laude, from Morehouse College and a juris doctorate degree from the State University of New York at Buffalo.

Atlanta's

COMMUNITY LEADERS

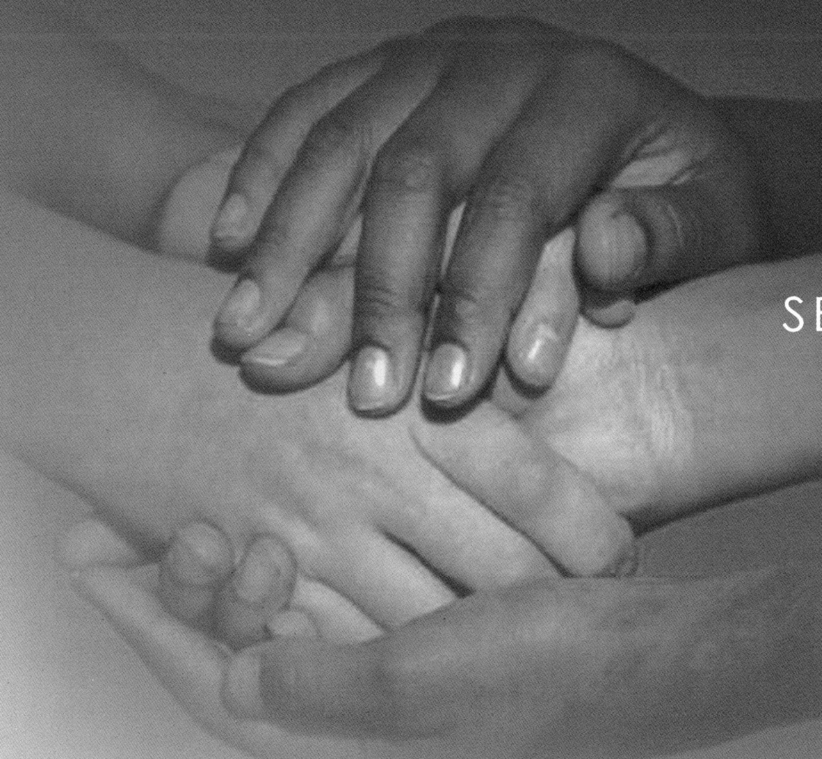

NOBLE

CARING

SELF-SACRIFICING

GENEROUS

EMPOWERING

HEROIC

PHILANTHROPIC

HUMANITARIAN

ALTRUISTIC

Deloris Baskin

Chief of Staff to
William "Bill" Edwards

Kimberly Boykin

Founder & Chief Executive Officer
boys who d.a.r.e., Inc.

Deloris Baskin has been appointed as chief of staff to Fulton County vice chair William "Bill" Edwards. Previously, she served as District 7 representative, where she worked to create and maintain a customer center office designed to support and serve the citizens of District 7. Deloris is responsible for handling issues related to zoning, seniors, code enforcement, building inspections, erosion, public safety and parks. Additionally, she will assume the responsibility of staff, budget and intergovernmental relations.

Deloris handles community and constituent issues for District 7 residents. One of her primary responsibilities is to help developers understand Commissioner Edwards' vision for South Fulton. Her office, located at the South Fulton Service Center, affords her the opportunity to be easily accessible to South Fulton County residents.

Deloris' motto is "to always try to enhance the quality of life in South Fulton by serving citizens professionally and with compassion." She is a member of Cascade United Methodist Church, where she serves as an usher, and is a member of the Lay Speakers Ministry and the Gospel Choir. She is the proud mother of one daughter, Shannon.

Kimberly Boykin is founder and chief executive officer of boys who d.a.r.e., Inc., a program designed to promote literacy among young males between the ages of 4 and 17 by providing thematic literacy events created to offer early literacy intervention, designed to expand educational experiences and cultural learning. She developed the program to empower young boys and to restore faith in the men of the community as they uplift young boys by demonstrating the importance of literacy while encouraging them to dream.

Kimberly received the National Coalition of 100 Black Women, Inc. Unsung Heroine Award 2004 and the 2005 Presidential Award for Volunteerism. She is also a 2007 Hands On Georgia Gallery of Service honoree.

Kimberly received a bachelor's degree in human resource development from Georgia State University. She is currently working on a Master of Business Administration degree at the University of Phoenix.

An Atlanta native, Kimberly has dedicated her life to serving others. An active member of Hunter Hill First Baptist Church, her most treasured gift is her son, Evann-Lawrence. She is the proud daughter of Larry and Margaret Boykin.

H. Ron Brashear

Founder & President
Youth of Honor Foundation

Dara Broadus

Professional Golfer & Founder
Impact Youth Development Initiative

H.Ron Brashear founded the Youth of Honor Foundation in 2006 and coined the phrase, "GET YOH JUMP ON LIFE." A motivational speaker, philanthropist and author, he is passionate about seeing at-risk youth turn toward the path of a new perspective and new opportunities in life.

Brashear received a Bachelor of Arts degree from National Louis University and is the author of *BOUNCING BACK...Living Life the Right Way.* This book chronicles his life and how he was able to rise above the impact of negative influences to become an IT director at Telcordia. Brashear is also executive vice president and managing editor for InsideBoxing, Inc., a position that afforded him the opportunity to meet and subsequently nurture a special relationship with his hero, Muhammad Ali.

A native of Elizabethtown, Kentucky, he is the nephew of Carl Brashear, the first African-American Navy master diver whose life was depicted in the 20th Century Fox Motion Picture *Men of Honor,* starring Cuba Gooding Jr. and Robert DeNiro.

Bashear resides in Atlanta with his wife, Audrey, and their daughters, Olivia and Jillian.

Dara Broadus is a professional golfer and founder of the Impact Youth Development Initiative (IYDI). Dara's experience on the Ladies Professional Golf Association Futures Tour helped propel her into her current roles as one of the most sought-after golf professionals in south Atlanta, and executive director of IYDI. She manages the development and three youth centers, all featuring golf academies for underserved youth. The locations include Atlanta, Georgia; Jacksonville, Florida; and Savannah, Georgia.

Dara plays an integral part in the production of several fundraisers, including the Impact Celebrity Golf & Tennis Challenge, and the Impact the Community Food and Toy Drive. She has been recognized in several golf publications, including Pete McDaniel's *Uneven Lies: The Heroic Story of African-Americans in Golf.* She is also a contributing writer for the *African American Golfer's Digest* magazine.

Dara earned a place among the elite list of black females qualified to play in the prestigious U.S. Women's Amateur Championship. She holds a Bachelor of Arts degree in business from Furman University, and attended The Westminster Schools in Atlanta and the David Leadbetter Golf Academy in Florida.

Naomi Brown

Environmental Chemist
Department of Watershed Management
City of Atlanta

Sam D. Burston

Regional Development Director
Atlanta Region
United Negro College Fund

Naomi Brown is an environmental chemist with the City of Atlanta. In this position, she manages the Nutrient Laboratory and provides analytical testing of water and wastes for phosphorus and nitrogen compounds. Naomi also services the instrumentation, keeping up with inventory and ordering. She is a certified laboratory analyst in the state of Georgia. The 2003 recipient of the Water Environment Federation's Laboratory Excellence Award, she serves on the Laboratory Committee of the Georgia Association of Water Professionals.

Naomi received a Bachelor of Science degree from Georgia College & State University and a teacher certification from Georgia State University.

A foster parent since 1990, Naomi has fostered more than 20 children. She is an advocate for children and presently serves as the subregional vice president for Fulton County with the Adoptive and Foster Parents Association of Georgia. Her duties as subregional vice president include serving as an advocate for the rights of foster parents, coordinating training activities and workshops, and helping with the grievance procedures associated with the Foster Parents Bill of Rights.

A native Atlantan, Sam D. Burston is a seasoned fundraising professional. He is responsible for raising critical funds for the UNCF's 39 HBCUs.

Prior to joining the UNCF, Burston spent many years in Atlanta's hospitality industry as director of sales and marketing, and hotel manager for a number of major and independent chains. While manager of the Radisson Hotel, he hosted the launch of the very first *Who's Who In Black Atlanta*® publication.

Burston's civic involvements include the Clayton County School Board Ethics Commission (vice chairman), African Americans for the Arts and the NAACP ACT-SO competition (annual judge). A graduate of Morris Brown College, he is a member of Ben Hill United Methodist Church and Iota Phi Theta Fraternity, Inc.

When not developing fundraising strategies for the UNCF, Burston is in his studio perfecting his gift as an accomplished visual artist. He recently participated in a one-man exhibition at The Lucy Craft Laney Museum of Black History in Augusta. He believes that the best hope for a good quality of life for today's youth is through education.

Gwendolyn Campbell

Executive Director
Atlanta Federal Executive Board

Joe Carn

Vice Mayor
City of College Park

Gwendolyn (Gwenne) Campbell, the executive director of the Atlanta Federal Executive Board, works directly with the 100 federal agencies' heads in Atlanta, representing 47,000 federal employees. Her responsibilities include serving as a catalyst to produce interagency communication, shared resources and workforce education relative to emergency preparedness, security and employee safety, facilitating interagency human capital readiness. She is also responsible for advancing local and national initiatives through intergovernmental and community partnerships in a manner that inspires public trust and confidence.

Gwenne created a governmentwide leadership program to equip future government leaders with executive competencies. She also provides oversight to the Combined Federal Campaign, where more than $4.6 million was raised for nonprofit organizations in 2008.

She is a member of Cascade United Methodist Church, where she serves on the Staff Pastor Parish Relations Committee and the Stewardship Committee. Her community activities include the UNCF, the Clark Atlanta University Guild, the Atlanta Fisk Club and Leadership Atlanta.

Gwenne received a degree in history and took graduate studies in public administration at Fisk University. A prolific writer, her hobbies include reading, traveling and creating games/puzzles.

Joe Carn truly represents the next generation of leadership in College Park. As the city's youngest elected official, he takes pride in challenging the status quo, moving in new and positive directions. Listed as one of the *Georgia Informer*'s 40 Under 40, Carn currently oversees $1.2 billion in new development and construction.

Carn serves on the board of directors for the Concerned Black Clergy and is the youngest board member of the National Organization to Insure a Sound Environment (N.O.I.S.E.). During his tenure, he set out to empower the community, demanding more from young people. He also serves locally as chairman of the Local School Advisory Council School Board, and volunteers with nonprofit organizations Metamorphasis Inc. and LIFT Community Development.

The son of R&B vocalist Jean Carn, Carn attended Benjamin E. Mays High School and completed graduate studies at Harvard University's John F. Kennedy School of Government. A devoted father and author, he is currently finishing his second book. In his spare time, he enjoys music and bike riding.

Greg Clay

Special Assistant to the City Manager
City of East Point

Dr. Joyce J. Dorsey

President & Chief Executive Officer
Fulton Atlanta Community
Action Authority

A native of southwest Atlanta, Greg Clay serves as special assistant to the city manager of East Point, Georgia. He assists the city manager with daily operations, working with internal departments and external entities to advance the goals of the city council.

Greg's recent honors include the Apex Society's Atlanta Power 30 Under 30™, and being one of 12 Black Men to Watch by *Clutch Magazine*. A local government management fellow with the International City/County Management Association, his other professional affiliations include the National Forum for Black Public Administrators, where he serves as a national board member, and in other capacities. Greg is a member of the Urban League, The Kiwanis Club of Peachtree-Atlanta, Big Brothers Big Sisters, and is a mentor with the Georgia State University Student Support Services Freshman Institute. He also founded and manages It Is Up To Us, a positive initiative-based company.

Greg received a business administration degree from Florida A&M University as a McNair scholar, and a Master of Public Administration degree from The University of Kansas, where he graduated Pi Alpha Alpha Honor Society.

F or more than 32 years, Dr. Joyce Dorsey has fought for the well-being of others. Commonly and appropriately referred to as a "champion for change," she speaks with authority on issues that affect humankind, particularly the poor and disenfranchised.

The Fulton Atlanta Community Action Authority (FACAA) is a nonprofit organization that annually serves 30,000 individuals and families by helping them become self-sufficient. Employed by the FACAA since its inception in 1991, Dorsey reconstituted the community action organization into one that is viable and financially sound. Such leadership brilliantly illuminates her efficient use of public funds and her ability to create a team to effectively implement the strategic plan of the organization.

Dorsey earned a bachelor's degree from Spelman College, a master's degree from Atlanta University and a doctorate degree in biblical studies from the North Carolina College of Theology. Her career reflects significant strides in social work, corrections, entrepreneurship and the nonprofit sector. Dorsey is active in numerous community organizations, and is a proud mother and grandmother.

Catherine Foster-Rowell

Senior Program Director, Title XX
Atlanta Renewal Community
Coordinating Responsible Authority

Michael German

National Team Leader
U.S. Interagency Council on
Homelessness

Catherine Foster-Rowell is a senior program director with the Atlanta Renewal Community Coordinating Responsible Authority (ACoRA), responsible for overseeing the investment of $46.7 million in program funds remaining from the City of Atlanta's former Atlanta Empowerment Zone designation. Her duties include overseeing the agency's procurement, which involves issuing requests for proposals/qualifications, evaluating proposal submissions to select vendors and service providers, making funding recommendations to the board of directors and monitoring grantee and contractor performance.

Prior to joining ACoRA, Foster-Rowell was a regional director for the Bronner Group. She was responsible for government relations, and providing consulting services to health and human service agencies and public housing authorities in the southeastern United States. Foster-Rowell also worked for the MAXIMUS consulting firm for five years. At her departure, she held the position of director in the Revenue Services Division.

Foster-Rowell has served on numerous boards. Her current volunteer activities include serving on a founding board of the Young Leaders Collegiate Academy, a proposed charter middle school for south Fulton County. She is also president of her homeowners' association.

Michael German is the national team leader for the U.S. Interagency Council on Homelessness, which is comprised of 20 cabinet secretaries and federal agency directors who convene regularly at the White House to ensure that federal resources are more available and accessible to homeless people. In 2007 Harvard University's John F. Kennedy School of Government named the council one of the Top 50 Government Innovations in the nation through its national partnership of 20 federal agencies, 49 states, three territories, and more than 300 commitments from mayors and county executives.

German serves in the U.S. Department of Housing and Urban Development. He was previously district manager to Congressman John Lewis; director of the Office of Grants Development under Atlanta Mayor Maynard Jackson; and deputy executive director of the Atlanta Housing Authority.

German's entrepreneurial endeavors include international commerce and travel to France, Germany, Spain, Canada, the United Kingdom, Mexico, the Republic of China and the Netherlands. He is a graduate of Alabama State University and has completed studies at the John F. Kennedy School of Government Executive Program at Harvard University.

Howard W. Grant, Ph.D.

Executive Director
Atlanta Board of Education

Kathy Hood

District Representative
Fulton County Commission

Dr. Howard W. Grant is executive director of the Atlanta Board of Education. He is responsible for the administration and policy vision of the board. He is also a scholar-practitioner in the field of public policy, and is currently on faculty at Clark Atlanta University.

Grant is a graduate of Morehouse College. He earned master's and doctorate degrees from Clark Atlanta University.

A member of Omega Psi Phi Fraternity, Inc., Grant was named in *Atlanta Business Chronicle*'s 40 Under 40 Up & Comers and received the Concerned Black Clergy Education Award. A fellow of the Charles Kettering Foundation and the Diversity Leadership Academy, he is also a member of the Leadership Atlanta Class of 2006 and the 100 Black Men of Atlanta.

Grant currently serves on the boards of directors for Atlanta Victims Assistance, Inc., the Fulton Atlanta Community Action Authority, VSA arts of Georgia and Men in Action, Inc. He, his daughter, Madison, and son, Carrington, are members of Cascade United Methodist Church and reside in the Cascade Heights area.

Kathy Hood is a district representative for Fulton County Commission vice chairman William "Bill" Edwards, South Fulton County, District Seven.

Kathy has worked with citizens and organizations in the Fulton Industrial, Cascade, Sandtown and Old National Highway areas for the past eight years. She enjoys assisting the constituents, acting as a liaison between the citizens and the county departments. Kathy also works closely with several Fulton County departments such as Public Works, the Fulton County Housing Authority, Human Services (Office of Children and Youth, Workforce Development), Parks and Recreation, Tax Commissioner and Tax Assessors. Additionally, she is the coordinator for Fulton County's Call To Womanhood and Call To Manhood annual teen conferences.

Kathy brings a wealth of expertise to this position with years of experience in the hotel management arena combined with years of special events and customer service experience. She is also the chief executive officer and founder of the Marvelous Light Empowerment Association, the Dare To Be Beautiful annual women's retreat and the Daughters of Zion leadership mentoring group.

Kathy is the proud mother of a son and daughter.

Garland R. Hunt

Board Member
Georgia Parole Board

Eric L. Jackson

Fire Suppression Captain &
Public Information Officer
DeKalb County Fire Rescue Department

Garland R. Hunt presently serves as a board member of the Georgia Parole Board. He was appointed in January of 2004 by Governor Sonny Perdue and served as chairman from July of 2006 to June of 2008. His background as a lawyer and minister provides a unique perspective to the board.

Garland obtained undergraduate and law degrees at Howard University. Upon graduation, he served as a staff attorney for the U.S. Court of Appeals, Fourth Circuit.

An ordained minister, he co-pastors The Father's House in Norcross, and serves as general counsel and executive vice president of the Fellowship of International Churches. His ministry has included overseeing the New Generation Campus Ministries, an outreach for students on historically black college campuses committed to developing faith-based leaders for the marketplace.

Garland is vice president of the Association of Paroling Authorities International. He was elected president of the 2004 class of The Coverdell Leadership Institute, and is a graduate of the Leadership Georgia class of 2006.

Garland and his wife, Eileen, reside in Alpharetta with their three children, Garland Jr., Christa and Jeremy.

Eric L. Jackson is a fire captain with the DeKalb County Fire Rescue Department (DCFR) in Tucker, Georgia, where he serves as public information officer. As spokesperson, he is responsible for the dissemination of all facets of fire department-related news and information to local media outlets, stakeholders, businesses and residents of DeKalb County.

Jackson's professional career with the fire service spans more than 20 years, and he spearheaded the creation of the DCFR Public Information Office. In 2000 he was named Firefighter of the Year by the West DeKalb Rotary Club, followed by receiving the first 2008 Public Information Officer of the Year Award given by Commissioner John Oxendine out of the Georgia State Office of Insurance and Safety Fire Commission. He will receive a bachelor's degree in organization leadership in December of 2009 from Mercer University in Macon, Georgia.

A native of Altadena, California, and a deacon at Beulah Missionary Baptist Church in Decatur, Jackson is married to his lovely wife, Shelbia. They are the proud parents of two young boys, Eric Lance II and William Laymon.

Ivory Latta

Professional Basketball Player
Atlanta Dream

Camille Russell Love

Director
Office of Cultural Affairs
City of Atlanta

With her high-energy play and bubbly personality, Atlanta Dream point guard, No. 12 Ivory Latta, is a fan favorite at Philips Arena. At 5 feet 6 inches, she has proven all of her doubters wrong, emerging as one of the brightest young talents in the WNBA.

A native of McConnells, South Carolina, Latta is the all-time leading scorer in state history with a total of 4,319 career points. After shattering records at York Comprehensive High School, she took her game to The University of North Carolina, where she led the Tar Heels to back-to-back Final Four appearances in 2006 and 2007. Originally drafted by the Detroit Shock in the 2007 WNBA Draft, she was acquired by the Dream in the 2008 expansion draft.

Latta was excited to return home to the Southeast, where she was already a recognizable face to fans. With her infectious personality and undeniable passion for the game always on display, she became an instant crowd favorite in the Atlanta Dream's inaugural season. She looks to be at the start of a very successful career in the league.

Camille Russell Love is the director of the City of Atlanta's Office of Cultural Affairs. Since 1998 she has directed the arts and culture programs for the City of Atlanta, including the Public Art Program, Contract for Art Services, Atlanta Reads and ARTSCooL. Camille manages the Atlanta Cyclorama, the South Bend Center for Arts and Culture and the Chastain Art Center and Gallery. She oversees the Cultural Experience Project in collaboration with the Atlanta Public School System and also produces the annual Atlanta Jazz Festival.

Currently, Camille is a board member of the United States Urban Arts Federation, the National Black Arts Festival, APEX Museum and the Metropolitan Atlanta Arts Fund. She was a participant in the 2006 Atlanta Regional Commission's Regional Leadership Institute and the 2008 Project Interchange in Israel.

Camille received a Bachelor of Arts degree from Wake Forest University and attended the Duke University School of Law.

She is the proud mother of three and the grandmother of two.

David T. Manuel

Director, Community Relations
Woodruff Arts Center
Diversity Initiative

Brian M. Morgan

President & Chief Executive Officer
Foundation for Men Awareness Inc.

As director of community relations for the Woodruff Arts Center Diversity Initiative, David T. Manuel is responsible for organizing and facilitating programs that promote art and serves as a spokesman for special events and community activities. In this capacity, he has managed several programs that promote education and diversity, including the Celebrate Diversity Initiative, which celebrates Atlanta's multicultural fabric and its role within the art community by offering resources that build awareness and participation within the arts center's diverse audience.

Currently, Manuel hosts HBO's Atlanta premiere screenings and the Urban Film Review, which showcases independent films monthly at Woodruff Arts Center. He has served on the executive boards of Callanwolde Fine Arts Center, the Atlanta Business League and the Boys & Girls Clubs of America.

Manuel's belief in celebrating art, life and community is evident in his book, *I Am A Father*. The book is designed to shine a positive light on the achievements and dedication of African-American fathers. In addition, he is a member of Berean Christian Church and lives in Lilburn, Georgia, with his sons, Branden and Blake.

Brian M. Morgan is president and chief executive officer of the Foundation for Men Awareness Inc., a Georgia nonprofit focused on helping homeless men, assisting sexually exploited youth and creating awareness of domestic violence against men. He is responsible for the oversight of programs and development issues related to improving and meeting the needs of the community.

Morgan is a graduate of the University of Phoenix Business Management Program, and has been employed by CBS and NBC. A recipient of the 2007 U.S. Presidential Volunteer Award, he is an Americorps Network member and has served as a logistic coordinator for the Hands On Atlanta Leadership Development Committee.

A native of Atlanta, Morgan is the proud father of Kiara Morgan, a fourth-grade honor roll student. In addition, he is a member of the High Museum of Art Atlanta, attends Maranatha Seventh-day Adventist Church and enjoys traveling and rafting.

Natasha Munson

Chief Executive Officer
Be Magic, Inc

Elisabeth Omilami

Chief Executive Officer
Hosea Feed The Hungry and Homeless

Natasha Munson is chief executive officer of Be Magic, Inc., based in Atlanta, Georgia. In this position, she manages the nonprofit organization's programs for teens and single mothers.

Natasha is the best-selling author of a series of books dedicated to empowering African-American women. She was featured in *USA Today* as one of the top self-published authors in the country and has been deemed a women's expert by *Publishers Weekly*.

A native of Plainfield, New Jersey, Natasha is the mother of two girls, Mecca and Kenya.

Elisabeth Omilami is chief executive officer of one of the largest female, African-American-operated human service organizations in the southeast region of Georgia, Hosea Feed The Hungry and Homeless. Hosea Feed The Hungry and Homeless provides for the basic needs of the homeless and working poor around the globe.

Elisabeth has expanded operations from every four months to year-round. She has developed the budget from $250,000 yearly to a whopping $2 million. It is the 40th year (2009) that the organization's signature holiday festival of services and dinners, held on Thanksgiving, Christmas, Martin Luther King Jr. Day and Easter, have received widespread attention. The dinners and the organization have progressed from providing meals to also providing human services, including clothing, barbers and beauticians, medical clinic screenings, job referrals, legal aid counseling, free long-distance phone calls and transportation.

Elisabeth has increased human services programming from 20,000 people a year to more than 140,000, extended internationally to include medical distribution and feeding programs in Haiti, Uganda, the Philippines and the Ivory Coast. Additionally, she received awards for servicing more than 4,000 Hurricane Katrina survivors.

Rev. James C. Polite Jr.

Chaplain Director &
Public Information Officer
Atlanta Police Department

Lee A. Ransaw

President
The National Alliance of
Artists from Historically Black
Colleges and Universities

Officer James C. Polite Jr. serves as public information officer for the Atlanta Police Department. In this position, he speaks with local, state, national and international media outlets on behalf of the Atlanta chief of police. Polite has become the face and voice of the Atlanta Police Department while receiving many accolades for his crisp and articulate speaking abilities. Additionally, he is the first African-American male to hold this position.

Polite appeared on CNN and has been featured in *Jet*, among several other publications. A licensed and ordained preacher, he also serves as chaplain director. In this position, he is responsible for 18 volunteer chaplains of all faiths and takes care of the spiritual needs of officers, civilians and their families.

Polite attended Florida A&M University and was a member of the Marching 100 Band. In addition, he is an active member of Omega Psi Phi Fraternity, Inc.

Lee Ransaw is president of The National Alliance of Artists from Historically Black Colleges and Universities, which has grown to include more than 70 professional artists and arts administrators from 30 HBCUs. He has managed a tight network of major exhibitions and conferences in major cities throughout the eastern region of the United States. A recent traveling exhibition on display at The APEX Museum in Atlanta, "Coming by Force: Overcoming by Choice," was mentioned in *The New York Times*.

Lee served as chair of the fine arts department, and dean of arts and letters at Morris Brown College. He was also adjunct professor of education at Spelman College. Among his many honors are the UNCF Distinguished Scholars Award, The Rockefeller Foundation Fellowship to the Metropolitan Museum of Art in New York, the Ford Foundation Fellowship and a Bronze Jubilee Award for Artistic Achievement.

A member of the DeKalb County Chapter of 100 Black Men of America, Inc., Lee received bachelor's and Master of Arts degrees from Indiana University, and a doctorate degree from Illinois State University. He is married to Cheryl Johnson.

Susan J. Ross

Vendor Development Manager
Department of Watershed Management
City of Atlanta

Leo Smith

Director
Bishop Eddie L. Long Family Life Center
Samson's Health and Fitness Club

Susan "Sue" J. Ross is vendor development manager of the City of Atlanta Department of Watershed Management (DWM). Sue currently manages the Vendor Development Program, designed to increase the quantity and quality of companies doing business with the $3.9 billion Clean Water Atlanta Program to rebuild Atlanta's water and sewer system. She directs an outreach program to raise the profile of DWM with potential vendors and manages the Small Business Development Program, an intensive ten-week training and technical assistance program for small, minority and/or female businesses.

Sue received a Bachelor of Arts degree in government and Afro-American studies from Pomona College. She is also an award-winning photographer who has documented the Atlanta community for more than 30 years. Her documentary photography has appeared in numerous books, publications and exhibitions.

Sue serves on the board of trustees at First Congregational Church, United Church of Christ. She also works closely with the National Black Arts Festival and other cultural institutions.

Leo Smith directs the Bishop Eddie L. Long Family Life Center along with Samson's Health and Fitness Club. He applies his extensive corporate health and wellness experience to develop membership/fee-based health clubs and sports centers. The New Birth campus center has become an Atlanta resource for cutting-edge personal and corporate fitness solutions, hosting sports tournaments and fitness camps, certifying personal trainers and inspiring congregational wellness initiatives.

Smith is president and co-founder of the 12-team, faith-based Southern Kings Amateur Athletic Union mentoring program. He is partnered with Nike, Inc. to develop elite youth basketball in Georgia. Additionally, he is a charter sponsor of the Georgia Summit on Faith and Fitness.

Smith's career began more than 30 years ago, opening and managing abandoned recreation facilities. His corporate experiences include Virginia Tech, Aries Technologies, Diligent Consulting, Equinox and LA Fitness. Smith's leadership was key in acquiring a $35 million bond referendum for Virginia Tech.

The African Methodist Episcopal Church licensed Smith to preach in 1997. In his spare time, Smith consults, volunteers, plays golf and enjoys his growing family.

Yolanda L. Watson Spiva, Ph.D.

Executive Director
Project GRAD Atlanta

Camille G. Stephens

Business Development Officer
Development Authority of Fulton County

Dr. Yolanda L. Watson Spiva currently serves as executive director for the nonprofit organization Project GRAD Atlanta. Project GRAD Atlanta works with students in economically disadvantaged communities in Atlanta and serves one-third of the schools in the Atlanta Public Schools system. GRAD begins working with students in kindergarten and sticks with them through college.

Prior to joining GRAD, Spiva served as assistant dean for academic affairs at Trinity College for Women, and director of research and programs for the American Association of University Women, both in Washington, D.C. She also served in various capacities within the U.S. Department of Education's Office of Postsecondary Education (Washington, D.C.) and the Region IV Office of the Secretary's Regional Representative (Atlanta).

As the author of numerous research articles and an academic text, Spiva has been consistently engaged as a consultant with several institutions of higher education and support organizations affiliated with academe. She earned an undergraduate degree in economics from Spelman College, a master's degree in public policy from The University of Chicago and a Doctor of Philosophy degree in higher education from Georgia State University.

Camille G. Stephens is a business development officer for the Development Authority of Fulton County. In this capacity, she works with many major corporations and not-for-profit entities looking to expand development opportunities or locate their business in Fulton County using bond financing. She works with many community groups and affiliate organizations on various economic development activities that include promoting growth through business attraction, job retention and expansion to those individuals or corporations with interest.

She currently holds the certified economic developer certification, which is the most esteemed in this field, as well as the economic development finance professional certification, which is also a highly renowned certification. She is presently pursuing the certified commercial investment member designation, which will recognize her as an expert in the disciplines of commercial and investment real estate.

Camille received a Bachelor of Arts degree in communications from Howard University and a Master of Public Administration degree from Troy State University. An aspiring entrepreneur and Atlanta native, Camille is the proud mother of three children, Jordan, Arayah and Malik.

Carla E. Stokes, Ph.D.

Founder, President &
Chief Executive Officer
Helping Our Teen Girls
In Real Life Situations, Inc.

D r. Carla Stokes is founder, president and chief executive officer of Helping Our Teen Girls In Real Life Situations, Inc. (HOTGIRLS), a youth-driven, 501(c)(3) nonprofit organization dedicated to advancing the health and lives of black young women and girls. She speaks nationally and provides consulting services to nonprofit organizations, youth-serving organizations, educational institutions, government agencies and corporations.

Stokes graduated, cum laude, from Spelman College with a Bachelor of Arts degree in psychology. She earned Doctor of Philosophy and Master of Public Health degrees from the University of Michigan, where she taught courses on black women's health and women in hip-hop.

Stokes' research on hip-hop, sexuality and identity construction in black adolescent girls' Internet profiles on social networking Web sites won honorable mention in the University of Michigan Distinguished Dissertation Awards competition. In addition, she completed a postdoctoral research fellowship at the U.S. Centers for Disease Control and Prevention Division of HIV/AIDS Prevention.

A member of Alpha Kappa Alpha Sorority, Inc., Stokes is currently developing books and products devoted to motivating, empowering and inspiring young women and girls to reach their fullest potential.

Kwame Tutuh

Program Director & Franchisee
Ident-A-Kid/Metro Atlanta

K wame Tutuh is program director/franchisee for Ident-A-Kid, the nation's largest child identification program. As such, he works with families in the north and south portions of Fulton County, and within Atlanta's city limits. The program allows participating parents to have easy access to the vital information needed by law enforcement in the case of a missing child emergency or other unforeseen crisis.

Of Ghanaian descent, Tutuh was born and raised in Washington, D.C. He formerly worked with the National Council of Negro Women as a mentor coordinator. Later, he spent several years with School-Aged Child Care and many summers working with autistic youth. Tutuh also volunteered for three seasons as a defensive coordinator for the McLean Mustangs Youth Football Team. Most notably, his tenure with Fairfax County Public Schools as an 8th grade teacher gave him the ability to launch his signature program, Men of Honor, a mentoring program for at-risk youth.

Tutuh attended Montgomery College in Takoma Park, Maryland. A devoted family man, he has two sons, Christian and Cameron.

Lisa Williams

Founder
Circle of Friends, Inc.

Nikema Williams

Chair, 13th Congressional District
Democratic Party of Georgia

Living Water for Girls, a program of Circle of Friends, Inc., a 501(c)(3) not-for-profit organization under the leadership of Lisa Williams, combats human trafficking and the rape-for-profit of American girls. Living Water for Girls is committed to providing safe, long-term residential care, therapeutic, medical, educational and vocational services, and life skills training for victimized 12 to 17-year-old girls, with the intent of seeing them filled with dignity, hope and a future.

Child sexual exploitation lies close to Williams' heart. As a throwaway child, she too was exploited. After enduring years of neglect and physical, mental and sexual abuse, Williams was abandoned and homeless at the age of 12. However, through God's grace, the kind acts of others and a can-do attitude, she now stands and speaks boldly as an advocate for child victims of commercial sexual exploitation, i.e., rape-for-profit.

Williams is wife to her best friend of 21 years and the mother of biological and adopted children. She lives on her farm in Georgia, and continuously thanks God for this good life and the opportunity to serve.

Nikema Williams is public policy manager for Planned Parenthood of Georgia, Inc. (PPG). In this position, she tracks and monitors key bills relevant to the mission of PPG. Weekly, she coordinates Women in the Halls, a citizen lobbying program that allows her to teach everyday women the art of lobbying their elected officials.

A delegate to the 2008 Democratic National Convention, Nikema serves as political director for the Young Democrats of Georgia, as well as the deputy regional director for the Young Democrats of America. The Apex Society designated her as one of their Power 30 Under 30 in the field of politics for 2008. She is a member of Leadership Atlanta's LEAD class of 2009 and an active member of Alpha Kappa Alpha Sorority, Inc.

In 2007 Nikema was elected chair of the 13th Congressional District for the Democratic Party of Georgia. Upon election, she became the youngest congressional district chair in the state.

A native of Smiths, Alabama, Nikema received a Bachelor of Arts degree from Talladega College in Talladega, Alabama.

Atlanta's

SPIRITUAL LEADERS

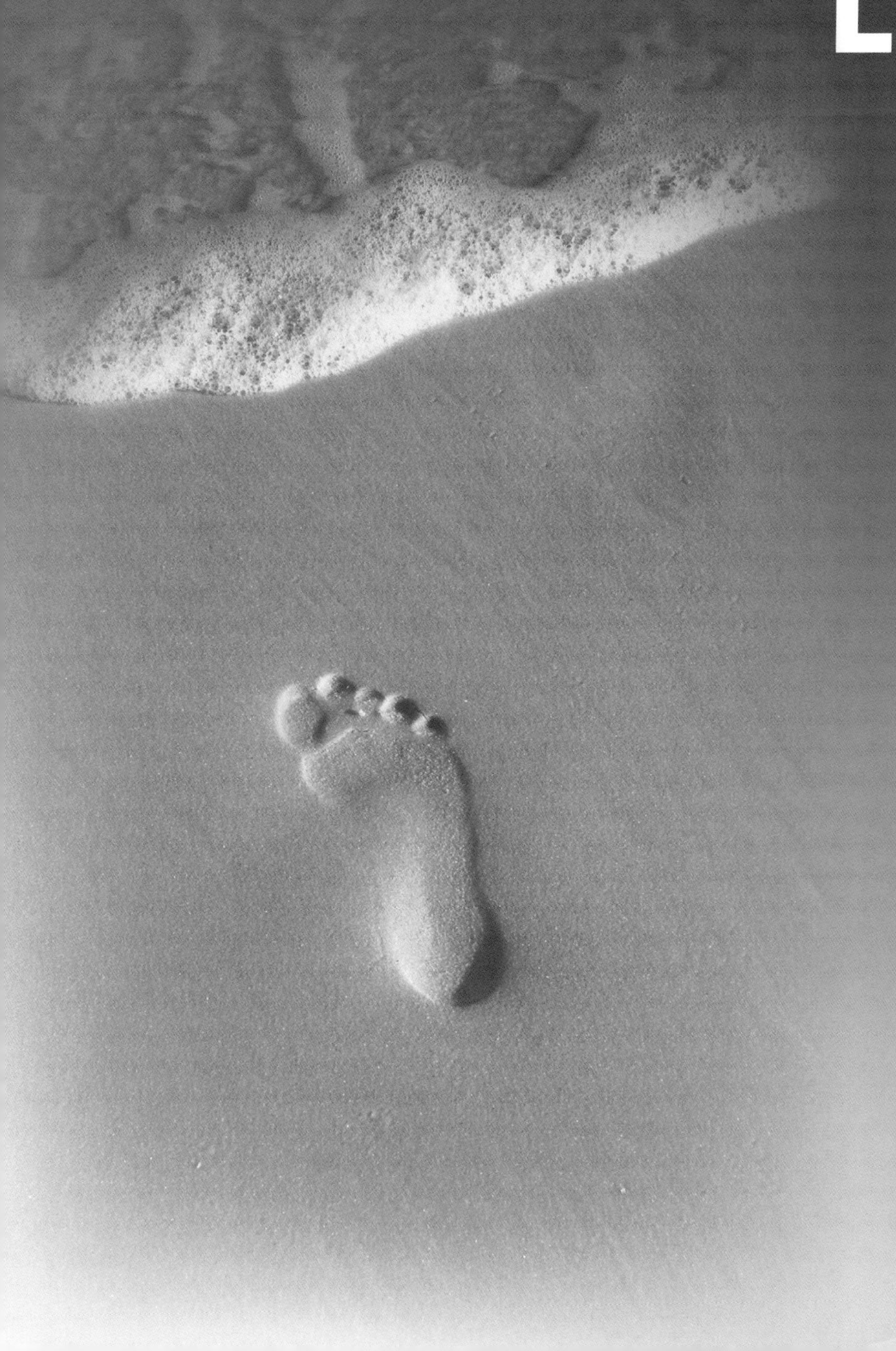

EARNEST

MERCIFUL

FAITHFUL

CONSECRATED

VIRTUOUS

DEDICATED

WISE

BENEVOLENT

HONORABLE

Diana Branch, D.Div.

Executive Pastor
Pilgrim Cathedral of Atlanta

D r. Diana Branch is executive pastor of Pilgrim Cathedral of Atlanta, where she ministers with her husband, Bishop Kent David Branch Sr. She also operates as senior vision builder and director of administration and finance.

As a sought-after speaker, Branch has ministered nationally and abroad with trademark sermons such as "Paper Plates and China," "Battle of the Sexes" and "The Role of a Man." Facilitating at seminars and conferences, she has helped develop leaders in the areas of leadership, spiritual protocol and the balance of work and life.

For tireless ministerial and civic service, Branch has been recognized by *Who's Who In Black Atlanta®*, and was awarded an honorary Doctor of Divinity degree in 2004. She has been featured in *The Atlanta Journal-Constitution* and Atlanta's *Good News Magazine*, as well as on the Trinity Broadcasting Network and as a return guest on Praise 97.5 FM shows, including CoCo Brother and Rhodell Lewis.

Branch is the loving and devoted wife of Bishop Kent David Branch Sr. They are the proud parents of three children.

Bishop Kent David Branch

Senior Pastor
Pilgrim Cathedral of Atlanta

B ishop Kent David Branch is the senior pastor of Pilgrim Cathedral of Atlanta in Decatur, Georgia, where he serves a thriving nondenominational Christian congregation. Consecrated to the Episcopal office of bishop in 1999, his prophetic vision impacts the local community and global world at large.

With more than 25 years in ministry, Branch travels abroad ministering the word of God. A sought-after motivational speaker, he is known for his unique ability to motivate people to move beyond mediocrity and to embrace excellence in their lives. Branch earned bachelor's and master's degrees in business administration from Pace University, a Master of Divinity degree from Emory University and a Doctor of Ministry degree from Drew University.

Branch also serves as an adjunct professor at Emory University and Beulah Heights University in Atlanta. He is the author of *Identifying and Affirming Your Call and Gifts* and currently serves on several executive boards. His spirit-filled television broadcast is aired weekly, offering relevant and practical teaching for life experiences. Branch resides in Atlanta with his wife Diana, his two daughters and son.

Dr. Carlton P. Byrd is senior pastor of the 3,400-member Berean Seventh-day Adventist Church of Atlanta, the largest Seventh-day Adventist congregation in the south Atlantic region.

Since his arrival in August of 2006, more than 800 people have been baptized, church attendance has doubled, the church has been completely remodeled and a weekly television ministry that airs on two Atlanta television stations was launched. He received the prestigious Chosen Pastor Award from Atlanta's 2007 Gospel Choice Awards and was inducted into the Morehouse College Martin Luther King Jr. Board of Preachers in 2008.

A graduate of Oakwood University with dual bachelor degrees in theology and business management, Byrd also graduated from Tennessee State University with a Master of Business Administration degree. In addition, he graduated from Andrews University and earned Master of Divinity and Doctor of Ministry degrees.

Byrd and his lovely wife, Danielle, are the proud parents of two girls, Christyn and Caileigh.

Carlton P. Byrd, D. Min.

Senior Pastor
Berean Seventh-day Adventist
Church of Atlanta

Bishop C. L. Carter Sr. is spiritual bishop and founder of First Missionary Baptist Church of Atlanta, Georgia. Married to Elder Deborah V. Carter, Carter was born in Atlanta and attended Atlanta Public Schools. He also attended the Carver Bible Institute and furthered his studies at the Morehouse College School of Continuing Education. He currently holds two honorary doctorate degrees, one from World Changers Church International and the other from United Pentecostal Churches of Christ.

Through a vision, God challenged Carter to establish a Bible institute that would fully train men and women to carry out Jesus' final words to his followers, as stated in Matthew 28:19. From that challenge, The Carter Theological Institute of Ministry was officially established and consecrated on May 27, 1990.

Carter has made an incalculable contribution to the promotion and maintenance of a healthy spiritual atmosphere by teaching, training and offering guidance to ministers, elders and pastors under his care and leadership. He is currently penning his autobiography, in which he commemorates 50 years of being in ministry.

Bishop C. L. Carter Sr.

Spiritual Bishop & Founder
First Missionary Baptist Church

Rev. Jeffery Bernard Cooper

Senior Pastor
Trinity AME Church

The Reverend Jeffery Bernard Cooper is senior pastor of Trinity AME Church in Atlanta, Georgia. He is also board chairman of the Trinity Day Care and Early Learning Center.

Cooper received a Bachelor of Arts degree (1980) and a Master of Public Administration degree (1983) from The University of Georgia. He received theological training from the Interdenominational Theological Center (Atlanta), the Emory University Candler School of Theology (Atlanta) and the Graduate Theological Seminary (South Bend, Indiana).

Cooper's honors include recognition in *Who's Who in Religion in America*; being named Outstanding Young Man in America; receiving the Atlanta Gospel Choice Chosen Award in 1998; and being named one of the *Atlanta Business Journal*'s 100 Most Influential Pastors in Atlanta. Previously, he was a consultant to the CIA, and director of minority admissions at The University of Georgia from 1984 to 1995.

Currently a member of the Atlanta Conference board of trustees, Cooper is a state accountant for the AME Church in Georgia. Married to Joanne E. Williams-Cooper, he is the father of Ako, Ethan, Charity and Jeffery II, and proud grandparent of Alex.

Rev. Alice Greene

Organizer
Supernatural Healing &
Deliverance Ministry

With a heart that is truly for the people of God, the Reverend Alice Greene has spent nearly three decades in ministry, serving as a pastor and evangelist. She also earned a distinct reputation for the effectiveness of her healing and deliverance ministry, as well as for her unique ability to reach those in prison, the homeless and hungry, and others in dire need. Greene's ministry launched with a simple gathering of teenagers, primarily her own children. Before she knew it, there were more than 50 teenagers involved.

Outside of her ministry, Greene worked many years as a certified nurse's assistant and home health aide. There were many days when she would come in three or four hours early to offer prayer and counseling for those who needed it.

A gifted researcher, Greene is currently writing a Bible commentary and a book called "Almost Persuaded," regarding her experience working with false television prophets. The former model and recording artist has been married to Allen Greene Sr. for 40 years. They are the parents of three adult children and grandparents of four.

The Reverend Dr. Cynthia L. Hale is founder and senior pastor of Ray of Hope Christian Church in Decatur. Ray of Hope has an active membership of 5,000 and an average of 1,500 in worship each Sunday morning.

A native of Roanoke, Virginia, Hale received a Bachelor of Arts degree from Hollins College in Virginia, a Master of Divinity degree from Duke University in North Carolina and a Doctor of Ministry degree from United Theological Seminary in Ohio. She has received five honorary Doctor of Divinity degrees.

Hale was selected by Senator Barack Obama and the Democratic Party to give the opening invocation at the 2008 Democratic National Convention. In January of 2009 she participated in the National Prayer Service for the inauguration of President Obama.

Throughout her 30 years in ministry, Hale has received many honors for making her contributions to the state of Georgia and beyond. Her ministerial gifts have drawn thousands to witness the power of God upon a woman with a mission to impact and transform this present world into the kingdom of God.

Rev. Dr. Cynthia L. Hale

Founder & Senior Pastor
Ray of Hope Christian Church

Minister BaSean Jackson grew up in DeSoto, Texas, and graduated from DeSoto High School in 1993. He attended Morehouse College in Atlanta, where he earned a Bachelor of Arts degree in religion in 1997. Jackson continued his theological education at the Morehouse School of Religion of the Interdenominational Theological Center, where he obtained a Master of Divinity degree, with a double concentration in New Testament and theology. He graduated, with honors, as a member of the International Honors Society of Theta Phi. He received a Master of Theology degree from the Candler School of Theology at Emory University and is now working on a Doctor of Philosophy degree in theological studies at Emory University.

Jackson has devoted his life to the understanding, imitation, emulation and proclamation of the life and ministry of Jesus Christ, and has preached throughout the country. He now serves as pastor and organizer of the Fellowship of Love Church in Fayetteville, Georgia. Jackson is the devoted and loving father of a wonderful son, Bryson, and resides in Smyrna, Georgia.

BaSean Jackson

Pastor & Organizer
Fellowship of Love Church

Rev. Dr. Barbara Lewis King

Founder & Chief Executive Officer
Spiritual Leader
Hillside International Truth Center, Inc.

The Reverend Dr. Barbara Lewis King, also known as Nana Yaa Twumwaah I, is founder, spiritual leader and chief executive officer of Hillside International Truth Center, Inc. The center encompasses more than 13 acres, several thousand members, a school of ministry, a scholarship foundation, a learning center, more than 30 service auxiliaries, a school in Ghana, a community development in Brazil and teaches children and adults in South Africa.

Author of the widely acclaimed *Transform Your Life*, King's autobiography, "Spirit Said to Me: The Healing and Spiritual Journey of Barbara Lewis King," is scheduled for publication. She has written articles and essays, and has hosted and appeared on television programs.

Often sought as counselor to world leaders, King has received honors from the Martin Luther King, Jr. Chapel, Morehouse College and the International Hall of Honor. She received the Interdenominational Theological Center Trail Blazer Award and is included in the portrait gallery of Women in the Pulpit at the Smithsonian Museum. King received the highest honor bestowed upon a woman when enstooled as the first female chief at Assin Nsuta, Ghana, West Africa.

André Landers

Senior Pastor
Higher Living Christian Church

Pastor André Landers is the senior pastor of Higher Living Christian Church (HLCC), with two locations in Jonesboro and McDonough, Georgia. Aiming to always be relevant, HLCC serves as a beacon of light for the community, promotes spiritual growth and lifts the total family unit towards higher living.

Under his leadership, the membership of HLCC has grown to more than 12,000 members in eight years. As a dynamic visionary, he provides his congregation with the biblical and practical teachings needed to address the real issues of today's society.

With a heart for community and the next generation, Landers serves on several community action boards, including the Clayton County Gang Awareness Task Force and the McDonald's Wheels of Dream Foundation advisory board.

A native of Atlanta, Georgia, Landers and his wife, Kimberley, are the proud parents of twin daughters, Devin and Morgan. He received a bachelor's degree in administration and marketing at the State University of West Georgia in 1988.

The Reverend Eugene Leonard Jr. is the senior pastor and teacher of Zion Missionary Baptist Church in Jackson. He is the former pastor of the Good Shepherd Full Gospel Baptist Church in Dothan, Alabama, which was founded by Jesus Christ and organized by Overseer Leonard in November of 1996. He is spirit-filled, and his soul-searching sermons inspire, uplift and challenge his listeners.

He has served as the Gulf South District overseer for the state of Alabama's Full Gospel Baptist Church Fellowship. His other areas of service in the Full Gospel Baptist Church Convention have included first assistant to State Bishop Ernest L. Palmer, first assistant to Regional General Overseer Dennis E. Joel, first assistant to Bishop Sherman L. Young Sr. and provost of the church planning and development of Christian education.

Leonard's preaching and pastoral experiences spans more than 40 years. He was licensed to preach in November of 1968. He is married to Elder Jacqueline James Leonard and has nine sons, six who are preachers. Leonard also has nine grandchildren.

Rev. Eugene Leonard Jr.

Senior Pastor & Teacher
Zion Missionary Baptist Church

The Reverend Dr. Curtis L. Lester has served as pastor of Greater Bethany Baptist Church for 35 years. Under his dynamic leadership, Greater Bethany has remained a beacon of hope in the Vine City community through outreach initiatives to inlude its Feed the Homeless and Hungry ministry, a special weekly community Bible study and a clothes bank.

Lester has served in the U.S. Army Reserve as a chaplain since 1974. He was promoted to lieutenant colonel in 1994. He served in the Iraqi Freedom operation as a troupe chaplain, and he retired from the Reserve in May of 2004 after 30 years of service.

Lester holds a degree in economics from Florida A&M University, a Master of Divinity degree, and a Doctor of Ministry degree in pastoral care and parish ministry from the Morehouse School of Religion Interdenominational Theological Center.

Lester and his wife, Sheila Ann Hamilton Lester, are the proud parents of Cicely Latrese Lester, Cadarren Linus Lester and Mrs. Chandra Briggs, as well as son-in-law Billy Briggs. They are the grandparents of Jazmine Nicole and Billy Ashton Briggs.

Rev. Dr. Curtis L. Lester

Pastor
Greater Bethany Baptist Church

Rev. Anthony McMichael

Pastor
Mt. Nebo Baptist Church & Life Center

Atlanta native the Reverend Anthony James McMichael pastors Mt. Nebo Baptist Church and Life Center and Mt. Nebo Cathedral South, a thriving congregation in the Atlanta and Jonesboro communities. Pastoring since 1981, he has played a phenomenal role in establishing a ray of hope, preaching, "The church cannot live apart from the community." In establishing a $7 million campus, including an academy, gymnasium, fitness club, 1,100-seat sanctuary, administrative building and a mission house, McMichael has reached more than 7,000 souls. All became a frequent site for life-changing outreach services.

McMichael holds a degree in theology from Mercer University and a Master of Divinity degree from the Morehouse School of Religion of the Interdenominational Theological Center. His recognition includes receiving the Atlanta Gospel Choice and Morehouse Distinguished Alumnus awards and being inducted into the Morehouse College Preachers' Hall of Fame. He is a member of Alpha Phi Alpha Fraternity, Inc., and chairman of the southeast region of the National Action Network.

He is married to Brenda McMichael, a retired DeKalb principal. They are the proud parents to Andria and William.

Bishop William L. Sheals

Senior Pastor
Hopewell Missionary Baptist Church

Bishop William L. Sheals is the senior pastor of Hopewell Missionary Baptist Church in Norcross, Georgia. Since 1980, under his leadership, Hopewell has grown from 200 members to more than 10,000, with more than 60 ministries and auxiliaries. The 32-acre complex called The City of Hope includes a 500-member youth church, a credit union, the Hopewell Christian Academy with pre-kindergarten through 12th grade, a senior citizens' center, a mall, a child development center and an onsite Bible college.

Sheals received a business degree from New York University. He also received theological degrees from Florida Memorial Seminary and the International Bible College, with studies at Luther Rice Seminary University, the ITC, Morehouse College and the Candler School of Theology at Emory University.

Sheals has been cited extensively for his civic leadership and service. He currently serves as the ambassador of reconciliation and goodwill of Israel. Additionally, he has received the Friend of Israel Award from the Israel Diplomatic Network of the Consulate General of Israel to the Southeastern United States in Atlanta. Sheals is married to the former Patricia Kim.

Elder A. Maurice Waddell has served as chief operating officer of New Birth Missionary Baptist Church (NBMBC) since January 21, 1999. He is responsible for the day-to-day operations of NBMBC, which includes the New Birth Cathedral, the Bishop Eddie L. Long Family Life Center, the Samson Health and Fitness Center, the Call to Conquer Bookstore, New Birth Christian Academy and other properties owned by the church.

Prior to becoming chief operating officer, Waddell was executive officer for the Atlanta regional director of the Social Security Administration. During the course of his 25-year federal career with the Social Security Administration, he held various management and supervisory positions and received numerous awards, including the Commissioner's Citation.

Waddell earned a Bachelor of Arts degree in sociology from North Carolina Central University. He has been married for more than 32 years to Sylvia (Jones) Waddell, and they are blessed with two children, Ashley and Andre.

Elder A. Maurice Waddell

Chief Operating Officer
New Birth Missionary Baptist Church

The Reverend Dr. Raphael G. Warnock serves as the fifth senior pastor of historic Ebenezer Baptist Church, spiritual home of the Reverend Dr. Martin Luther King Jr. Warnock is part of a new generation of up-and-coming ministers who are reaching out to young African Americans. His outreach and activism have addressed such issues as voting rights, HIV/AIDS and disparities in the criminal justice system.

A sought-after preacher and scholar, Warnock is a member of the American Academy of Religion, Alpha Phi Alpha Fraternity, Inc. and various other civic and social organizations. His dedication and commitment to the teachings of Christ and concern for the community provide a holistic ministry perspective on the work of the church. He has picked up the mantle and is leading his church family to a new phase: From Heritage to Horizon – From Horizon to Higher Ground.

Warnock graduated, cum laude, from Morehouse College in 1991 with a Bachelor of Arts degree in psychology. He also holds Master of Divinity, Master of Philosophy and Doctor of Philosophy degrees from Union Theological Seminary.

Rev. Raphael G. Warnock, Ph.D.

Senior Pastor
Ebenezer Baptist Church

Grace C. Washington

Senior Pastor & Organizer
Love Life Christian Fellowship Church

Love Life Christian Fellowship Church of Ellenwood, Georgia, is led by a spirit-filled woman of God who is totally committed to walking in the spirit of excellence. With more than 33 years of ministry experience, 21 of which have been served as a pastor, Pastor Grace C. Washington is an authoritative teacher, preacher and leader. She is skilled in all aspects of ministry, and her international experiences include China, Bethlehem, the Virgin Islands and Soweto. The West Palm Beach, Florida, native is author of three books related to marriage.

Washington holds degrees from Georgia State University and the Interdenominational Theological Center's Gammon Theological Seminary. She founded the Grace C. Washington Institute to teach and train people in biblical, theological and ethical procedures of Christian education.

Known as a fiery preacher, Washington's sermon, "The Dawning of a New Day," was selected for inclusion in the American Folklife Center's Inauguration 2009 Sermons and Orations Project. Devoted to family, she has been married to Robert Washington for 39 years. They are the parents of two daughters and have four grandchildren.

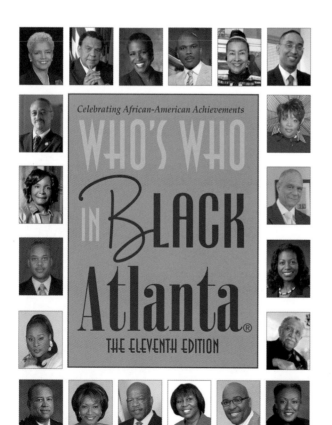

Atlanta's
CORPORATE SPOTLIGHT

INTEREST

LIMELIGHT

ATTENTION

PROMINENCE

 AGL Resources

HIGHLIGHT

CELEBRATE

HEADLINE

FOCUS

RECOGNITION

Myra Coleman Bierria

Vice President, Corporate Secretary &
Securities Counsel
AGL Resources

Ralph Cleveland

Executive Vice President
Engineering & Operations
AGL Resources

Myra Coleman Bierria was appointed vice president, corporate secretary and securities counsel at AGL Resources in March of 2008. She is responsible for all corporate governance and securities law compliance and disclosure matters. Previously, she served as executive director, corporate governance and securities counsel for the company, and lead governance counsel for Atlanta Gas Light.

Bierria is a member of the Georgia Asian Pacific American, National Asian Pacific American, American, New York State and Atlanta bar associations. She recently completed a two-year term as an ambassador for the Business Law Section of the American Bar Association.

Additionally, she is a member of the American Association of Blacks in Energy, the Society of Corporate Secretaries and Governance Professionals, and the Association of Corporate Counsel. In 2006 Bierria received the *Atlanta Business Chronicle*'s 40 Under 40 Up and Comer Award. She also serves on the boards of the AGL Resources Private Foundation, AID Atlanta, Inc. and the Girl Scouts of Greater Atlanta, Inc.

Bierria received a law degree from the Georgetown University Law Center and an undergraduate degree from the University of California, Berkeley.

Ralph Cleveland was named executive vice president of engineering and operations of AGL Resources in December of 2008. His primary responsibilities include executive oversight of the policy direction for the engineering and operations activities of the company and pivotal energy development. Prior to this role, Cleveland served as senior vice president of engineering and operations and as vice president of engineering and construction.

Cleveland is vice chair of the North American Energy Standards Board, a national board member of the American Association of Blacks in Energy, a board member for the American Institute for Managing Diversity, and a regional board member for Junior Achievement and Teach for America. Additionally, he is president and founder of the Capital Formation and Enterprise Development Foundation and Network, which are nonprofit and collaborative endeavors.

A native of Macon, Georgia, Cleveland received an undergraduate degree in mechanical engineering from Georgia Tech, completed postgraduate studies in mechanical engineering at Rice University in Houston, and received a master's degree in business administration from Tulane University in New Orleans.

Randy E. Cobb

Organizational Development &
Human Resources Manager
AGL Resources

Wendell Dallas

Vice President & General Manager
Atlanta Gas Light Company

Randy E. Cobb has worked for AGL Resources for more than 25 years in a variety of positions in operations, corporate communications, marketing and human resources. He is currently the organizational development and HR manager. Randy is responsible for the corporate diversity programs and activities. He provides enhancements to the talent review/succession planning process, and designs and manages organizational surveys relating to performance, diversity, culture and the organizational pulse.

In past roles, Randy managed AGL Resources' Visual Services Department where he developed, designed and implemented the company's first corporate intranet site. He also managed the company's external Web site. As manager of new business development, he was responsible for generating revenue outside of the normal business operations. Randy received the Flame Keepers Award and the Most Valuable Award for outstanding work.

Randy received an Executive Level MBA degree from Georgia State University. He is married with two adult children and six grandchildren. He enjoys reading, photography, public speaking and traveling.

Wendell Dallas is vice president and general manager of Atlanta Gas Light. He is responsible for the day-to-day operations and market development of AGL. Prior to this role, he served as general manager. Dallas has more than 17 years of operations, management and engineering experience in the natural gas industry.

Dallas began AGL as service area manager in Macon and region manager for Southeast Georgia in Savannah. Prior to AGL, he was operations supervisor for El Paso Energy's Macon office and responsible for the operations of the natural gas transmission pipeline facilities in central Georgia.

A graduate of Leadership Georgia's class of 2006 and Leadership Savannah's class of 2004, Dallas is a gubernatorial appointee to the State of Georgia's Workforce Investment Board and serves as vice chairman. He is chairman of Auburn University's Engineering Alumni Council, serves on the Academic Assessment Committee and the boards of the Atlanta Neighborhood Development Partnership and Gwinnett Technical College.

Dallas grew up in Opelika, Alabama, and earned a degree in mechanical engineering from Auburn University. Dallas, his wife and three children reside in Gwinnett County.

Eric K. Greenwood

Region Manager,
Atlanta Metro
Atlanta Gas Light Company

Tarece L. Johnson Hassell

Manager of Supplier Diversity
AGL Resources

Eric Greenwood joined Atlanta Gas Light in 2003 and was appointed as Atlanta Metro regional manager. His responsibilities include managing all utility activities associated with distribution, service and meter reading functions, ensuring the safe, reliable and economical delivery of natural gas to more than 343,000 customers, and service center compliance with all applicable federal, state, local and company rules and regulations.

Eric participates in charitable events and organizations, including Kiwanis International, the American Association of Blacks in Energy, Alpha Phi Alpha Fraternity, Inc., Habitat for Humanity, the Atlanta Union Mission, the American Heart Foundation and Frank Ski Kids Foundation. A board member of the Eastlake YMCA and the University of West Georgia-African American Success and Leadership, Eric serves the boards of directors of the DeKalb Chamber of Commerce and the Atlanta Business League. Additionally, he sits on the Andrews Chapel United Methodist Church board of trustees.

Members of Andrews Chapel United Methodist Church, Eric and Veronica Greenwood have been married for 20 years and have two children, Elijah and Velecity. He is from Meridian, Mississippi, and received an engineering degree from Tuskegee University.

A native of Houston, Texas, Tarece L. Johnson Hassell graduated cum laude from La Universidad del Sagrado Corazon in Santurce, Puerto Rico. Shortly after graduation, she moved to New York City to earn a master's degree in public policy and administration from Columbia University's School of International & Public Affairs.

Previously, Hassell worked for JPMorgan Chase as an assistant treasurer in the Supplier Diversity Program. In 2001 she was recruited to work as director of diversity at the New York City Fire Department (FDNY). While working at the FDNY, Hassell earned a certificate in diversity management from Cornell University's School of Industrial and Labor Relations. She relocated to Georgia in 2005 and was hired as the manager of supplier diversity at AGL Resources. In 2006 Hassell earned a certificate in supplier diversity management from Rutgers University.

As a diversity professional at AGL Resources, Hassell quickly assessed the organization and developed a comprehensive supplier diversity program. With year-over-year increase in spend and development opportunities for diverse suppliers, she has produced exceptional results. Additionally, Hassell developed a Business Development Mentoring Program.

Jesse W. Killings

Region Manager,
Northeast Georgia
Atlanta Gas Light Company

Shareka L. Nelson

Manager,
Talent Acquisition
AGL Resources

Jesse Killings is region manager of Northeast Georgia for Atlanta Gas Light Company, a subsidiary of AGL Resources. He has worked for AGL Resources' companies for 15 years and has held several management positions in marketing, safety and training and field operations. In his current position, Jesse is responsible for all distribution operations within the corporation's second-largest territory, and serves as the liaison for local community agencies and officials.

Jesse takes special interests in organizations that support the education, mentoring and leadership of children. He works with the boards or committees of 100 Black Men of Atlanta, Inc., the Jesse Draper Boys & Girls Club, the Fulton Education Foundation and the South Fulton Chamber of Commerce.

Jesse received a Bachelor of Science degree in mechanical engineering from Tuskegee University in 1992 and immediately began work for Atlanta Gas Light Company. A native of Tuscaloosa, Alabama, Jesse is married to Brigitte Killings and the proud father of two children, Christopher and Dominique.

Shareka L. Nelson is talent acquisition manager for AGL Resources. She is responsible for developing, implementing and administering consistent talent acquisition strategies necessary to recruit talented and diverse candidates for the organization and its subsidiaries. Shareka previously served as the senior regional recruiter for First Data Corporation.

Involved in several civic and community organizations, including the American Cancer Society – Relay for Life, Junior Achievement and Delta Sigma Theta Sorority Inc. – Marietta Roswell Alumni Chapter, Shareka is also active with the Boys & Girls Clubs of America, the United Way, the Georgia Multiple Sclerosis Society and serves as a mentor. Shareka serves on an alumni task force for Albany State University and is a 2008 graduate of L.E.A.D. Atlanta.

Shareka is involved with the SHRP, the National Association of African-Americans in HR, the Georgia Association of Colleges and Employers and AABE. She is also a member of the Atlanta Recruiting Directors Roundtable.

Shareka received a bachelor's degree from Albany State University, and has completed graduate work in the area of human resource development. She holds a SPHR certification and an ABA-approved paralegal certification.

Opal S. Reed

Director
Call Center Operations
AGL Resources

Mickey Wade

Liaison, Utility Operations
AGL Resources

Opal S. Reed enjoys the privilege of leading and serving others, having earned this distinction by consistently applying the art of leadership and accomplishing more than the science of management. In a management career that spans more than two decades, she is an ardent practitioner and student of servant leadership. Opal firmly believes that the organization's success is firmly rooted in the quality, diversity and discretionary effort of the company's workforce.

She holds a Bachelor of Science degree and graduated, with honors, from Bowie State University and a Master of Business Administration degree from California Coast University. Opal joined AGL in 2003, after spending 20 years with the FedEx Corporation. She is currently the director of call center operations.

An enthusiastic community business leader, she serves on the board of the Women Resource Center to End Domestic Violence. As a career management professional, Opal holds the view that in order to achieve excellence in big things, one must develop the habit in little matters. She currently lives in Winston with her family and enjoys an active and healthy lifestyle.

Mickey Wade currently serves as the utility operations liaison for AGL Resources. Her personality, professionalism and resourcefulness have been rewarded by her selection as AGL's first African-American female lobbyist registered at the Georgia State Legislature.

Mickey earned a degree in economics with a minor concentration in management and organization from Spelman College. She was also selected for American Honda Motor Company's National Management Trainee program, an honor given to only six outstanding individuals nationwide annually.

A United Way Cole Society member, Mickey has consistently volunteered with Junior Achievement, Habitat for Humanity, Hands on Atlanta, Hosea Feed the Hungry and Homeless, the American Red Cross and the American Heart Association's Heart Walk.

Mickey serves on the executive committee for the American Association of Blacks in Energy as chair of Legislative and Regulatory Affairs, as well as on the advisory board for the International Rescue Committee. She earned a certificate from the Georgia Institute of Technology's Management Program, and is a member of the 2009 class of the Atlanta Women's Foundation Destiny Fund and the Buckhead Business Association's Leadership Development Institute.

Atlanta's

MEDIA
PROFESSIONALS

ENLIVEN

RECREATE

INSPIRE

CAPTIVATE

DELIGHT

IMAGINE

AMUSE

ILLUMINATE

INNOVATIVE

Silas Alexander III

On-Air Personality
Majik 107.5/97.5

Silas Alexander III, also known as "SiMan Baby", is a native of Eatonton, Georgia. He has been in the field of broadcasting, both in radio and television, for 29 years.

Former weatherman and news director for the NBC TV station in Macon, Georgia, SiMan Baby also worked as a videotape editor and field host for 11Alive in Atlanta. He has worked in many formats of radio, including country, heavy metal, jazz, gospel, top 40 and urban music.

To date, he is with Radio One Atlanta as the host of the evening show on Majik 107.5/97.5. Previously, he was the evening host of *SiMan After Dark*, on 102.5 Grown Folks Radio. SiMan Baby is very active in the community and is committed to making a difference in Atlanta.

He and his wife, Sandra, have one son, Silas IV.

Nina Brown

Producer
The Frank & Wanda Morning Show
WVEE V-103 FM

Nina Brown is producer of V-103's *The Frank & Wanda Morning Show* and CW 69's *Frank & Wanda Show*. While Frank and Wanda have maintained a No. 1 status since their Atlanta arrival, the energetic and spunky show producer enjoys keeping them on time, organized, and always in front of the local and national happenings. Nina admits that while the business is extremely fast-paced, she loves every bit of the excitement that comes with working for Frank Ski, Wanda and Miss Sophia.

In the industry since 2003, Nina is proud of her "intern to producer" story that exemplifies her dedication and drive, which has led her to mainstream success and respect from veterans and fans alike. She humbly uses her media and public leverage to capture the attention of the youth and inspire those afraid to follow their dreams.

A native of Northern California, Nina is proud of her African-American and Samoan heritage. She is the mother of an 8-year-old, Jaylen Johnson.

Commitment, drive and dedication come to mind when you think of USA Track & Field star Monica Cabbler. However, her talents expand beyond the lines, as she has also made a profound mark in the media arena. A reporter for *The 411 in Health* on My WSE-TV, she has also teamed up with FOX during national live coverage of NFL matchups.

Cabbler's work as a corporate spokesperson has been a catalyst toward her media success. She has made appearances representing the American Lung Association, Coca-Cola Company, Blue Cross Blue Shield and the National Football League. She uses the stage of sports and media as a platform for community outreach.

Her professional background is in sports marketing under the company umbrella Cabbler & Associates. She aligns other athletes and corporations with opportunities to impact their communities, and her personal initiative promotes the importance of healthy lifestyles and targets the childhood obesity epidemic.

The Roanoke, Virginia, native received a Bachelor of Business Administration degree in marketing from The University of Georgia.

Monica Cabbler

Reporter
MY WSE-TV

Brian Clay is the host of the gospel jazz broadcast on Praise 102.5 every Sunday from 5 to 8 p.m. He is also creator and program director of an Internet radio station called Jazzspirations that streams inspirational jazz 24 hours a day, 7 days a week.

Brian is a keyboardist/vocalist/songwriter/producer based in Atlanta, Georgia. Originally from Chicago, he began playing piano at age 5, and continued when he moved with his family to Atlanta in 1972.

As he creates a name for himself as a headliner, Brian has been featured as an opening act and shared the stage with the biggest names in the industry. He has opened for Stanley Clark, Najee, Euge Groove, Kirk Whalum, The Rippingtons, Alex Bugnon, Gerald Albright and Norman Brown.

Brian Clay

On-air Personality
Praise 102.5 FM

Cory "Co Co Brother" Condrey

On-air Personality
Hot 107.9 FM

Cory Condrey, better known as "CoCo Brother," is more than your average radio personality. CoCo Brother first came to Atlanta after graduating from high school in Nashville, Tennessee, marking the beginning of his career in radio.

CoCo Brother came full circle on September 11, 2001, when he returned to Hot 107.9, Atlanta, in the 6 to 10 p.m. time slot. It didn't take long before CoCo Brother and the Home Team made their presence known. When the first book came out, the show was No. 1 with 12–17 year olds. It also made history for Hot 107.9, ranking No. 1 with 18–34 year olds for the first time.

In addition to being an on-air personality, he has also hosted *Vibe*'s TV show and BET's *Talent Search*, made appearances on MTV and hosted a video show on UPN. CoCo Brother hosted Michael Vick's Shoe Release for three consecutive years and appeared in *Vibe, Source, Creative Loafing* and *rolling out*. Currently he is the new host of BET's *Lift Every Voice* (2008).

D'Vine

International Recording Artists

For 16 years, D'Vine has traveled the world, delivering songs that linger in the hearts of audiences long after they have left the stage. The group consists of Paula McGuire Saunders, Pamela McGuire Deas and Sheryl Pollard Riggins, two sisters and a friend whose voices have taken them from the White House to worldwide schoolhouses.

D'Vine has performed in Brazil, Argentina, Chile, Honduras and Europe for the American Embassy. Officials share that the group gives the country the opportunity to strengthen ties of friendship and respect. D'Vine performed at the 53rd Presidential Inauguration, at the Olympic Games with the Atlanta Symphony Orchestra and Northwest Florida Symphony, and at schools and corporate events nationally.

In addition to performing more than 150 dates annually, the members of D'Vine are employed as a legal analyst at The Coca-Cola Company, a bone marrow transplant social worker at Emory Healthcare and a staffing consultant at CreekSide Dental. Former students of Avondale High School, DeVry University and The University of Georgia, the trio has recorded three projects, *Two Sisters & A Friend, Perfect Timing* and *Simply D'Vine*.

Julian Davis is director of urban outreach at Arbitron, Inc., a media and marketing research firm. His primary focus is to work with clients (urban media outlets, ad agencies and advertisers), community leaders, educational facilities and political figures to enhance the brand of Arbitron in minority communities and to communicate to advertisers to take a fresh look at radio. He joined Arbitron in 1989 as an account executive for radio station services and has worked his way up the ranks.

Prior to Arbitron, Davis ran the gamut in the entertainment industry as a co-owner of KYEA-FM in Monroe, Louisiana, to concert promoter, stage manager and artist manager. He is a co-founder and national scholarship chair of the National Black Programmers Coalition, an organization of radio programmers and record executives throughout the U.S. that has awarded more than $200,000 in scholarships since its creation in 1975.

Locally, Davis is involved with Hosea Feed the Hungry and Homeless, which provides food to the homeless and hungry in Atlanta. He serves as one of the dinner operations managers.

Julian Davis

Director, Urban Outreach
Arbitron, Inc.

Elle Duncan, midday host on Atlanta's WVEE V-103 FM, is the biggest female sports fan you will ever find. She has dreamed about entertaining people since she was a small child singing and acting for her family. Born in Atlanta, Elle had the opportunity to be involved in various plays, musicals and performing arts productions. She attended McEachern High School and West Georgia College, majoring in broadcasting.

In 2003 Elle was granted a great opportunity to intern for a year at 790 The Zone with the popular brother duo the *2 Live Stews*. She gained a wealth of radio broadcasting knowledge during her internship. In 2005 she joined V-103 as the afternoon drive traffic girl. Her energy, quick wit, comic delivery and great chemistry with Ryan Cameron cemented her a permanent position on *The Ryan Cameron Show* in 2006.

Elle has been selected as One of Atlanta's Most Beautiful People by *JEZEBEL Magazine*. She was also selected by the Gospel Music Channel to host *The Kitchen Sink*.

Elle Duncan

Midday On-Air Personality
WVEE V-103 FM

Rebecca J. Franklin

Founder & Chief Executive Officer
Women Works Publishing, Inc.

Rebecca J. Franklin has built a publishing empire by writing about women who have succeeded in their respective business industries and within their communities. As founder and chief executive officer of Women Looking Ahead Publications (WLAP), Rebecca ensures that women receive deserving exposure through her publication, *Women Looking Ahead* news magazine. A believer in equal time, she also created *Men Looking Ahead*, which has been met with equal success.

Rebecca's belief in empowering oneself and others to be the best is the secret behind the success of her company, which for more than a decade has brought together the best people in the best places in Atlanta and around the country. WLAP sponsors a series of annual empowerment events that attract nationally known speakers, authors and entertainers. Her contributions have earned her the respect of organizations such as the YWCA of Greater Atlanta, which inducted her into its 2004 Academy of Women Achievers, in addition to countless other awards and accolades for her accomplishments.

Donna Frazier

Executive Producer & Host
MCTV-Channel 25

Former model Donna Frazier is one of Atlanta's rising talents in the media industry. Donna serves as the executive producer and host for Atlanta's MCTV-Channel 25 (Metro Café Television). A magazine-style television show dedicated to exploring the attractions, entertainment and interesting people of Atlanta, MCTV produces family-friendly television that empowers, educates and entertains all audiences.

A native of Philadelphia, Donna moved to Atlanta in 2003. In 2004 she interned as an associate producer at the now-defunct Black Family Channel, where Hollywood's Robert Townsend was director of programming.

A true renaissance woman, Donna is a prominent stakeholder in one of Atlanta's exclusive event planning companies, Family Matters Event Planning Company, which coordinates special events for families, corporations, celebrity entertainers and professional athletes.

Donna is a graduate of Virginia Union University and member of Delta Sigma Theta Sorority, Inc., the National Coalition of 100 Black Women, Women in Film & Television Atlanta and the National Academy of Television Arts & Sciences.

Sharmen May Gowens is community engagement manager for *The Atlanta Journal-Constitution* (AJC), the southeast's largest media solutions company. The AJC is the leading print and digital source of news, information and advertising for Metro Atlanta, reaching a total print and online audience of more than 2.2 million people weekly.

Managing AJC's initiatives and programs committed to enriching the community, Gowens is responsible for developing and administering charitable giving guidelines, overseeing AJC's partnerships with nonprofit organizations and representing the AJC within the community. She creates opportunities for the AJC to build connections through innovative outreach efforts, and emerging online and social networking tools.

An AJC employee since 1976, Gowens has led her company's efforts in several community-related capacities, including employee drives for the United Way and The Empty Stocking Fund. Named one of Atlanta's Top 100 Women of Influence from 2006 to 2009, she serves on the boards of the Better Business Bureau, the Atlanta Business League and the YWCA of Greater Atlanta.

A graduate of The University of Georgia, Gowens and husband Don have two sons, Donald Jr. and Nicholas.

Sharmen May Gowens

Community Engagement Manager
The Atlanta-Journal Constitution

Karyn Greer joined *11Alive News* in 1999. A reporter for 11Alive's special projects unit, she is also an anchor for *11Alive Weekend* at 6 and 11 p.m. Karyn came to 11Alive from WGNX-TV, where she completed a ten-year tenure in the primary co-anchor position for that station's weeknight newscasts.

Beginning her broadcast career in 1983 at WCIA-TV in Champaign, Illinois, Karyn moved to WICD-TV the following year, where she worked as a weekend anchor and reporter. She then spent three years in Charleston, South Carolina, where she was the solo anchor for the highest-rated newscast in the market.

A longtime Atlanta resident, Karyn has a history of hands-on community involvement. She is the past president of the Atlanta Press Club and currently serves on the board of governors for the National Academy of Television Arts & Sciences. She is the recipient of numerous awards honoring both her professional work and her community contributions. A native of Chicago, Illinois, Karyn and her husband, Tony, have two sons, Kyle and Tyler.

Karyn Greer

Anchor & Reporter
WXIA-TV 11Alive

Derek Harper

Program Director
Majik 107.5/97.5 &
Praise 102.5

Derek Harper is program director for Majik 107.5/97.5 and Praise 102.5. Prior to coming to Radio One, Atlanta, Derek joined WVEE V-103 as producer of its No. 1-rated morning show in April of 1994, not long after graduating from the prestigious School of Business and Industry at Florida A&M University with a Bachelor of Science degree in business administration.

In August of 1998, he accepted the operations manager/morning drive personality position with WFXM in Macon, Georgia. Over the next four years he would make the fledgling station the second-most listened to urban station in Middle Georgia.

Radio One brought Derek back to Atlanta in August of 2002 as assistant program director/co-host/producer of the *Si-Man in the Morning* morning show. In 2005 he was named program director of Majik 107.5/97.5. In 2006 he added programming duties for Praise 102.5 FM.

Mark Hayes

Co-Host
FOX 5 Morning News &
Good Day Atlanta

Mark Hayes joined FOX 5 Atlanta as *FOX 5 Morning* News and *Good Day Atlanta* co-host in April of 2002. Before that, he anchored Detroit's top-ranked 5 p.m. newscast at WXYZ-TV. Mark's on-air career began in Albany, Georgia, at WALB-TV. He has also worked at WOKR in Rochester, New York, KMGH-TV in Denver and WBAL in Baltimore.

Mark's proudest accomplishment was anchoring coverage of the Fulton County courthouse shootings. From the Friday morning he began alerting viewers on the whereabouts of the suspect, right through Saturday afternoon's surprising and intriguing arrest of Brian Nichols, it was a story he will never forget.

Active in his community, Mark is a member of Omega Psi Phi Fraternity, Inc. He graduated from Howard University in 1989 with a bachelor's degree in communications.

Mark's two sons are both avid hockey players, and his eldest hopes to play football in college. The family lives in North Fulton County, enjoys traveling and has journeyed to the beautiful island of Kauai, which they describe as the closest thing to paradise on earth.

I t can truthfully be said that Rick Joyner is a voice in more ways than one. Embodying the elements of class, wit and compassion for humanity, he tactfully makes a difference wherever he goes. Known nationwide as an eloquent broadcaster, speaker and businessman, Joyner's broadcast career began in Memphis, Tennessee, where he was reared, more than 28 years ago.

Joyner attended Memphis State University, where he majored in broadcast journalism. He later honed his skills by working for several Memphis radio stations, including WHRK 97.1, 1340 WLOK and Magic 101.

Joyner has served in many capacities within the industry, including as music director and program director in Jackson, Tennessee; Nashville; St. Louis; and Tupelo, Mississippi. In Atlanta, he served as music director and host of "The Praise Party" for *The Light* on the Sheridan Gospel Network for seven years.

Joyner has been well-lauded for his accomplishments. Some of his honors include induction into the National Broadcasters Hall of Fame in 2004 and receiving of the Favorite Network Personality of the Year Award for four consecutive years.

Rick Joyner
National Broadcaster

T om Joyner Sr. is one of the most influential, inspirational and dynamic personalities in the country. He is founder of REACH Media, Inc., the Tom Joyner Foundation and BlackAmericaWeb. com, and hosts the nationally syndicated *Tom Joyner Morning Show*.

From Tuskegee, Alabama, this 1999 Radio Hall of Fame inductee ignites a sense of pride in the hearts of eight million listeners in more than 115 radio markets, and can be heard weekdays from 6 to 10 a.m. on KISS 104.1, WALR-FM.

A graduate of the Tuskegee Institute, now Tuskegee University, he began his broadcasting career in Montgomery at WRMA-AM. In the mid-1980s, Joyner made his claim to fame accepting simultaneous positions as a morning drive man at Dallas' KKDA and an afternoon drive man at Chicago's WGCI. Flying every day between the two cities to work eventually earned him national recognition as the "Fly Jock."

He resides in Dallas with his wife, fitness guru Donna Richardson. Joyner has two sons, Thomas Jr., chief executive officer of the Tom Joyner Foundation, and Oscar, president and chief operating officer of REACH Media, Inc.

Tom Joyner Sr.
Host
Tom Joyner Morning Show

Eric Lee

Account Manager
WALR KISS 104.1 FM

With 22 years' experience in radio and television, Eric Lee is an account manager for Cox Radio. His focus on customer service and strategic and creative thinking consistently makes him a million-dollar-producing marketing professional for WALR KISS 104.1 FM.

Eric's career began at his alma mater's station, WVST-FM. He enjoyed stints at WANT-FM as an afternoon drive personality, WPLZ-FM as a midday personality and as assistant program/music director at WCDX-FM, receiving Billboard's Music Director of the Year Award in 1993. That same year, he won the Richmond Association of Broadcasters' Commercial of the Year award. He spent five years at two Virginia television stations as executive producer/host of music video program *Video Connection*, interviewing hip-hop and R&B icons.

In 2000 Eric transitioned from programming to sales, where he has excelled. He held positions with Sinclair Communications, Clear Channel and Radio One before making his home at Atlanta-based Cox.

The Newport News native holds a business information systems degree from Virginia State University and minored in mass communications. His favorite pastimes include cycling, golf and fundraising for the MS Foundation.

Diamond Miller Lewis

Director
DCTV Channel 23

Emmy Award-winning journalist Diamond Miller Lewis commands the post as one of the youngest news directors in the country, skillfully transforming a nearly obsolete cable station into a fully-programmed, award-winning powerhouse. As DCTV's news director, Diamond has won nearly 70 national broadcasting awards before the age of 30.

She is also the executive producer and creative mind behind such projects as the reality podcast series for Usher Raymond, the *Rights of Passage* civil rights documentary and a successful homeownership marketing campaign with spokesperson Dominique Wilkins. Additionally, Diamond co-produced the Wayne Williams news exclusive.

She earned a Master of Science degree from the Columbia University Graduate School of Journalism and a Bachelor of Arts degree from Spelman College. Her extensive ten-year journalism background includes anchoring and reporting for local television stations and working for *ABC World News Tonight with Peter Jennings*.

Diamond is a member of the National and Atlanta associations of black journalists, NATAS, NATOA, the Columbia University Club of Atlanta and the National Association for Multi-Ethnicity In Communications. She continues to pursue her passion for news, entertainment and women's issues.

Joyce Littel is host of WVEE V-103 FM's popular programs *The Quiet Storm* and *Love & Relationships*. With more than 21 years of radio experience, she has held a variety of positions for various stations in Georgia.

Joyce's dedication lies in her community. She has organized benefit concerts and events to raise thousands of dollars for her alma mater, as well as the National Council of Negro Women, Aid to Imprisoned Mothers and I AM, Inc. She is the renowned author of *Poetic Moments*, a collection of poetry and affirmations from *The Quiet Storm*.

On her numerous awards and honors, Joyce holds the Outstanding Alumni and Community Service Award from the Women of Morris Brown College most dear to her heart. A graduate of Morris Brown College with a Bachelor of Arts degree in mass communications, she has created several successful annual events, including The Love Cruise (nine years strong), Passion & Poetry (eight years strong) and the Got Word? Youth Poetry Slam, now in its fourth year.

Joyce is married to James Jackson and has one son, Jamal Christopher.

Joyce Littel

Host, *The Quiet Storm*
WVEE V-103 FM

As promotions manager for Praise 102.5, Atlanta native Cie Cie Wilson McGhee is responsible for the station's creative event marketing. She produces the annual Praise in the Park, which attracts more than 4,000 attendees and major artists such as Deitrick Haddon, Donald Lawrence and Regina Bell.

McGhee has made her mark in the gospel music community for two years as co-producer of The Stone Mountain Gospel Celebration, which has featured headliners Donnie McClurkin, Dorinda Clark Cole and Hezekiah Walker. With more than 20 years in entertainment, her mission is to connect the community with issues that matter. She has a passion for working with women and children's organizations and Hosea Feed the Hungry.

She recognized her niche for grassroots promotion while working with UniverSoul Circus as media production/promotion manager creating advertising campaigns marketed to millions of people in major cities.

McGhee worked with Warner Bros. Records to assist in the early career development of artists on the music charts today. Her work with Intersound promoted the resurgence of live music projects featuring George Clinton, The Dazz Band, Lakeside and more.

Cie Cie Wilson McGhee

Promotions Manager
Praise 102.5 FM

Evelyn Deloise Mims

Program Coordinator
WXIA-TV 11Alive

Evelyn Deloise Mims has an extensive career in television, with experience in syndication, programming, promotion, production and special events. She brings to the team a national reputation for project management and program development, with emphasis on involvement with the National Academy of Television Arts & Sciences (NATAS), the organization that sponsors the annual Emmy Awards. In fact, Mims served several terms as NATAS president for the southeast chapter. NATAS is one of the most influential organizations in the broadcast industry. She is also a three-time Emmy nominee.

As part of her current position as program coordinator for WXIA-TV Atlanta, Mims deals consistently with every major syndication company in America, such as Paramount, Viacom and Warner Bros. Her knowledge includes familiarization with all kinds of syndications, from religious to sports and entertainment. Mims knows what works best in different regions of the country, at what time, for what age groups and during whatever climate may be in the world at the time. She interacts regularly with all the publications syndication companies use, such as *TV Guide*, *TV Data* and *Nielsen Media Marketing*.

Parquita Nassau

Account Manager
Cox Radio

A talented, multifaceted, 20-year veteran within the radio and media industry, Parquita Nassau is currently an award-winning senior level account manager with Cox Radio Atlanta.

This former Miss Black Georgia began her radio career at age 19. A graduate of Spelman College, Nassau was well-known for many years as radio personality "Marie Stevens," hostess of the popular *Kiss Classic Café* on KISS 104.1 FM. She has served as media relations manager for the Georgia Lottery Corporation, and in 2001 she formed the Nassau Media Group. Additionally, she is founder and president of the Black Radio Hall of Fame.

A native of Liberia, West Africa, Nassau was raised in Atlanta. Her professional achievements include hosting a cable television program, having syndicated radio shows, and freelance writing for local magazines. She has been featured on *The Joan Rivers Show*, and in *Ebony* and *Jet*.

Nassau served on the National Black Programmers Coalition board, and has been involved with several organizations, including Big Brothers Big Sisters, the National Association of Black Journalists, and the National Coalition of 100 Black Women – Metropolitan Atlanta Chapter.

Monica Pearson joined WSB-TV Channel 2 in 1975, and currently serves as a 6 and 11 p.m. Action News anchor. The University of Louisville graduate was a reporter with *The Louisville Times* for five years.

Monica is a member of the Society of Professional Journalists, the National Association of Black Journalists, the Atlanta Association of Black Journalists, and The Junior League of Atlanta, Alpha Kappa Alpha Sorority, Inc., Our Lady of Lourdes Catholic Church and Gospel Tabernacle Church. A native of Louisville, Kentucky, Monica is a life member of the NAACP. Additionally, she serves on the True Colors Theatre Company and the High Museum of Art boards of directors, and the Alliance Theatre advisory committee.

She has received numerous awards, such as 28 local and southern regional Emmy awards for talent, reporting and close-ups. In 2002 Monica received an Emmy for Best Feature Program, *Monica Kaufman Closeups*, and *JEZEBEL* magazine named her one of the 50 Most Beautiful Women in 2003.

Married to John E. Pearson Sr., Monica has a daughter, Claire Patrice, and a stepson, John E. Pearson II.

Monica Pearson

Anchor
WSB-TV Channel 2

Corey A. Punzi is the promotions director for Radio One Atlanta's MAJIC 107.5/97.5, home of *The Steve Harvey Morning Show* and Michael Baisden. He is responsible for all promotional endeavors relative to this new stellar station.

A native New Yorker, Corey's radio interests commenced growing up listening to historic radio craftsmen of the city. While in college, Corey had his own radio show, which segued into a Bachelor of Arts degree in television/radio broadcasting.

In 1996 Corey began his career as an intern at an Atlanta radio station during the summer Olympics. He later became promotions assistant and gospel morning show producer. Moving on to another popular Atlanta station, Corey became director of marketing. With the endorsement of one of his greatest mentors, Kathy Daniels Jenkins, coupled with his creativity and passion for the business, Corey found his way to Radio One in 2004. He specializes in events, public relations and marketing.

Corey spends his quality time with partner Tim and their dog, Barrington, while also working on obtaining a Master of Business Administration degree from Georgia State University.

Corey A. Punzi

Promotions Director
MAJIC 107.5/97.5

J ean Ross is news director of 1380 WAOK AM/WVEE V-103 FM and operations manager of 1380 WAOK AM. She now anchors the morning news on *The Frank & Wanda Morning Show* on WVEE V-103 FM.

Ross was one of the first voices on Baltimore's V-103 FM (WXYV), where she worked as news anchor, public affairs director, morning show co-host with Frank Ski and host of *Jean Ross and Co.* She was also host and producer of the nationally syndicated program *Focus on Women*, airing in 50 U.S. cities and the Caribbean, in 1990. In 2002 she worked as a media relations specialist for the NAACP.

Ross is a graduate of Morgan State University in Baltimore, Maryland. She has won many awards, including the Crystal Award from the National Association of Broadcasters and National Public Service Director of the Year from *BRE* magazine.

Jean Ross

News Director
WVEE V-103 FM &
1380 WAOK AM

D ena J. Smith serves as press secretary and director of the Office of Communications for the Georgia Department of Human Resources (DHR). DHR is the largest agency in state government, employing more than 20,000 Georgians. In her roles, she is responsible for media and public relations for DHR's four divisions, including the Division of Family and Children Services, the Division of Mental Health, Developmental Disabilities and Addictive Diseases and others which provide 80 human services programs in 1,000 locations statewide.

Prior to joining DHR, Smith headed her own strategic consulting firm, Smith Communications, specializing in media relations and crisis management. Her other noted experience includes serving as director of media relations for the Alisias Group, an Atlanta-based PR agency. She also served as spokesperson for the City of Detroit's Housing Commission during former Mayor Dennis Archer's administration. Smith began her professional career as a reporter for *The Atlanta Journal-Constitution*.

Smith is also a member of the National Association of Black Journalists and the Black Public Relations Society of America.

Dena J. Smith

Press Secretary &
Director of Communications
Georgia Department of Human Resources

Shelice M. Smith is director of marketing and promotions for CBS Radio East, Inc. in Atlanta, which includes radio stations WVEE V-103 FM and 1380 WAOK AM. She is in charge of leading the companies' initiatives in developing new and innovative programs for station promotions, and generating nontraditional revenue. She joined the WAOK/WVEE management team in 1999 as director of promotions before taking the helm of the business development department, which includes event marketing, promotions, Web site marketing and client-driven campaigns.

Smith began her career in media 20 years ago in her hometown of Buffalo, New York, at the heritage urban radio station, WBLK, where she established the promotions and marketing department. Her professional journey brought her to Atlanta in 1995 as marketing director at WALR-FM, then to the Atlanta Urban Radio Alliance and Kicks 101.5 as a sales account executive.

Smith has been selected by the Atlanta Business League as one of the Top 100 Women of Influence and was voted as one of the Most Powerful & Influential Women in Media by *Women Looking Ahead* magazine.

Shelice M. Smith

Director, Marketing & Promotions
CBS Radio East, Inc.

Ryan Stewart, half of the nationally syndicated *2 Live Stews*, can be heard across the country via *Sporting News Radio*. A former NFL player, he and his brother convinced 790 The Zone's program director to let them work on the air without pay. As their fans, affectionately known as the "dogs and poodles," will tell you, the rest is history.

Ryan started playing football as a youngster in Moncks Corner, South Carolina, he gained recognition and was drafted by the NFL at his alma mater, the Georgia Institute of Technology, in 1996. He retired from football in 2001.

The *2 Live Stews* were featured in *Sports Illustrated* magazine. ESPN2 viewers also got a glimpse of the *2 Live Stews* during a 30-minute show that chronicled "a day in the life of the 2 Live Stews." Since becoming syndicated, the duo has become a regular on ESPN2's *First Take*. In 2004 the Stews were named Air Talent of the Year by ESPN.

When Ryan is not talking sports, he loves riding his motorcycle, traveling, exercising and spending time with his lovely wife, Jevonne.

Ryan Stewart

Sports Radio Personality
WQXI-AM, 790 The Zone

Willie Stewart

Publisher & Chief Executive Officer
Trendsetters to Trendsetters Magazine

Willie Stewart is the chief executive officer and publisher of *Trendsetters to Trendsetters Magazine*, a national publication based in Atlanta. Born in Canton, Ohio, he attended McKinley High School, where he received many honors. Willie attended Tiffin University and received a Bachelor of Arts degree in marketing.

After graduating from college, Willie moved to Columbus, Ohio, where he became involved in several marketing ventures. He has also lived in Fairfield, California, Des Moines, Iowa and Atlanta, Georgia.

Willie is also the creator of *On the Radar*, a professional online television show. *Trendsetters to Trendsetters Magazine* is currently distributed in Atlanta; Birmingham; Columbia; Charlotte; Columbus, Ohio; Houston; and parts of Florida.

Greg Street

On-Air Personality
WVEE V-103 FM

Greg Street is WVEE V-103 FM's evening personality from 6 to 10 p.m. He is an entrepreneur, marketing specialist, record mogul and community activist. He has been instrumental in the radio industry, launching the careers of successful hip-hop rap artists.

On V-103, Greg attracts a large and loyal audience of all ages. His passion for the community and children spills over into his daily life. A founder of the Street Academy, Greg works to provide opportunities for at-risk youth to achieve extraordinary accomplishments. He established the Greg Street Scholarship Fund, and donates his personal time and money to make a difference.

Hailing from Hattiesburg, Mississippi, Greg began his radio career at WORV and WJMG. His journey took him to Mobile and Houston, as well as commuting between Dallas and Atlanta for three years, working at KKDA-FM and WVEE simultaneously. Greg is one of the country's most known and respected on-air personalities, earning him his own exclusive tennis shoe from Reebok in 2004.

W hen it comes to laughs, Joe Taylor, or "Miss Sophia" McIntosh, is a real queen of comedy. A Texas native, Miss Sophia has been making people laugh until they cry for years.

Miss Sophia is one of the most widely known comedians in Atlanta. With a one-of-a-kind style that brings together Flip Wilson's Geraldine, Martin Lawrence's Sheneneh and every church's church lady, Miss Sophia creates a style that is all his (or her) own.

Born in Calvert, Texas, Miss Sophia has lived in Atlanta since 1999, where she has become the premier host of GLBT pageants and club parties all around the region. She can also be heard every day as co-host and entertainment correspondent on Atlanta's No. 1 morning show, *The Frank & Wanda Morning Show*, on The People's Station, WVEE V-103 FM.

Miss Sophia has been featured in several stage plays and travels nationally with her wild and hilarious comedy shows. She wants the whole world to be one big happy family, and by bringing people together through comedy, she is definitely doing her part to make that happen.

Joe Taylor "Miss Sophia"

Host, *Girl Talk*
WVEE V-103 FM

A tlanta native Art Terrell embraces the expansion of urban community, radio and music within the Greater Atlanta area. No stranger to the urban radio scene or Atlanta's African-American community, his radio career affords him the opportunity to do what he loves while donating time to causes such as Atlanta's homeless, among others.

Terrell hosts WALR's *Afternoon Drive*, providing listeners with entertainment news, light comic relief and an excellent mix of music. Upon his arrival to the afternoon slot in 2004, WALR saw its highest daypart (25-54) ratings ever. Additionally, station listeners once nominated him as the Sexiest Voice in Atlanta Radio.

Terrell interned at WVEE-FM while attending Mays High School and continued his employment while attending Georgia State University. He hosted Atlanta's first hip-hop show, *The Fresh Party, Reggae Jammin' with Lil' John, The Quiet Storm* and *The House Party*. While at WHTA, Terrell hosted *The Morning Party – The Art Terrell and Felesha Love Show,* and served as co-host and co-producer of *The Ryan Cameron Morning Show* while working alongside and training, then intern, Chris "Ludacris" Bridges.

Art Terrell

Host, *Afternoon Drive*
KISS 104.1 WALR-FM

Chandra R. Thomas

Journalist & Co-Founder
TalkBLACK

Chandra R. Thomas is an award-winning journalist whose work has appeared in *People, Essence, Ebony, Newsweek, Upscale* and *Atlanta* magazines, as well as on Time.com. She was named Journalist of the Year for 2007 by Region III of the National Association of Black Journalists for a body of work she produced in 2006, including a feature story about Hurricane Katrina victims exiled in Atlanta and the first in-depth account of the controversial Genarlow Wilson teen sex case. The latter ultimately helped contribute to a change in Georgia law and Wilson's 2007 release from prison. The same year, she was named Print Journalist of the Year by the Atlanta Press Club.

Thomas recently completed a Rosalynn Carter Mental Health Journalism Fellowship project that focused on mental health challenges in the African-American community. The Clark Atlanta University graduate and New Orleans native has previously served as an associate producer for FOX 5's *Good Day Atlanta* program, a producer for the ABC television affiliate in Birmingham and a reporter for the *Birmingham Post-Herald* newspaper. Thomas is co-founder of an Atlanta-based discussion group, TalkBLACK.

Tara Thomas

Event Marketing Coordinator
WVEE V-103 FM & 1380 WAOK

Tara Thomas is event marketing coordinator for The People's Station, Atlanta's WVEE V-103 FM, and News & Talk 1380 WAOK. She came to Atlanta from Seat Pleasant, Maryland.

Thomas began her career in 1994 as an intern for the *Frank and Jean Morning Show* at WXYV V-103 in Baltimore while attending Towson State University. A year later, she was hired as assistant producer.

After graduating with a Bachelor of Science degree in mass communications, Thomas performed a short stint at WUST-AM, a foreign language station in Virginia. She rejoined Frank Ski as the producer of his own morning show on Baltimore's 92Q Jams FM. When the *Frank Ski Morning Show* moved to Atlanta, she became the entertainment reporter and fill-in morning show host.

After nine years in broadcasting, Thomas stepped down as morning show producer for the *Frank Ski Morning Show* in 2003 to pursue a personal goal of event marketing, a position she has held with V-103 for six years. In addition, she has also started her own company, Privy Events, which consults local and national companies' grassroots events and marketing strategies.

arry Tinsley gives listeners *Sunday Morning Inspiration* every Sunday morning from 6 a.m. to 12 p.m. on WVEE V-103 FM and 1380 WAOK AM. He is regarded as one of America's top gospel announcers and has received the coveted Stellar Award as Gospel Announcer of the Year.

Larry was born in Decaturville, Tennessee. At the age of 5, he moved to Knoxville, Tennessee. He received a diploma from Riverside High School in Parsons, Tennessee, and later received a Bachelor of Science degree from Lambuth University in Jackson, Tennessee. Upon graduation, he worked as on-air announcer for WJBE radio, which was owned by legendary soul singer James Brown.

In June of 1971, Larry accepted an offer to work as an on-air announcer for WAOK in Atlanta. In 1981 he was elevated to the position of program director.

Larry is married with two children and attends New Birth Missionary Baptist Church in Lithonia, Georgia, where Bishop Eddie Long serves as pastor. He is a devoted Christian who lives each day according to the word of God and the Holy Spirit that dwells within him.

Larry Tinsley

On-Air Personality
WVEE V-103 FM &
1380 WAOK AM

orraine Jacques White hosts *PowerTalk* on 1380 WAOK AM Monday through Friday, from 8 a.m. to 12 p.m. She and her guests provide the knowledge, and the community gains the power.

Lorraine is an honor graduate of the Interdenominational Theological Center with a Master of Divinity degree. She serves as director of Christian education at Mt. Ephraim Baptist Church, where her husband, Dr. R.L. White Jr., pastors.

Lorraine also hosted a popular radio talk show, *Ministerial Insight*, which was heard every Monday evening on 1380 WAOK. The show became a hit with listeners for its hard-hitting, issues-oriented topics and celebrity guests. *Ministerial Insight* was host to some of the nation's most recognized public figures, including Kweisi Mfume, the Reverend Jesse Jackson, the Reverend Al Sharpton, Dick Gregory, John Lewis and Coretta Scott King.

Lorraine has been recognized as a trailblazer for women in ministry, and she is one of the co-authors of the inspirational book *Sister-to-Sister*. Additionally, she has been named one of the 100 Most Influential Women in Atlanta.

Lorraine Jacques White

Host, *PowerTalk*
1380 WAOK AM

hristine Willis began her early broadcasting career under the guiding hand of her father, assisting him in the daily operation of corporate responsibilities in the chain's numerous radio stations. Her broadcasting skills include sales, collections and management.

In August of 2001, Christine moved to Atlanta to assume management of WTJH 1260 Radio, a 5,000-watt AM gospel music/ministry station. Under her guidance, WTJH radio was relocated from East Point to more modern studio facilities in southwest Atlanta. The new complex includes three separate broadcast studios and state-of-the-art equipment.

Christine's current plans include the acquisition of several FM stations. Her mission is to better serve Metro Atlanta with great music, ministries and fresh and vital information in every capacity.

Christine is the mother of two handsome sons, Steven G. Felton Jr. and Alexander "Alex" Lashawn Felton. She is the daughter of media mogul Bishop Levi and Mrs. Hortense Willis Sr. of Norfolk, Virginia.

Christine Willis

General Manager
WTJH 1260 AM Radio

his quintessential radio personality with a silky smooth voice is Cynthia Young. Her warmth and sense of humor make her listeners feel comfortable with her from the very moment her voice is heard. This Buffalo-born Scorpio and Who's Who in Atlanta Radio has been a radio personality for more than 20 years.

Cynthia has been an air personality with KISS 104.1 since 1997 and plays a major role in the consistency of this top-rated station. She also co-hosted the *Blue Lights in the Basement House Party Live* with Mitch Faulkner. She was the voice of a syndicated weekly entertainment program, *The Industry*, with a segment entitled "Hot and Happening."

Off the air, Cynthia enjoys playing percussions in open jam sessions, catching productions at local theatres and participating in the choir at Ray of Hope Christian Church. She has a strong commitment for community with annual contributions to local and national organizations. With a full schedule as a radio personality, Cynthia is never too busy to serve and give back to the very audience that enjoys her talents on KISS 104.1.

Cynthia Young

Radio Personality
KISS 104.1 WALR-FM

Ryan Young joined the Channel 2 Action News team in July of 2005. The Miami native got his first big television break while hosting a syndicated sports show as a college student. After graduating from Florida State University with a bachelor's degree in media production, Ryan joined WTXL-TV in Tallahassee, Florida, where he kept local viewers in touch with a wide variety of stories, including the 2002 Florida elections and Florida State's national championship run.

As a reporter for WTOC-TV in Savannah, Ryan provided viewers with crucial, up-to-the-minute late-night reports, earning two Associated Press awards, one for best investigative piece that exposed dangerous cigarette lighters and the other for best spot news coverage of a major street collapse. While working for Raleigh, North Carolina's WNCN-TV, Ryan told the stories of people whose lives were torn apart by hurricanes Ivan and Frances. While covering the problem of gangs in the state, Ryan gained national recognition by producing a groundbreaking report on gangs in the military.

In his spare time, Ryan enjoys reading, football and playing a game of fetch with his dog.

Ryan Young

Reporter
WSB-TV, Channel 2

BE HEARD
your world, your voice, our work

INTEGRATED MARKETING   MULTI-MEDIA   EXTENDED NETWORK

Let Real Times Media create unique and innovative marketing experiences for your brand.

Real Times Media 535 Griswold, Suite 1300, Detroit, MI 48226 ■ 313-963-8100

BIOGRAPHICAL INDEX

ADVERTISER'S INDEX